Sweet Endings

Beta Sigma Phi

EDITORIAL STAFF

Executive Editor	Paul Stansberry
Project Editor	Anna Watson; Kim O'Connor
Editorial Consultant	Georgia Brazil
Award Selection Judge	Paul Stansberry
Art Director	Steve Newman
Illustrator	Barbara Ball
Book Design	Travis Rader
Production Design	Jessie Anglin, Sara Anglin
Test Kitchen	Ron Hartman

© Favorite Recipes® Press, A Division of Heritage House, Inc. 2006
  P.O. Box 305141, Nashville, Tennessee 37230

ISBN: 0-87197-528-9

Manufactured in the United States of America

First Printing 2006

Contents

Dear Friends,

International is proud to present to you, during the 76th year of your wonderful organization, the *Sweet Endings* cookbook.

We all love desserts, be it cookies, cakes, or pies— won't it be fun to find old friends and their favorite recipes as you browse through this book?

One of our favorite things here at International is our pot-luck luncheons. What a great time we have tasting and trading recipes with each other!

Bill and Marilyn Ross

 We have had replies from many, many members who have enjoyed using the cookbooks throughout the years. The cookbooks make wonderful Secret Sister gifts, presents for Mom or Daughter, or just "Special Friends."

My very best wishes to you for an enjoyable Beta Sigma Phi cooking year.

Sincerely,

Bill Ross

Walter W. Ross III

P.S. Once again, I would like to remind you that by the purchase of this cookbook, you have allowed the members of Beta Sigma Phi to raise money for worthy causes and contribute to their favorite charities.

Express Lane

FIVE INGREDIENTS OR LESS

ANISE BISCOTTI

2 eggs
2/3 cup sugar

1 teaspoon anise seeds
1 cup all-purpose flour

Beat the eggs and sugar in a bowl until light and fluffy. Stir in the anise seeds. Stir in the flour gradually. Spoon the batter into a nonstick 5×9-inch loaf pan. Bake at 375 degrees for 20 minutes or until a wooden pick inserted in the center comes out clean. Cool in the pan for 10 minutes. Remove to a cutting board. Cut diagonally with a serrated knife into 1/2-inch slices. Arrange the slices on a greased cookie sheet. Bake at 375 degrees for 5 minutes or until the bottom of the slices are golden brown. Turn the slices over and bake for 5 minutes longer. Remove to a wire rack to cool completely. Yield: 16 biscotti.

Cindy Montalbano-Johns, Laureate Iota
Raleigh, North Carolina

CAKE COOKIES

1 (2-layer) package cake
  mix (any flavor)
1 egg

2 cups whipped topping
Confectioners' sugar or
  finely chopped nuts

Mix the cake mix, egg and whipped topping in a bowl. Shape into small balls. Roll in confectioners' sugar or nuts and place on a foil-lined cookie sheet. Press the balls lightly to flatten slightly. Bake at 350 degrees for 10 to 12 minutes or until firm. Cool on the cookie sheet for 1 minute. Remove to a wire rack to cool completely. Yield: 2 to 3 dozen cookies.

Ione FitzGerald, Lambda Lambda
Redford, Michigan

BIG CHOCOLATE COOKIES

2 (2-layer) packages
  chocolate cake mix
1 (19 1/2-ounce) package
  brownie mix

3 eggs
3/4 cup vegetable oil
3/4 cup water

Combine the cake mix, brownie mix, eggs, oil and water in a bowl and mix well. Drop by tablespoonfuls 3 inches apart onto a greased cookie sheet. Bake at 325 degrees for 8 to 10 minutes or until firm. Cool on the cookie sheet for 1 minute. Remove to a wire rack to cool completely. Yield: 6 dozen cookies.

Sharon M. Goins, Xi Rho Gamma
Vernon, Texas

COCONUT PECAN FINGERS

These cookies are quick and easy to make, and so good. Kids love them.

3/4 cup flaked coconut
1/3 cup chopped pecans
2 slices bread

1/2 cup sweetened
  condensed milk

Mix the coconut and pecans in a shallow dish. Cut each bread slice into four strips. Pour the condensed milk into a shallow dish. Dip each bread strip into the condensed milk and coat with the coconut mixture. Arrange on a greased cookie sheet. Bake at 375 degrees for 10 to 12 minutes or until golden brown. Remove to a wire rack to cool.
Yield: 4 servings.

Eddie Cox, Preceptor Delta Gamma
Camarillo, California

CRISPY LEMON COOKIES

1 (2-layer) package
   lemon cake mix
1 cup crisp rice cereal

1 cup butter or
   margarine, melted
1 egg, slightly beaten

Combine the cake mix, cereal, butter and egg in a bowl and mix well. Drop by teaspoonfuls 2 inches apart onto a nonstick cookie sheet. Bake at 350 degrees for 9 to 12 minutes or until light brown. Cool on the cookie sheet for 1 minute. Remove to a wire rack to cool completely. Yield: 2 to 3 dozen cookies.

Patsy Rene Baggett, Laureate Gamma Chi
Jacksonville, Texas

"M & M" DROP COOKIES

1 (2-layer) package
   yellow cake mix
1/3 cup butter or
   margarine, melted
1/4 cup all-purpose flour

1 egg
1 1/2 cups (9 ounces)
   "M & M's" Chocolate
   Candies

Combine the cake mix, butter, flour and egg in a bowl. Beat at medium speed until a stiff dough forms. Stir in 1 cup of the candies. Shape by 1 1/2 table-spoonfuls into balls. Place 2 inches apart on an ungreased cookie sheet and press each ball lightly to flatten slightly. Press the remaining candies into the cookies. Bake at 350 degrees for 11 to 12 minutes. Cool on the cookie sheet for 1 minute. Remove to a wire rack to cool completely. Yield: 3 dozen cookies.

Sandra Morley, Preceptor Alpha Upsilon
Tacoma, Washington

MELTING MOMENTS

1 cup all-purpose flour
2 tablespoons
   cornstarch
1/2 cup confectioners'
   sugar

1 cup (2 sticks)
   margarine, softened
1 1/3 cups flaked coconut

Combine the flour, cornstarch and confectioners' sugar in a bowl and mix well. Add the margarine and stir until a soft dough forms. Chill, covered, until firm. Shape into 3/4-inch balls and roll in the coconut. Place 1 1/2 inches apart on an ungreased cookie sheet. Bake at 300 degrees for 20 to 25 minutes or until lightly browned. Cool on the cookie sheet for 1 minute. Remove to a wire rack to cool completely. Yield: 3 dozen cookies.

Marie Bray, Alpha Omega Master
Orlando, Florida

EASY MERINGUE COOKIES

2 egg whites
Dash of salt
2/3 cup sugar

1 cup (6 ounces)
   chocolate chips

Beat the egg whites and salt in a bowl until foamy. Add the sugar and beat until stiff peaks form. Fold in the chocolate chips. Drop by spoonfuls onto a foil-lined cookie sheet. Place in a 350 degree oven and turn off the heat. Leave in the oven for 5 hours or longer without opening the oven door.
Yield: 2 to 3 dozen cookies.

Deborah Newton, Xi Mu Beta
Zanesville, Ohio

EASY PEANUT BUTTER COOKIES

1 (2-layer) package
   yellow cake mix
1 cup peanut butter

1/3 cup water
2 eggs

Combine the cake mix, peanut butter, water and eggs in a bowl and mix well. Drop by spoonfuls onto a nonstick cookie sheet. Flatten with a fork dipped in sugar to form a crosshatch design. Bake at 375 degrees for 10 to 15 minutes or until firm. Cool on the cookie sheet for 1 minute. Remove to a wire rack to cool completely. Yield: 3 to 4 dozen cookies.

Sharon Miller, Preceptor Mu Eta
Encino, California

HEAVENLY PEANUT BUTTER COOKIES

2 egg whites
1 cup sugar
1 cup chunky peanut
   butter

1/2 teaspoon almond
   extract

Beat the egg whites in a bowl until stiff peaks form. Fold in the sugar, peanut butter and almond extract. Drop by spoonfuls onto a parchment paper-lined cookie sheet. Bake at 350 degrees for 15 minutes. Cool on the cookie sheet for 1 minute. Remove to a wire rack to cool completely. Yield: 2 dozen cookies.

Barbara Kent, Xi Delta Psi
Sequim, Washington

PECAN MERINGUES

2 egg whites
1/4 cup sugar
1 cup chopped pecans

1/2 teaspoon vanilla
   extract
1/4 cup sugar

Beat the egg whites in a mixer bowl until soft peaks form. Beat in 1/4 cup sugar gradually until stiff peaks form. Fold in the pecans, vanilla and 1/4 cup sugar. Drop by teaspoonfuls onto a parchment paper-lined cookie sheet. Bake at 200 degrees for 45 minutes. Cool on the cookie sheet for 1 minute. Remove to a wire rack to cool. Yield: 2 to 3 dozen cookies.

Margie Kelarek, Laureate Eta Beta
Hilltop Lakes, Texas

RICH REFRIGERATOR COOKIES

2 cups (4 sticks) butter, softened	3 tablespoons vanilla extract
1 cup sugar	4 cups all-purpose flour
	1 cup chopped nuts

Beat the butter and sugar in a bowl until light and fluffy. Beat in the vanilla. Add the flour and mix well. Stir in the nuts. Divide the dough in half. Shape each portion into a log and wrap in plastic wrap. Chill until firm. Cut into 1/4-inch slices and place on a non-stick cookie sheet. Bake at 350 degrees for 12 minutes or until light brown. Cool on the cookie sheet for 1 minute. Remove to a wire rack to cool completely. Dust with confectioners' sugar if desired.
Yield: 7 to 8 dozen cookies.

Norma Pierce, Alpha Psi
Spokane, Washington

FOOD PROCESSOR SHORTBREAD

2 cups (4 sticks) butter, cut into pieces	3 cups all-purpose flour
1 cup confectioners' sugar	Melted chocolate (optional)

Process the butter in a food processor until smooth. Add the confectioners' sugar and process until light and fluffy. Add the flour gradually and process until well blended. Drop by tablespoonfuls onto a non-stick cookie sheet. Bake in the center of the oven at 300 degrees for 14 minutes. Cool on the cookie sheet for 1 minute. Remove to a wire rack to cool completely. Dip one end of each cookie in melted chocolate and place on waxed paper. Let stand until firm. Yield: 4 dozen cookies.

Wendy Horton, Xi Epsilon Theta
Port Perry, Ontario, Canada

SHORTBREAD THUMBPRINTS

1 cup (2 sticks) butter, softened	2/3 cup sugar
1/2 teaspoon almond extract	2 cups all-purpose flour
	Jam (any flavor)

Beat the butter, 1/2 teaspoon almond extract and sugar in a bowl until light and fluffy. Beat in the flour gradually and mix well. Shape into 1-inch balls and place 2 inches apart on an ungreased cookie sheet. Make an indentation in each cookie with your thumb.

Fill each indentation with 1/4 teaspoon jam. Bake at 350 degrees for 15 minutes or until the edges are light brown. Cool on the cookie sheet for 1 minute. Remove to a wire rack to cool completely.
Yield: 3 1/2 dozen cookies.

Bonnie Schroeder, Alpha Gamma Delta
North Ft. Myers, Florida

SHORTBREAD WEDGES

1 1/2 cups (3 sticks) butter, softened	1 cup confectioners' sugar
	3 cups all-purpose flour

Beat the butter and confectioners' sugar in a bowl at medium speed until light and fluffy. Stir in the flour gradually and mix well. Press into an ungreased large pie plate or 9×13-inch baking pan. Prick the surface of the dough with a fork. Score the dough 1/8-inch deep with a sharp knife to mark wedges. Bake at 300 degrees for 40 to 45 minutes or until golden brown. Remove to a wire rack to cool completely. Cut along the scored lines and remove from the pan. Yield: 10 to 12 servings.

Natalia Bialkowski, Laureate Beta Theta
Sierra Vista, Arizona

BROWNIE DELIGHT

1 (19 1/2-ounce) package brownie mix	8 ounces whipped topping
1 (6-ounce) package chocolate instant pudding mix	2 or 3 (2-ounce) Butterfinger candy bars, chopped

Prepare and bake the brownie mix using the package directions for an 8×8-inch baking pan. Cool completely in the pan. Prepare the pudding mix using the package directions. Spread over the cooled brownies in the pan. Spread the whipped topping evenly over the pudding and sprinkle with the crushed candy. Chill, covered, until ready to serve. Cut into squares just before serving. Yield: 12 servings.

Patricia Bleick, Xi Alpha Gamma Lambda
Palestine, Texas

---

*Elaine C. Olson, Chi Master, Lake Havasu City, Arizona, prepares **Fluffy Rice Dessert** by draining one 20-ounce can crushed pineapple and reserving the juice. She dissolves one small package sugar-free cherry gelatin in 1 cup boiling water in a bowl and stirs in the reserved pineapple juice and 1 1/2 cups hot cooked rice. The mixture is chilled slightly. She then folds in the pineapple and 1 cup light whipped topping. The dessert is chilled, covered, for 1 hour.*

MILKY WAY BROWNIES

2 (18-ounce) rolls
    refrigerated chocolate
    chip cookie dough
1 (2-pound) package
    Milky Way miniature
    candy bars
$^{1}/_{2}$ cup chopped walnuts
    or pecans

Press the cookie dough into a nonstick 9×13-inch baking pan. Bake at 350 degrees for 20 to 25 minutes or until light brown. Cut each candy bar into thirds. Sprinkle the candy evenly over the hot cookie. Bake for 5 minutes longer or until the candy melts. Spread the candy with a knife or spatula. Sprinkle with the walnuts. Cool completely in the pan. Cut into squares just before serving. Yield: 2 dozen brownies.

Betty Kelly, Laureate Beta Pi
Jenison, Michigan

SURPRISE BROWNIES

This is a fun recipe to make with children.

1 (19$^{1}/_{2}$-ounce) package
    fudge brownie mix
12 vanilla wafers
12 caramels

Prepare the brownie mix using the package directions. Place vanilla wafers in the bottoms of 12 greased muffin cups. Spoon 3 tablespoons of brownie batter over each vanilla wafer. Place one caramel on top of the batter in each muffin cup. Top with 1 teaspoon batter. Bake at 350 degrees for 22 minutes. Cool in the pan for 10 minutes. Remove to a wire rack to cool. Cut into squares. Serve warm with a scoop of vanilla ice cream. Yield: 1 dozen brownies.

Bonnie Carroll, Xi Nu
Evansville, Indiana

TRIPLE CHOCOLATE BROWNIES

1 (4-ounce) package
    cook and serve
    chocolate pudding mix
2 cups milk
1 (2-layer) package
    chocolate cake mix
1 cup (6 ounces)
    semisweet
    chocolate chips
1 cup chopped walnuts

Prepare the pudding mix using the package directions, using 2 cups milk. Pour into a bowl and cool to lukewarm, stirring frequently. Add the cake mix and mix well. Pour into a greased 9×13-inch baking pan. Sprinkle with the chocolate chips and walnuts. Bake at 350 degrees for 25 to 30 minutes or until the brownies test done. Remove to a wire rack to cool completely. Cut into squares.
Yield: 2 to 3 dozen brownies.

Patricia Elliott-Pugh, Laureate Delta Nu
Placentia, California

CARAMEL LAYER CHOCOLATE BARS

1 (12-ounce) can
    evaporated milk
1 (14-ounce) package
    caramels
1 (2-layer) package
    German chocolate
    cake mix
$^{3}/_{4}$ cup (1$^{1}/_{2}$ sticks)
    margarine, melted
2 cups (12 ounces)
    semisweet chocolate
    chips

Combine $^{1}/_{3}$ cup of the evaporated milk and the caramels in a double boiler. Cook until smooth, stirring frequently. Combine the cake mix, margarine and remaining evaporated milk in a bowl and mix well. Press half the dough into the bottom of a greased and floured 9×13-inch baking pan. Bake at 350 degrees for 6 minutes. Sprinkle with the chocolate chips. Pour the caramel mixture evenly over the chocolate chips. Crumble the remaining dough and sprinkle over the caramel mixture. Bake for 15 to 16 minutes longer. Remove to a wire rack to cool completely. Cut into bars. Yield: 2 dozen bars.

Kathryn Dotson, Preceptor Beta Beta
Arapaho, Oklahoma

CHOCOLATE BUTTER CRACKER SQUARES

1 (12-ounce) box butter
    crackers, crushed
1 (14-ounce) can
    sweetened
    condensed milk
1 (10-ounce) package
    toffee bits
1 container chocolate
    frosting (or to taste)

Combine the crushed crackers, condensed milk and toffee bits in a bowl and mix well. Spoon into a greased 9×9-inch baking pan. Bake at 350 degrees for 15 minutes. Remove to a wire rack to cool completely. Spread with the chocolate frosting. Cut into squares. Yield: 3 dozen bars.

Lorene Macphee, Laureate Delta Kappa
Oakville, Ontario, Canada

CHOCOLATE SQUARES

37 unsalted saltine
    crackers
1 cup (2 sticks)
    margarine
1 cup sugar
2 cups (12 ounces)
    chocolate chips
$^{1}/_{2}$ cup finely chopped
    pecans (optional)

Fit the crackers closely in a single layer in a buttered 10×15-inch baking pan. Bring the margarine and sugar to a boil in a saucepan over medium heat, stirring frequently. Boil for 3 minutes, stirring constantly. Pour over the crackers. Bake at 400 degrees for 4 minutes. Remove from the oven and turn off the heat.

Sprinkle the chocolate chips evenly over the baked layer. Return to the oven for 2 minutes. Spread the chocolate evenly with a knife or spatula and sprinkle with the pecans. Cool completely in the pan. Cut into squares. Yield: 3 dozen squares.

Florence Marie Short, Preceptor Alpha Epsilon
Melbourne, Florida

GERMAN CHOCOLATE BARS

1 (2-layer) package
  German chocolate
  cake mix
2/3 cup margarine,
  softened
1 cup (6 ounces)
  semisweet
  chocolate chips

1 (15-ounce) container
  coconut pecan
  frosting
1/4 cup milk

Place the cake mix in a bowl. Cut in the margarine until crumbly. Press half the mixture into the bottom of a greased 9×13-inch baking pan. Bake at 350 degrees for 10 minutes. Sprinkle the chocolate chips over the baked layer. Drop the frosting by tablespoonfuls over the chocolate chips. Stir the milk into the remaining cake mixture. Drop by tablespoons over the frosting layer. Bake for 25 to 30 minutes longer or until the cake layer is slightly dry to the touch. Cool completely in the pan. Chill, covered, until firm. Cut into bars. Yield: 4 dozen bars.

Claudia M. Long, Kappa Kappa
Meriden, Kansas

LEMON SQUARES

These squares were the specialty of a local restaurant in the small town where I lived in high school.

1 (16-ounce) package
  graham crackers
4 (14-ounce) cans
  sweetened condensed
  milk
Juice of 4 lemons

1 container vanilla
  frosting
Juice of 1 lemon
Chopped walnuts
  (optional)

Fit half the graham crackers in a single layer in a 10×15-inch baking pan. Combine the condensed milk and the juice of 4 lemons in a bowl and beat until very thick. Pour evenly over the graham crackers in the pan. Top with the remaining graham crackers. Combine the frosting and juice of 1 lemon in a bowl and mix well. Pour evenly over the top. Sprinkle with chopped walnuts. Chill, covered, for 4 to 6 hours. Cut into squares. Yield: 5 to 6 dozen squares.

Ann Kilpatrick, Preceptor Tau
Sheridan, Wyoming

PEANUT BUTTER CRISPY BARS

1 cup sugar
1 cup light corn syrup
1 cup peanut butter
6 cups crisp rice cereal
  or rice-and-wheat
  cereal

1 cup (6 ounces)
  chocolate chips or
  peanut butter chips

Combine the sugar and corn syrup in a large saucepan. Bring to a boil over medium-high heat, stirring constantly. Add the peanut butter and stir until smooth. Remove from the heat. Add the cereal and mix well. Press into a buttered 8×8-inch baking pan. Sprinkle with the chocolate chips and press lightly. Cut into bars. Yield: 2 dozen bars.

Judi Tippin, Laureate Delta
Las Vegas, Nevada

PEANUT MARSHMALLOW BARS

1 (14-ounce) can
  sweetened
  condensed milk
2 cups (12 ounces)
  semisweet
  chocolate chips

2 tablespoons butter or
  margarine
2 cups dry-roasted
  peanuts
1 (10-ounce) package
  miniature
  marshmallows

Combine the condensed milk, chocolate chips and butter in a saucepan. Cook over medium heat until smooth, stirring frequently. Remove from the heat. Stir in the peanuts and marshmallows. Press into a greased 9×13-inch baking pan. Chill, covered, until firm. Cut into bars. Yield: 12 servings.

Naomi E. Golden, Alpha Nu Master
Van Buren, Ohio

TOFFEE BARS

1 (16-ounce) package
  graham crackers
2 (5-ounce) packages
  sliced almonds

2 cups (4 sticks) butter
1/2 cup granulated sugar
1/2 cup packed brown
  sugar

Fit the graham crackers in a single layer in two foil-lined 10×15-inch baking pans. Sprinkle evenly with the almonds. Melt the butter in a saucepan. Stir in the granulated sugar and brown sugar. Bring to a boil over medium heat, stirring frequently. Boil for 3 minutes; do not stir. Pour evenly over the crackers and almonds. Bake at 350 degrees for 8 to 10 minutes. Cool completely in the pans. Dust with confectioners' sugar if desired. Cut into bars.
Yield: 15 to 20 servings.

Sandra Dwyer, Laureate Alpha Beta
Placentia, California

TOFFEE CRACKER BARS

2 (10-ounce) packages
   toffee bits
90 butter crackers,
   crushed
2 (14-ounce) cans
   sweetened condensed
   milk

Reserve ½ cup toffee bits. Combine the remaining toffee bits, crushed crackers and condensed milk in a bowl and mix well. Spoon into a greased 9×13-inch baking pan. Sprinkle with the reserved toffee bits. Bake at 350 degrees for 30 minutes. Cool in the pan. Cut into small bars while warm.
Yield: 9 to 10 dozen bars.

Janet English, Laureate Delta Kappa
Mississauga, Ontario, Canada

WHITE CHOCOLATE PEPPERMINT SQUARES

1 (2-layer) package
   white cake mix
3 ounces white
   chocolate, melted
¼ cup crushed
   candy canes
3 ounces white
   chocolate, melted
¼ cup crushed
   candy canes

Prepare the cake mix batter using the package directions. Stir in 3 ounces white chocolate and ¼ cup crushed candy canes. Pour into a nonstick 9×13-inch baking pan. Bake at 350 degrees for 30 minutes or until the cake tests done. Cool in the pan for 15 minutes. Spread 3 ounces white chocolate on the cake and sprinkle with ¼ cup crushed candy canes. Cut into squares. Yield: 20 squares.

Carol Underwood, Laureate Xi
Goldsboro, North Carolina

APPLESAUCE CAKE

¼ cup sugar
1 tablespoon cinnamon
1 (2-layer) package
   yellow cake mix
1⅔ cups applesauce
3 eggs

Combine the sugar and cinnamon. Grease a bundt pan and dust it with a small amount of the cinnamon-sugar. Combine the cake mix, applesauce and eggs in a bowl and mix well. Pour half the batter into the pan. Sprinkle with the cinnamon-sugar and top with the remaining batter. Bake at 350 degrees for 45 minutes. Cool in the pan for 15 minutes. Invert onto a serving plate. Yield: 12 to 16 servings.

Gladys Weems, Laureate Eta Iota
Highland, California

STRAWBERRY DELIGHT

This dessert can also be made with raspberries.

1 angel food cake
1 cup cubed strawberry
   gelatin
12 ounces whipped
   topping
1 (8-ounce) jar
   strawberry jam
Sliced strawberries

Slice the cake in half horizontally. Remove the center of the bottom layer with a fork, leaving a 1-inch shell. Spoon the gelatin into the cake base. Combine the whipped topping and jam in a bowl and spoon it over the gelatin until the mixture is level with the top of the base. Replace the top of the cake. Spread the remaining whipped topping mixture over the top and side of the cake. Garnish with strawberries. Chill before serving. Yield: 10 servings.

Lois Ebel, Preceptor Beta Rho
Hillsboro, Oregon

BERRY CAKE

1 cup frozen berries
1 (2-layer) package
   yellow cake mix
1 (12-ounce) can
   diet cola

Arrange the fruit in a greased and floured 9×13-inch cake pan. Cover with the cake mix. Pour the cola over the cake mix; do not stir. Cover the pan with aluminum foil. Bake at 350 degrees for 20 minutes. Remove the foil and bake for an additional 20 minutes. Cool in the pan for 10 minutes. Remove to a wire rack to cool completely. Yield: 12 servings.

Sandi Kent, Alpha Rho
Crookston, Minnesota

BLUEBERRY DUMP CAKE

I fixed this wonderful cake for my 8-year-old grandson, Grisha, who lives in France, when he came here on his school break for 10 days.

2 cups fresh or frozen
   blueberries
1 (8-ounce) can crushed
   pineapple
1 (2-layer) package
   yellow cake mix
½ cup chopped pecans
¾ cup (1½ sticks)
   butter, melted

Layer the blueberries, pineapple, cake mix and pecans in a greased and floured 9×13-inch cake pan; do not stir. Drizzle with the butter. Bake at 350 degrees for 45 to 60 minutes or until the cake tests done. Cool in the pan for 10 minutes. Remove to a wire rack to cool completely. Yield: 12 servings.

Nancy E. Clapp, Preceptor Xi Sigma
Houston, Texas

BLACK FOREST CAKE

1 (2-layer) package chocolate cake mix	2 (16-ounce) cans cherry pie filling
1 (12-ounce) diet cola	8 ounces whipped topping

Combine the cake mix and the cola in a bowl and mix well. Pour into a greased and floured 9×13-inch cake pan. Bake at 350 degrees for 30 minutes. Cool in the pan for 10 minutes. Remove to a wire rack to cool completely. Combine the pie filling and whipped topping in a bowl. Spread on the cooled cake. Yield: 9 to 12 servings.

Dorothy Holbrook, Alpha Omega Master
Winter Park, Florida

BUTTERSCOTCH SURPRISE CAKE

1 (2-layer) package German chocolate cake mix	8 ounces whipped topping
1 cup butterscotch syrup	Toffee pieces or crushed chocolate-covered toffee bar

Prepare the cake mix using the package directions. Pour into a greased and floured 9×13-inch cake pan. Bake at 350 degrees for 25 to 30 minutes or until the cake tests done. Pierce the warm cake with a fork and drizzle with the butterscotch syrup. Cool completely in the pan. Spread with the whipped topping and sprinkle with toffee pieces. Chill until just before serving. Yield: 12 to 15 servings.

Dotti Celso, Alpha Nu Master
Jacksonville, Florida

CHERRY CHOCOLATE CAKE

3 eggs	1/3 cup vegetable oil
1 (2-layer) package devil's food cake mix	1 (4-ounce) package chocolate instant pudding
1 (21-ounce) can cherry pie filling	

Beat the eggs in a large bowl. Stir in the cake mix, pie filling and oil until blended. Pour into a greased and floured 9×13-inch pan. Bake for 35 to 40 minutes or until the cake tests done. Cool in the pan for 10 minutes. Remove to a wire rack to cool completely. Prepare the pudding mix using the package directions and spread evenly on the cake. Garnish with whipped cream, chopped nuts and maraschino cherries. Chill, covered, until just before serving. You may omit the pudding if desired. Yield: 12 to 15 servings.

Barbara Swedenburg, Preceptor Alpha Omicron
Columbus, Nebraska

LIGHT AND LUSCIOUS CHOCOLATE CAKE

1 (2-layer) package chocolate cake mix	8 ounces low-calorie whipped topping
1 (12-ounce) diet cola or diet cherry cola	Fresh or frozen raspberries

Combine the cake mix and cola in a bowl and mix well. Pour into 2 greased and floured 9-inch cake pans. Bake at 350 degrees for 30 minutes. Cool in the pans for 10 minutes. Remove to a wire rack to cool completely. Combine the whipped topping and raspberries in a bowl. Spread the whipped topping mixture between the layers and over the top and side of the cooled cake. Chill until just before serving. Yield: 12 to 15 servings.

Mary Stuhr, Preceptor Alpha
Council Bluffs, Iowa

CHOCOLATE CAKE

1 (2-layer) package German chocolate cake mix	12 ounces whipped topping
1 (14-ounce) can sweetened condensed milk	4 Butterfinger candy bars, crushed

Prepare and bake the cake mix using the package directions for a 9×13-inch cake pan. Pierce the warm cake with a fork and drizzle with the condensed milk. Cool completely in the pan. Frost with the whipped topping and sprinkle with Butterfingers. Chill until just before serving. Yield: 12 to 15 servings.

Rene Ann Kennedy, Xi Beta Sigma
Sulphur, Oklahoma

CHERRY FUDGE CAKE

1 (2-layer) package fudge cake mix	1 teaspoon almond extract
2 eggs	1 (21-ounce) can cherry pie filling

Combine the cake mix, eggs, almond extract and pie filling in a bowl and mix well. Pour into a greased and floured 9×13-inch cake pan. Bake at 350 degrees for 30 to 35 minutes or until the cake tests done. Cool in the pan for 10 minutes. Remove to a wire rack to cool completely. Yield: 12 to 15 servings.

Jeri Lou Herbert, Xi Eta Zeta
Terre Haute, Indiana

GRASSHOPPER CAKE

1 (2-layer) package
  white cake mix
¼ cup crème de menthe
  liqueur
1 jar fudge topping
¼ cup crème de menthe
  liqueur
8 ounces whipped
  topping

Prepare the cake mix using the package directions. Stir ¼ cup crème de menthe into the batter. Bake the cake using the package directions for a 9×13-inch cake pan. Cool in the pan for 5 minutes. Spread with the fudge topping. Cool completely in the pan. Fold ¼ cup crème de menthe into the whipped topping. Spread on the cake. Chill until just before serving. Yield: 15 servings.

Catherine (Kay) Lynch, Xi Alpha Omicron
Necedah, Wisconsin

LEMON CAKE

1 (2-layer) package
  white cake mix
3 eggs
1 (21-ounce) can lemon
  pie filling
1 container cream cheese
  frosting

Combine the cake mix and eggs in a bowl and mix well. Stir in the pie filling. Pour into a greased and floured bundt pan. Bake at 350 degrees for 50 minutes or until the cake tests done. Cool in the pan for 10 minutes. Invert onto a serving plate. Frost the cooled cake. Yield: 12 to 15 servings.

Bronna Lyon, Laureate Delta Beta
Newtown, Missouri

ORANGE CAKE

1 (2-layer) package
  yellow cake mix
1 (12-ounce) can diet
  orange soda
8 ounces whipped
  topping

Combine the cake mix and soda in a bowl and mix well. Pour into a greased and floured 9×13-inch cake pan. Bake at 350 degrees for 25 minutes or until the cake tests done. Cool in the pan for 15 minutes. Remove to a wire rack to cool completely. Cover with the whipped topping. Yield: 12 servings.

Glenda Carlson, Preceptor Xi Zeta
West Sacramento, California

PEACH CAKE

1 (16-ounce) package
  frozen sliced peaches
1 (2-layer) package
  yellow cake mix
22 ounces diet lemon-
  lime soda

Place the peaches in a greased and floured 9×13-inch cake pan. Sprinkle with the cake mix. Pour the soda evenly over the cake mix; do not stir. Bake at 350 degrees for 35 minutes. Cool in the pan for 10 minutes. Remove to a wire rack to cool completely. Chill until just before serving. Serve with fat-free whipped topping if desired. Yield: 12 servings.

Beth A. Burns, Psi Pi
Mazon, Illinois

PECAN APPLE DUMP CAKE

2 (16-ounce) cans apple
  pie filling
1 (2-layer) package
  yellow cake mix
1½ cups (3 sticks)
  margarine, melted
1¼ cups chopped pecans

Pour the pie filling in a greased and floured 9×13-inch cake pan. Sprinkle with the cake mix. Drizzle with the margarine and sprinkle with the pecans; do not stir. Bake at 350 degrees for 1½ hours. Cool in the pan for 10 minutes. Serve warm with whipped topping or ice cream. Yield: 12 servings.

Sue Peters, Xi Nu
Winter Haven, Florida

PINEAPPLE ANGEL FOOD CAKE

1 (16-ounce) package
  angel food cake mix
1 (20-ounce) can crushed
  pineapple

Combine the cake mix and crushed pineapple in bowl and mix well; do not use an electric mixer. Pour into a greased and floured tube pan. Bake at 350 degrees or until firm to the touch. Invert on a funnel to cool completely. Loosen the cake from the side of the pan. Invert onto a serving plate. Serve with berries, whipped topping or ice cream if desired. Yield: 8 to 10 servings.

Barbara Oller, Laureate Zeta Lambda
Orlando, Florida

BLUEBERRY POUND CAKE

1 (2-layer) butter
  cake mix
8 ounces cream cheese,
  softened
½ cup vegetable oil
3 eggs
1 cup blueberries

Combine the cake mix, cream cheese, oil and eggs in a bowl and mix well. Fold in the blueberries. Pour into a greased and floured bundt pan. Bake at 300 degrees for 1 hour. Cool in the pan for 10 minutes. Invert onto a serving plate. Yield: 12 to 15 servings.

Annette Guillory, Lambda Beta
Natchitoches, Louisiana

POUND CAKE

1 cup (2 sticks) butter, softened	**2 cups flour**
1²/₃ cups sugar	**¹/₂ teaspoon vanilla, almond or rum extract**
5 eggs	

Beat the butter and sugar in a bowl until light and fluffy. Add the eggs 1 at a time, mixing well after each addition. Add the flour and vanilla and mix well. Pour into a greased and floured 5×8-inch loaf pan. Bake at 300 degrees for 1¹/₂ hours. Cool in the pan for 10 minutes. Remove to a wire rack to cool completely. Yield: 10 servings.

Bobbie J. Quick, Alpha Lambda Master
Mentor, Ohio

PUMPKIN SPONGE CAKE

1 angel food cake mix	**1 teaspoon pumpkin pie spice**
1 (15-ounce) can pumpkin	**Fat-free whipped topping**
1 cup water	

Combine the cake mix, pumpkin, water and pumpkin pie spice in a bowl and mix well. Pour into an ungreased 9×13-inch cake pan. Bake at 350 degrees for 25 or 30 minutes or until the cake tests done. Cool in the pan for 10 minutes. Remove to a wire rack to cool completely. Serve with whipped topping. Yield: 16 to 24 servings.

Jana Johnson, Xi Mu Beta
Stuart, Florida

RED VELVET CAKE

1 (2-layer) red velvet cake mix (without pudding)	**9 ounces diet cherry vanilla cola**
	Low-fat whipped topping

Combine the cake mix and cola in a bowl and mix well. Pour into a greased and floured 9×13-inch cake pan. Bake at 350 degrees for 30 minutes. Cool in the pan for 10 minutes. Remove to a wire rack to cool completely. Serve with whipped topping. Yield: 12 to 15 servings.

Diana K. Adams, Theta
Vincennes, Indiana

RICOTTA CHEESE CAKE

This recipe took second place at a county fair in 1998.

1 (2-layer) package yellow cake mix	**³/₄ cup sugar**
4 cups ricotta cheese	**¹/₄ teaspoon vanilla extract**
2 eggs	

Prepare the cake mix using package directions, using only 2 eggs instead of 3. Pour into a greased and floured 9×13-inch cake pan. Combine the ricotta cheese, eggs, sugar and vanilla in a bowl and mix well. Pour over the cake batter. Bake at 350 degrees for 1 hour. The cheese will rise to the top after baking. Cool in the pan for 10 minutes. Remove to a wire rack to cool completely. Yield: 12 to 15 servings.

Linda Wilmoth, Laureate Gamma Xi
St. Petersburg, Florida

APPLE PIE

1 (6-ounce) can frozen apple juice concentrate, thawed	**2 teaspoons cinnamon**
	6 Golden Delicious apples, sliced
2 tablespoons cornstarch	**1 (2-crust) pie pastry**

Mix the first 3 ingredients in a bowl. Add the apples and mix well. Unfold 1 pastry into a pie plate. Spoon in the fruit mixture. Top with the remaining pastry, sealing the edge and cutting vents. Bake at 350 degrees for 1 hour. Yield: 6 to 8 servings.

Cheri Kent, Preceptor Gamma Upsilon
Austin, Colorado

OPEN-FACED BLUEBERRY PIE

My family enjoys picking blueberries, which grow wild here. You can also use strawberries in this recipe.

4 cups blueberries	**1 cup sugar**
1 baked (9-inch) pie shell	**2 tablespoons cornstarch**
1 tablespoon lemon juice	

Place 2 cups of the blueberries in the pie shell. Combine the remaining 2 cups blueberries, lemon juice, sugar, and cornstarch in a saucepan. Cook over low heat until thickened, stirring often. Remove from the heat and cool slightly. Pour the mixture into the pie shell. Cool completely. Serve with whipped cream or ice cream. Yield: 6 to 8 servings.

Beverly Goranson, Delta Eta
Elliot Lake, Ontario, Canada

Charlene A. Schilling, Xi Epsilon Epislon, Evansville, Indiana, prepares **Peach Cobbler** *by beating 2 cups baking mix, 1¹/₂ cups milk and 1¹/₂ cups sugar in a bowl until smooth. She then pours ¹/₂ cup (1 stick) melted butter into a 9×13-inch baking pan and spreads the batter evenly over the butter, topping with two (16-ounce) cans drained peaches. The cobbler is baked at 375 degrees for 45 minutes and cooled on a wire rack. She serves with ice cream or whipped topping.*

CANDY BAR PIE

I bought this pie at a church auction and fell in love with it!

8 ounces cream cheese, softened
1/2 cup confectioners' sugar
8 ounces whipped topping
6 large Butterfinger candy bars, crushed
1 (9-inch) graham cracker pie shell

Beat the cream cheese and confectioners' sugar in a bowl until light and fluffy. Fold in the whipped topping and 4 of the crushed candy bars. Pour the mixture into the pie shell. Sprinkle with the remaining crushed candy bars. Chill for 4 hours. Yield: 6 to 8 servings.

Kali Erdman, Alpha Delta Epsilon
Higginsville, Missouri

CREAMY CHEESECAKE PIE

You can top this pie with glazed strawberries.

16 ounces cream cheese, softened
1 (14-ounce) can sweetened condensed milk
1 teaspoon vanilla extract
1/4 cup lemon juice
1 (9-inch) graham cracker pie shell

Beat the cream cheese in a bowl until light and fluffy. Add the condensed milk, vanilla and lemon juice and mix well. Pour into the pie shell. Chill for several hours. Yield: 6 to 8 servings.

Sharon A. Heiman, Laureate Beta Psi
Harper Woods, Michigan

CHERRY PIE CUPS

These pie cups are a good alternative to traditional cherry pie.

1 (2-crust) pie pastry, at room temperature
1 (21-ounce) can cherry pie filling
8 ounces whipped topping

Cut six rounds from each pie shell with a 3 1/2- or 4-inch round cutter; discard the scraps. Press the rounds into ungreased muffin cups. Spoon the pie filling into the cups. Bake at 425 degrees for 14 to 18 minutes or until the pie shell edges are golden brown and the filling is bubbly. Cool completely. Top with the whipped topping just before serving. Yield: 12 pie cups.

Barbara Allen, Laureate Alpha
Brewer, Maine

CHOCOLATE DELIGHT PIE

This pie is easy to make and is a favorite of young and old.

1/2 cup milk
15 large marshmallows
1 (4-ounce) milk chocolate bar
1 cup whipped cream
1 (9-inch) chocolate crumb pie shell

Pour the milk in a saucepan and cook over low heat until warmed through. Add the marshmallows and chocolate and cook until smooth, stirring constantly. Remove from the heat and cool completely. Fold in the whipped cream. Pour into the pie shell. Chill until just before serving. Yield: 6 to 8 servings.

Elsie Wagler, Iota Master
Cody, Wyoming

FRENCH SILK CHOCOLATE PIE

This pie has been a sorority favorite for 25 years!

1 cup (2 sticks) butter, softened
1 1/2 cups sugar
2 ounces unsweetened chocolate, melted
4 eggs
1 (9-inch) graham cracker pie shell

Beat the butter and sugar in a bowl until light and fluffy. Stir in the chocolate. Add the eggs 2 at a time, beating for 5 minutes after each addition. Pour into the pie shell. Chill for 2 hours or longer. Serve with whipped topping. Yield: 8 servings.

Victoria E. Butcher, Preceptor Alpha Gamma
Buford, Georgia

COCONUT CREAM PIE

There are three Weight Watchers points in each piece of pie.

1 small box sugar-free vanilla instant pudding mix
1 3/4 cup fat-free half-and-half
1/4 cup shredded coconut
1 (9-inch) reduced-fat graham cracker pie shell
6 ounces fat-free whipped topping

Beat the pudding mix and half-and-half in a bowl for 2 minutes. Stir in 2 tablespoons of the coconut. Pour the mixture into the pie shell. Toast the remaining coconut. Top with the whipped topping and sprinkle with toasted coconut. Chill until just before serving. Yield: 8 servings.

Betty Phillips, Delta Iota Master
Farmers Branch, Texas

NO-BAKE LEMON PIE

1 egg
1 (14-ounce) can
   sweetened
   condensed milk
Juice of 3 lemons

1 (8-inch) graham
   cracker pie shell
8 ounces whipped
   topping

Combine the egg, condensed milk and lemon juice in a bowl and mix well. Pour the mixture into the pie shell. Chill for 2 hours or longer. Serve with whipped topping. Yield: 6 servings.

Yvonne Norris, Laureate Delta Alpha
Aurora, Colorado

LEMONADE PIE

1 (6-ounce) can frozen
   lemonade
   concentrate, thawed
9 ounces whipped
   topping

1 (14-ounce) can
   sweetened condensed
   milk
1 (9-inch) graham
   cracker pie shell

Combine the lemonade, whipped topping and condensed milk in a bowl and mix well. Pour into the pie shell. Chill until just before serving.
Yield: 4 to 6 servings.

Theresa (Malinda) Lysinger, Alpha Delta Phi
Lowry City, Missouri

FIVE-MINUTE KEY LIME PIE

1 small package sugar-
   free lime gelatin
1/4 cup boiling water
16 ounces Key lime pie
   light yogurt

8 ounces fat-free
   whipped topping
1 (9-inch) reduced-fat
   graham cracker
   pie shell

Combine the gelatin and water in a large heat-resistant bowl, stirring until the gelatin dissolves. Whisk in the yogurt. Fold in the whipped topping. Spoon the mixture in the pie shell. Chill for 2 hours or longer. Store in the refrigerator. Yield: 6 to 8 servings.

Dana L. Harris, Alpha Gamma Alpha
Warsaw, Missouri

MILK PIE

This is one of my husband's favorite pies. His mom made it for them all the time. It was cheap and easy when times were tough.

1 cup sugar
1/4 cup cornstarch
2 tablespoons butter

2 cups milk
1 (9-inch) pie shell,
   baked for 10 minutes

Combine the sugar, cornstarch, butter and milk in a saucepan. Bring to a boil over medium heat. Reduce the heat and cook for 20 minutes, stirring constantly. Pour into the pie shell. Bake at 350 degrees for 20 to 25 minutes until the shell is golden brown. Sprinkle with cinnamon if desired. Yield: 6 to 8 servings.

Linda Rehmert, Xi Delta Tau
Dove Creek, Colorado

PARFAIT PIE

1 (3-ounce) package
   raspberry or
   strawberry gelatin
1/4 cup boiling water
1 pint vanilla ice cream

1 1/2 cups raspberries or
   sliced strawberries
1 (9-inch) baked
   pie shell

Combine the gelatin and water in a bowl, stirring until the gelatin dissolves. Add the ice cream 1 spoonful at a time, mixing well after each addition. Chill until thickened but not set. Fold in the fruit. Spoon into the pie shell. Chill until firm.
Yield: 6 to 8 servings.

Linda Thoma, Xi Theta
Dover, Delaware

NO-BAKE PUMPKIN CREAM PIE

1 quart vanilla ice
   cream or low-fat
   frozen yogurt,
   softened
1 (16-ounce) can
   pumpkin

2 (3 1/2-ounce) packages
   vanilla instant
   pudding
2 (9-inch) graham
   cracker pie shells
8 ounces whipped
   topping

Combine the ice cream and pumpkin in a bowl and mix gently. Add the pudding and mix well. Pour into the pie shells. Chill, covered, overnight. Serve with whipped topping. Yield: 16 servings.

Michaela Wells, Gamma Upsilon
Prairie View, Kansas

RASPBERRY YOGURT PIE

12 ounces low-fat
   raspberry yogurt
1/2 cup raspberries
8 ounces whipped
   topping

1 (9-inch) graham
   cracker pie shell

Combine the yogurt and raspberries in a bowl and mix well. Fold in the whipped topping. Spoon into the pie shell. Freeze, covered, until just before serving. Yield: 6 servings.

Betty Gotte, Alpha Omicron Master
Cañon City, Colorado

STRAWBERRY MINUTE PIE

This is an old recipe of my mom's. She would make it as a little treat for my sisters and me.

1 (3-ounce) package
    strawberry gelatin
1 cup boiling water
1 (16-ounce) package
    frozen sliced
    strawberries
1 (8-inch) baked
    pie shell

Mix the gelatin and water in a bowl, stirring until the gelatin dissolves. Add the frozen strawberries, breaking them up with a fork. Stir until thickened. When the gelatin is partially set, pour the mixture into the pie shell. Chill until set. Garnish with sweetened whipped cream or whipped topping.
Yield: 6 to 8 servings.

Marylove Jacobs, Laureate Delta
Phoenix, Arizona

NO-BAKE STRAWBERRY PIE

My dad dislikes yogurt but loves this pie. I still haven't divulged the ingredients to him!

1/2 to 1 cup sliced
    strawberries
1 (9-inch) graham
    cracker pie shell
8 ounces strawberry
    yogurt
8 ounces whipped
    topping

Arrange half the strawberries in the pie shell. Combine the remaining strawberries with the yogurt and whipped topping in a bowl and mix well. Spoon the mixture into the pie shell. Garnish with additional sliced strawberries. Chill for 2 hours or longer.
Yield: 6 to 8 servings.

Sherilynn Paul, Xi Sigma Zet
Granada Hills, California

AMBROSIA PARFAIT

2 cups plain fat-free
    yogurt
1 teaspoon vanilla
    extract
2 cups sliced fruit
2 tablespoons
    chopped nuts
1 tablespoon flaked
    coconut (optional)

Combine the yogurt and vanilla in a bowl and mix well. Place one-quarter of the fruit in a parfait glass. Top with one-quarter of the yogurt mixture. Repeat the layers. Sprinkle with half the nuts and half the coconut. Repeat the process with the remaining ingredients and another parfait glass.
Yield: 2 servings.

Karen Asselin, Xi Zeta
Dover, New Hampshire

EASY AMBROSIA

2 (11-ounce) cans
    mandarin oranges,
    drained
2 (20-ounce) cans
    crushed pineapple
1 (10-ounce) package
    miniature
    marshmallows
4 cups sour cream
2 cups flaked coconut

Combine the oranges, pineapple, marshmallows, sour cream and coconut in a bowl and mix gently. Spoon into a 9×13-inch baking dish. Chill, covered, until cold. Yield: 12 to 24 servings.

Judy Ann Evans, Alpha Beta Master
Fairmont, West Virginia

FRIED APPLES

This tastes just like apple pie without the crust.

12 to 15 apples, peeled
    and sliced
1/2 cup (1 stick)
    margarine
1 cup sugar
Cinnamon or nutmeg
    to taste

Sauté the apples in the margarine in a skillet just until tender. Stir in the sugar and cinnamon. Spoon into serving dishes and top with whipped cream or vanilla ice cream. Yield: 12 servings.

Shirley J. Davidson, Preceptor Xi
Devils Lake, North Dakota

MICROWAVE APPLE DESSERT

Put this in the microwave when you sit down to dinner and it's ready in time for dessert.

1 cup Spenda
1/2 cup Splenda Brown
    Sugar Blend
1/2 teaspoon cinnamon
2 tablespoons
    cornstarch
4 to 5 apples, sliced

Combine the Splenda, Splenda Brown Sugar Blend, cinnamon and cornstarch in a bowl and mix well. Add the apples and toss to coat. Spoon into a microwave-safe baking dish coated with nonstick cooking spray. Microwave, covered, on Medium for 15 minutes. Serve with fat-free whipped topping.
Yield: 4 servings.

Theresa (Malinda) Lysinger, Alpha Delta Phi
Lowry City, Missouri

Molly Todd, Xi Eta Xi, Merritt Island, Florida, makes **No-Guilt Pistachio Fluff** *by mixing 1 small package fat-free sugar-free pistachio instant pudding mix, one 20-ounce can undrained crushed pineapple and 2 cups plain fat-free yogurt in a bowl. She folds in 1 cup light whipped topping and chills, covered, until cold.*

CARAMEL FRUIT DIP

16 ounces cream cheese, softened	1 cup packed brown sugar
	1/2 cup caramel topping

Combine the cream cheese, brown sugar and caramel topping in a bowl. Beat until smooth. Serve with fresh fruit or use as a frosting for cake. Yield: 3 cups.

Dianna Hartman, Xi Omega
Paul, Idaho

DREAMSICLE DESSERT

24 ounces low-fat cottage cheese	1 large package sugar-free orange gelatin
12 ounces fat-free whipped topping	1 (15-ounce) can mandarin oranges, drained

Combine the cottage cheese and whipped topping in a bowl and mix well. Add the gelatin and mix well. Stir in the oranges. Yield: 6 to 8 servings.

Judy Osborne, Laureate Epsilon
Montgomery, Alabama

BLUSHED PEARS

4 cups water	4 pears, peeled
1 (3-ounce) package raspberry gelatin	

Bring the water to a boil in a saucepan. Add the gelatin and stir until it dissolves. Add the pears and simmer, covered, for 10 minutes. Turn the pears over and simmer for 10 minutes or until tender. Remove the pears with a slotted spoon to serving bowls. Serve warm or chilled with vanilla yogurt or vanilla pudding and topped with oats or crunchy cereal. Yield: 4 servings.

Paula Roberts, Laureate Epsilon Theta
St. Petersburg, Florida

BAKED PINEAPPLE

This tastes like pineapple upside down cake and is so much easier to make.

2 (20-ounce) cans pineapple chunks, drained	3/4 cup crushed butter crackers
1 cup packed brown sugar	3 tablespoons butter, cut into small pieces

Arrange half the pineapple over the bottom of a 7×11-inch baking dish. Sprinkle with half the brown sugar and half the crushed crackers. Dot with half the butter. Repeat the layers. Bake at 300 degrees for 45 to 50 minutes. Remove to a wire rack to cool. Serve warm. Yield: 8 to 10 servings.

Kathy Fishel, Eta Beta
Gainesville, Florida

STRAWBERRY GELATIN DESSERT

I have taken this dessert to Beta potlucks to accommodate diabetic sisters.

1 (20-ounce) can crushed pineapple or pineapple tidbits	2 cups boiling water
	4 cups frozen sliced strawberries, thawed
2 small packages sugar-free strawberry gelatin	2 bananas, mashed

Drain the pineapple, reserving 1/4 cup juice. Dissolve the gelatin in the boiling water in a bowl. Stir in the strawberries, bananas, pineapple and reserved juice. Pour into a 9×13-inch baking dish. Chill, covered, for several hours. Serve with whipped cream or whipped topping. Yield: 12 servings.

Doreen J. Balint, Laureate Alpha
Sarasota, Florida

MARSHMALLOW APPLESAUCE DESSERT

4 cups applesauce	2 cups miniature marshmallows
1/2 teaspoon cinnamon	
1/4 teaspoon nutmeg	

Combine the applesauce, cinnamon and nutmeg in a bowl and mix well. Pour into a nonstick 9×13-inch baking pan. Sprinkle with the marshmallows. Bake at 350 degrees for 10 minutes. Remove to a wire rack to cool. Serve warm. Yield: 15 servings.

Beverly Schwab, Laureate Omega
Memphis, Tennessee

APRICOT BAKE

5 to 6 (16-ounce) cans apricot halves, drained	35 butter crackers, crumbled
1 (1-pound) package brown sugar	1/2 cup (1 stick) margarine, thinly sliced

Arrange the apricot halves, cut side up, in a nonstick 9×13-inch baking pan. Sprinkle evenly with the brown sugar and crumbled crackers. Arrange the margarine slices evenly over the top. Bake at 300 degrees for 1 hour. Serve warm with vanilla ice cream if desired. Yield: 12 servings.

Dianna Hanzelka, Alpha Kappa Rho
Yoakum, Texas

BLACKBERRY CHERRY CRUMBLE

**1 (21-ounce) can
    blackberry pie filling**
**1 (21-ounce) can cherry
    pie filling**
**1 (2-layer) package
    yellow cake mix**
**1/2 cup (1 stick) butter,
    softened**
1/2 cup chopped pecans

Spoon the blackberry pie filling and cherry pie filling into a greased 9×13-inch baking dish; do not mix. Mix the cake mix, butter and pecans in a bowl until crumbly. Sprinkle evenly over the pie fillings. Bake at 350 degrees for 45 minutes or until golden brown. Serve warm with whipped topping or ice cream. Yield: 18 servings.

*Marla Egbert, Laureate Omega
American Falls, Idaho*

QUICK AND EASY COBBLER

2 cups baking mix
1 cup milk
**1/2 cup (1 stick) butter or
    margarine, melted**
**2 (21-ounce) cans pie
    filling (any flavor)**
1/2 cup sugar

Beat the baking mix and milk in a bowl until smooth. Pour the butter in an 8×12-inch baking pan. Pour the batter over the butter. Spoon the pie filling evenly over the batter and sprinkle with the sugar. Bake at 350 degrees for 45 minutes or until golden brown. Remove to a wire rack to cool. Yield: 8 to 12 servings.

*Mickey Taylor, Preceptor Alpha Epsilon
Edmond, Oklahoma*

MELT-IN-YOUR-MOUTH PEACH COBBLER

**1 (29-ounce) can sliced
    peaches**
**1 (2-layer) package
    yellow cake mix**
**1/2 cup (1 stick) butter or
    margarine, melted**
1/2 cup chopped pecans

Pour the peaches into a greased 9×13-inch baking pan. Sprinkle with the cake mix. Pour the butter evenly over the cake mix and sprinkle with the pecans. Bake at 350 degrees for 40 minutes. Serve warm with ice cream. Yield: 12 servings.

*Janet Chapman, Xi Beta
Marshall, Minnesota*

CORNFLAKE CAKE

**1 cup packed brown
    sugar**
**1 cup peanut butter
    (may use chunky)**
1 cup light corn syrup
6 cups cornflakes

Combine the brown sugar, peanut butter and corn syrup in a saucepan. Bring to a boil over medium heat, stirring frequently. Pour over the cornflakes in a large bowl and mix well. Press lightly into a nonstick 9×11-inch baking pan. Let stand until firm. Yield: 24 servings.

*Crystal Neudorf, Delta
Edwin, Manitoba, Canada*

CORNFLAKE COOKIES

1/2 cup sugar
1/2 cup light corn syrup
1/2 cup peanut butter
3 to 4 cups cornflakes

Combine the sugar and corn syrup in a saucepan. Cook over medium heat until the sugar dissolves, stirring constantly. Add the peanut butter and cook until smooth, stirring constantly. Remove from the heat. Add the cornflakes and mix well. Drop by large spoonfuls onto waxed paper. Let stand until firm. Break into bite-size pieces. Yield: 24 servings.

*Rebekka Bicart, Xi Alpha Tau
Twin Falls, Idaho*

MOCK CHOCOLATE ÉCLAIRS

**2 (3 1/2-ounce) packages
    vanilla instant
    pudding mix**
3 1/2 cups milk
**8 ounces whipped
    topping**
**1 (16-ounce) package
    club crackers**
**1 container chocolate
    frosting**

Whisk the pudding mix and milk in a bowl for 2 minutes. Fold in the whipped topping. Fit one-third of the crackers in a single layer in a 9×13-inch baking pan. Spread half the pudding evenly over the crackers. Top with half the remaining crackers. Spread with the remaining pudding. Top with the remaining crackers. Heat the frosting in a microwave-safe bowl in the microwave for 30 seconds or just until melted; stir. Pour evenly over the cracker layer. Chill, covered, overnight. Yield: 12 servings.

*Kelli Clevenger, Preceptor Delta Rho
Wakarusa, Kansas*

FRUIT BALLS

Grated zest of 1 orange
1/2 cup chopped nuts
1/2 cup shredded coconut
3 cups dried fruit

Combine the orange zest, nuts, coconut and dried fruit in a food processor and process until finely chopped. Shape into balls. Store in an airtight container in the refrigerator. Yield: 5 to 6 dozen balls.

*Joyce Ann Trojan, Laureate Theta Eta
Camden, Texas*

GUILT-FREE DESSERT

12 ounces light whipped
    topping
8 ounces cottage cheese
1 (8-ounce) can crushed
    pineapple, drained

1 small package
    sugar-free lemon
    gelatin
1/4 cup pecan pieces

Combine the whipped topping, cottage cheese and pineapple in a bowl and mix gently. Sprinkle with the gelatin and mix gently to combine. Sprinkle with the pecans. Chill, covered, for 2 hours.
Yield: 8 to 10 servings.

Janis M. Halstead, Xi Delta Iota
Tucson, Arizona

EASY DONUTS

1 (10-count) can
    refrigerated biscuits
2 cups vegetable oil

Confectioners' sugar,
    cinnamon-sugar or
    chocolate glaze

Separate the biscuits and make a hole in the center of each biscuit. Heat the oil in a heavy saucepan until hot. Add the biscuits and fry until golden brown, turning once during frying. Remove to paper towels to drain. Coat in confectioners' sugar or cinnamon-sugar while warm or drizzle with chocolate glaze when cool. Yield: 10 servings.

Glenda Wall, Xi Alpha Delta Zeta
Schertz, Texas

LEMON FLUFF

1 (6-ounce) package
    lemon gelatin
4 teaspoons lemon juice
1 cup heavy whipping
    cream

1 cup sugar
4 cups graham cracker
    crumbs

Prepare the gelatin using the package directions. Chill until almost set. Add the lemon juice and beat until fluffy. Whip the cream in a large bowl. Beat in the sugar. Add the gelatin mixture and beat until fluffy. Spread half the graham cracker crumbs in a 9×13-inch baking pan. Top with the lemon mixture. Sprinkle evenly with the remaining graham cracker crumbs. Chill, covered, until set. Yield: 15 servings.

Mardele Toth, Laureate Iota
Havre, Montana

MACAROON DESSERT

12 ounces whipped
    topping
3 bananas, sliced

1 to 1 1/2 cups crushed
    macaroon cookies
1/2 cup chopped pecans

Spread half the whipped topping in a glass bowl. Top with the bananas. Sprinkle with the cookie crumbs, reserving a small amount for garnish. Sprinkle with the pecans. Spread with the remaining whipped topping and sprinkle with the remaining cookie crumbs. Chill, covered, for 4 hours or longer. Yield: 8 servings.

Nina Jane Hickman, Laureate Delta Beta
Princeton, Missouri

OAT SLICE

2 cups rolled oats
3/4 cup packed brown
    sugar

1/2 cup (1 stick) butter or
    margarine
1 teaspoon vanilla
    extract

Combine the oats and brown sugar in a bowl and mix well. Cut in the butter until crumbly. Stir in the vanilla. Press into a nonstick 8×8-inch baking pan. Bake at 375 degrees for 12 to 20 minutes or until golden brown and the edges are bubbly. Remove to a wire rack. Score with a sharp knife. Cool completely. Cut along the scored lines and remove from the pan. Yield: 16 servings.

Janet Clatney-Bertsch, Laureate Delta
Saskatoon, Saskatchewan, Cananda

ORANGE SMOOTHIE

This smoothie is quick and easy. No sugar is added so my diabetic friends can enjoy it.

1 cup cold water
1/4 cup dry milk powder
1 cup ice cubes

1 (6-ounce) can frozen
    orange juice
    concentrate, partially
    thawed

Combine all the ingredients in a blender. Process until smooth and foamy. Serve immediately.
Yield: 3 to 4 servings.

Cari Goebel Frahm, Zeta Master
Havre, Montana

PEANUT BUTTER BALLS

1/2 cup peanut butter
1/2 cup honey
3/4 to 1 1/2 cups dry milk
    powder

Flaked coconut,
    sunflower kernels or
    chopped nuts
    (optional)

Combine the peanut butter, honey and dry milk in a bowl and mix well. Shape into balls. Roll in coconut, sunflower kernels or chopped nuts.
Yield: 3 dozen balls.

Roberta Viau, Xi Gamma Eta
Hudsonville, Michigan

RASPBERRY FLUMMERY

Any fresh or frozen berry will work in this recipe.

2 cups raspberries
1/2 cup cold water
1/3 cup sugar

1/4 cup cornstarch
1/2 teaspoon salt

Combine the raspberries and water in a 2-quart saucepan. Cook, covered, over medium heat for 10 minutes or until the berries are soft. Combine the sugar, cornstarch and salt in a small bowl and mix well. Stir into the raspberry mixture gradually. Reduce the heat to low. Cook for 5 minutes or until thickened, stirring constantly. Spoon into heatproof glasses. Chill, covered, until cold. Yield: 4 servings.

*Sharon Wiggins, Preceptor Alpha Omicron
Deer Park, Texas*

RICOTTA AND BLUEBERRY PARFAIT

1 cup low-fat ricotta
   cheese
1 tablespoon
   confectioners' sugar

Grated zest of 1 lemon
1 1/2 cups blueberries

Combine the ricotta cheese, confectioners' sugar and lemon zest in a bowl and mix well. Place 3 tablespoons blueberries into each of 4 parfait glasses. Divide the cheese mixture evenly among the glasses. Top each with 3 tablespoons blueberries. Garnish with additional grated lemon zest, chopped pecans or slivered almonds. Yield: 4 servings

*Roxanne Bowell, Laureate Eta
Palmer, Alaska*

KAHLÚA BROWNIE TRIFLE

1 (19 1/2-ounce) package
   brownie mix
1/4 cup Kahlúa
1 (3 1/2-ounce) package
   chocolate instant
   mousse mix

8 (1 1/4-ounce) chocolate-
   covered toffee bars,
   crushed
12 ounces whipped
   topping

Prepare and bake the brownie mix using the package directions for a 9×13-inch baking pan. Pierce the warm brownie with a fork. Brush with the Kahlúa. Cool completely in the pan. Crumble the cooled brownie. Prepare the chocolate mousse using the package directions; do not chill. Spread half of the crumbled brownies over the bottom of a trifle bowl. Top with half the mousse and sprinkle with half the crushed candy. Spread with half the whipped topping. Repeat the layers. Garnish with additional crushed candy. Chill, covered, for 8 hours. Yield: 16 servings.

*Deborah A. Miller, Laureate Lambda
Wichita, Kansas*

CHERRIES ON A CLOUD TRIFLE

8 ounces cream cheese,
   softened
1 cup sugar
6 ounces whipped
   topping

1 angel food cake, torn
   into pieces
1 (21-ounce) can cherry
   pie filling

Beat the cream cheese and sugar in a bowl until light and fluffy. Fold in the whipped topping. Fold in the cake pieces. Spoon the pie filling evenly over the top. Chill, covered, until ready to serve. Yield: 12 servings.

*Savanah Hargraves, Laureate Eta
Wasilla, Alaska*

LEMON TRIFLE

You may use sugar-free instant lemon pudding mix or canned lemon pie filling in this recipe.

1 (6-ounce) package
   lemon pudding mix
1 angel food cake

8 ounces whipped
   topping

Prepare the pudding mix using the package directions; cool slightly. Cut the cake into 3/4-inch pieces. Arrange half the cake pieces over the bottom of a 9×13-inch baking pan. Add the remaining cake pieces and half the whipped topping to the pudding and mix well. Spread over the cake in the baking pan. Spread with the remaining whipped topping. Chill, covered, until ready to serve. Yield: 16 servings.

*Sandra Martin, Laureate Delta Xi
Niagara Falls, Ontario, Canada*

MOCHA WALNUT TRUFFLES

1/2 cup heavy cream
1 tablespoon instant
   coffee granules
8 ounces bittersweet or
   semisweet chocolate,
   finely chopped

2 teaspoons vanilla
   extract
1 1/2 cups ground walnuts

Heat the cream in a saucepan just until boiling. Add the coffee granules and stir until dissolved. Pour over the chocolate in a bowl. Let stand for 30 seconds. Whisk until smooth. Stir in the vanilla. Lay a sheet of plastic wrap over the filling and press gently to prevent a skin from forming. Chill for 6 hours or longer. Spread the walnuts in a shallow dish. Shape the chocolate mixture by rounded teaspoonfuls into balls. Coat with the walnuts and place on a waxed paper-lined or parchment paper-lined baking sheet. Cover with plastic wrap. Chill for 1 hour or longer. Yield: 2 dozen truffles.

*Sharon M. Goins, Xi Rho Gamma
Vernon, Texas*

Rolling Pin

PIES AND PASTRIES

ANGEL NUT PIE

4 egg whites
2 teaspoons baking powder
1 cup sugar
1 cup graham cracker crumbs

1 cup chopped nuts
1 teaspoon vanilla extract
Whipped cream
1 cup chopped nuts

Beat the egg whites in a bowl until soft peaks form. Add the baking powder and sugar gradually, beating until stiff peaks form. Fold in the graham cracker crumbs, 1 cup chopped nuts and vanilla. Pour into a greased pie plate. Bake at 325 degrees for 30 minutes or until a wooden pick inserted in the center comes out clean. Remove to a wire rack to cool. Top with whipped cream and sprinkle with nuts just before serving. Yield: 8 to 10 servings.

Paula Roberts, Laureate Epsilon Theta
St. Petersburg, Florida

APPLE PIE

6 Granny Smith apples, peeled and sliced
3/4 cup granulated sugar
1 teaspoon cinnamon
1/4 teaspoon ground cloves
2 tablespoons cornstarch
1/4 cup (1/2 stick) butter or margarine, cut into small pieces

1 (9-inch) unbaked pie shell
1/2 cup packed brown sugar
1/3 cup all-purpose flour
1/2 cup chopped nuts
1/3 cup quick-cooking oats
2 1/2 tablespoons butter or margarine, softened

Place the apples in a large bowl. Add the granulated sugar, cinnamon, cloves and cornstarch and toss to coat. Add 1/4 cup butter and mix well. Spoon into the pie shell. Combine the brown sugar, flour, nuts and oats in a bowl. Cut in 2 1/2 tablespoons butter until crumbly. Sprinkle over the apples. Bake at 325 degrees for 55 minutes. Remove to a wire rack to cool. Serve warm with vanilla ice cream if desired. Yield: 6 to 8 servings.

Frances Wright, Laureate Tau
Tarboro, North Carolina

MICROWAVE APPLE PIE

1 (12-ounce) can frozen apple juice concentrate, thawed
3 tablespoons quick-cooking tapioca
1/8 teaspoon salt
1 teaspoon cinnamon
1/2 teaspoon nutmeg
2 tablespoons butter or margarine

5 Golden Delicious apples, peeled and sliced
1 (9-inch) baked pie shell
1/2 cup chopped nuts (optional)

Pour the apple juice concentrate into an 8×8-inch baking dish. Stir in the tapioca, salt, cinnamon and nutmeg. Let stand for 10 minutes or longer. Add the butter and apples and stir to coat. Microwave on Medium for 8 minutes or until bubbly and thickened, stirring occasionally. Cool completely. Spoon into the pie shell. Sprinkle with chopped nuts. Chill, covered, until just before serving. Serve with whipped cream or ice cream if desired. Yield: 6 to 8 servings.

Maxine Birdsong, Laureate Delta Tau
Wentzville, Missouri

NORWEGIAN APPLE PIE

1 egg, beaten	1/4 teaspoon salt
3/4 cup sugar	1 teaspoon cinnamon
1 teaspoon vanilla	1/2 cup all-purpose flour
extract	1/2 cup chopped walnuts
1 teaspoon baking	or pecans
powder	2 tart apples, chopped

Mix the first 7 ingredients in a bowl. Add the walnuts and apples and mix well. Spoon into a buttered 9-inch pie plate. Bake at 350 degrees for 30 to 35 minutes or until brown. Serve with whipped cream or ice cream if desired. Yield: 6 to 8 servings.

Virginia Mullen, Alpha Lambda Master
Hummelstown, Pennsylvania

PAPER BAG APPLE PIE

5 or 6 apples, sliced	5 tablespoons
1 (9-inch) unbaked	all-purpose flour
pie shell	3 tablespoons water
1 1/2 cups sugar	1/2 cup flour
1/8 teaspoon salt	1/2 cup (1 stick) margarine

Arrange the apples in the pie shell. Sprinkle with the sugar, salt, 5 tablespoons flour and water. Place 1/2 cup flour in a bowl. Cut in the margarine until crumbly. Sprinkle over the pie. Slide the pie in a large oven-cooking bag. Close the bag with paper clips or staples. Place on a baking sheet. Bake at 425 degrees for 1 hour. Split the bag carefully. Remove to a wire rack to cool. Yield: 8 servings.

Barbara Black, Preceptor Eta Upsilon
Cheshire, Ohio

❖ SOUR CREAM APPLE PIE

1 (2-crust) pie pastry	1 teaspoon lemon juice
2/3 cup packed	1/4 teaspoon cinnamon
brown sugar	1/3 teaspoon nutmeg
1 tablespoon cornstarch	1 cup sour cream
4 1/2 cups sliced	
tart apples	

Fit 1 pie pastry into a 9-inch pie plate. Mix the brown sugar and cornstarch. Sprinkle 1/4 of the mixture over the pie pastry. Cover with the apples. Sprinkle with the lemon juice, cinnamon, nutmeg and the remaining brown sugar mixture. Spoon the sour cream over the top. Cover with the remaining pie pastry, sealing the edge and cutting vents. Bake at 450 degrees for 15 minutes. Reduce the heat to 350 degrees. Bake for 30 minutes or until the apples are tender. Remove to a wire rack to cool. Yield: 8 servings.

Gloria Thrasher, Laureate Delta Kappa
Mississauga, Ontario, Canada

APPLE PIE WITH SOURDOUGH CRUST

7 tart apples, peeled	2 tablespoons butter, cut
and sliced	into small pieces
3/4 cup sugar	2 cups all-purpose flour
2 tablespoons	1 cup shortening
all-purpose flour	1/4 cup milk
1 teaspoon cinnamon	2 tablespoons white or
Dash of salt	apple cider vinegar

Combine the apples, sugar, 2 tablespoons flour, cinnamon, salt and butter in a bowl and mix well. Place 2 cups flour in a medium bowl. Cut in the shortening until crumbly. Add the milk and vinegar, mixing with a fork until the mixture forms a ball. Roll into two 12-inch circles on a lightly floured surface, handling as little as possible. Fit one pastry into a pie plate. Spoon in the apple mixture. Top with the remaining pastry, sealing the edge and cutting vents. Brush with additional milk and sprinkle with additional sugar. Cover the edge with foil. Bake at 400 degrees for 10 minutes. Remove the foil. Bake for 30 minutes or until golden brown. Remove to a wire rack to cool. Yield: 8 servings.

Judy Ridgway, Xi Theta
Annapolis, Maryland

UPSIDE-DOWN APPLE PIE

1/4 cup (1/2 stick) butter,	5 cups peeled and sliced
softened	Granny Smith apples
1/2 cup pecan halves	1/3 cup granulated sugar
1/2 cup packed brown	2 tablespoons
sugar	all-purpose flour
1 (2-crust) pie pastry	1/2 teaspoon cinnamon
	or to taste

Spread the butter on the bottom and side of a pie plate. Press the pecan halves round side-down into the butter. Sprinkle with the brown sugar. Cover with 1 pie pastry. Combine the apples, granulated sugar, flour and cinnamon in a bowl and mix well. Spoon over the pastry in the pie plate. Cover with the remaining pastry, sealing the edge and cutting vents. Cover the edge with foil. Bake at 375 degrees for 25 minutes. Remove the foil. Bake for 20 to 25 minutes or until golden brown. Cool for 5 minutes on a wire rack. Loosen the edge carefully with a sharp knife. Invert onto a serving plate. Serve warm with whipped cream or ice cream if desired.
Yield: 8 servings.

Judy Wagner, Laureate Beta Tau
Buckeye, Arizona

BANANA BLUEBERRY CREAM PIE

2 bananas, sliced
2 (9-inch) baked
  pie shells
12 ounces cream cheese,
  softened
1 1/2 cups sugar

Juice of 1 lemon
16 ounces whipped
  topping
1 (21-ounce) can
  blueberry pie filling

Divide the bananas between the 2 pie shells. Combine the cream cheese, sugar and lemon juice in a bowl and mix well. Fold in the whipped topping. Spoon half the mixture into each pie shell and spread evenly. Top each pie with half the pie filling. Chill, covered, until just before serving. Yield: 12 servings.

Betty Ann Murphy-Rivera, Laureate Theta Tau
Colleyville, Texas

BANANA BUTTERSCOTCH PIE

3/4 cup packed
  brown sugar
1/3 cup all-purpose flour
1/4 teaspoon salt
2 cups milk
2 eggs
1 tablespoon butter or
  margarine

1 teaspoon vanilla
  extract
2 or 3 bananas, sliced
1 (9-inch) baked pie
  shell or graham
  cracker pie shell

Combine the brown sugar, flour and salt in a saucepan. Stir in 1 cup of the milk. Bring to a boil over medium heat, stirring constantly. Boil for 2 minutes, stirring constantly. Remove from the heat. Beat the eggs and the remaining 1 cup milk in a bowl. Stir into the hot mixture gradually. Boil for 1 minute or until thickened over medium heat, stirring constantly. Remove from the heat. Stir in the butter and vanilla. Cool completely. Arrange the bananas in the pie shell. Pour the cooled mixture over the bananas. Chill until just before serving. Serve with whipped cream if desired. Yield: 6 to 8 servings.

Dorothy Armstrong Lang, Xi Gamma
Miles City, Montana

BANANA CHOCOLATE PIE

1 banana, sliced
1 (9-inch) baked pie
  shell
1 1/4 cups sugar
1/3 cup cornstarch
1/2 teaspoon salt
4 egg yolks, slightly
  beaten

3 cups milk
2 tablespoons butter
2 ounces unsweetened
  chocolate, melted
2 teaspoons almond
  extract
1 cup flaked coconut

Arrange the banana in the pie shell. Combine the sugar, cornstarch and salt in a saucepan. Stir in the

egg yolks and milk. Bring to a boil over medium heat, stirring constantly. Boil for 1 minute, stirring constantly. Remove from the heat. Stir in the butter and chocolate until smooth. Stir in the almond extract and coconut. Pour over the bananas in the pie shell. Cool for 2 hours or longer. Chill, covered, until just before serving. Serve with whipped cream if desired. Yield: 8 servings.

Bertie Farabee, Laureate Beta Kappa
Haysville, Kansas

BANANA CREAM PIE

3/4 cup sugar
1/3 cup all-purpose flour
1/4 teaspoon salt
2 cups milk
3 egg yolks, slightly
  beaten

2 tablespoons butter
3 bananas, sliced
1 (9-inch) baked
  pie shell

Combine the sugar, flour and salt in a saucepan. Stir in the milk gradually. Cook for 2 minutes over medium heat, stirring often. Stir a small amount of the hot mixture into the beaten eggs; stir the eggs into the hot mixture. Cook for 2 minutes, stirring constantly. Remove from the heat. Stir in the butter and the bananas. Pour into the pie shell. Cool completely. Top with whipped cream or meringue. Store in the refrigerator. Yield: 6 servings.

Lee Ann Jenson, Beta Rho
Rapid City, South Dakota

FRENCH VANILLA BANANA CREAM PIE

1 banana, sliced
1 (9-inch) graham
  cracker pie shell
2 cups milk

2 (4-ounce) packages
  vanilla instant
  pudding mix
2 cups French vanilla
  whipped topping

Arrange the banana in the pie shell. Combine the milk and pudding mix in a large bowl. Whisk for 2 minutes. Fold in 1 cup of the whipped topping. Spoon over the bananas. Chill for 4 hours or until set. Cover with the remaining whipped topping just before serving. Yield: 8 servings.

Yvonne Nitz, Laureate Beta Lambda
Topeka, Kansas

---

*Pat Love, Preceptor Delta, San Andreas, California, makes a **No-Bake Cranberry Pie**. She combines one 16-ounce can whole cranberries, one drained 16-ounce can crushed pineapple and 6 ounces whipped topping in a bowl and mixes gently. She pours the mixture into a 9-inch baked pie shell.*

BUTTERMILK PIE

This is a great substitute for those who find chess pie too sweet. I love to serve it to my Yankee friends, who can't believe buttermilk can taste so good!

6 tablespoons butter or
   margarine, softened
1¹/2 cups sugar
3 eggs
2 tablespoons
   all-purpose flour

¹/2 cup buttermilk
1 teaspoon vanilla
   extract
1 (9-inch) unbaked
   pie shell

Beat the butter and sugar in a bowl until light and fluffy. Add the eggs and flour and mix until smooth. Add the buttermilk and vanilla and mix well. Pour into the pie shell. Bake at 450 degrees for 15 minutes. Reduce the heat to 300 degrees. Bake for 45 minutes. Remove to a wire rack to cool. Yield: 6 to 8 servings.

Betsy Fisher, Delta Master
Nashville, Tennessee

BUTTERNUT SQUASH PIE

1¹/2 cups boiled and
   mashed butternut
   squash
1 tablespoon butter,
   softened
1 teaspoon cinnamon
¹/4 cup honey
¹/4 cup maple syrup

¹/2 teaspoon salt
3 eggs
¹/2 cup sugar
1 teaspoon vanilla
   extract
³/4 cup chopped walnuts
1 (9-inch) unbaked
   pie shell

Mix the butternut squash, butter, cinnamon, honey, maple syrup, salt and eggs in a bowl. Add the sugar, vanilla and walnuts and mix well. Spoon into the pie shell. Bake at 350 degrees for 1 hour. Remove to a wire rack to cool. Yield: 8 servings.

Terrie Stamey, Preceptor Kappa
Social Circle, Georgia

BUTTERSCOTCH PIE

³/4 cup packed brown
   sugar
5 tablespoons
   all-purpose flour
¹/2 teaspoon salt
¹/3 cup milk
1 (12-ounce) can
   evaporated milk
2 egg yolks

2 tablespoons butter
1 teaspoon vanilla
   extract
1 (9-inch) baked
   pie shell
2 egg whites
¹/4 cup granulated sugar
Dash of salt

Combine the brown sugar, flour, ¹/2 teaspoon salt, the milk and evaporated milk in a saucepan. Stir in the egg yolks. Bring to a boil over medium heat, stirring constantly. Remove from the heat. Stir in the butter and vanilla. Pour into the pie shell. Beat the egg whites in a bowl until soft peaks form. Add the sugar and a dash of salt gradually, beating until stiff peaks form. Top the pie with the meringue, sealing to the edge. Bake at 350 degrees for 15 minutes or until golden brown. Remove to a wire rack to cool. Yield: 8 servings.

Sue A. McClellan, Xi Beta Upsilon
Decatur, Alabama

CARAMEL PIE

This recipe came from a special hometown restaurant.

¹/4 cup (¹/2 stick) butter
7 ounces shredded
   coconut
1 cup chopped pecans
1 (14-ounce) can
   sweetened
   condensed milk

8 ounces cream cheese,
   softened
16 ounces whipped
   topping
3 (9-inch) baked
   pie shells
12 ounces melted
   caramel

Melt the butter in a skillet over medium heat. Add the coconut and pecans and stir until brown. Remove from the heat. Combine the condensed milk and cream cheese in a bowl and beat until smooth. Fold in the whipped topping. Spoon an equal amount of the mixture into each pie shell. Drizzle with the caramel. Sprinkle with the coconut mixture. Freeze, covered, for 6 hours or longer. Yield: 8 servings.

Kimberly Lyon, Lambda Phi
Jupiter, Florida

CHERRY PIE

1 (2-crust) pie pastry
1¹/3 cups sugar
¹/4 cup sifted all-purpose
   flour
¹/8 teaspoon salt
¹/8 teaspoon almond
   extract

3 or 4 drops red food
   coloring
4 cups cherries, pitted
1 tablespoon butter or
   margarine

Fit 1 pastry into a 9-inch pie plate. Combine the sugar, flour, salt, almond extract and food coloring in a bowl and mix well. Place half the cherries in the pie plate. Sprinkle with half the sugar mixture. Repeat the layers. Dot with the butter. Cover with the remaining pie pastry, sealing the edge and cutting vents. Bake at 400 degrees for 40 to 50 minutes or until the crust is golden brown. Remove to a wire rack to cool. Serve with whipped cream or ice cream if desired. Yield: 6 to 8 servings.

Audrey Pemberton, Xi Chi
Port Alberni, British Columbia, Canada

MACAROON CHERRY PIE

1 (9-inch) unbaked pie shell	1 egg, beaten
3 (14-ounce) cans pitted tart cherries	2 tablespoons milk
1 cup sugar	1 tablespoon butter, melted
1/3 cup cornstarch	1/4 teaspoon almond extract
1/4 teaspoon cinnamon	1/8 teaspoon salt
1/4 teaspoon red food coloring	1 cup flaked coconut
	1/2 cup sliced almonds

Bake the pie shell at 400 degrees for 6 minutes. Remove to a wire rack to cool. Drain the cherries, reserving 1 cup of the liquid. Combine the sugar and cornstarch in a saucepan. Stir in the reserved liquid gradually. Bring to a boil over medium heat, stirring constantly. Boil until thickened, stirring constantly. Remove from the heat. Stir in the cinnamon and food coloring and cherries. Pour into the pie shell. Cover the edge with foil. Bake at 400 degrees for 20 minutes. Remove to a wire rack. Reduce the heat to 350 degrees. Combine the egg, milk, butter, almond extract and salt in a bowl and beat for 2 minutes. Stir in the coconut and almonds. Spoon the mixture over the hot pie. Remove the foil. Bake at 350 degrees for 20 minutes. Remove to a wire rack to cool completely. Chill for 4 hours or longer. Yield: 6 to 8 servings.

Patricia Cracchiola, Xi Lambda Pi
St. Charles, Missouri

BUTTERMILK CHESS PIE

1/2 cup (1 stick) butter, melted	3 eggs, beaten
2 cups sugar	1 teaspoon vanilla extract
3 tablespoons all-purpose flour	1 (9-inch) unbaked pie shell
1 cup buttermilk	

Combine the butter, sugar and flour in a bowl and mix well. Add the buttermilk, eggs and vanilla and mix well. Pour into the pie shell. Bake at 325 degrees for 45 to 50 minutes or until a wooden pick inserted in the middle comes out clean. Remove to a wire rack to cool. Yield: 8 servings.

Joeddye Robinson, Laureate Omega
Cordova, Tennessee

LEMON CHESS PIE

1 3/4 cups sugar	1/4 cup evaporated milk
2 tablespoons yellow cornmeal	3 tablespoons lemon juice
1/4 teaspoon salt	4 eggs
1/3 cup butter, melted	1 (9-inch) unbaked pie shell

Combine the sugar, cornmeal and salt in a bowl and mix well. Add the butter, evaporated milk and lemon juice and mix well. Add the eggs 1 at a time, mixing well after each addition. Pour into the pie shell. Bake at 350 degrees for 45 minutes or just until set. Remove to a wire rack to cool. Chill, covered, until just before serving. Yield: 8 servings.

Betty J. Tipton, Laureate Psi
Altus, Oklahoma

PINEAPPLE AND COCONUT CHESS PIE

1 1/2 cups sugar	1/4 cup (1/2 stick) butter, melted
3 tablespoons cornmeal	3 1/2 ounces flaked coconut
2 tablespoons all-purpose flour	1 (15-ounce) can crushed pineapple, drained
1/4 teaspoon salt	1 (9-inch) unbaked pie shell
4 eggs, slightly beaten	
1 teaspoon vanilla extract	

Combine the sugar, cornmeal, flour and salt in a bowl. Add the eggs and vanilla and mix well. Stir in the butter, coconut and pineapple. Pour into the pie shell. Bake at 350 degrees for 40 minutes. Cover the edge with foil. Bake for 20 minutes longer or until set. Remove to a wire rack to cool. Yield: 8 servings.

Louise F. Borchelt, Preceptor Gamma Omicron
Cape Girardeau, Missouri

CHERRY CREAM PIE

1 cup cream or milk	1 (9-inch) baked pie shell
1 cup sugar	3 egg whites
2 heaping tablespoons all-purpose flour	1/4 teaspoon cream of tartar
2 egg yolks	6 tablespoons sugar
1 1/2 cups canned tart cherries with juice, warmed	1/2 teaspoon vanilla extract
1/2 to 1 teaspoon almond extract	

Combine the cream, sugar, flour and egg yolks in a double boiler. Cook until thickened, stirring constantly. Add the cherries and almond extract and mix well. Pour into the pie shell. Beat the egg whites and cream of tartar in a bowl until soft peaks form. Add the sugar 1 tablespoon at a time, beating until stiff peaks form. Stir in the vanilla. Top the pie with the meringue, sealing to the edge. Bake at 400 degrees for 10 minutes or until golden brown. Remove to a wire rack to cool. Yield: 8 servings.

Marcia Jansonius, Laureate Nu
Stilwell, Kansas

CHOCOLATE ALMOND PIE

16 to 20 large
   marshmallows
4 (1½-ounce) chocolate
   bars with almonds,
   chopped
½ cup milk

1 cup heavy whipping
   cream
1 teaspoon vanilla
   extract
1 (8-inch) graham
   cracker pie shell

Combine the marshmallows, chocolate bars and milk in a double boiler. Cook until smooth, stirring often. Cool completely. Whip the cream in a bowl until stiff peaks form. Fold in the chocolate mixture. Stir in the vanilla. Pour into the pie shell. Chill, covered, until just before serving. Serve with whipped cream or whipped topping if desired. Yield: 6 to 8 servings.

Daryl Reyner, Xi Alpha
Los Lunas, New Mexico

CHOCOLATE CHIP PIE

2 eggs
½ cup all-purpose flour
½ cup granulated sugar
½ cup packed brown
   sugar
¾ cup (1½ sticks)
   butter, softened

1 cup (6 ounces)
   chocolate chips
1 cup chopped nuts
1 (9-inch) unbaked
   pie shell
Whipped cream or
   ice cream

Beat the eggs at high speed in a bowl until foamy. Add the flour, granulated sugar and brown sugar and mix well. Add the butter and mix well. Stir in the chocolate chips and nuts. Spoon into the pie shell. Bake at 325 degrees for 55 to 60 minutes or until the crust is golden brown. Remove to a wire rack to cool. Serve with whipped cream or ice cream. Yield: 8 servings.

Ruth Ann Costa, Laureate Iota Sigma
Vallejo, California

CHOCOLATE TRUFFLE PIE

17 wrapped caramel
   squares, unwrapped
¼ cup evaporated milk
1 (9-inch) chocolate
   crumb pie shell
1½ cups (9 ounces)
   semisweet
   chocolate chips

1 cup heavy whipping
   cream
3 tablespoons butter
Whipped topping

Combine the caramels and evaporated milk in a microwave-safe bowl. Microwave on High until smooth, stirring occasionally. Pour into the pie shell. Combine the chocolate chips, cream and butter in a microwave-safe bowl. Microwave on High until smooth, stirring occasionally. Pour over the caramel.

Chill for 4 hours or longer. Garnish with whipped topping just before serving. Yield: 8 servings.

Evelyn Hutton, Zeta Zeta
Pine, Arizona

EASY CHOCOLATE PIE

1 cup (2 sticks) butter
   or margarine,
   softened
1½ cups sugar
3 ounces unsweetened
   chocolate, melted

4 eggs or an equivalent
   amount of egg
   substitute
2 teaspoons vanilla
   extract
1 (9-inch) graham
   cracker pie shell

Beat the butter and sugar in a bowl until light and fluffy. Add the chocolate and mix well. Add the eggs 2 at a time, beating for 5 minutes after each addition. Add the vanilla and mix well. Pour into the pie shell. Chill, covered, until just before serving. Garnish with chocolate shavings if desired. Yield: 8 servings.

Cynthia Keene, Xi Chi Kappa
McKinleyville, California

COCOA CREAM PIE

½ cup baking cocoa
1¼ cups sugar
⅓ cup cornstarch
¼ teaspoon salt
3 cups milk

3 tablespoons butter
1½ teaspoons vanilla
   extract
1 (9-inch) baked
   pie shell

Combine the baking cocoa, sugar, cornstarch and salt in a saucepan. Stir in the milk gradually. Bring to a boil over medium heat, stirring constantly. Boil for 1 minute, stirring constantly. Remove from the heat. Stir in the butter and vanilla. Pour into the pie shell. Cool completely. Press plastic wrap directly onto the filling. Chill for 3 to 4 hours. Yield: 8 servings.

Pam Wallace, Xi Phi
Council Bluffs, Iowa

NO-CRUST COCONUT PIE

4 eggs
1¾ cups sugar
½ cup self-rising flour
7 ounces shredded
   coconut

¼ cup (½ stick) butter
   or margarine, melted
2 cups milk
1 teaspoon vanilla
   extract

Beat the eggs in a bowl until thick and pale yellow. Stir in the remaining ingredients. Pour into a greased 10-inch glass pie plate. Bake at 350 degrees for 50 minutes or until golden brown. Remove to a wire rack to cool. Yield: 8 to 10 servings.

Barbara Mims, Iota
Bessemer, Alabama

COCONUT CREAM PIE

2/3 cup sugar
1/2 teaspoon salt
2 1/2 tablespoons
  cornstarch
2 tablespoons
  all-purpose flour
3 cups milk
3 egg yolks
1 tablespoon butter
1 teaspoon coconut
  flavoring

1 cup shredded coconut
1 (9-inch) baked
  pie shell
3 egg whites
1 tablespoon cornstarch
3 tablespoons sugar
Pinch of salt
1/2 teaspoon vanilla
  extract

Combine the sugar, salt, 2 1/2 tablespoons cornstarch and the flour in a saucepan. Stir in the milk gradually. Bring to a boil over low heat, stirring constantly. Stir a small amount of the hot mixture into the egg yolks; stir in the eggs into the hot mixture. Boil for 1 minute, stirring constantly. Remove from the heat. Stir in the butter until smooth. Stir in the coconut flavoring and shredded coconut. Pour into the pie shell. Beat the egg whites in a bowl until soft peaks form. Add 1 tablespoon cornstarch and the sugar gradually, beating until stiff peaks form. Stir in the salt and vanilla. Top the pie with the meringue, sealing to the edge. Bake at 275 degrees for 30 minutes. Remove to a wire rack to cool. Yield: 6 to 8 servings.

Donise Peterson, Laureate Gamma Alpha
Manhattan, Kansas

CRANBERRY WALNUT PIE

I enjoy using cranberries in my cooking because I buy them from a marsh near my home.

2 1/2 cups cranberries
1 (9-inch) unbaked
  pie shell
1/2 cup packed brown
  sugar
1/2 cup chopped walnuts

2 to 3 tablespoons
  butter (optional)
2 eggs
1 cup granulated sugar
2/3 cup butter, melted
1 cup all-purpose flour

Place the cranberries in the pie shell. Combine the brown sugar and walnuts in a small bowl. Cut in 2 to 3 tablespoons butter until crumbly. Sprinkle over the cranberries. Whisk together the eggs, granulated sugar, 2/3 cup butter and flour in a bowl. Spoon over the pie and spread lightly. Bake at 350 degrees for 45 minutes. Remove to a wire rack to cool.
Yield: 6 to 8 servings.

Carolyn Pittman, Laureate Alpha Alpha
Merrill, Wisconsin

CRÈME DE MENTHE PIE

This is a cool pie for summer entertaining.

3 tablespoons butter
3 1/2 ounces flaked
  coconut
1/2 cup chopped pecans
4 egg yolks
3/4 cup sugar
1 tablespoon unflavored
  gelatin

1/4 cup cold water
1/4 cup plus 1 tablespoon
  crème de menthe
1 1/2 cups heavy
  whipping cream,
  whipped (may use
  12 ounces whipped
  topping)

Melt the butter in a skillet over medium heat. Stir in the coconut and pecans. Cook until brown, stirring constantly. Press the hot mixture into a 9-inch pie plate. Cool completely. Beat the egg yolks in a bowl until thick and pale yellow. Add the sugar gradually, beating until light and fluffy. Soften the gelatin in the water in a small bowl. Remove to a double boiler and cook until the gelatin dissolves, stirring often. Add to the egg mixture. Stir in the crème de menthe. Fold in the whipped cream. Pour into the prepared pie shell. Chill, covered, several hours to overnight. Note: If you are concerned about using raw eggs, use eggs pasteurized in their shells, which are sold at some specialty food stores, or use an equivalent amount of pasteurized egg yolk substitute.
Yield: 6 to 8 servings.

Wanda E. Dudley, Upsilon Master
Alburquerque, New Mexico

NO-BAKE CRÈME DE MENTHE PIE

1 (2-ounce) package lime
  gelatin
1 (10 1/2-ounce) package
  miniature
  marshmallows
1 cup milk
6 tablespoons crème
  de menthe

2 tablespoons white
  crème de cacao
1 cup heavy whipping
  cream, whipped
1 (9-inch) chocolate
  crumb pie shell

Prepare and chill the gelatin using the package directions. Place the marshmallows and milk in a saucepan. Cook over medium heat until smooth, stirring often. Remove from the heat. Stir in the liqueurs. Cool completely. Fold in the whipped cream. Beat the gelatin. Fold into the whipped cream mixture. Pour the mixture into the pie shell. Chill, covered, for several hours to overnight. Garnish with chocolate cookie crumbs, maraschino cherries and peppermint candy if desired. Yield: 8 servings.

Vera Woronchanka, Xi Theta Alpha
Grimsby, Ontario, Canada

CUSTARD PIE

4 eggs
2/3 cup sugar
1/2 teaspoon salt
1/4 teaspoon nutmeg
2 2/3 cups milk

1 teaspoon vanilla
  extract
1 (9-inch) unbaked
  pie shell

Beat the eggs in a bowl. Add the sugar, salt, nutmeg, milk and vanilla and mix well. Pour into the pie shell. Sprinkle with additional nutmeg. Bake at 350 degrees for 45 minutes or until a wooden pick inserted in the center comes out clean. Remove to a wire rack to cool. Yield: 6 servings.

Kim Smith, Gamma Pi
Kirksville, Missouri

EGG CUSTARD PIE

3 tablespoons butter,
  melted
2/3 cup sugar
1 tablespoon
  all-purpose flour
1/8 teaspoon salt
1 cup milk

2 egg yolks
1 teaspoon vanilla
  extract
2 egg whites
1 (9-inch) unbaked
  pie shell

Combine the butter and sugar in a bowl and mix well. Add the flour, salt, milk, egg yolks and vanilla and mix well. Beat the egg whites in a mixing bowl until stiff peaks form. Fold into the butter mixture. Pour into the pie shell. Bake at 350 degrees for 30 minutes. Remove to a wire rack to cool.
Yield: 6 servings.

Betty Parsons, Laureate Rho
Jasper, Alabama

NO-CRUST CUSTARD PIE

4 eggs
1 cup sugar
2 cups milk
1 teaspoon vanilla
  extract

1/4 cup (1/2 stick) butter,
  melted
1/2 cup baking mix
Nutmeg

Combine the eggs, sugar, milk, vanilla, butter and baking mix in a mixing bowl and mix well. Pour into an ungreased 9-inch pie plate. Sprinkle with nutmeg. Bake at 350 degrees for 55 minutes. Remove to a wire rack to cool. Yield: 8 to 10 servings.

Patricia Grant, Preceptor Kappa Epsilon
Arlington, Texas

FRUIT PIE

1 (21-ounce) can cherry
  pie filling
1 (20-ounce) can crushed
  pineapple
3/4 cup sugar
1 tablespoon cornstarch
1 teaspoon red food
  coloring

1 (3-ounce) package
  raspberry gelatin
6 bananas, sliced
1 cup chopped pecans
2 (9-inch) baked
  pie shells
8 ounces whipped
  topping

Combine the pie filling, pineapple, sugar, cornstarch and food coloring in a saucepan. Cook over low heat until thickened, stirring often. Remove from the heat and stir in the gelatin. Cool completely. Stir in the bananas and pecans. Divide the mixture between the 2 pie shells. Cover with whipped topping. Chill until just before serving. Yield: 12 to 16 servings.

Lavada Harrison, Laureate Delta Sigma
Poplar Bluff, Missouri

JAPANESE FRUIT PIE

1/2 cup raisins
1/2 cup (1 stick)
  margarine, softened
1 cup sugar
2 eggs, slightly beaten
1/2 cup chopped nuts

1/2 cup shredded coconut
1 teaspoon vanilla
  extract
1 (9-inch) unbaked
  pie shell

Soak the raisins in water in a small bowl for 5 minutes. Drain. Beat the margarine and sugar in a bowl until light and fluffy. Add the eggs and mix well. Add the raisins, nuts, coconut and vanilla and mix well. Spoon the mixture into the pie shell. Bake at 325 degrees for 45 minutes. Remove to a wire rack to cool. Yield: 6 to 8 servings.

Martha Batson, Laureate Rho
Greenville, South Carolina

FRUIT COCKTAIL CREAM PIE

2 cups graham cracker
  crumbs
1/3 cup butter, melted
1/4 cup sugar
2 cups sour cream
2/3 cup sugar

1 teaspoon grated
  lemon zest
1 teaspoon lemon juice
1 teaspoon vanilla
  extract
1 (14-ounce) can fruit
  cocktail, drained

Combine the graham cracker crumbs, butter and 1/4 cup sugar in a bowl and mix until crumbly. Reserve 2 tablespoons for garnish. Press the remaining crumb mixture into an 8-inch pie plate. Bake at 350 degrees for 10 minutes. Cool on a wire rack. Combine the sour cream, 2/3 cup sugar, lemon zest, lemon juice and vanilla in a bowl and mix well. Reserve 1/4 cup of the fruit cocktail. Fold the remaining fruit cocktail into the sour cream mixture. Pour into the prepared pie crust. Garnish with the reserved crumb mixture and reserved fruit cocktail. Chill, covered, until just before serving. Yield: 8 servings.

Lynn Timpson, Laureate Beta Tau
Simcoe, Ontario, Canada

LIGHT FRUIT PIE

1 (3-ounce) package gelatin (any flavor)	1 cup fresh or canned fruit
2/3 cup boiling water	1 (9-inch) graham cracker pie shell
2 cups ice cubes	
8 ounces whipped topping	

Dissolve the gelatin in boiling water in a bowl. Let stand for 3 minutes. Add the ice cubes and stir until thickened. Whisk in the whipped topping. Fold in the fruit. Pour into the pie shell. Chill for 2 hours. Yield: 8 servings.

Janet John, Beta
Terre Haute, Indiana

GRAPEFRUIT PIE

4 red grapefruits	1/8 teaspoon salt
1 cup sugar	1 (3-ounce) package strawberry or raspberry gelatin
2 tablespoons cornstarch	
1 3/4 cups water	1 (9-inch) baked pie shell

Peel and section the grapefruit. Combine the sugar, cornstarch, water and salt in a saucepan. Bring to a boil over medium heat and cook until clear and thickened, stirring often. Remove from the heat. Stir in the gelatin. Cool until thickened. Spoon a small amount of the mixture into the pie shell. Top with the grapefruit. Cover with the remaining gelatin mixture. Chill for 4 hours or until set. Yield: 8 servings.

Katy Burke, Preceptor Xi Epsilon
Harlingen, Texas

GRASSHOPPER PIE

24 large marshmallows	5 drops green food coloring
1/2 cup milk	
1 1/2 ounces white crème de cocoa	12 ounces whipped topping
1 ounce crème de menthe	1 (9-inch) chocolate crumb pie shell

Combine the marshmallows and milk in a saucepan. Cook over low heat until smooth, stirring often. Cool completely. Stir in the liqueurs and the food coloring. Fold in the whipped topping. Pour into the pie shell. Chill for 4 hours or longer. Yield: 8 servings.

Marie Trepinski, Xi Theta Mu
Port Charlotte, Florida

ITALIAN EASTER PIE

My grandmother brought this recipe from Italy in the early 1900s.

8 eggs	24 ounces cottage cheese
1 cup sugar	2 (9-inch) unbaked pie shells
3/4 cup half-and-half	
1/4 cup vanilla extract	1 (1-crust) pie pastry
2 cups cooked rice	1 egg yolk
2/3 cup raisins	2 tablespoons milk

Beat the eggs in a bowl until thick and pale yellow. Beat in the sugar, half-and-half and vanilla gradually. Pour over the rice in a large bowl. Stir in the raisins and cottage cheese. Pour half the mixture into each pie shell. Cut the pie pastry into strips. Arrange lattice-fashion over the pies. Combine the egg yolk and milk in a small bowl and mix well. Brush over the pastry. Bake at 350 degrees for 35 to 40 minutes or until a wooden pick inserted in the center comes out clean. Remove to a wire rack to cool. Yield: 12 servings.

Carolyn Marshall, Laureate Beta Beta
Colorado Springs, Colorado

❖ TRIPLE LEMON PIE

1 (3-ounce) package lemon gelatin	2 tablespoons lemon juice
1/2 cup sugar	12 ounces whipped topping
1 cup boiling water	
8 ounces cream cheese, softened	1 (9-inch) graham cracker pie shell or baked pie shell
1 cup lemon yogurt	

Dissolve the gelatin and sugar in the boiling water in a bowl. Chill for 25 minutes. Beat the cream cheese in a bowl until light and fluffy. Add the yogurt and lemon juice and mix well. Add the gelatin and mix just until combined. Fold in half the whipped topping. Spoon into the pie shell. Chill until firm. Top with the remaining whipped topping just before serving. Garnish with mint sprigs and lemon slices if desired. Yield: 8 servings.

Juanita W. Gray, Xi Omicron
Bluefield, West Virginia

LEMON CHEESECAKE PIE

1/2 cup skim milk
8 ounces fat-free cream
 cheese, softened
1 1/2 cups skim milk
1 large package sugar-
 free instant pudding
 mix (any flavor)

1 (9-inch) graham
 cracker pie shell
Fat-free whipped
 topping

Combine 1/2 cup milk and cream cheese in a bowl and mix until smooth. Add 1 1/2 cups milk and the pudding mix and mix well. Pour into the pie shell. Chill until just before serving. Serve with whipped topping. Yield: 6 to 8 servings.

Kathy Lee Harris, Xi Omicron
Harlingen, Texas

LEMON PINEAPPLE PIE

1 (20-ounce) can crushed
 pineapple
1 (3 1/2-ounce) package
 lemon instant
 pudding mix

8 ounces whipped
 topping
1 (9-inch) graham
 cracker pie shell

Combine the pineapple and pudding mix in a bowl and mix well. Fold in the whipped topping. Pour into the pie shell. Chill several hours to overnight. Yield: 8 servings.

Marilyn Hartl, Laureate Delta
Long Beach, California

LEMON RASPBERRY RIBBON PIE

1 (10-ounce) package
 frozen raspberries,
 thawed and drained
1 tablespoon cornstarch
1 (14-ounce) can
 sweetened
 condensed milk

1/2 cup lemon juice
Yellow food coloring
 (optional)
2 cups heavy whipping
 cream, whipped
1 (9-inch) baked
 pie shell

Combine the raspberries and cornstarch in a sauce-pan. Cook over low heat until thickened, stirring often. Cool for 10 minutes. Chill for 20 minutes. Combine the condensed milk, lemon juice and food coloring in a bowl and mix well. Fold in the whipped cream. Spoon half the lemon mixture into the pie shell. Top with the raspberry mixture and spread lightly. Cover with the remaining lemon mixture. Chill until just before serving. Garnish with raspberries and twists of lemon rind if desired. Yield: 6 to 8 servings.

Nancy K. Dodge, Beta Chi
Independence, Iowa

LEMON ICEBOX PIE

1 (3-ounce) package
 sugar-free lemon
 gelatin
1 cup boiling water
2 tablespoons Splenda
12 ounces sugar-free
 lemon yogurt

8 ounces light sour
 cream
8 ounces sugar-free
 whipped topping
1 (9-inch) graham
 cracker pie shell

Combine the gelatin, water and Splenda in a large bowl and mix well. Stir in the yogurt and sour cream. Fold in the whipped topping. Pour into the pie shell. Chill for 2 hours or longer. Yield: 6 to 8 servings.

Janelle Williamson, Xi Phi Sigma
Texarkana, Texas

LIME MARGARITA PIE

1 1/4 cups finely crushed
 pretzels
1/2 cup (1 stick) butter or
 margarine, melted
1/4 cup sugar
Grated zest of 2 limes
Juice of 2 limes

1/4 cup orange juice
1 (14-ounce) can
 sweetened
 condensed milk
8 ounces whipped
 topping

Combine the pretzels, butter and sugar in a bowl and mix until crumbly. Press into a 9-inch pie plate. Combine the lime zest, lime juice, orange juice and condensed milk in a bowl and mix well. Fold in the whipped topping. Pour into the prepared pie shell. Chill for 20 to 25 minutes. Yield: 6 to 8 servings.

Joyce DuFeu, Preceptor Epsilon Omega
Chillicothe, Ohio

LIME PIE

12 ounces whipped
 topping
1 (14-ounce) can
 sweetened
 condensed milk
1 (3-ounce) can frozen
 limeade concentrate,
 thawed

3 tablespoons lemon or
 lime juice
Dash of nutmeg
1/2 to 1 teaspoon green
 food coloring
 (optional)
2 (9-inch) baked
 pie shells

Combine the whipped topping and condensed milk in a bowl and mix well. Add the limeade, lemon juice, nutmeg and food coloring and mix well. Divide the mixture evenly between the pie shells. Chill until just before serving. Yield: 16 servings.

Carolyn K. Sowers, Laureate Alpha Rho
Christiansburg, Virginia

MISSISSIPPI MUD PIE

This was my favorite recipe from a cooking class attended by my Omega sisters. What great fun we had!

10 tablespoons butter, melted
1 ounce semisweet chocolate, chopped
6 tablespoons baking cocoa, sifted
2 teaspoons instant espresso powder
3 eggs

1 cup sugar
2 tablespoons sour cream
3 tablespoons corn syrup
1 teaspoon vanilla extract
1 (1-crust) pie pastry
Chocolate curls for garnish

Place a baking sheet on the lower rack of a 350-degree oven. Combine the butter, chocolate, baking cocoa and espresso in a bowl and mix until smooth. Beat the eggs and sugar in a mixing bowl until creamy. Add the sour cream, corn syrup and vanilla and mix well. Stir in the chocolate mixture. Pour into a pastry-lined pie plate. Bake on the baking sheet at 350 degrees for 35 to 40 minutes or until puffed. Remove to a wire rack to cool. Garnish with chocolate curls. Store in the refrigerator for up to 2 days. Yield: 8 servings.

Sue Gress, Omega
Waterloo, Iowa

MANDARIN PIE

1 (14-ounce) can sweetened condensed milk
1/4 cup lemon juice
2 (11-ounce) cans mandarin oranges, drained

1 cup chopped walnuts
8 ounces whipped topping
1 (9-inch) baked pie shell

Combine the condensed milk, lemon juice, oranges and walnuts in a bowl and mix well. Fold in the whipped topping. Spoon into the pie shell. Chill until just before serving. Yield: 8 servings.

Martha Clark, Alpha Tau Master
Lakeland, Florida

OATMEAL PIE

1/4 cup (1/2 stick) butter, melted
2 eggs
1/2 cup milk
3/4 cup corn syrup
3/4 cup rolled oats

1 teaspoon vanilla extract
1 cup shredded coconut
1/8 teaspoon salt
1 (9-inch) unbaked pie shell

Combine the butter and eggs in a bowl and mix well. Add the milk, corn syrup, oats, vanilla, coconut and salt and mix well. Spoon into the pie shell. Bake at

350 degrees for 1 hour. Remove to a wire rack to cool. Yield: 8 servings.

Brenda Fishel, Nu Lambda
Stafford, Kansas

PEANUT BUTTER CREAM PIE

3 cups milk
3 egg yolks
1 cup sugar
1/2 cup cornstarch
1/4 teaspoon salt
1/2 cup chunky peanut butter

2 teaspoons vanilla extract
1 (9-inch) baked pie shell
1 cup heavy whipping cream, whipped
1/2 cup chopped peanuts

Combine the milk and egg yolks in a double boiler. Add the sugar, cornstarch and salt and cook until thickened, stirring constantly. Pour into a bowl and cover with buttered waxed paper. Chill until cold. Beat until creamy. Add the peanut butter and vanilla and mix well. Pour into the pie shell. Cover with whipped cream and sprinkle with peanuts. Yield: 6 to 8 servings.

Eleanor V. Hatch, Phi Master
Joseph, Oregon

PEANUT BUTTER AND BANANA CREAM PIE

3/4 cup peanut butter
1/4 cup (1/2 stick) butter, softened
3/4 cup confectioners' sugar
3/4 cup whipped topping
1 (9-inch) chocolate crumb pie shell
2 (3-ounce) packages vanilla instant pudding mix

1 cup milk
1 (6-ounce) jar baby food bananas
1 1/2 cups whipped topping
2 bananas, sliced
3 cups whipped topping
Chocolate-covered peanuts (optional)

Beat the peanut butter and butter in a mixing bowl until smooth. Add the confectioners' sugar and mix well. Fold in 3/4 cup whipped topping. Spoon into the pie shell. Combine the pudding mix and milk in a bowl and beat until smooth. Whisk in the baby food. Fold in 1 1/2 cups whipped topping. Spoon into the pie shell and spread lightly over the peanut butter layer. Chill, covered, for 4 hours or until set. Top with banana slices. Cover with 3 cups whipped topping. Sprinkle with peanuts. Yield: 8 to 10 servings.

Joyce Bjork, Preceptor Kappa Lambda
Portland, Texas

CHOCOLATE AND PEANUT BUTTER CREAM PIE

3/4 cup hot fudge topping
1 (9-inch) graham
   cracker pie shell
1/2 cup peanut butter
1 1/4 cups milk
2 (4-ounce) packages
   vanilla instant
   pudding mix
8 ounces whipped
   topping

Spoon 1/2 cup of the fudge topping into the pie shell and spread lightly. Freeze for 10 minutes. Whisk the peanut butter and milk in a large bowl until smooth. Add the pudding mix and whisk for 2 minutes. Stir in half of the whipped topping. Spoon into the pie shell. Cover with the remaining whipped topping. Chill for 3 hours. Drizzle with the remaining fudge topping just before serving. Yield: 8 servings.

Melissa Hrencher, Iota Beta
Medicine Lodge, Kansas

PEAR PIE

8 or 9 small Bartlett
   pears, peeled and
   sliced
3/4 cup sugar
2 tablespoons
   all-purpose flour
1/2 teaspoon nutmeg
1 teaspoon cinnamon
2 tablespoons honey
1 tablespoon lemon
   juice
1 (2-crust) pie pastry
Margarine to taste
1 tablespoon milk
Additional sugar for
   sprinkling

Combine the pears, sugar, flour, nutmeg and cinnamon in a saucepan. Cook over low heat until the sugar dissolves, stirring occasionally. Add the honey and lemon juice and mix well. Pour into a pastry-lined pie plate. Dot with margarine. Top with the remaining pastry, sealing the edge and cutting vents. Brush with milk and sprinkle with sugar. Bake at 350 degrees for 1 hour or until bubbly. Remove to a wire rack to cool. Yield: 6 to 8 servings.

Joy Whiteman, Sigma Master
Boise, Idaho

SOUR CREAM PEAR PIE

We are always looking for recipes to use the delicious pears from two trees we planted 20 years ago.

1/2 cup sugar
2 tablespoons
   all-purpose flour
1 cup sour cream
1 egg, beaten
1 teaspoon vanilla
   extract
3 cups chopped peeled
   pears
1 (9-inch) unbaked
   pie shell
1/4 cup all-purpose flour
1/2 teaspoon cinnamon
2 tablespoons sugar
1/4 cup (1/2 stick) butter
3/4 cup chopped walnuts
   or sliced almonds

Combine 1/2 cup sugar, 2 tablespoons flour, the sour cream, egg and vanilla in a bowl and mix well. Stir in the pears. Pour into the pie shell. Cover the edge with foil. Bake at 375 degrees for 30 minutes. Remove to a wire rack. Combine 1/4 flour, the cinnamon and 2 tablespoons sugar in a bowl. Cut in the butter until crumbly. Add the walnuts and mix well. Sprinkle over the hot pie. Bake for 25 to 30 minutes longer or until golden brown. Remove to a wire rack to cool. Yield: 8 servings.

Marian Stubbs, Preceptor Mu
Newton, Kansas

BUTTER CRACKER PECAN PIE

3 egg whites
2 cups crushed butter
   crackers
1 cup sugar
1 cup chopped pecans

Beat the egg whites in a bowl until stiff peaks form. Fold in the cracker crumbs, sugar and pecans. Spread in a greased 9-inch pie plate. Bake at 350 degrees for 45 minutes or until light brown. Remove to a wire rack to cool. Serve warm with ice cream if desired. Yield: 8 servings.

Sandy Hale, Xi Theta
Staunton, Virginia

CARAMEL PECAN PIE

28 vanilla caramel
   candies
1/2 cup water
1/4 cup (1/2 stick)
   margarine
2 eggs, slightly beaten
3/4 cup sugar
1/4 teaspoon salt
1/2 teaspoon vanilla
   extract
1 cup chopped pecans
1 (9-inch) unbaked
   pie shell

Combine the caramels, water and margarine in a double boiler. Cook until smooth, stirring frequently. Combine the eggs, sugar, salt and vanilla in a bowl and mix well. Stir in the caramel mixture gradually. Stir in the pecans. Pour into the pie shell. Bake at 400 degrees for 10 minutes. Reduce the heat to 350 degrees. Bake for 20 minutes. Remove to a wire rack to cool. Yield: 6 to 8 servings.

Jayne Hornsby, Xi Alpha Xi
Hueytown, Alabama

---

*Joyce Chriss, Laureate Beta Lambda, Katy, Texas, starts her **Hawaiian Pie** with a 9-inch graham cracker pie shell. She mixes one 5-ounce package vanilla instant pudding mix, one 20-ounce can crushed pineapple, and 8 ounces sour cream in a bowl and pours the mixture into the pie shell. She chills the pie for 2 hours or longer before serving.*

CHOCOLATE PECAN PIE

4 ounces German's
  sweet chocolate
3 eggs
1/3 cup sugar
2 tablespoons butter,
  melted

1 cup light corn syrup
1 teaspoon vanilla
  extract
1 1/2 cups chopped pecans
1 (9-inch) unbaked
  pie shell

Melt the chocolate in a heavy saucepan and cool. Mix with the next 5 ingredients in a bowl. Stir in the pecans. Pour into the pie shell. Bake at 350 degrees for 50 to 60 minutes or the crust is golden brown. Remove to a wire rack to cool. Yield: 8 servings.

Sharon Young, Laureate Beta Tau
Olathe, Kansas

MOCK PECAN PIE

2 eggs
1 cup dark corn syrup
1 cup sugar
1/2 cup (1 stick) butter,
  melted

1 cup quick-cooking
  oats
1 (9-inch) unbaked
  pie shell

Beat the eggs in a bowl. Add the corn syrup, sugar and butter and mix well. Stir in the oats. Pour into the pie shell. Bake at 350 degrees for 40 to 50 minutes or until set. Remove to a wire rack to cool. Serve with whipped cream if desired. Yield: 6 to 8 servings.

Eleanor Steber, Xi Iota Lambda
Claremont, Illinois

OATMEAL PECAN PIE

1/2 cup (1 stick) butter or
  margarine, melted
2/3 cup sugar
2/3 cup dark corn syrup
2/3 cup rolled oats
2 eggs

1 teaspoon vanilla
  extract
1 (9-inch) unbaked
  pie shell
1/2 cup chopped pecans

Combine the butter, sugar, corn syrup and oats in a bowl and mix well. Stir in the eggs and vanilla. Pour into the pie shell. Sprinkle with the pecans. Cover the edge with foil. Bake at 325 degrees for 25 minutes or until set. Remove the foil. Remove to a wire rack to cool. Yield: 8 servings.

Nadine Gentry, Laureate Gamma Iota
Springfield, Missouri

OKLAHOMA PECAN PIE

3 eggs
1 cup sugar
1 cup light corn syrup
1 tablespoon butter,
  melted

1 teaspoon vanilla
  extract
1 cup pecan halves
1 (9-inch) unbaked
  pie shell

Beat the eggs in a bowl. Add the sugar, corn syrup and butter and mix well. Stir in the vanilla and pecans. Pour into the pie shell. Bake at 350 degrees for 45 to 55 minutes or until a wooden pick inserted in the center comes out clean. Remove to a wire rack to cool. Serve with whipped cream if desired. Yield: 6 to 8 servings.

Barbara Ashlock, Xi Gamma Sigma
Ponca City, Oklahoma

RONALD REAGAN'S PUMPKIN PECAN PIE

When Ronald Reagan was governor of California, he came to San Diego for meetings that I attended. He always called me "Shirley" because he thought I looked like Shirley Temple!

4 eggs
2 cups canned pumpkin
1 cup sugar
1/2 cup dark corn syrup
1 teaspoon vanilla
  extract

1/2 teaspoon cinnamon
1/4 teaspoon salt
1 (9-inch) baked
  pie shell
1 cup chopped pecans

Beat the eggs in a bowl. Add the pumpkin, sugar, corn syrup, vanilla, cinnamon and salt and mix well. Pour into the pie shell. Sprinkle with the pecans. Microwave on Medium for 10 minutes. Rotate the pie plate. Microwave on Medium for 10 to 12 minutes longer or until set. Remove to a wire rack to cool. Yield: 6 servings.

Mabel Hartman, Preceptor Mu Sigma
Borrego Springs, California

PINEAPPLE PIE

1 (20-ounce) can crushed
  pineapple
1 small box sugar-free
  vanilla instant
  pudding mix

1 cup plain yogurt
8 ounces whipped
  topping
2 (9-inch) graham
  cracker pie shells

Combine the pineapple and pudding mix in a bowl and mix well. Fold in the yogurt and whipped topping. Divide the mixture evenly between 2 pie shells. Chill until just before serving. Freezes well. Yield: 16 servings.

R. Jean Zeigler, Preceptor Psi
Oakdale, California

Ida May Humke, Iota Master, Quincy, Illinois, makes **No-Roll Pie Crust** *by combining 1 cup all-purpose flour, 1/3 cup vegetable oil, and 3 tablespoons milk in a pie plate coated with nonstick cooking spray. She mixes the ingredients with her hands and presses the dough over the bottom and up the side of the pie plate.*

NO-CRUST PUMPKIN PIE

3/4 cup sugar	1 (12-ounce) can
1/2 cup baking mix	evaporated milk
2 tablespoons butter or	2 eggs
margarine, softened	2 teaspoons vanilla
1 (16-ounce) can	extract
pumpkin	2 teaspoons pumpkin
	pie spice

Mix the sugar, baking mix, butter, pumpkin, evaporated milk, eggs, vanilla and pumpkin pie spice in a large bowl until smooth. Pour into a greased 9-inch pie plate. Bake at 350 degrees for 50 to 60 minutes or until set. Remove to a wire rack to cool completely. Serve with ice cream, whipped topping or whipped cream if desired. Yield: 8 servings.

Mary DiBeneditto, Laureate Delta Eta
Lantana, Florida

SUPREME PUMPKIN PIE

2 egg whites	2 egg yolks
1 cup cooked pumpkin	1 cup cream
1 cup sugar	1 (9-inch) unbaked pie
1/2 teaspoon salt	shell
2 teaspoons cinnamon	8 ounces whipped
2 tablespoons	topping or
all-purpose flour	whipped cream

Beat the egg whites in a bowl until stiff peaks form. Combine the pumpkin, sugar, salt, cinnamon and flour in a bowl and mix well. Add the egg yolks and cream and mix well. Fold in the egg whites. Pour into the pie shell. Bake at 450 degrees for 12 minutes. Reduce the heat to 325 degrees. Bake for 40 minutes. Remove to a wire rack to cool. Serve with whipped topping. Yield: 8 servings.

Ruth York, Xi Iota Sigma
Archie, Missouri

LIGHT PUMPKIN PIE

1 (15-ounce) can	1/3 cup baking mix
pumpkin	2 tablespoons pumpkin
1 (12-ounce) can fat-free	pie spice
evaporated milk	1 (9-inch) unbaked
3/4 cup Splenda	pie shell
2 eggs	

Combine the pumpkin, evaporated milk, Splenda, eggs, baking mix and pumpkin pie spice in a bowl and mix well. Pour into the pie shell. Bake at 375 degrees for 35 to 40 minutes or until set. Remove to a wire rack to cool. Yield: 8 to 10 servings.

Heddy Hess, Preceptor Theta
Williamson, West Virginia

PUMPKIN CHIFFON PIE

1 envelope unflavored	1 teaspoon cinnamon
gelatin	3/4 cup skim milk
3/4 cup packed light	3 egg yolks
brown sugar	1 1/2 cups pumpkin
1/2 teaspoon salt	3 egg whites
1/2 teaspoon nutmeg	1/4 cup granulated sugar
1/4 teaspoon ginger	1 (9-inch) baked
1/4 teaspoon allspice	pie shell

Combine the gelatin, brown sugar, salt, nutmeg, ginger, allspice and cinnamon in a saucepan. Stir in the milk, egg yolks, and pumpkin. Cook over medium heat for 10 minutes or until the gelatin dissolves and the mixture is heated through, stirring constantly. Remove from the heat. Chill until partially set, stirring occasionally. Beat the egg whites in a bowl until soft peaks form. Add the granulated sugar gradually, beating until stiff peaks form. Fold in the pumpkin mixture. Pour into the pie shell. Chill until just before serving. Serve with whipped cream if desired. Note: If you are concerned about using raw eggs, use eggs pasteurized in their shells, which are sold at some specialty food stores, or use an equivalent amount of pasteurized egg substitute. Yield: 8 to 10 servings.

Freda Bush, Preceptor Gamma Kappa
Chesapeake, Virginia

RAISIN PIE

I had nine siblings. At Christmas, Mom would bake each of us our favorite pie. Raisin was my favorite.

1 (15-ounce) package	1 1/2 cups sugar
raisins	Dash of salt
4 1/2 cups water	1/3 cup all-purpose flour
1 teaspoon apple cider	2 (2-crust) pie pastries
vinegar	Butter to taste

Cover the raisins with 4 1/2 cups water in a saucepan. Add the vinegar, sugar and salt and mix well. Bring to a boil over medium heat, stirring occasionally. Boil for 5 minutes or until the raisins are tender, stirring often. Place the flour in a small bowl. Stir in enough of the boiling water to make a thin paste. Add the mixture to the raisins and boil several minutes or until thickened, stirring often. Remove from the heat. Divide the mixture between 2 pastry-lined pie plates. Dot both pies with butter. Top each pie with one of the remaining pastries, sealing the edge and cutting vents. Bake at 425 degrees for 45 minutes. Remove to a wire rack to cool.
Yield: 16 servings.

Barbara Smith, Xi Gamma Upsilon
Conway, Arkansas

RASPBERRY AND LEMON BUTTERMILK PIE

1 (1-crust) pie pastry	1 teaspoon grated
4 eggs	lemon zest
3/4 cup sugar	1/4 teaspoon salt
2 tablespoons	3/4 cup buttermilk
all-purpose flour	1 cup seedless
1/4 cup (1/2 stick) butter	raspberry jam
or margarine, melted	1 cup raspberries
1 teaspoon lemon	
extract	

Fit the pie pastry into a 9-inch pie plate. Beat the eggs in a bowl. Add the sugar, flour, butter, lemon extract, lemon zest and salt and mix well. Add the buttermilk and mix well. Pour into the pie plate. Bake at 350 degrees for 40 or 50 minutes or until a wooden pick inserted in the center comes out clean. Remove to a wire rack to cool. Reserve 2 tablespoons of the jam. Spread the remaining jam over the cooled pie. Arrange the raspberries in concentric circles over the jam. Warm the reserved jam in a saucepan over low heat. Drizzle over the raspberries. Yield: 8 servings.

Jeanne Caimano, Laureate Delta Tau
St. Petersburg, Florida

RASPBERRY PIE

6 cups raspberries	1 cup whipped topping
1 cup sugar	1 cup confectioners'
3 tablespoons cornstarch	sugar
1/2 cup water	1 (9-inch) graham
8 ounces cream cheese,	cracker pie shell
softened	

Mash 2 cups of the raspberries in a saucepan. Add the sugar, cornstarch and water and mix well. Bring to a boil over medium heat, stirring constantly. Boil for 2 minutes, stirring constantly. Remove from the heat and cool completely. Beat the cream cheese, whipped topping and confectioners' sugar in a bowl. Spread in the pie shell. Top with the remaining 4 cups raspberries. Pour the cooled raspberry mixture over the top. Chill for 3 hours or until set. Yield: 8 to 10 servings.

Shellie Hosch, Pi Pi
Gilbert, Iowa

RHUBARB PIE

1 cup all-purpose flour	2 cups sliced rhubarb
5 tablespoons	1/4 teaspoon salt
confectioners' sugar	1/4 cup all-purpose flour
1/2 cup (1 stick) butter or	1 1/2 cups granulated
margarine	sugar
2 eggs	

Combine 1 cup flour and the confectioners' sugar in a bowl. Cut in the butter until crumbly. Reserve 1/2 cup. Press the remaining mixture into a greased pie plate. Combine the eggs, rhubarb, salt, 1/4 cup flour and the granulated sugar in a large bowl and mix well. Pour into the prepared pie shell. Sprinkle with the reserved mixture. Bake at 350 degrees for 35 minutes. Remove to a wire rack to cool.
Yield: 6 to 8 servings.

Nicolle Murray
New Hampton, Iowa

SUGAR-FREE RHUBARB PIE

If you don't want to make the pastry, use a graham cracker pie shell.

3 cups sliced rhubarb	1 1/2 cups milk
1 small package sugar-	1 teaspoon vanilla
free strawberry	extract
gelatin	No-Roll Pie Shell
1 small package sugar-	8 ounces whipped
free vanilla instant	topping
pudding mix	

Combine the rhubarb and gelatin in a saucepan. Cook over low heat until the gelatin dissolves, stirring often. Cool completely. Combine the pudding mix, milk and vanilla in a bowl and mix well. Fold in half the whipped topping. Fold in the rhubarb mixture. Pour into the No-Roll Pie Shell. Cover with the remaining whipped topping. Yield: 8 servings.

NO-ROLL PIE SHELL

1 3/4 cups all-purpose	1/4 cup milk
flour	Salt to taste
1/2 cup vegetable oil	

Combine the flour, oil, milk and salt in a bowl and mix well. Divide the mixture in half. Freeze half the dough for later use. Pat the remaining dough into a greased pie plate.

Marjory Andrews, Preceptor Mu
Pleasantville, Iowa

*Susan Rae Wynans, Preceptor Omicron, Aberdeen, Washington, makes a light **Sugar-Free Cherry Pie** by combining 32 ounces fat-free yogurt and 2 small packages sugar-free cherry gelatin in a microwave-proof bowl. She microwaves the mixture for 3 minutes on High, stirring after 1 1/2 minutes. The mixture is then poured into a greased pie plate and chilled for 3 hours or until set. She serves slices of the pie with fat-free whipped topping.*

STRAWBERRY PIE

1 heaping cup all-purpose flour	1 cup water
2 tablespoons confectioners' sugar	1 cup granulated sugar
	3 tablespoons cornstarch
1/2 cup (1 stick) butter or margarine	1 (3-ounce) package strawberry gelatin
1 cup strawberries	Whipped topping or whipped cream
3 cups sliced strawberries	

Place the flour and confectioners' sugar in a bowl. Cut in the butter until crumbly. Knead on a floured surface until smooth. Press into a 9-inch pie plate. Bake at 350 degrees for 20 minutes. Remove to a wire rack to cool. Place 1 cup strawberries, hulled side down, inside the edge of the pie shell. Place the sliced strawberries in the prepared pie shell. Combine the water, granulated sugar and cornstarch in a saucepan. Bring to a boil over medium heat, stirring constantly. Boil until thickened. Stir in the gelatin. Pour the hot mixture over the strawberries in the pie shell. Chill until cold. Serve with whipped topping or whipped cream. Yield: 8 to 10 servings.

Diane K. Wilson, Alpha Zeta Master
Holland, Michigan

STRAWBERRY CREAM PIE

In 1956, the Eta Theta chapter was organized. As a chapter member, I served this pie at our first meeting at my house. I am now sponsor of Eta Theta.

1 1/2 cups vanilla wafer crumbs	2 eggs, beaten
1/3 cup butter, melted	1 1/2 cups sweetened sliced strawberries
1/2 cup (1 stick) butter, softened	1 to 2 cups heavy whipped cream, whipped (optional)
1 1/2 cups sifted confectioners' sugar	

Combine the vanilla wafer crumbs and 1/3 cup butter in a bowl and mix until crumbly. Press into a 9-inch pie plate. Chill for 45 minutes or until firm. Beat 1/2 cup butter in a mixing bowl until smooth. Add the confectioners' sugar gradually, beating until light and fluffy. Add the eggs and mix well. Spoon the mixture into the prepared pie shell. Fold the strawberries into the whipped cream. Spoon into the pie shell. Chill for 6 to 8 hours or until firm. Garnish with mint sprigs and additional strawberries if desired. Note: If you are concerned about using raw eggs, use eggs pasteurized in their shells, which are sold at some specialty food stores, or use an equivalent amount of pasteurized egg substitute. Yield: 8 servings.

Katherine H. Young, Laureate Gamma
Nevada, Missouri

SWEET POTATO PIE

1 cup buttermilk	1 cup sugar
1/2 teaspoon baking soda	2 eggs
Pinch of salt	1 teaspoon vanilla extract
2 tablespoons butter, melted	1 (9-inch) unbaked pie shell
2 cups mashed cooked sweet potatoes	

Combine the buttermilk, baking soda, salt, butter, sweet potatoes and sugar and mix well. Add the eggs and vanilla and mix well. Pour into the pie shell. Bake at 350 degrees for 30 to 40 minutes or until set. Remove to a wire rack to cool. Yield: 6 to 8 servings.

Alma Harrelson, Preceptor Gamma
Memphis, Tennessee

WHITE PIE

3/4 cup sugar	1/2 teaspoon almond extract
3 tablespoons cornstarch	2 egg whites
1/2 cup minus 3 tablespoons all-purpose flour	1/4 cup sugar
	1 baked (9-inch) pie shell
1/8 teaspoon salt	Whipped topping
2 cups milk	Chopped pecans or walnuts
2 teaspoons vanilla extract	

Combine 3/4 cup sugar, the cornstarch, flour and salt in a saucepan. Stir in the milk. Bring to a boil over medium heat, stirring constantly. Remove from the heat and stir in the vanilla and almond extract. Beat the egg whites in a bowl until soft peaks form. Add 1/4 cup sugar gradually, beating until stiff peaks form. Fold into the warm custard. Cover with plastic wrap and let stand until cool. Pour into the pie shell. Cover with whipped topping and sprinkle with pecans. Chill for several hours. Yield: 8 servings.

Freda F. Pirtle, Alpha Chi Master
West Frankfort, Illinois

WHITE CHRISTMAS PIE

1/2 cup sugar	1 cup flaked coconut
1/4 cup all-purpose flour	3 egg whites, stiffly beaten
1/4 teaspoon salt	1/4 teaspoon cream of tartar
1 3/4 cups milk	
1 envelope unflavored gelatin	1/2 cup heavy whipping cream
3/4 teaspoon vanilla extract	1/2 cup sugar
1/4 teaspoon almond extract	1 (9-inch) baked pie shell

Combine ½ cup sugar, flour, salt, milk and gelatin in a saucepan. Bring to a boil over medium heat, stirring constantly. Boil for 1 minute, stirring constantly. Remove from the heat and cool completely. Stir in the vanilla, almond extract and coconut. Fold in the egg whites and cream of tartar. Whip the cream and ½ cup sugar in a bowl until stiff peaks form. Fold into the egg white mixture. Pour into the pie shell. Yield: 8 servings.

Marybeth Syfert, Laureate Alpha Epsilon
Gainesville, Florida

APPLE CRISP FOR ONE

1 tablespoon butter or
  margarine, melted
2 tablespoons dark
  brown sugar
2 tablespoons quick-
  cooking oats
1 tablespoon
  all-purpose flour

⅛ teaspoon cinnamon
Pinch of nutmeg
1 apple, peeled and
  sliced
Whipped cream or ice
  cream

Combine the butter, brown sugar, oats, flour, cinnamon and nutmeg in a small bowl. Place the apple slices in a small microwave-proof bowl. Sprinkle with the brown sugar mixture. Microwave on High for 2½ minutes. Serve with whipped cream or ice cream. Yield: 1 serving.

Carmen Reinbold, Laureate Alpha Delta
Saginaw, Michigan

APPLE DUMPLINGS

2 (8-count) cans
  refrigerated
  crescent rolls
4 Golden Delicious
  apples, peeled and
  quartered

1 cup (2 sticks) butter,
  melted
2 cups sugar
2 teaspoons cinnamon
1 (12-ounce) can lemon-
  lime soda

Separate the rolls into triangles. Place an apple quarter at the large end of each triangle and roll up. Arrange in a 9×13-inch baking dish. Combine the butter, sugar and cinnamon in a small bowl and mix well. Drizzle over the dumplings. Pour the soda evenly over the dumplings. Bake at 350 degrees for 30 to 40 minutes or until golden brown. Remove to a wire rack to cool. Spoon the hot liquid in the dish over the dumplings. Serve warm. Yield: 16 servings.

Barbara Bearden, Preceptor Alpha Kappa
Ozark, Arkansas

BAKED APPLE DUMPLINGS

¼ cup pecans, chopped
¼ cup granulated sugar
¼ cup packed brown
  sugar
¼ cup crushed
  peppermint candy
4 baking apples, peeled
  and cored

4 sheets frozen puff
  pastry, thawed
Granulated sugar for
  sprinkling
1 cup cream
½ cup (1 stick) butter
1 cup granulated sugar
1 teaspoon vanilla
  extract

Combine the pecans, ¼ cup granulated sugar, brown sugar and peppermint candy in a bowl and mix well. Spoon the mixture into the cored apples. Place each apple on the end of a sheet of puff pastry and roll up carefully. Place in an 8×8-inch baking dish. Sprinkle with granulated sugar. Bake at 350 degrees for 20 to 30 minutes or until the apples are tender. Remove to a wire rack to cool. Combine the cream, butter, 1 cup granulated sugar and vanilla in a saucepan. Bring to a boil over medium heat, stirring constantly. Boil for 3 to 4 minutes or until thickened, stirring constantly. Spoon over the warm dumplings just before serving. Yield: 4 servings.

Judith Fields, Preceptor Iota Nu
Palm Coast, Florida

RUSTIC APPLE TART

1 (1-crust) pie pastry
1 egg, beaten
3 tablespoons chunky
  applesauce
4 Gala apples, peeled
  and sliced
½ cup raisins

½ cup chopped nuts
  (optional)
½ cup sugar
1 teaspoon cinnamon
1 teaspoon nutmeg
1 tablespoon sugar

Fit the pie pastry in a pie plate. Brush part of the egg over the center of the crust. Top with the applesauce and spread to within 1 inch of the crust edge. Top with the apples, raisins and nuts. Combine ½ cup sugar, cinnamon and nutmeg in a small bowl and mix well. Sprinkle evenly over the filling. Moisten the pastry edge with water and fold over the filling. Brush the edge with the remaining egg and sprinkle with 1 tablespoon sugar. Bake at 350 degrees for 55 minutes or until golden brown and the apples are tender. Let stand for 1 hour before removing to a serving plate. Yield: 8 servings.

Marcy Hauser, Preceptor Beta Psi
Bermuda Dunes, California

SCRUMPTIOUS APPLE TART

1 (1-crust) pie pastry
4 cups thinly sliced
    peeled apples
1 tablespoon cinnamon
2 tablespoons cornstarch
3/4 cup sugar
1 egg white, slightly
    beaten
1 teaspoon sugar

Unfold the pie pastry on a foil-lined baking sheet. Combine the apples, cinnamon, cornstarch and 3/4 cup sugar in a bowl and toss to coat. Spoon over the center of the pastry, leaving a 2-inch rim. Moisten the pastry edge with water and fold over the filling. Brush the egg white over the edge. Sprinkle with 1 teaspoon sugar. Bake at 425 degrees for 20 minutes or until the apples are tender. Remove to a wire rack to cool. Yield: 6 to 8 servings.

Gloria Swager, Xi Zeta Mu
Belle Glade, Florida

APPLE PIZZA

3 1/2 cups all-purpose
    flour
1 1/2 cups shortening
1 egg
4 tablespoons water
1 tablespoon vinegar
6 to 8 apples, peeled and
    thinly sliced
1 teaspoon cinnamon
1/2 cup sugar
1/4 teaspoon nutmeg
1/2 cup sugar
3/4 cup all-purpose flour
1/2 cup (1 stick) butter or
    margarine

Place 3 1/2 cups flour in a bowl. Cut in the shortening until crumbly. Mix the egg, water and vinegar in a small bowl. Add to the flour mixture and stir to form a dough. Roll into a 16-inch circle on a floured surface. Place on a greased baking sheet. Arrange the apples on the pastry, overlapping slightly. Sprinkle a mixture of the cinnamon, 1/2 cup sugar and nutmeg over the apples. Combine 1/2 cup sugar and 3/4 cup flour in a bowl. Cut in the butter until crumbly. Sprinkle over the apples. Bake at 400 degrees for 20 minutes. Cool on a wire rack. Yield: 12 servings.

Margaret C. Long, Preceptor Gamma Epsilon
Marysville, Ohio

BANANA CHOCOLATE SURPRISE

12 sheets frozen phyllo
    dough, thawed
4 bananas
1 cup raspberries or
    blueberries
2 ounces chocolate,
    chopped
1/4 cup (1/2 stick) butter,
    melted

Stack the phyllo dough. Cut the stack into a 6×14-inch rectangle with a sharp knife. Discard the scraps. Stack 3 sheets of the dough. Place a banana at one end of the stack. Sprinkle with one-quarter of the berries and one-quarter of the chocolate. Roll to enclose the filling. Brush with melted butter. Place in an 11×14-inch baking dish. Repeat the process with the remaining ingredients. Bake at 350 degrees for 10 to 12 minutes or until golden brown. Remove to a wire rack to cool. Serve with ice cream if desired. Yield: 4 servings.

Georgina McLaren, Laureate Beta Tau
Waterford, Ontario, Canada

BLACKBERRY DUMPLINGS

4 to 5 cups blackberries
3 cups sugar or to taste
3 cups water
1 tablespoon butter
1 teaspoon nutmeg
2 cups baking mix
2/3 cup milk

Combine the blackberries, sugar and water in a saucepan. Cook over low heat until soft, stirring often. Remove from the heat and stir in the butter and nutmeg. Combine the baking mix and milk in a bowl and mix well. Drop the dough over the blackberries by tablespoonfuls. Cook, covered, over low heat for 15 minutes. Stir gently. Cover and cook for 10 minutes. Serve warm with ice cream if desired. Yield: 10 to 12 servings.

Marilyn Wood, Preceptor Epsilon
Sullivan, Illinois

BUTTER TARTS

These tarts remind me of mincemeat.

1 1/2 cups raisins
1/4 cup corn syrup
1 cup packed brown
    sugar
2 tablespoons butter
2 eggs
1/2 teaspoon vanilla
    extract
1 teaspoon nutmeg
24 miniature unbaked
    tart shells

Place the raisins in a saucepan with enough water to cover. Bring to a boil over medium heat. Boil for 10 minutes, stirring occasionally. Drain and return the raisins to the saucepan. Add the corn syrup, brown sugar, butter, eggs, vanilla and nutmeg and mix well. Spoon the mixture into the tart shells. Bake at 400 degrees for 15 to 20 minutes. Yield: 24 servings.

Lorraine P. Fraess, Iota Master
Saskatoon, Saskatchewan, Canada

MINIATURE CHEESECAKE TARTS

1/2 teaspoon vanilla
    extract
1/2 cup sugar
8 ounces cream cheese,
    softened
1 egg
Vanilla wafers
1 (21-ounce) can cherry
    pie filling

Beat the vanilla, sugar, cream cheese and egg in a bowl until light and fluffy. Place 1 vanilla wafer in each paper-lined muffin cup. Top with 1 tablespoon of the cream cheese mixture. Bake at 300 degrees for 15 to 20 minutes or until set. Remove to a wire rack to cool. Top the warm tarts with a spoonful of pie filling. Yield: 24 servings.

Iris M. Rapko, Xi Theta Alpha
Grimsby, Ontario, Canada

CHOCOLATE BROWNIE TART

1 cup all-purpose flour
1/4 cup packed
  brown sugar
1 ounce unsweetened
  chocolate,
  finely chopped
1/2 cup (1 stick) butter,
  cut into 1/2-inch slices
2 tablespoons milk
1 teaspoon vanilla
  extract
3 ounces unsweetened
  chocolate

3 ounces semisweet
  chocolate
1/2 cup (1 stick) butter,
  softened
1 1/2 cups granulated
  sugar
3 eggs
2 teaspoons vanilla
  extract
3/4 cup all-purpose flour
1/2 cup chopped pecans
Frosting

Combine 1 cup flour, the brown sugar and 1 ounce unsweetened chocolate in a bowl. Cut in 1/2 cup butter until crumbly. Add the milk and 1 teaspoon vanilla and mix well. Pat into an 11-inch tart pan. Melt 3 ounces unsweetened chocolate and the semisweet chocolate in a double boiler, stirring occasionally. Remove from the heat. Stir in 1/2 cup butter 1 tablespoon at a time. Remove to a large bowl. Add the granulated sugar and mix well. Add the eggs 1 at a time, mixing well after each addition. Stir in 2 teaspoons vanilla. Add 3/4 cup flour gradually, mixing well after each addition. Stir in the pecans. Pour into the prepared tart pan. Bake at 350 degrees for 20 to 25 minutes or until a wooden pick inserted in the center comes out clean. Remove to a wire rack to cool. Spread with the Frosting. Yield: 8 to 10 servings.

FROSTING

4 ounces semisweet
  chocolate, melted
1/4 cup (1/2 stick) butter,
  softened

2 teaspoons vegetable
  oil

Combine the chocolate, butter and oil in a large bowl and mix until smooth.

Lana Pisansky, Laureate Pi
Rochester, Minnesota

CHOCOLATE HAZELNUT TART

This is not overly sweet and the pears add a refreshing taste and texture.

1 cup all-purpose flour
1/2 cup shortening
1/4 cup confectioners'
  sugar
3/4 cup finely chopped
  hazelnuts
8 ounces cream cheese,
  softened
1/4 cup granulated sugar
1 egg

3 ounces semisweet
  chocolate, melted
1 (14-ounce) can pears
  halves
1 tablespoon butter
1 ounce semisweet
  chocolate
1/4 cup coarsely chopped
  hazelnuts

Place the flour in a bowl. Cut in the shortening until crumbly. Stir in the confectioners' sugar and 3/4 cup hazelnuts. Press into the bottom and up the side of a 9-inch flan pan. Bake at 425 degrees for 15 minutes. Beat the cream cheese and granulated sugar in a bowl until light and fluffy. Beat in the egg and 3 ounces chocolate. Spread over the warm crust. Drain the pears and pat dry. Arrange the pear halves over the cream cheese layer. Bake at 375 degrees for 25 minutes. Cool in the pan on a wire rack for 3 hours. Melt the butter and 1 ounce chocolate in a small saucepan over low heat, stirring occasionally. Drizzle over the pears. Sprinkle with 1/4 cup hazelnuts. Yield: 8 to 12 servings.

Linda DellaRossa, Mu Pi
St. David's, Ontario, Canada

RUSTIC FRUIT TART

1 (1-crust) pie pastry
3 cups sliced fruit
3 to 4 tablespoons sugar

2 tablespoons cornstarch
1 teaspoon almond
  extract

Place the pie pastry on a baking sheet. Combine the fruit, sugar, cornstarch and almond extract in a bowl and mix well. Spoon the fruit on the center of the pastry, leaving a 2-inch rim. Moisten the edge of the pastry with water and fold up to partially cover the fruit. Bake at 450 degrees for 25 minutes or until bubbly. Remove to a wire rack to cool. Yield: 6 servings.

Sharon Gladish, Xi Zeta Omega
Petersburg, Indiana

Elizabeth Neisen, Preceptor Alpha Lambda, Oshkosh, Wisconsin, contributed her recipe for **Goof-Proof Pie Crust.** *She combines 3/4 cup vegetable oil, 1/4 cup boiling water, 2 tablespoons milk, 2 cups all-purpose flour, 1 teaspoon salt and 1 tablespoon sugar in a bowl and mixes well. She rolls the dough between two sheets of waxed paper before fitting it into a pie plate.*

MINIATURE KEY LIME TARTS

3 ounces cream cheese,
  softened
1/4 cup sweetened
  condensed milk
2 tablespoons Key
  lime juice

1/4 teaspoon grated
  lime zest
15 miniature baked
  tart shells

Beat the cream cheese and condensed milk in a bowl until light and fluffy. Add the lime juice and lime zest and mix well. Spoon the mixture into the tart shells. Serve immediately. Garnish with thin lime slices if desired. Yield: 15 servings.

T. Lynn Moerke, Preceptor Upsilon
Franklin, Wisconsin

PECAN PICK-UPS

1/2 cup (1 stick) butter,
  softened
3 ounces cream cheese,
  softened
1 cup all-purpose flour
3/4 cup packed brown
  sugar

1 egg, beaten
1/2 cup chopped pecans
1 teaspoon butter,
  softened
1 teaspoon vanilla
  extract

Beat 1/2 cup butter and the cream cheese in a bowl until smooth. Add the flour gradually, mixing well after each addition. Chill, wrapped in plastic wrap, for 30 minutes or longer. Shape the dough into 1-inch balls. Press over the bottoms and sides of greased miniature muffin cups. Combine the brown sugar, egg, pecans, 1 teaspoon butter and the vanilla in a bowl and mix well. Fill each muffin cup with 1 tablespoon of the pecan mixture. Bake at 350 degrees for 30 minutes. Remove to a wire rack to cool. Yield: 24 tarts.

Sheila Findley, Xi Theta Upsilon
Lutz, Florida

RASPBERRY TART

1/2 cup sugar
11/2 cups all-purpose
  flour
1/3 cup butter, cut into
  small pieces
3 cups frozen raspberries,
  thawed and drained

4 eggs
3/4 cup sugar
1/4 cup all-purpose flour
2 teaspoons vanilla
  extract
Confectioners' sugar

Place 1/2 cup sugar and 11/2 cups flour in a bowl. Cut in the butter until crumbly. Pat into a 9×9-inch baking pan. Bake at 400 degrees for 20 minutes or until light brown. Remove to a wire rack. Arrange the raspberries over the crust. Combine the eggs, 3/4 cup sugar, 1/4 cup flour and vanilla in a bowl and mix well. Pour over the berries in the pan. Bake at 325 degrees for 30 minutes or until set. Remove to a wire rack to cool. Dust with confectioners' sugar. Yield: 12 servings.

Brenda Hansen, Xi Alpha Nu
Baker, Montana

UPSIDE-DOWN PEAR TART

1/4 cup (1/2 stick)
  unsalted butter
1/2 cup sugar
2 pounds Bosc pears
  (3 to 5 pears), peeled
  and halved
1/2 teaspoon cinnamon
21/2 cups all-purpose
  flour

3 tablespoons sugar
1 cup (2 sticks) unsalted
  butter, cut into
  small pieces
2 egg yolks, slightly
  beaten
4 tablespoons ice water

Melt 1/4 cup butter in an ovenproof skillet over medium heat. Stir in 1/2 cup sugar. Arrange the pears, cut side up, in the center of the skillet. Sprinkle with the cinnamon. Cook for 10 to 25 minutes or until the liquid is caramel colored; do not stir. Remove from the heat and cool completely in the skillet. Combine the flour and 3 tablespoons sugar in a bowl. Cut in 1 cup butter until crumbly. Add the egg yolks and mix well. Add the water 1 tablespoon at a time, mixing with a fork until the mixture forms a ball. Chill, wrapped in plastic wrap, for 1 hour. Roll into an 11-inch circle on a floured surface. Arrange over the caramelized pears, tucking the edge. Bake at 425 degrees for 30 to 35 minutes or until golden brown. Invert the skillet onto a serving plate. Cool completely. Serve with whipped cream or ice cream if desired. Yield: 8 servings.

Gig Rose, Preceptor Kappa
Ludington, Michigan

WHITE CHOCOLATE MOUSSE PASTRIES

6 ounces premium white
  chocolate, melted
11/2 cups heavy
  whipping cream

1 ounce semisweet
  chocolate, melted
6 unbaked tart shells,
  baked and cooled

Combine the white chocolate and 1/4 cup of the cream in a large bowl and stir until smooth. Let stand for 20 minutes, stirring occasionally. Whip the remaining 11/4 cups cream in a bowl until stiff peaks form. Fold half of the whipped cream into the white chocolate mixture. Fold in the remaining whipped cream just until blended. Spoon into the prepared pastry shells and drizzle with the semisweet chocolate. Chill for 1 hour or longer. Yield: 6 servings.

Doris J. Bain, Xi Epsilon
Chattanooga, Tennessee

Slices
CAKES AND CHEESECAKES

ALMOND JOY CAKE

1 (2-layer) package
  devil's food cake mix
1 (12-ounce) can
  evaporated milk
1 1/2 cups sugar
25 large marshmallows
1 (14-ounce) package
  flaked coconut
1 cup sugar
1/2 cup (1 stick) butter
2 cups (12 ounces)
  semisweet
  chocolate chips
1/2 cup toasted almonds

Prepare and bake the cake mix using the package directions for a 9×13-inch cake pan. Combine half the evaporated milk and 1 1/2 cups sugar in a saucepan. Bring to a boil over medium heat, stirring often. Remove from the heat and stir in the marshmallows until smooth. Stir in the coconut. Pour over the cake. Combine 1 cup sugar and the remaining evaporated milk in a saucepan. Bring to a boil over medium heat, stirring often. Remove from the heat and stir in the remaining ingredients. Pour over the coconut layer. Chill, covered, for 2 hours or longer. Yield: 12 servings.

Maria Hedlund, Xi Zeta
Anthony, Kansas

AMARETTO DELIGHT

1 (2-layer) package
  yellow cake mix
1 (4-ounce) package
  pistachio instant
  pudding mix
1 cup vegetable oil
4 eggs
1/4 cup vodka
1/4 cup amaretto
2/3 cup orange juice
1 cup sugar
1/2 cup (1 stick) butter
1/4 cup orange juice
1/4 cup amaretto

Mix the cake mix, pudding mix and oil in a bowl. Beat in the eggs 1 at a time. Add the vodka, 1/4 cup amaretto and 2/3 cup orange juice and mix well. Pour into a greased and floured bundt pan. Bake at 340 degrees for 55 minutes. Combine the sugar, butter, 1/4 cup orange juice and 1/4 cup amaretto in a saucepan. Bring to a boil over medium heat, stirring often. Boil for 4 minutes, stirring constantly. Pierce the warm cake with a fork. Pour the glaze over the cake. Cool in the pan for 30 minutes. Invert onto a serving plate. Yield: 12 servings.

Donna Maddox, Beta Iota
Haughton, Louisiana

AMISH CAKE

2 cups sugar
2 eggs
2 teaspoons vanilla
  extract
1 (20-ounce) can crushed
  pineapple
2 cups all-purpose flour
2 teaspoons baking soda
1 cup pecans, chopped
1/4 cup (1/2 stick) butter,
  softened
4 ounces cream cheese,
  softened
1 teaspoon vanilla
  extract
Confectioners' sugar

Combine the sugar, eggs, 2 teaspoons vanilla and the pineapple in a bowl and mix well. Add the flour and baking soda and mix well. Stir in the pecans. Pour into a greased 9×13-inch cake pan. Bake at 350 degrees for 35 to 40 minutes or until the cake tests done. Cool in the pan for 10 minutes. Remove to a wire rack to cool completely. Beat the butter, cream cheese and 1 teaspoon vanilla in a bowl until light and fluffy. Beat in enough confectioners' sugar to make of spreading consistency. Spread on the cooled cake. Yield: 16 servings.

Joyce Williams, Preceptor Nu
Salina, Kansas

ANGEL FOOD STRAWBERRY CAKE ROLL

1 (16-ounce) package
   angel food cake mix
1 cup strawberry yogurt
1 small package sugar-
   free vanilla instant
   pudding

3 drops red food
   coloring
8 ounces low-fat
   whipped topping

Prepare the cake mix using the package directions. Pour into a waxed paper-lined 10×15-inch cake pan. Bake at 350 degrees for 15 to 20 minutes or until the top is brown and dry. Cool in the pan for 5 minutes. Dust a clean kitchen towel generously with confectioners' sugar. Invert the cake onto the towel. Remove the waxed paper. Roll the warm cake in the towel as for a jelly roll from the short side and place on a wire rack to cool. Combine the yogurt, pudding mix and food coloring in a bowl and mix well. Fold in the whipped topping. Unroll the cooled cake carefully and remove the towel. Spread the yogurt mixture within 1/2-inch of the edge and reroll. Wrap in plastic wrap and freeze. Remove 30 minutes before serving. Yield: 10 servings.

Charlene Gonzalez, Xi Beta Lambda
Derby, Kansas

CHOCOLATE ANGEL FOOD CAKE

1/4 cup baking cocoa,
   sifted
3/4 cup plus 2 tablespoons
   sifted cake flour
2/3 cup sugar
1 3/4 cups egg whites

1 1/2 teaspoons cream
   of tartar
1/2 teaspoon salt
1 teaspoon almond
   extract
1 cup sugar

Sift the baking cocoa, cake flour and 2/3 cup sugar together 6 times. Beat the egg whites at low speed in a mixing bowl until foamy. Add the cream of tartar and salt. Beat at medium speed until soft peaks form. Add the almond extract. Add 1 cup sugar gradually, beating constantly at high speed until stiff peaks form. Fold in the flour mixture. Spoon into an ungreased tube pan. Cut through the batter 1 inch from the center of the pan with a knife. Bake at 325 degrees on the bottom rack for 55 to 60 minutes or until the top is brown and dry. Invert on a funnel to cool completely. Loosen the cake from the side of the pan with a sharp knife. Invert onto a cake plate. Drizzle with chocolate and serve with whipped cream and raspberries if desired. Yield: 12 servings.

Sharon Cordani, Xi Delta Nu
Litchfield, Illinois

FROSTED ANGEL FOOD CAKE

3/4 cup sugar
1 tablespoon
   all-purpose flour
1 1/2 cups milk
1 envelope unflavored
   gelatin

1/4 cup cold water
1 cup heavy whipping
   cream
1 teaspoon vanilla
   extract
1 angel food cake

Combine the sugar, flour and milk in a saucepan. Place over simmering water. Cook until thickened, stirring often. Soften the gelatin in the water in a bowl. Add to the milk mixture and stir until smooth. Remove from the heat. Chill, covered, until firm. Whip the cream in a bowl until stiff peaks form. Add the vanilla and mix well. Fold in to the gelatin mixture. Slice the angel food cake horizontally into 3 layers. Spread the frosting between the layers and over the top and side of the cooled cake. Yield: 12 servings.

Dorothy Stohlman, Laureate Beta Beta
Cave Junction, Oregon

STUFFED ANGEL FOOD CAKE

1 (16-ounce) package
   angel food cake mix
1 (4-ounce) package
   strawberry gelatin
1 cup hot water
1 (16-ounce) package
   frozen strawberries

8 ounces cream cheese,
   softened
1 teaspoon vanilla
   extract
1 1/2 cups confectioners'
   sugar

Prepare and bake the cake mix using the package directions. Slice off the top of the cake, about 1 inch, reserving the slice. Remove the center of the remaining cake with a fork, leaving a 1-inch shell. Combine the gelatin, hot water and strawberries in a bowl and mix well. Add the cake pieces and stir gently to coat. Spoon the mixture into the cake base. Replace the top slice. Combine the cream cheese, vanilla and confectioners' sugar in a bowl and mix until smooth. Spread the mixture over the top and side of the cake. Store in the refrigerator. Yield: 12 servings.

Marie A. Robinson
Denver, Colorado

APPLE CAKE

We have three apple trees, so I make this often.

2 cups sugar
2 eggs
1/2 cup canola oil
2 cups all-purpose flour
2 teaspoons baking soda

1 teaspoon salt
1 heaping teaspoon
   cinnamon
4 cups sliced peeled
   apples

Combine the sugar, eggs and oil in a bowl and mix well. Stir in the flour, baking soda, salt and cinnamon. Stir in the apples. Pour into a greased and floured 9×13-inch glass baking dish. Bake at 350 degrees for 55 minutes. Cool in the pan for 10 minutes. Remove to a wire rack to cool completely. Serve warm with vanilla ice cream or serve at room temperature with whipped topping.
Yield: 15 servings.

Judy Westbrook, Xi Alpha Delta
Elmira, Oregon

APPLE CAKE WITH NUTS

4 cups chopped peeled apples	2 teaspoons vanilla extract
2 cups sugar	2 cups all-purpose flour
1/2 cup applesauce	1 teaspoon salt
1/4 cup chopped nuts	2 teaspoons baking soda
2 eggs	2 teaspoons cinnamon

Combine the apples and sugar in a bowl and mix well. Add the applesauce, nuts, eggs and vanilla and mix well. Sift the flour, salt, baking soda and cinnamon into the bowl and mix well. Pour into a greased and floured 9×13-inch cake pan. Bake at 350 degrees for 1 hour or until the cake tests done. Cool in the pan for 10 minutes. Remove to a wire rack to cool completely. Yield: 12 to 15 servings.

Bernadette Kleinsmith, Laureate Gamma Alpha
DeWitt, Iowa

APPLE TUBE CAKE

2 cups sliced peeled apples	1/3 to 1/2 cup orange juice
2 tablespoons sugar	2 cups all-purpose flour
2 tablespoons cinnamon	2 cups sugar
4 eggs	4 teaspoons baking powder
1 cup vegetable oil	Confectioners' sugar
2 1/2 teaspoons vanilla extract	

Combine the apple slices, 2 tablespoons sugar and cinnamon in a small bowl and mix well. Combine the eggs, oil, vanilla and orange juice in a mixing bowl and mix well. Add the flour, 2 cups sugar and baking powder and mix well. Pour 1/2 the batter into a greased and floured tube pan. Layer with 1/2 the apple slices. Repeat the layers. Bake at 350 degrees for 1 hour and 5 minutes. Cool in the pan for 10 minutes. Invert onto a serving plate. Dust with confectioners' sugar. Yield: 10 servings.

Edith Sklar, Preceptor Delta
Honolulu, Hawaii

GERMAN APPLE CAKE

3 eggs	4 cups chopped Pippin or Granny Smith apples
1 cup vegetable oil	
2 cups granulated sugar	8 ounces cream cheese, softened
2 cups all-purpose flour	
1 teaspoon baking soda	3 tablespoons butter, melted
1/2 teaspoon salt	
3 teaspoons cinnamon	1/2 cup confectioners' sugar
1 cup chopped walnuts	

Combine the eggs and oil in a small bowl and mix well. Combine the granulated sugar, flour, baking soda, salt and cinnamon in a large bowl. Add the oil mixture and mix well. Stir in the walnuts and apples. Pour into a greased and floured 9×13-inch cake pan. Bake at 350 degrees for 50 minutes. Cool in the pan for 10 minutes. Remove to a wire rack to cool completely. Combine the cream cheese, butter and confectioners' sugar in a mixing bowl and beat until light and fluffy. Spread on the cooled cake.
Yield: 24 servings.

Marilynn Grahn, Xi Epsilon Xi
Port Orange, Florida

GLAZED APPLE CAKE

1 1/2 cups vegetable oil	1 teaspoon baking soda
2 cups sugar	1 teaspoon salt
3 eggs	3 cups chopped peeled apples
1 teaspoon vanilla extract	
3 cups all-purpose flour	1 1/2 cups chopped pecans
1/4 teaspoon cinnamon	Glaze

Combine the oil, sugar, eggs and vanilla in a bowl and mix well. Stir in the flour, cinnamon, baking soda and salt. Stir in the apples and pecans. Pour into a greased and floured tube pan. Bake at 325 degrees for 1 hour. Cool in the pan for 5 minutes. Invert onto a serving plate. Drizzle with warm Glaze.
Yield: 12 servings.

GLAZE

1 cup packed light brown sugar	1/4 cup milk
	1 teaspoon vanilla extract
1/2 cup (1 stick) butter or margarine	

Combine the brown sugar and butter in a saucepan. Bring to a boil over low heat, stirring often. Stir in the milk and vanilla.

Jane F. McDonald, Gama Alpha Master
Fort Worth, Texas

HOT APPLE CAKE WITH CARAMEL PECAN SAUCE

1 cup (2 sticks) unsalted butter, softened
1 cup sugar
2 eggs, at room temperature
1½ cups all-purpose flour
¼ teaspoon nutmeg
1½ teaspoons cinnamon
1 teaspoon baking soda
¼ teaspoon salt
1 teaspoon vanilla extract
3 tart apples, peeled and chopped
¾ cup chopped pecans
1 quart vanilla ice cream
Caramel Pecan Sauce

Beat the butter and sugar in a bowl until light and fluffy. Add the eggs 1 at a time, mixing well after each addition. Add the flour, nutmeg, cinnamon, baking soda and salt and mix well. Stir in the vanilla, apples and pecans. Spoon into a 9-inch cake pan. Bake at 350 degrees for 35 to 45 minutes or until the cake tests done. Cool in the pan for 10 minutes. Remove to a wire rack to cool completely. Serve with a scoop of vanilla ice cream and drizzled with Caramel Pecan Sauce. Yield: 10 servings.

CARAMEL PECAN SAUCE

¼ cup (½ stick) unsalted butter
½ cup pecan halves
1 cup packed dark brown sugar
1 cup heavy whipping cream

Melt the butter in a saucepan over medium heat. Add the pecans. Cook until the butter is light brown, stirring constantly. Add the brown sugar and cream. Bring to a boil.

Patricia Soard, Theta Psi
Cookeville, Tennessee

SWISS APPLE CAKE

1 (2-layer) package German chocolate cake mix
1 (21-ounce) can apple pie filling
3 eggs
3 tablespoons fat-free mayonnaise
½ cup chopped pecans or walnuts
½ cup (3 ounces) chocolate chips
3 tablespoons sugar

Combine the cake mix, pie filling, eggs and mayonnaise in a bowl and mix well. Pour into a greased and floured 9×13-inch cake pan. Sprinkle with pecans, chocolate chips and sugar. Bake at 350 degrees for 45 to 55 minutes or until the cake tests done. Cool in the pan on a wire rack. Serve with whipped cream if desired. Yield: 12 servings.

Fran Trainer, Xi Lambda Sigma
Osceola, Missouri

APPLE CARAMEL CAKE

1 (2-layer) package yellow cake mix
1 (4-ounce) package vanilla or French vanilla instant pudding mix
1 cup water
4 eggs
⅓ cup vegetable oil
3 Granny Smith apples, peeled and chopped
Chopped pecans
20 caramel candies
¼ cup milk

Combine the cake mix, pudding mix, water, eggs and oil in a large bowl. Beat at low until blended. Beat at high speed for 2 minutes. Stir in the apples and pecans. Pour into a greased and floured bundt pan. Bake at 350 degrees for 50 to 60 minutes or until a wooden pick inserted in the center comes out clean. Cool in the pan for 20 minutes. Invert onto a serving plate. Microwave the candies and milk in a bowl on High for 1 to 1½ minutes, stirring every 30 seconds. Cool for 10 minutes or until slightly thickened. Drizzle over the cake. Yield: 16 servings.

Fran Bogar, Laureate Delta Tau
St. Charles, Missouri

APPLE CINNAMON CAKE

You can change the flavors by using orange cake mix and pineapple pie filling.

1 (2-layer) package spice cake mix
1 (21-ounce) can apple pie filling
3 eggs
3 tablespoons sugar
1 teaspoon cinnamon

Combine the cake mix, pie filling and eggs in a bowl. Beat at medium speed for 2 minutes. Pour half the batter into a greased and floured 9×13-inch cake pan. Combine the sugar and cinnamon in a small bowl. Sprinkle half the cinnamon-sugar over the batter. Repeat the layers. Bake at 350 degrees for 30 to 35 minutes or until a wooden pick inserted in the center comes out clean. Cool in the pan for 10 minutes. Remove to a wire rack to cool completely. Yield: 12 servings.

Mary Nita Wing, Xi Master
Lake Jackson, Texas

APPLE COCONUT CAKE

3 cups all-purpose flour
1 teaspoon baking soda
1 teaspoon salt
1 cup vegetable oil
3 eggs
2¼ cups sugar
2 teaspoons vanilla extract
2 cups chopped pecans or walnuts
3 cups chopped peeled cooking apples
½ cup flaked coconut
Glaze

Combine the flour, baking soda and salt. Combine the oil, eggs, sugar and vanilla and beat at medium speed for 2 minutes. Add the flour mixture and beat just until mixed. Fold in the pecans, apples and coconut; batter will be stiff. Spoon into a greased and floured 10-inch tube pan. Bake at 350 degrees for 1 1/3 hours or until the cake tests done. Drizzle the cake with hot Glaze. Cool in the pan for 10 minutes. Invert onto a serving plate. Yield: 12 servings.

GLAZE

1/2 cup packed light brown sugar
1/4 cup milk

1/2 cup (1 stick) butter or margarine

Combine the brown sugar, milk and butter in a saucepan. Bring to a boil over medium heat, stirring constantly. Boil for 2 minutes, stirring constantly.

Kathleen M. Melton, Preceptor Kappa Epsilon
Forth Worth, Texas

APPLE CRANBERRY UPSIDE-DOWN CAKE

1/2 cup packed brown sugar
1/4 cup (1/2 stick) butter, melted
1 large apple, peeled and sliced
1/4 cup sweetened dried cranberries

1 (16-ounce) package cranberry quick bread mix
3/4 cup water
2 tablespoons vegetable oil
2 eggs

Combine the brown sugar and butter in a bowl and mix well. Spread in a greased and floured deep-dish pie plate. Arrange the apple slices and cranberries over the brown sugar mixture. Combine the bread mix, water, oil and eggs in a bowl. Stir just until moistened. Spoon the batter over the fruit. Bake at 350 degrees for 35 to 40 minutes or until a wooden pick inserted in the center comes out clean. Cool in the pan for 2 minutes. Invert onto a serving plate. Yield: 8 to 10 servings.

Christine Soard, Theta Psi
Cookeville, Tennessee

APPLE CRISP CAKE

1 3/4 cups sugar
1 cup vegetable oil
3 eggs
2 cups all-purpose flour
1 teaspoon baking soda
1 teaspoon cinnamon

1 teaspoon salt
2 cups chopped peeled apples
1 cup nuts
1/2 cup raisins

Combine the sugar, oil and eggs in a bowl and mix well. Sift the flour, baking soda, cinnamon and salt into the bowl and mix well. Stir in the apples, nuts and raisins. Pour into a greased and floured 9×13-inch cake pan. Bake at 350 degrees for 40 minutes. Cool in the pan for 10 minutes. Remove to a wire rack to cool completely. Yield: 12 servings.

Marjorie A. Travis, Laureate Beta Upsilon
Grand Blanc, Michigan

APPLESAUCE SOUR CREAM CAKE

1 1/2 cups all-purpose flour
3/4 cup packed brown sugar
1 teaspoon baking soda
1/2 teaspoon baking powder
1 teaspoon cinnamon

1/2 teaspoon salt
3/4 cup fat-free sour cream
2 tablespoons vegetable oil
1 cup unsweetened applesauce

Combine the flour, brown sugar, soda, baking powder, cinnamon and salt. Combine the sour cream, oil and applesauce in a bowl and mix well. Stir in the dry ingredients just until moistened. Pour into a greased and floured 9×9-inch cake pan. Bake at 350 degrees for 40 to 45 minutes or until a wooden pick inserted in the center comes out clean. Cool in the pan for 10 minutes. Remove to a wire rack to cool completely. Serve with fat-free whipped topping if desired. Yield: 16 servings.

Rhonda Wassenberg, Preceptor Zeta
Blue Rapids, Kansas

APPLE SPICE CAKE

1 (2-layer) package spice cake mix
1 (21-ounce) can apple pie filling
1/3 cup apple butter
3 eggs
8 ounces cream cheese, softened

1/2 cup (1 stick) butter, softened
1 cup confectioners' sugar
4 tablespoons apple butter

Combine the cake mix, pie filling, 1/3 cup apple butter and the eggs in a bowl and mix well. Bake using the package directions. Cool in the pan for 10 minutes. Remove to a wire rack to cool completely. Combine the cream cheese, butter and confectioners' sugar in a bowl and beat until light and fluffy. Add 4 tablespoons apple butter and mix well. Spread on the cooled cake. Yield: 12 servings.

Joanne Farmer, Preceptor Delta Sigma
Bedford, Texas

APRICOT CRISP

My mother-in-law, Mildred Sodeman Burns, came up with this recipe.

1 (15-ounce) can apricot halves
1 egg
1 cup sugar
1 cup all-purpose flour
1 teaspoon baking powder

Drain the apricots, reserving the liquid. Place the apricots in a greased and floured 9-inch cake pan. Measure 1/3 cup of the reserved liquid and discard. Combine the egg and the remaining reserved liquid in a bowl and mix well. Add the sugar, flour and baking powder and mix well. Pour over the apricots. Bake at 325 degrees for 55 minutes to 1 hour or until the cake tests done. Cool in the pan for 10 minutes. Remove to a wire rack to cool completely. Dust with confectioners' sugar if desired. Yield: 8 servings.

Ruby Burns, Lambda Mu
Lathrop, Missouri

APRICOT NECTAR CAKE

1 (2-layer) package lemon cake mix
1 cup apricot nectar (apricot juice)
3/4 cup vegetable oil
1/2 cup granulated sugar
4 eggs
1 1/2 cups confectioners' sugar
3 tablespoons apricot nectar (apricot juice)
Juice of 1 lemon

Combine the cake mix, 1 cup apricot nectar, the oil, sugar and eggs in a bowl and mix well. Pour into a greased and floured 9×13-inch cake pan. Bake at 350 degrees for 30 to 40 minutes or until the cake tests done. Combine the confectioners' sugar, 3 tablespoons apricot nectar and the lemon juice in a medium bowl and mix well. Pour over the warm cake. Cool completely in the pan. Yield: 5 to 10 servings.

Brenda Davis, Iota Sigma
Decatur, Tennessee

FROSTED BANANA CAKE

1 1/4 teaspoons baking soda
2/3 cup buttermilk
1 1/4 cups mashed bananas
2 eggs, beaten
2/3 cup chopped nuts (optional)
1/3 cup vegetable oil
1 (2-layer) package white or yellow cake mix
Frosting

Mix the first 6 ingredients in a bowl. Add the cake mix and mix well. Pour into a greased 9×13-inch cake pan. Bake at 350 degrees for 35 to 40 minutes or until the cake tests done. Cool in the pan for 10 minutes. Remove to a wire rack to cool completely. Spread the Frosting on the cooled cake. Yield: 16 servings.

FROSTING

1/2 cup (1 stick) butter
1 cup packed brown sugar
1/4 cup milk
2 cups confectioners' sugar

Melt the butter in saucepan over medium heat. Stir in the brown sugar. Bring to a boil and boil for 5 minutes, stirring constantly. Stir in the milk. Bring to a boil, stirring constantly. Remove from the heat. Cool to lukewarm. Add the confectioners' sugar and beat until the mixture is of spreading consistency.

June M. Clark, Alpha Zeta Alpha
Deepwater, Missouri

BLACK RUSSIAN CAKE

1 (2-layer) package yellow cake mix
1 (6-ounce) box chocolate instant pudding mix
1/2 cup sugar
1 cup vegetable oil
4 eggs
1/4 cup vodka
1/4 cup Kahlua
3/4 cup water
1/2 cup confectioners' sugar
1/3 cup Kahlua

Combine the cake mix, pudding mix, sugar, oil, eggs, vodka, 1/4 cup Kahlua and the water in a large bowl. Mix at low speed for 1 minute. Mix at medium speed for 4 minutes. Pour into a greased and floured tube pan. Bake at 350 degrees for 1 hour to 70 minutes or until the cake tests done. Cool in the pan for 10 minutes. Invert onto a serving plate. Pierce the cake with a fork. Combine the confectioners' sugar and 1/3 cup Kahlua in a bowl and mix until smooth. Drizzle over the cake. Yield: 16 servings.

Lorna Webb, Beta Kappa Mu
Hilltop Lakes, Texas

BLACKBERRY CAKE

3/4 cup (1 1/2 sticks) butter or margarine, softened
1 cup packed brown sugar
3 eggs
2 1/2 cups all-purpose flour
1 teaspoon baking powder
1 teaspoon allspice
1 teaspoon cinnamon
1 teaspoon nutmeg
3/4 cup buttermilk
2 cups blackberry jam
Whipped cream
Freshly grated nutmeg

Beat the butter in a bowl until light and fluffy. Add the brown sugar gradually, beating well after each addition. Add the eggs 1 at a time, beating well after each addition. Combine the flour, baking powder, allspice, cinnamon and nutmeg. Add to the butter mixture alternately with the buttermilk, ending with the flour mixture. Fold in 3/4 cup of the blackberry jam. Pour into 2 greased and floured 9-inch cake

pans. Bake at 350 degrees for 25 minutes or until a wooden pick inserted in the center comes out clean. Cool in the pans for 10 minutes. Remove to a wire rack to cool completely. Melt the remaining 1¼ cups jam in a saucepan over low heat, stirring often. Brush the jam between the layers and over the top and side of the cooled cake. Top with whipped cream and sprinkle with nutmeg just before serving.
Yield: 12 servings.

Virginia (Ginny) Thomas, Preceptor Gamma Eta
Merritt Island, Florida

BLACKBERRY JAM CAKE

1 cup (2 sticks) butter, softened	2 teaspoons cinnamon
2 cups sugar	1 cup seedless blackberry jam
4 egg yolks	1 teaspoon vanilla extract
1 cup buttermilk	
1 teaspoon baking soda	4 egg whites, stiffly beaten
3 cups all-purpose flour	

Beat the butter in a bowl until light and fluffy. Add the sugar gradually, beating well after each addition. Add the egg yolks and mix well. Combine the buttermilk and baking soda in a small bowl and mix well. Sift the flour and cinnamon together. Add to the butter mixture alternately with the buttermilk, beating well after each addition. Beat on medium speed for 2 minutes. Add the jam and vanilla and mix well. Fold in the egg whites with a rubber spatula. Pour into a greased and floured tube pan. Bake at 350 degrees for 15 minutes. Lower the heat to 325 degrees. Bake for 1 hour longer or until the cake tests done. Cool in the pan for 10 minutes. Invert onto a serving plate. Yield: 16 to 20 servings.

Rosemary Souleyrette, Xi Beta Iota
Nevada, Iowa

BLACKBERRY WINE CAKE

1 (2-layer) package white cake mix	1 cup blackberry wine
1 (3-ounce) package blackberry gelatin	½ cup chopped pecans
4 eggs	½ cup (1 stick) butter
½ cup vegetable oil	½ cup blackberry wine
	1 cup confectioners' sugar

Combine the cake mix, gelatin, eggs, oil and 1 cup wine in a mixing bowl. Beat at low speed for 30 seconds. Beat at medium speed for 2 minutes. Sprinkle the pecans in a greased and floured bundt pan. Pour the batter into the pan. Bake at 325 degrees for 45 to 50 minutes or until the cake tests done. Melt the butter in a saucepan over medium heat. Stir in ½ cup wine and confectioners' sugar. Bring to a boil, stirring

often. Pierce the cake with a fork. Drizzle with half the glaze. Cool in the pan. Invert onto a serving plate. Drizzle with the remaining glaze.
Yield: 10 to 12 servings.

Paula Lyens, Laureate Epsilon Theta
Treasure Island, Florida

BROWNIE CAKE

1 (4-ounce) box chocolate pudding mix	½ cup vegetable oil
2 cups milk	1 cup (6 ounces) chocolate chips
1 (2-layer) package yellow cake mix	½ cup chopped nuts

Combine the pudding mix and milk in a large saucepan over medium heat, stirring constantly. Bring to a boil. Remove from the heat. Stir in the cake mix and oil. Pour into a greased and floured 9×13-inch cake pan. Sprinkle with chocolate chips and nuts. Bake at 350 degrees for 30 minutes. Cool in the pan. Yield: 10 servings.

Roxanne Saathoff, Laureate Kappa
Beatrice, Nebraska

BUTTERSCOTCH CAKE

1 (4-ounce) package butterscotch pudding mix	1 (11-ounce) package butterscotch chips
2 cups milk	½ cup chopped pecans or walnuts
1 (2-layer) package yellow cake mix	

Combine the pudding mix and milk in a large saucepan over medium heat. Bring to a boil, stirring constantly. Remove from the heat. Stir in the cake mix. Pour into a greased and floured 9×13-inch cake pan. Sprinkle with butterscotch chips and pecans. Bake at 350 degrees for 35 to 40 minutes or until the cake tests done. Serve warm with whipped cream or ice cream if desired. Yield: 16 servings.

Juanita Schmidt, Gamma Mu
Benton City, Missouri

*Mary M. Fronczak, Alpha Omega Master, Oviedo, Florida, makes **Angel Lush Cake** by slicing an angel food cake into three layers horizontally. She mixes one 4-ounce package vanilla instant pudding mix and one 20-ounce can crushed pineapple in a bowl. She folds in 1 cup whipped topping and spreads the mixture between the layers and over the top and side of the cake. The cake should be chilled for 1 hour or longer before serving.*

CALAMONDIN CAKE

I have a calamondin tree in my backyard. The cake is not very sweet and has a nice tang.

1 (2-layer) package
    yellow cake mix
1 (3-ounce) package
    lemon or lime gelatin
1/3 cup milk
4 eggs
1/2 cup calamondin purée
1 tablespoon lemon
    extract or lemon juice
3/4 cup vegetable oil
Calamondin Glaze

Combine the cake mix, gelatin and milk in a bowl and mix well. Add the eggs 1 at a time, mixing well after each addition. Combine the calamondin purée, lemon extract and oil in a bowl and mix well. Add gradually to the batter, mixing well after each addition. Pour into a greased and floured tube pan. Bake at 350 degrees for 50 minutes to 1 hour or until the cake tests done. Cool in the pan for 20 minutes. Remove to a wire rack to cool completely. Drizzle Calamondin Glaze over the cooled cake.
Yield: 12 to 15 servings.

CALAMONDIN GLAZE

1/4 cup (1/2 stick) butter
    or margarine, melted
2 tablespoons
    calamondin purée
1/4 teaspoon lemon juice
2 cups confectioners'
    sugar

Combine the butter, calamondin purée, lemon juice and confectioners' sugar in a bowl and mix until smooth.

Lillian (Bunny) Van Natta, Xi Lambda Psi
Englewood, Florida

CARAMEL SURPRISE CAKE

1 (2-layer) package
    caramel or
    butterscotch cake mix
1 large jar caramel,
    butterscotch or fudge
    topping, warmed
12 ounces whipped
    topping
10 ounces English
    toffee bits

Prepare and bake the cake mix using the package directions for a 9×13-inch cake pan. Cool in the pan for 10 minutes. Pierce the cake with the handle of a wooden spoon. Pour the caramel topping over the cake. Cool completely. Cover with whipped topping. Sprinkle with toffee bits. Yield: 12 servings.

Sherri Brandt, Lambda Chi
Danville, Pennsylvania

BABY FOOD CARROT CAKE

4 eggs, beaten
1 1/4 cups vegetable oil
2 large jars baby food
    carrots
2 cups all-purpose flour
2 cups sugar
1 tablespoon plus
    1 teaspoon cinnamon
2 teaspoons baking soda
1 teaspoon salt
Vanilla Frosting
Chopped pecans

Combine the eggs, oil and carrots in a bowl and mix well. Combine the flour, sugar, cinnamon, baking soda and salt. Add to the carrot mixture and mix well. Pour into a greased and floured 10×15-inch cake pan. Bake at 350 degrees for 30 minutes. Cool in the pan for 10 minutes. Remove to a wire rack to cool completely. Spread the Vanilla Frosting on the cooled cake. Sprinkle with pecans. Store in the refrigerator. Yield: 16 servings.

VANILLA FROSTING

8 ounces cream cheese,
    softened
1/2 cup (1 stick) butter,
    softened
2 cups confectioners'
    sugar
2 teaspoons vanilla
    extract

Combine the cream cheese, butter, confectioners' sugar and vanilla in a bowl and beat until smooth.

Jane Sommers, Xi Theta Tau
Robinson, Kansas

CARROT CAKE

2 cups all-purpose flour
2 cups granulated sugar
2 teaspoons salt
2 teaspoons baking soda
2 teaspoons cinnamon
1 1/2 cups vegetable oil
4 eggs
3 cups grated peeled
    carrots
6 ounces cream cheese,
    softened
1 (1-pound) package
    confectioners' sugar
1/2 cup (1 stick) butter,
    melted
2 teaspoons vanilla
    extract
1 cup chopped nuts

Sift the flour, granulated sugar, salt, baking soda and cinnamon into a large bowl. Add the oil and mix well. Add the eggs 1 at a time, mixing well after each addition. Stir in the carrots. Pour into two greased and floured 10-inch cake pans. Bake at 350 degrees for 40 to 45 minutes or until the cake tests done. Cool for 10 minutes in the pans. Remove to a wire rack to cool completely. Beat the cream cheese and confectioners' sugar in a bowl until light and fluffy. Add the butter and vanilla and mix well. Stir in the nuts. Spread the frosting between the layers and over the top and side of the cooled cake. Yield: 15 servings.

Rita Hofsheier, Xi Gamma Alpha
Banks, Oregon

CARROT PINEAPPLE CAKE

2¹/₂ cups unbleached
  flour
1¹/₃ cups sugar
2 teaspoons baking soda
2 teaspoons cinnamon
2 (8-ounce) cans crushed
  pineapple
4 egg whites, lightly
  beaten

2 teaspoons vanilla
  extract
2 cups grated peeled
  carrots
¹/₂ cup golden raisins
¹/₃ cup chopped pecans
Cream Cheese Frosting

Combine the flour, sugar, baking soda and cinnamon. Combine the pineapple, egg whites and vanilla extract in a bowl and mix well. Add the dry ingredients and mix well. Stir in the carrots, raisins and pecans. Pour into a greased 9×13-inch cake pan. Bake at 325 degrees for 35 minutes or until a wooden pick inserted in the center comes out clean. Cool in the pan for 10 minutes. Remove to a wire rack to cool completely. Spread the Cream Cheese Frosting on the cooled cake. Yield: 12 servings.

CREAM CHEESE FROSTING

8 ounces fat-free or
  reduced-fat cream
  cheese, softened
1 cup fat-free ricotta
  cheese

¹/₂ cup confectioners'
  sugar
1 teaspoon vanilla
  extract

Combine the cream cheese, ricotta cheese, confectioners' sugar and vanilla extract in a food processor and process until smooth.

Bev Zaborski, Xi Theta Alpha
Stoney Creek, Ontario, Canada

CARROT, PINEAPPLE AND WALNUT BUNDT CAKE

2 cups sifted cake flour
2 cups sugar
2 teaspoons cinnamon
1¹/₂ teaspoons baking
  soda
1¹/₂ teaspoons salt
1 teaspoon baking
  powder
1 (8-ounce) can crushed
  pineapple

3 eggs, beaten
1¹/₂ cups vegetable oil
2 teaspoons vanilla
  extract
2 cups grated peeled
  carrots
1¹/₂ cups chopped black
  walnuts
Walnut Frosting

Combine the flour, sugar, cinnamon, baking soda, salt and baking powder in a large bowl. Drain the pineapple, reserving the liquid. Add the liquid to the dry ingredients and mix well. Add the eggs, oil and vanilla and mix well. Stir in the pineapple, carrots and walnuts. Pour into a greased and floured bundt pan. Bake at 325 degrees for 1¹/₂ hours. Cool in the pan for 10 minutes. Invert onto a serving plate. Spread the Walnut Frosting on the cooled cake. Yield: 12 servings.

WALNUT FROSTING

4¹/₂ cups confectioners'
  sugar
¹/₄ cup (¹/₂ stick) butter,
  softened
8 ounces cream cheese,
  softened

2 tablespoons milk
2 tablespoons vanilla
  extract
¹/₄ cup chopped black
  walnuts

Combine the confectioners' sugar, butter, cream cheese, milk and vanilla in a bowl and beat until smooth. Stir in the walnuts.

Marjorie M. Douglas, Xi Phi Theta
Schertz, Texas

ORANGE CARROT CAKE

1 (2-layer) package
  yellow cake mix
1 (3-ounce) package
  vanilla instant
  pudding mix
2 teaspoons cinnamon
4 eggs
²/₃ cup orange juice

¹/₂ cup vegetable oil
3 cups grated peeled
  carrots
¹/₂ cup sweetened dried
  cranberries
¹/₂ cup chopped pecans
Orange Frosting

Combine the cake mix, pudding mix and cinnamon in a large bowl. Combine the eggs, orange juice and oil in a medium bowl and mix well. Add to the dry ingredients and mix well. Stir in the carrots, cranberries and pecans. Batter will be thick. Pour into 2 greased and floured 9-inch cake pans. Bake at 350 degrees for 30 to 35 minutes or until the cake tests done. Cool in the pans for 10 minutes. Remove to a wire rack to cool completely. Spread the Orange Frosting between the layers and over the top and side of the cooled cake. Yield: 12 to 14 servings.

ORANGE FROSTING

8 ounces cream cheese,
  softened
¹/₂ cup (1 stick) butter,
  softened
3 cups confectioners'
  sugar

2 tablespoons orange
  juice
1 tablespoon grated
  orange zest

Beat the cream cheese and butter in a bowl until light and fluffy. Add the confectioners' sugar, orange juice and orange zest and mix well.

Karil E. Kirschner, Theta
Vincennes, Indiana

CHARDONNAY CAKE

I decorate this cake with edible flowers.

4 eggs	2¼ tablespoons baking
2 cups sugar	powder
1 tablespoon vanilla	2 cups sour cream
extract	1 cup confectioners'
1 cup Chardonnay	sugar
1 cup canola oil	3 cups flaked coconut
2½ cups all-purpose	
flour	

Line two 8-inch cake pans with parchment paper. Grease and flour the paper. Combine the eggs and sugar in a bowl and mix for 1 minute. Add the vanilla, Chardonnay, oil, flour and baking powder and mix until smooth. Pour into the prepared pans. Bake at 350 degrees for 35 minutes. Cool in the pans. Remove to a wire rack to cool completely. Combine the sour cream and confectioners' sugar in a bowl and mix well. Stir in the coconut. Spread the mixture between the layers and over the top and side of the cooled cake. Serve with fruit if desired.
Yield: 12 servings.

Barbara Summerfield, Gamma Alpha
Darby, Montana

VALENTINE CHERRY CAKE

2½ cups sifted cake	1 teaspoon vanilla
flour	extract
1½ cups sugar	2 teaspoons almond
3½ teaspoons baking	extract
powder	4 egg whites
1 teaspoon salt	18 maraschino cherries
½ cup shortening	½ cup chopped walnuts
¾ cup milk	Creamy Frosting
¼ cup maraschino	
cherry juice	

Sift the flour, sugar, baking powder and salt into a mixing bowl. Add the shortening and mix well. Combine the milk and cherry juice in a small bowl. Reserve ¼ cup. Pour the remainder into the flour mixture and mix well. Beat for 2 minutes at low speed. Add the reserved cherry juice mixture, vanilla, almond extract and egg whites and mix well. Stir in the cherries and walnuts. Divide the batter between 2 greased and floured 9-inch cake pans. Bake at 350 degrees for 20 to 25 minutes or until the cake tests done. Cool in the pans for 10 minutes. Remove to a wire rack to cool completely. Spread the Creamy Frosting between the layers and over the top and side cooled cake. Yield: 8 to 10 servings.

CREAMY FROSTING

2 tablespoons	4 cups sifted
shortening	confectioners' sugar
¼ cup (½ stick) butter,	9 tablespoons scalded
softened	cream
1 teaspoon vanilla	2 or 3 drops red food
extract	coloring
½ teaspoon salt	

Combine the shortening, butter, vanilla and salt in a bowl and mix well. Add half of the confectioners' sugar and mix well. Add the cream alternately with the remaining confectioners' sugar, mixing well after each addition. Stir in the food coloring.

Sonjie Bowles, Preceptor Kappa
Lilburn, Georgia

CHERRY UPSIDE-DOWN CAKE

½ cup (1 stick) butter,	2 cups all-purpose flour
softened	1 cup milk
1 cup sugar	2 (16-ounce) cans pitted
2 teaspoons baking	sour cherries
powder	1 cup sugar

Beat the butter and 1 cup sugar in a bowl until light and fluffy. Add the baking powder and flour and mix well. Gradually add the milk, mixing well after each addition. Batter will be lumpy. Pour into a greased and floured 9×13-inch cake pan. Spoon the cherries evenly over the top. Sprinkle with 1 cup sugar. Bake at 375 degrees for 45 minutes. Cool in the pan on a wire rack. Yield: 12 servings.

Jean Michel, Preceptor Beta Omega
Parker, Colorado

BLACK FOREST CHOCOLATE CAKE

1 (2-layer) package	1¼ cups water
devil's food cake mix	4 eggs
1 (4-ounce) package	1 (21-ounce) can cherry
chocolate instant	pie filling
pudding mix	Whipped topping
½ cup vegetable oil	Chopped almonds

Combine the cake mix, pudding mix, oil, water and eggs in a bowl and mix well. Pour into a greased and floured bundt pan. Bake at 350 degrees for 55 minutes. Cool in the pan for 25 minutes. Invert onto a serving plate. Serve with a large spoonful of pie filling. Top with whipped topping and sprinkle with almonds. Yield: 12 servings.

Colleen Burrichter, Laureate Sigma
Ottawa, Kansas

CHERRY CHOCOLATE CAKE

1 (2-layer) package fudge cake mix	1 cup sugar
1 teaspoon almond extract	1/4 cup (1/2 stick) margarine
2 eggs	1/3 cup milk
1 (21-ounce) can cherry pie filling	1 cup (6 ounces) chocolate chips

Combine the cake mix, almond extract and eggs in a bowl and mix well. Stir in the pie filling. Pour into a greased and floured 9×13-inch cake pan. Bake at 350 degrees for 30 to 35 minutes or until the cake tests done. Cool in the pan for 10 minutes. Remove to a wire rack to cool completely. Combine the sugar, margarine and milk in a saucepan. Bring to a boil over medium heat, stirring often. Boil for 1 minute, stirring constantly. Stir in the chocolate chips until smooth. Pour over the warm cake. Yield: 12 servings.

Betty Montgomery, Rho Sigma Phi
Joplin, Missouri

CHOCOLATE CAKE

1 (2-layer) package chocolate cake mix with pudding	3 eggs
1 cup water	1 container chocolate frosting
1 cup mayonnaise	1/2 cup peanut butter

Combine the cake mix, water, mayonnaise and eggs in a bowl. Mix at low speed for 30 seconds. Mix at medium speed for 2 minutes. Bake using the package directions. Cool in the pan for 10 minutes. Remove to a wire rack to cool completely. Combine the chocolate frosting and peanut butter in a bowl and mix well. Frost the cooled cake. Yield: 12 servings.

Madeleine Dobranski, Preceptor Gamma
Dollard Des Ormeaux, Quebec, Canada

CHOCOLATE CHIFFON CAKE

3/4 cup cake flour	1/4 teaspoon salt
1/4 cup baking cocoa	1 1/2 teaspoons vanilla extract
12 egg whites	
1 1/2 teaspoons cream of tartar	3/4 cup sugar
	Chocolate Frosting

Sift the flour and baking cocoa together 3 times. Beat the egg whites at low speed in a mixing bowl until foamy. Add the cream of tartar, salt and vanilla. Beat at medium speed until soft peaks form. Add the sugar 2 tablespoons at a time, beating constantly at high speed until stiff peaks form. Fold in the flour mixture. Spoon into an ungreased tube pan. Cut through the batter 1 inch from the center of the pan with a knife. Bake at 350 degrees for 30 to 35 minutes or until the cake tests done. Cool in the pan for 10 minutes. Invert onto a serving plate. Spread the Chocolate Frosting on the cooled cake. Yield: 12 servings.

CHOCOLATE FROSTING

2 cups heavy whipping cream	1/4 cup baking cocoa
	1/3 cup sugar

Whip the cream in a large bowl until soft peaks form. Add the baking cocoa and sugar and whip until stiff peaks form.

Mary La Mantia, Mu Eta
Brechin, Ontario, Canada

CHOCOLATE CHIP CAKE

8 ounces cream cheese, softened	1 (4-ounce) package chocolate instant pudding mix
1 cup sour cream	
1/2 cup coffee liqueur or water	1 cup (6 ounces) semisweet chocolate chips
2 eggs	
1 (2-layer) package chocolate cake mix	Confectioners' sugar

Combine the cream cheese, sour cream, liqueur and eggs in a bowl and mix well. Add the cake mix and pudding mix and mix well. Stir in the chocolate chips. Batter will be stiff. Pour into a greased and floured tube pan. Bake at 325 degrees for 60 to 65 minutes or until a wooden pick inserted in the center comes out clean. Cool in the pan for 5 minutes. Remove to a wire rack and cool completely. Dust with confectioners' sugar. Garnish with fruit if desired. Yield: 10 to 12 servings.

Marlene Graves, Xi Delta Omicron
Muscatine, Iowa

CHOCOLATE COCONUT CAKE

Baking cocoa for dusting	1 (21-ounce) can coconut pie filling
1 (2-layer) package chocolate cake mix	2 eggs, beaten
2 tablespoons vegetable oil	

Grease a bundt pan and dust with baking cocoa. Combine the cake mix, oil, pie filling and eggs in a large bowl and mix well. Pour into the prepared pan. Bake at 350 degrees for 50 minutes. Cool in the pan for 10 minutes. Invert onto a serving plate. Glaze or frost if desired. Yield: 10 to 12 servings.

Roberta Sweeney, Preceptor Eta
Taylorsville, Utah

CHOCOLATE CUPCAKES

1 (2-layer) package chocolate cake mix	Dash of salt
8 ounces cream cheese, softened	1 egg
1/3 cup sugar	1 cup (6 ounces) semisweet or milk chocolate chips

Prepare the cake mix using the package directions. Pour into 30 paper-lined muffin cups. Combine the cream cheese, sugar, salt and egg in a bowl and mix well. Stir in the chocolate chips. Drop by teaspoonfuls into each muffin cup. Bake at 350 degrees for 15 to 25 minutes or until cupcakes test done. Frost if desired. Yield: 30 servings.

Sue Jedlicka, Xi Master
Beatrice, Nebraska

CHOCOLATE RUM CAKE

1 (2-layer) package yellow cake mix	1/2 cup vegetable oil
1 (4-ounce) package chocolate instant pudding mix	1 teaspoon vanilla extract
	1/2 cup dark rum
4 eggs	2 cups chopped nuts
1 cup sour cream	1 cup (6 ounces) chocolate chips

Combine the cake mix, pudding mix, eggs, sour cream, oil, vanilla and rum in a mixing bowl. Beat at medium speed for 2 minutes. Stir in the nuts and chocolate chips. Pour into a greased and floured bundt pan. Bake at 325 degrees for 1 hour or until a wooden pick inserted in the center comes out clean. Cool in the pan for 10 minutes. Invert onto a serving plate. Yield: 12 to 14 servings.

Bess Drake, Xi Mu
Mooringsport, Lousiana

CHOCOLATE SHEET CAKE

1 cup (2 sticks) butter	2 cups sugar
1/4 cup baking cocoa	1 teaspoon baking soda
1 cup water	2 eggs, beaten
2 cups all-purpose flour	1 cup sour cream
1/2 teaspoon salt	Vanilla Nut Frosting

Combine the butter, baking cocoa and water in a large saucepan. Bring to a boil over medium heat, stirring often. Remove from the heat. Combine the next 4 ingredients. Combine the eggs and sour cream in a small bowl. Add the flour mixture and egg mixture alternately to the cooled chocolate mixture, mixing well after each addition. Pour into a greased 10×15-inch baking pan. Bake at 375 degrees for 20 minutes. Cool in the pan for 10 minutes. Remove to a wire rack to cool completely. Spread the Vanilla Nut Frosting on the cooled cake. Yield: 12 servings.

VANILLA NUT FROSTING

1/2 cup (1 stick) butter	1 (1-pound) package confectioners' sugar
6 tablespoons milk	1 teaspoon vanilla
1 cup chopped nuts	
1/4 cup baking cocoa	

Combine the butter, milk and nuts in a saucepan. Bring to a boil over medium heat, stirring constantly. Remove from the heat. Add the baking cocoa, confectioners' sugar and vanilla and mix well.

Helen Lambert, Omicron Eta
Chico, California

CHOCOLATE SYRUP CAKE

1/2 cup (1 stick) butter, softened	1 (16-ounce) can chocolate syrup
1 cup sugar	Chocolate Frosting
4 eggs	1/2 cup chopped pecans (optional)
1 cup self-rising flour	

Beat the butter and sugar in a bowl until light and fluffy. Add the eggs 1 at a time, mixing well after each addition. Add the flour and chocolate syrup and mix well. Pour into a greased and floured 9×13-inch cake pan. Bake at 350 degrees for 30 minutes. Cool in the pan for 10 minutes. Remove to a wire rack to cool completely. Spread the Chocolate Frosting on the cooled cake. Sprinkle with pecans. Yield: 12 servings.

CHOCOLATE FROSTING

1 1/3 cups sugar	1/2 cup (3 ounces) semisweet chocolate chips
6 tablespoons butter	
6 tablespoons evaporated milk	

Combine the sugar, butter and evaporated milk in a saucepan. Bring to a boil over medium heat, stirring often. Boil for 1 minute. Remove from the heat and stir in the chocolate chips until smooth.

Patricia A. Lindon, Delta Beta
Hazard, Kentucky

DOUBLE CHOCOLATE BUNDT CAKE

1 (2-layer) package chocolate cake mix	3/4 cup vegetable oil
1 container chocolate fudge frosting	4 eggs
	1 cup water

Mix the cake mix, frosting, oil, eggs and water in a bowl. Pour into a greased and floured bundt pan. Bake at 350 degrees for 45 to 50 minutes or until the cake tests done. Cool in the pan for 15 minutes. Invert onto a serving plate. Yield: 12 servings.

Ruth Baker, Alpha Xi
Hazard, Kentucky

DOUBLE CHOCOLATE CAKE

1 (2-layer) package chocolate cake mix	8 ounces whipped topping
1 jar caramel topping, warmed	Chopped walnuts
2 cups (12 ounces) chocolate chips, melted	

Prepare and bake the cake mix using the package directions for an 11×13-inch cake pan. Cool in the pan. Pierce the cake with a fork. Pour the caramel topping over the cake. Pour the chocolate over the cake. Cover with whipped topping and sprinkle with walnuts. Chill, covered, until just before serving. Yield: 16 to 20 servings.

Linda L. Plake, Laureate Beta Tau
Elwood, Indiana

"FLOURLESS" CHOCOLATE CAKE

My daughter was insulin-dependent during her second pregnancy. She said this cake was delicious, and we have made it ever since. The small amount of flour also makes it good for those who must restrict gluten.

6 tablespoons margarine, softened	1½ cups Splenda
4 ounces unsweetened chocolate	3 egg whites
⅓ cup skim milk	⅛ teaspoon cream of tartar
⅓ cup raspberry jam	¼ cup all-purpose flour
1 egg yolk	⅛ teaspoon salt
1 teaspoon vanilla extract	Chocolate Frosting

Combine the margarine, chocolate, milk and jam in a saucepan. Cook over medium heat until smooth, stirring often. Whisk in the egg yolk and vanilla. Whisk in the Splenda. Remove from the heat. Beat the egg whites at low speed in a mixing bowl until foamy. Add the cream of tartar. Beat at high speed until stiff peaks form. Fold in the chocolate mixture. Fold in the flour and salt. Pour into a greased and floured 9-inch cake pan. Bake at 350 degrees for 18 to 20 minutes or until cake springs back when lightly touched. Cool completely on a wire rack. Loosen from the side of the pan with a sharp knife and invert onto a serving plate. Spread the Chocolate Frosting over the top and side of the cake. Yield: 12 servings.

CHOCOLATE FROSTING

2 ounces unsweetened chocolate, chopped	¼ cup skim milk
	½ cup Splenda

Combine the chocolate and milk in a saucepan. Cook over medium heat until almost smooth, whisking often. Remove from the heat and whisk until smooth. Whisk in the Splenda. Cool completely.

Elizabeth K. Dennis, Laureate Beta Rho
Pitt Meadows, British Columbia, Canada

FLOURLESS CHOCOLATE ALMOND CAKE

2 cups slivered almonds, ground	1 teaspoon almond extract
1 cup packed brown sugar	½ teaspoon salt
½ cup canola oil	4 egg yolks
⅓ cup baking cocoa	4 egg whites

Grease a springform pan and line the bottom with waxed paper or parchment paper. Combine all the ingredients except the egg whites in a large bowl and mix well. Beat the egg whites in a mixing bowl at high speed until stiff peaks form. Fold in the almond mixture in 4 batches. Spoon into the prepared pan. Bake at 350 degrees for 40 to 50 minutes or until the cake tests done. Cool for 15 minutes on a wire rack. Loosen from the side of the pan with a sharp knife and remove the side. Invert onto a serving plate. Serve with whipped topping if desired. Yield: 10 to 12 servings.

Lila Duff, Alpha Mu
Preeceville, Saskatchewan, Canada

CARAMEL FUDGE CAKE

1 (2-layer) package chocolate cake mix	14 ounces caramel candies
1 (14-ounce) can sweetened condensed milk	½ cup (1 stick) margarine
	1 cup chopped pecans

Prepare the cake mix using the package directions. Pour 2 cups of the batter into a greased and floured 9×13-inch cake pan. Bake at 350 degrees for 15 minutes. Combine the next 3 ingredients in a saucepan. Cook over low heat until smooth, stirring constantly. Spread over the baked layer. Top with the remaining batter and sprinkle with pecans. Bake for 30 to 35 minutes or until cake springs back when lightly touched. Cool in the pan on a wire rack. Yield: 12 servings.

Betty Pruett, Phi Master
Morgantown, West Virginia

DECADENT FUDGE CAKE

1 cup (2 sticks) butter or margarine, softened
1½ cups sugar
4 eggs
½ teaspoon baking soda
1 cup buttermilk
2½ cups all-purpose flour
1 cup (6 ounces) miniature semisweet chocolate chips
8 ounces German's sweet chocolate, melted
⅓ cup chocolate syrup
2 teaspoons vanilla extract
4 ounces white chocolate, chopped
2 tablespoons shortening
½ cup (3 ounces) miniature semisweet chocolate chips
2 teaspoons shortening

Beat the butter in a mixing bowl. Gradually add the sugar, beating well after each addition. Add the eggs 1 at a time, mixing well after each addition. Dissolve the baking soda in the buttermilk in a small bowl. Add the flour to the butter mixture alternately with the buttermilk, ending with the flour. Stir in the 1 cup chocolate chips, the sweet chocolate, chocolate syrup and vanilla. Spoon into a greased and floured bundt pan. Bake at 300 degrees for 85 to 95 minutes or until the cake springs bake when lightly touched. Cool in the pan for 10 minutes. Invert onto a serving plate. Combine the white chocolate and 2 tablespoons shortening in a double boiler and stir until smooth. Drizzle over the cooled cake. Melt ½ cup chocolate chips and 2 teaspoons shortening in a small saucepan over low heat, stirring until smooth. Cool. Drizzle over the cake. Yield: 12 servings.

Susan Farmer, Laureate Epsilon
Montgomery, Alabama

GERMAN CHOCOLATE SHEET CAKE

This is lower in fat than traditional recipes.

1 (2-layer) package German chocolate cake mix
1 egg
2 egg whites
1¾ cups water
⅓ cup chopped pecans
1 (14-ounce) can fat-free sweetened condensed milk
⅓ cup sweetened flaked coconut
Frosting

Combine the cake mix, egg, egg whites and water in a large bowl and mix well. Pour into a greased and floured 10×15-inch baking pan. Bake at 350 degrees for 15 minutes. Mix the pecans, condensed milk and coconut in a bowl. Spread over the warm cake. Broil on the lowest rack in the oven until golden, about 2 minutes. Remove to a wire rack to cool. Spread the Frosting on the cooled cake. Yield: 48 servings.

FROSTING

¼ cup (½ stick) margarine, softened
1 (1-pound) package confectioners' sugar
⅓ cup baking cocoa
1 teaspoon vanilla extract
3 to 4 tablespoons skim milk

Mix the margarine, confectioners' sugar, baking cocoa, vanilla and milk in a bowl until smooth.

Kay Chadick, Preceptor Alpha Epsilon
Edmond, Oklahoma

GERMAN CHOCOLATE UPSIDE-DOWN CAKE

1 cup chopped nuts
2 cups shredded coconut
1 (2-layer) package German chocolate cake mix
8 ounces cream cheese, softened
½ cup (1 stick) margarine, softened
1 (1-pound) package confectioners' sugar

Sprinkle the nuts in a greased and floured 9×13-inch cake pan. Sprinkle with the coconut. Prepare the cake mix using the package directions. Pour into the prepared pan. Combine the cream cheese, margarine and confectioners' sugar in a bowl and mix well. Drop by tablespoonfuls over the batter. Bake at 350 degrees for 45 minutes to 1 hour or until the cake tests done. Cool in the pan for 10 minutes. Remove to a wire rack to cool completely. Yield: 12 to 15 servings.

Doris White, Preceptor Epsilon Iota
Memphis, Missouri

LOW-FAT CHOCOLATE CHIP CAKE

1 (2-layer) package low-fat devil's food cake mix
1 small package chocolate fat-free pudding mix
1 cup fat-free sour cream
1 cup egg whites
½ cup water
2 tablespoons vegetable oil
1 cup (6 ounces) semisweet chocolate chips
Confectioners' sugar

Combine the cake mix, pudding mix, sour cream, egg whites, water and oil in a large bowl. Beat at medium speed for 2 minutes. Stir in the chocolate chips. Pour into a greased and floured bundt pan. Bake at 350 degrees for 40 to 50 minutes. Cool in the pan for 10 minutes. Remove to a wire rack and cool completely. Dust with confectioners' sugar. Yield: 12 servings.

Janelle Edwards, Delta Sigma
Oshawa, Ontario, Canada

❖ MEXICAN CHOCOLATE CAKE

Every time we bake this cake we think of wonderful sunny trips to the beaches of Mexico. The surprising thing is that the recipe came from friends in Minnesota!

2 teaspoons all-purpose
  flour
1 cup all-purpose flour
1/3 cup baking cocoa
1 teaspoon cinnamon
3/4 teaspoon baking
  powder
1/2 teaspoon baking soda
1/4 teaspoon salt
1/4 cup (1/2 stick) unsalted
  butter, softened
1 cup packed light
  brown sugar

3 egg whites
1 cup fat-free plain
  yogurt
1 teaspoon vanilla
  extract
1 egg
1 tablespoon skim milk
1 ounce Mexican
  chocolate, chopped
2 tablespoons
  confectioners' sugar

Grease an 8-inch cake pan and line the bottom with waxed paper. Sprinkle with 2 teaspoons flour. Sift 1 cup flour, the baking cocoa, cinnamon, baking powder, baking soda and salt together. Beat the butter and brown sugar in a bowl until light and fluffy. Beat in the egg whites 1 at a time. Add the yogurt, vanilla and egg and mix well. Add the flour mixture gradually, mixing well after each addition. Pour into the prepared pan. Bake at 350 degrees for 35 minutes or until a wooden pick inserted in the middle comes out clean. Cool in the pan for 10 minutes. Invert onto a serving plate. Peel off the waxed paper. Combine the milk and chocolate in a microwave-safe bowl. Microwave on High for 30 seconds or until the chocolate melts. Stir until smooth. Cool slightly. Drizzle over the cake. Cool completely and dust with confectioners' sugar. Serve with raspberries if desired. Yield: 8 servings.

Ann Walters, Xi Alpha Omicron
Roy, Utah

MOIST CHOCOLATE CAKE

2 cups all-purpose flour
1 1/2 cups sugar
3 tablespoons baking
  cocoa
2 teaspoons baking soda

1 teaspoon vanilla
  extract
1 cup water
1 cup mayonnaise

Combine all the ingredients in a large bowl and mix well. Pour into a greased and floured 9×13-inch cake pan. Bake at 350 degrees for 30 minutes. Cool in the pan for 10 minutes. Remove to a wire rack to cool completely. Yield: 12 servings.

Linda Conwell, Preceptor Alpha Epsilon
Edmond, Oklahoma

MOLTEN CHOCOLATE CAKES

1 cup (2 sticks)
  margarine, softened
1 1/3 cups (8 ounces)
  semisweet
  chocolate chips
5 eggs

1/2 cup sugar
Pinch of salt
4 teaspoons all-purpose
  flour
Whipped topping

Place paper liners in 12 muffin cups and spray with nonstick cooking spray. Melt the margarine and chocolate chips in a microwave-safe bowl in the microwave. Stir until smooth. Combine the eggs, sugar and salt in a bowl and mix well. Add the flour and mix well. Add the chocolate mixture and mix well. Pour into the prepared muffin cups. Bake at 450 degrees for 10 minutes or until the cakes puff but have not set. Cool for 1 minute or longer. Transfer to individual serving plates and remove the paper liners. Serve with whipped topping. Yield: 12 servings.

Linda Shaver, Kappa Kappa
Meriden, Kansas

WACKY CHOCOLATE CAKE

This cake will fall, so be careful not to slam doors while it's baking.

3 cups all-purpose
  flour
2 cups sugar
6 tablespoons baking
  cocoa
2 teaspoons baking soda
1 teaspoon salt

2 tablespoons white
  vinegar
3/4 cup (1 1/2 sticks)
  butter, melted
2 teaspoons vanilla
  extract
2 cups cold water

Combine the flour, sugar, baking cocoa, baking soda and salt in an ungreased 9×13-inch cake pan. Make 3 wells in the dry mixture. Pour the vinegar, butter and vanilla into separate wells. Cover with the cold water. Mix until smooth. Bake at 350 degrees for 40 to 50 minutes or until a wooden pick inserted in the center comes out clean. Cool completely in the pan. Yield: 12 servings.

Gini Liveley, Rho Sigma
Gardner, Kansas

*Marcella Younker, Preceptor Mu, Knoxville, Iowa, makes **Chocolate Cupcakes** by combining 1 package devil's food cake mix, 1 cup water, and one 15-ounce can pumpkin in a bowl and mixing well. She stirs in 1/2 cup chocolate chips and spoons the batter into 24 paper-lined muffin cups. The cupcakes are baked at 350 degrees for 18 to 22 minutes or until they test done.*

WESTERN CHOCOLATE CAKE

2 cups sugar	2 eggs
2 cups all-purpose flour	1/2 cup buttermilk
1/2 teaspoon salt	1 teaspoon baking soda
1 cup water	2 teaspoons vanilla
1 cup (2 sticks) butter	Chocolate Frosting
1/3 cup baking cocoa	

Combine the sugar, flour and salt in a large mixing bowl. Bring the water, butter and baking cocoa to a boil in a saucepan over medium heat, stirring often. Add to the sugar mixture gradually, beating constantly on medium speed. Add the eggs and mix well. Combine the buttermilk, baking soda and vanilla in a small bowl and add to the batter. Mix until smooth. Pour into 2 greased and floured 9-inch cake pans. Bake at 350 degrees for 25 minutes. Cool in the pans for 10 minutes. Remove to a wire rack to cool completely. Spread the Chocolate Frosting between the layers and over the top and side of the cooled cake. Yield: 12 servings.

CHOCOLATE FROSTING

1 cup (6 ounces) semisweet chocolate chips	1 teaspoon vanilla extract
1/4 cup (1/2 stick) butter	1/4 teaspoon salt
3 cups confectioners' sugar	1/3 cup evaporated milk (may use milk)

Melt the chocolate chips and butter in a saucepan over low heat, stirring until smooth. Add the confectioners' sugar, vanilla and salt and mix well. Add the evaporated milk 1 tablespoon at a time until of spreading consistency, mixing well after each addition.

Dorrita Hottel, Delta Sigma
Burleson, Texas

COCA-COLA CAKE

This cake is best if you make it a few days before you plan to eat it.

2 cups all-purpose flour	1/2 cup buttermilk
2 cups sugar	2 teaspoons vanilla extract
1/2 cup (1 stick) margarine	1 teaspoon baking soda
1/2 cup shortening	2 eggs, beaten
5 tablespoons baking cocoa	1 1/2 cups miniature marshmallows
1 cup Coca-Cola	Chocolate Frosting
1/4 teaspoon salt	

Sift the flour and sugar together. Combine the margarine, shortening, baking cocoa, Coca-Cola and salt in a large saucepan. Bring to a boil over medium heat, stirring often. Cool completely. Add the buttermilk, vanilla, baking soda and eggs and mix well. Stir in the marshmallows. Pour into a greased and floured 9×13-inch cake pan. Bake at 300 degrees for 35 to 40 minutes or until the cake tests done. Pierce the warm cake with a fork. Spread the Chocolate Frosting on the cake. Cool in the pan. Yield: 15 servings.

CHOCOLATE FROSTING

1/2 cup (1 stick) margarine	6 tablespoons Coca-Cola
2 tablespoons baking cocoa	1 (1-pound) package confectioners' sugar

Combine the margarine, baking cocoa and Coca-Cola in a saucepan. Bring a boil over medium heat, stirring often. Remove from the heat. Add the confectioners' sugar and mix well.

Betty C. Landrum, Delta Omicron
Kennett, Missouri

COCOA CHIFFON CAKE

3/4 cup boiling water	7 egg yolks
1/2 cup baking cocoa	1/2 teaspoon vanilla extract
1 3/4 cups sifted all-purpose flour	1/4 teaspoon red food coloring
1 3/4 cups sugar	1 cup egg whites
3 teaspoons baking powder	1/2 teaspoon cream of tartar
1 teaspoon salt	
1/2 cup vegetable oil	

Combine the water and baking cocoa in a bowl and mix until smooth. Cool completely. Sift the flour, sugar, baking powder and salt together into a large bowl. Make a well and add the oil, egg yolks, cocoa mixture, vanilla and food coloring. Beat with a wooden spoon until smooth. Beat the egg whites at low speed in a mixing bowl until foamy. Add the cream of tartar. Beat at high speed until stiff peaks form. Fold in the batter gently with a rubber spatula. Bake at 325 degrees for 55 minutes. Increase the heat to 350 degrees. Bake for 10 to 15 minutes longer or until the cake tests done. Yield: 12 servings.

Deborah Tyler, Laureate Iota Omega
Lake Isabella, California

---

*Linda Thiele, Preceptor Epsilon Phi, Delaware, Ohio, submitted her recipe for **Pudding Frosting**, which can be made with any flavor of pudding. She beats 1 envelope instant whipped topping mix with 1 package instant pudding mix and 1 1/2 cups milk in a chilled mixing bowl until stiff peaks form. She then spreads the frosting on a cooled cake and stores it in the refrigerator.*

COCONUT CAKE

1 (2-layer) package
   yellow cake mix
2 (14-ounce) packages
   shredded coconut
1 cup sour cream

1 cup sugar
1 teaspoon almond
   extract
2 cups whipped topping

Prepare and bake the cake mix using the package directions for three 8-inch cake pans. Cool in the pans for 10 minutes. Remove to a wire rack to cool completely. Combine 21 ounces of the coconut, the sour cream, sugar and almond extract in a bowl and mix well. Spread between the layers of the cake. Combine the remaining 7 ounces coconut and the whipped topping in a bowl and mix well. Spread over the top and side of the cake. Yield: 12 servings.

Linda N. Smiley, Xi Beta Gamma
North Augusta, South Carolina

COCONUT PECAN CAKE

1 cup (2 sticks) butter,
   softened
2 cups sugar
2 cups all-purpose flour
1 teaspoon baking soda
5 egg yolks
1 cup buttermilk
1 teaspoon vanilla
   extract

1 cup chopped pecans
2 cups shredded coconut
5 egg whites,
   stiffly beaten
Frosting
Additional shredded
   coconut
Additional chopped
   pecans

Beat the butter and sugar in a bowl until light and fluffy. Sift the flour and baking soda into the bowl and mix well. Combine the egg yolks and buttermilk in a small bowl and mix well. Stir into the batter. Stir in the pecans and coconut. Fold in the egg whites. Pour into 3 greased and floured 9-inch cake pans. Bake at 325 degrees for 30 minutes. Cool in the pans for 10 minutes. Remove to a wire rack to cool completely. Spread the Frosting between the layers and over the top and side of the cooled cake. Sprinkle with coconut and pecans. Yield: 16 servings.

FROSTING

8 ounces cream cheese,
   softened
2 teaspoons vanilla
   extract

1¹/2 cups (3 sticks)
   butter, softened
1 (1-pound) package
   confectioners' sugar

Combine the cream cheese, vanilla, butter and confectioners' sugar and mix until smooth.

Doris Toole, Preceptor Gamma
Omaha, Nebraska

CREAMY COCONUT CAKE

1 (2-layer) package
   yellow cake mix
1¹/2 cups milk
¹/2 cup sugar

2 cups shredded coconut
8 ounces whipped
   topping

Prepare and bake the cake mix using the package directions for a 9×13-inch cake pan. Remove to a wire rack. Pierce the warm cake with a fork. Combine the milk, sugar and ¹/3 cup of the coconut in a saucepan. Bring to a boil over low heat, stirring occasionally. Boil for 1 minute, stirring constantly. Pour over the warm cake. Cool completely. Fold ¹/2 cup of the coconut into the whipped topping. Spread over the cake. Sprinkle with the remaining coconut. Chill, covered, overnight. Store in the refrigerator. Yield: 12 servings.

Orlene Biggert, Psi Master
Loveland, Colorado

CRÈME DE MENTHE CAKE

1 (2-layer) package
   white cake mix
2 tablespoons crème
   de menthe
1 (16-ounce) can
   chocolate syrup

12 ounces whipped
   topping
1 tablespoon crème
   de menthe

Prepare the cake mix using the package directions. Stir in 2 tablespoons crème de menthe. Bake using the package directions for a 9×13-inch cake pan. Cool in the pan for 10 minutes. Remove to a wire rack to cool completely. Spread the chocolate syrup over the cooled cake. Combine the whipped topping and 1 tablespoon crème de menthe in a bowl and mix well. Spread over the cake. Store in the refrigerator. Yield: 12 servings.

Sharon Peine, Pi Iota
Shawnee, Kansas

CRUMB CAKE

2 cups packed brown
   sugar
2 cups all-purpose flour
¹/2 cup (1 stick) butter

1 egg
1 cup sour milk
1 teaspoon baking soda

Combine the brown sugar and flour in a bowl. Cut in the butter until crumbly. Reserve 1 cup of the butter mixture. Add the egg, sour milk and baking soda to the remaining butter mixture and mix well. Pour into a greased and floured 9×13-inch cake pan. Sprinkle with the reserved butter mixture. Bake at 350 degrees for 25 to 30 minutes or until the cake tests done. Cool in the pan on a wire rack. Yield: 15 servings.

Sandra Childs, Laureate Lambda
Wichita, Kansas

FRAGRANT FRUITCAKE

1½ cups sifted
   all-purpose flour
1½ cups sugar
1 teaspoon baking
   powder
1 teaspoon salt
2 (7-ounce) packages
   pitted dates, sliced

8 ounces candied
   pineapple
2 (16-ounce) jars
   maraschino cherries,
   drained
5½ cups pecan halves
6 eggs
⅓ cup orange juice
¼ cup light corn syrup

Grease two 5×9-inch loaf pans with shortening. Line the pans with aluminum foil, leaving a 2-inch overhang on each side. Grease with shortening. Sift the flour, sugar, baking powder and salt into a mixing bowl. Add the dates, pineapple, cherries and pecans and toss to coat. Mix the eggs and orange juice in a bowl. Add to the fruit mixture and mix well. Pour into the prepared loaf pans. Bake at 300 degrees for 1¾ hours or until the loaves test done. Cool in the pans for 15 minutes. Invert onto serving plates and remove the foil. Brush the warm loaves with corn syrup. Yield: 48 servings.

Janet Harden, Delta Master
Frostburg, Maryland

LEMON FRUITCAKE

2 cups (4 sticks) butter,
   softened
2⅓ cups sugar
6 eggs
3 ounces lemon extract
4 cups sifted all-purpose
   flour

½ teaspoon salt
1½ teaspoons baking
   powder
8 ounces each candied
   cherries and candied
   pineapple
1 pound chopped pecans

Beat the butter and sugar in a bowl until light and fluffy. Add the eggs and mix well. Add the lemon extract and mix well. Sift the flour, salt and baking powder into the bowl and mix well. Stir in the candied fruit and pecans. Spoon into 8 greased small loaf pans. Bake at 300 degrees for 1½ to 2 hours or until the cake tests done. Freezes well. Yield: 72 servings.

Fluff Stephens, Laureate Iota Psi
Banning, California

---

*Shelley Wimberly, Omega Chi, LaBelle, Florida, makes an easy **Chess Cake** by pouring ½ cup melted butter in a 9×13-inch baking pan. She combines 1 package yellow cake mix and 1 egg in a bowl and mixes until crumbly. She adds 8 ounces softened cream cheese, one 1-pound package confectioners' sugar, and 2 eggs, beating constantly at low speed until smooth. She pours the batter in the prepared pan and bakes the cake at 350 degrees for 35 minutes.*

MEXICAN FRUITCAKE

2 cups granulated sugar
2 eggs
2 cups all-purpose flour
2 teaspoons baking
   soda
1 (20-ounce) can crushed
   pineapple
1 cup chopped nuts

8 ounces cream cheese,
   softened
½ cup (1 stick) butter,
   melted
2 cups confectioners'
   sugar
1 teaspoon vanilla
   extract

Combine the granulated sugar, eggs, flour, baking soda and pineapple in a bowl and mix well. Stir in the nuts. Pour into a greased and floured 9×13-inch cake pan. Bake at 350 degrees for 45 minutes. Cool in the pan for 10 minutes. Combine the cream cheese, butter, confectioners' sugar and vanilla in a mixing bowl and mix until smooth. Spread over the warm fruitcake. Yield: 12 servings.

Nancy Tillette, Laureate Alpha
Lansing, West Virginia

MINIATURE FRUITCAKES

¾ cup sugar
¼ cup all-purpose flour
½ teaspoon baking
   powder
⅛ teaspoon salt
1½ cups chopped
   walnuts
1 cup chopped dates

¾ cup chopped mixed
   candied fruit
2 egg yolks, beaten
½ teaspoon vanilla
   extract
2 egg whites, stiffly
   beaten
Candied cherries, halved

Combine the sugar, flour, baking powder, salt, walnuts, dates and candied fruit in a large bowl and mix well. Add the egg yolks and vanilla and mix well. Fold in the egg whites. Spoon into 12 greased and floured muffin cups. Cover with aluminum foil. Bake at 275 degrees for 1 hour. Remove the foil. Top the fruitcakes with candied cherries. Bake for 5 minutes longer or until a wooden pick inserted in the center comes out clean. Cool in the pan for 5 minutes. Remove to a wire rack to cool completely.
Yield: 1 dozen fruitcakes.

Mary Honsberger, Laureate Zeta
Nome, Alaska

FRUIT MARBLE CAKE

Use different flavors of cake mix and pie filling to customize the recipe.

¼ cup vegetable oil
2 eggs
½ cup water
1 (2-layer) package
   white cake mix

1 (21-ounce) can cherry
   pie filling
Confectioners' sugar

Pour the oil into a 9×13-inch cake pan, coating the bottom of the pan. Add the eggs, water and cake mix. Mix with a fork until smooth. Drop the pie filling by spoonfuls over the batter. Swirl with a knife to marbleize. Bake at 350 degrees for 40 to 45 minutes or until a wooden pick inserted in the center comes out clean. Cool in the pan for 10 minutes. Remove to a wire rack to cool completely. Dust with confectioners' sugar. Yield: 16 servings.

Aislinn Smith, Lambda Lambda
Wixom, Michigan

WHITE FRUITCAKE

1 (20-ounce) can crushed pineapple
1¹/2 cups raisins
4 ounces chopped mixed peel (orange, lemon and lime)
1 cup red maraschino cherries, quartered
1 cup green maraschino cherries, quartered
1 cup shredded coconut
2³/4 cups all-purpose flour
2 teaspoons baking powder
1 teaspoon salt
1 teaspoon mace
1 cup (2 sticks) butter, softened
1¹/2 cups sugar
3 eggs
1 teaspoon vanilla extract
1 teaspoon lemon extract
1 teaspoon almond extract

Drain the pineapple and reserve the juice. Measure the juice and if necessary, add enough water to equal ¹/2 cup. Grease a loaf pan and line with parchment paper or 2 layers of waxed paper. Combine the raisins, peel, cherries and coconut in a bowl and mix well. Sprinkle with ¹/2 cup of the flour and toss to coat. Combine the remaining 2¹/4 cups flour, the baking powder, salt and mace. Beat the butter and sugar in a mixing bowl until light and fluffy. Add the eggs 1 at a time, mixing well after each addition. Add the vanilla, lemon extract and almond extract and mix well. Add the pineapple and mix well. Add the dry ingredients in 4 batches, mixing well after each addition. Stir in the fruit mixture, the pineapple and the reserved pineapple juice. Pour into the prepared pan. Bake at 300 degrees for 2³/4 to 3 hours or until a wooden pick inserted in the center comes out clean. Cool in the pan on a wire rack for 30 minutes. Invert onto a serving plate and cool completely. Wrap in aluminum foil and store in a cool place. Freezes well. Yield: 10 to 12 servings.

Muriel McLaughlin, Beta Master
Fredericton, New Brunswick, Canada

FUDGE CUPCAKES

1 cup (2 sticks) butter, melted
2/3 cup (4 ounces) chocolate chips, melted
1³/4 cups sugar
1 cup all-purpose flour
4 eggs
1 teaspoon vanilla extract
1 cup chopped nuts

Combine the butter and chocolate chips in a bowl and mix well. Add the sugar, flour, eggs and vanilla and mix well. Stir in the nuts. Spoon into 15 greased and floured muffin cups. Bake at 325 degrees for 35 minutes. Cool in the pan for 10 minutes. Remove to a wire rack to cool completely. Yield: 15 servings.

Karen Knox, Omicron Gamma
Altus, Oklahoma

GINGERBREAD PUMPKIN CAKE

2 (14-ounce) packages gingerbread mix
1 (15-ounce) can pumpkin pie filling
¹/2 cup packed brown sugar
¹/3 teaspoon cinnamon
1 (6-ounce) box vanilla instant pudding mix
8 ounces whipped topping

Prepare and bake the gingerbread mix using the package directions for a 9×13-inch baking pan. Cool completely. Combine the pumpkin pie filling, brown sugar and cinnamon in a bowl and mix well. Spread the mixture on the cooled cake. Prepare the pudding mix using the package directions. Spread over the cake. Top with an even layer of whipped topping. Yield: 24 servings.

Marcella Backherms, Beta Rho Preceptor
Salem, Indiana

HARVEY WALLBANGER CAKE

1 (2-layer) package yellow cake mix
1 (4-ounce) package vanilla instant pudding mix
¹/2 cup vegetable oil
4 eggs
¹/4 cup vodka
¹/4 cup galliano
³/4 cup orange juice
Confectioners' sugar

Combine the cake mix, pudding mix, oil, eggs, vodka, galliano and orange juice in a bowl and mix well. Pour into a greased and floured bundt pan. Bake at 350 degrees for 45 to 50 minutes or until the cake tests done. Cool in the pan for 10 minutes. Invert onto a serving plate. Dust with confectioners' sugar. Yield: 10 servings.

Sharon McGinnis, Xi Rho Beta
Grand Prairie, Texas

HAWAIIAN CHIFFON CAKE

2 cups sifted all-purpose
  flour
1½ cups sugar
3 teaspoons baking
  powder
1 teaspoon salt
½ cup vegetable oil
7 egg yolks

¾ cup cold water
2 teaspoons vanilla
  extract
Grated zest of 1 lemon
1 cup egg whites
½ teaspoon cream of
  tartar
Pineapple Frosting

Sift the flour, sugar, baking powder and salt into a large bowl. Make a well. Add the oil, egg yolks, water, vanilla and lemon zest. Beat with a wooden spoon until smooth. Beat the egg whites and cream of tartar in a bowl until stiff peaks form. Fold in the batter with a rubber spatula. Pour into an ungreased tube pan. Bake at 325 degrees for 65 to 70 minutes. Invert on a funnel to cool completely. Loosen the cake from the side of the pan with a sharp knife. Invert onto a serving plate. Spread the Pineapple Frosting on the cooled cake. Yield: 12 servings.

PINEAPPLE FROSTING

2 teaspoons shortening
1 tablespoon butter,
  softened
1 teaspoon salt

3 cups sifted
  confectioners' sugar
½ cup drained crushed
  pineapple

Combine the shortening, butter, salt and ½ cup of the confectioners' sugar in a bowl and beat until light and fluffy. Add the remaining 2½ cups confectioners' sugar and the the pineapple alternately, mixing well after each addition.

Nancy Smith, Xi Alpha Mu
Terre Haute, Indiana

SOUR CREAM HUCKLEBERRY CAKE

½ cup (1 stick) butter,
  softened
1 cup granulated sugar
3 eggs
2 cups all-purpose flour
1 teaspoon baking soda
1 teaspoon baking
  powder
½ teaspoon salt
1 cup sour cream
1 teaspoon vanilla
  extract

3 cups huckleberries
½ cup packed brown
  sugar
8 ounces cream cheese,
  softened
¼ cup (½ stick) butter,
  softened
1 (1-pound) package
  confectioners' sugar
1 teaspoon vanilla
  extract
½ cup chopped walnuts

Beat ½ cup butter and the granulated sugar in a bowl until light and fluffy. Add the eggs 1 at a time, mixing well after each addition. Sift the flour, baking soda, baking powder and salt together. Combine the sour cream and 1 teaspoon vanilla in a small bowl and mix well. Add the dry ingredients and sour cream mixture alternately to the batter, mixing well after each addition. Fold in 1½ cups of the huckleberries. Pour half the batter into a greased and floured 9×13-inch cake pan. Sprinkle with the remaining 1½ cups huckleberries. Sprinkle with the brown sugar. Top with the remaining batter. Bake at 325 degrees for 45 to 50 minutes or until the cake tests done. Cool in the pan for 10 minutes. Remove to a wire rack to cool completely. Beat the cream cheese and ¼ cup butter in a bowl until light and fluffy. Add the confectioners' sugar and 1 teaspoon vanilla and mix well. Stir in the walnuts. Spread on the cooled cake. Yield: 12 to 15 servings.

Barb Strevy, Preceptor Beta Beta
Colfax, Washington

ITALIAN DREAM CAKE

½ cup shortening
½ cup (1 stick)
  margarine, softened
2 cups sugar
5 egg yolks
1 teaspoon baking soda
2 cups cake flour
½ teaspoon salt

1 cup buttermilk
1 teaspoon vanilla
  extract
2 cups shredded coconut
1 cup chopped pecans
5 egg whites, stiffly
  beaten
Frosting

Beat the shortening, margarine and sugar in a bowl until light and fluffy. Add the egg yolks 1 at a time, mixing well after each addition. Combine the baking soda, flour and salt. Add to the batter alternately with the buttermilk, mixing well after each addition. Stir in the vanilla, coconut and pecans. Fold in the egg whites. Pour into 3 greased and floured 8-inch cake pans. Bake at 325 degrees for 35 to 40 minutes or until the cake tests done. Cool in the pans for 10 minutes. Remove to a wire rack to cool completely. Spread the Frosting between the layers and over the top and side of the cooled cake. Yield: 10 to 12 servings.

FROSTING

½ cup (1 stick) butter or
  margarine, softened
8 ounces cream cheese,
  softened
1½ teaspoons milk
Dash of salt

1 (1-pound) package
  confectioners' sugar,
  sifted
1 cup chopped nuts
  (optional)

Beat the butter and cream cheese in a bowl until light and fluffy. Add the milk, salt and confectioners' sugar and mix until smooth. Stir in the nuts.

Patricia Fils, Laureate Tau
Creston, Iowa

ITALIAN LOVE CAKE

1 (2-layer) package
    fudge marble cake mix
4 cups ricotta cheese
3/4 cup sugar
4 eggs
1 teaspoon vanilla
    extract

1 (4-ounce) box
    chocolate instant
    pudding mix
1 cup milk
8 ounces whipped
    topping

Prepare the cake mix using the package directions. Pour into a greased and floured 9×13-inch cake pan. Combine the ricotta cheese, sugar, eggs and vanilla in a bowl and mix well. Spread over the batter. Bake at 350 degrees for 1 hour. Cool in the pan for 10 minutes. Remove to a wire rack to cool completely. Whisk the pudding mix and milk in a bowl for 2 minutes. Fold in the whipped topping. Spread the mixture on the cooled cake. Chill for 1 hour or longer. Yield: 12 servings.

Linda Cozzi, Xi Rho
Tucson, Arizona

LEMON CAKE

1 (3-ounce) package
    lemon gelatin
1 cup boiling water
4 eggs
3/4 cup vegetable oil

1 (2-layer) package
    lemon cake mix
2 cups confectioners'
    sugar
Juice of 2 lemons

Combine the gelatin and water in a bowl. Cool. Beat the eggs in a bowl. Add the oil and mix well. Add the cake mix and gelatin and mix well. Pour into a greased and floured 9×13-inch cake pan. Bake at 350 degrees for 40 to 45 minutes or until the cake tests done. Pierce the hot cake with a fork. Combine the confectioners' sugar and lemon juice in a small bowl and mix until smooth. Pour over the warm cake. Cool completely in the pan. Yield: 12 servings.

Marilyn Vincent, Laureate Beta
Essex Junction, Vermont

LIGHT LEMON CAKE

1 (2-layer) package
    yellow cake mix
1¼ cups water
1/4 cup fat-free vanilla
    yogurt
3/4 cup egg substitute

2 tablespoons grated
    lemon zest
1/2 cup confectioners'
    sugar
2 to 3 teaspoons water
1 cup sliced strawberries

Combine the cake mix, water, yogurt, egg substitute and lemon zest in a mixing bowl and mix well. Beat at high speed for 2 minutes. Pour into a greased and floured tube pan. Bake at 350 degrees for 45 minutes. Cool in the pan on a wire rack for 30 minutes. Invert onto a serving plate. Combine the confectioners'

sugar and water and mix until smooth. Drizzle over the cake. Serve with strawberries. Yield: 12 servings.

Wilma Hamm, Preceptor Gamma Theta
Camano Island, Washington

FILLED LEMON CAKE

1 (2-layer) package
    lemon cake mix
Juice of 4 lemons
3 eggs, beaten

2 cups sugar
1 cup applesauce
1/2 cup (1 stick)
    margarine

Prepare and bake the cake mix using the package directions for two 9-inch cake pans. Cool in the pans for 10 minutes. Remove to a wire rack to cool completely. Slice each cake layer horizontally in half. Combine the remaining ingredients in a saucepan. Bring to a boil over low heat, stirring constantly. Boil for 2 minutes, stirring constantly. Cool slightly. Spread between the cake layers. Yield: 16 servings.

Ethel Manuel, Laureate Theta
Stone Mountain, Georgia

LEMON APRICOT CAKE

1 cup apricot nectar
    (apricot juice)
1 (2-layer) package
    lemon cake mix
3/4 cup vegetable oil

1/2 cup sugar
4 eggs
1 cup confectioners'
    sugar
Juice of 1 lemon

Mix the apricot nectar, cake mix, oil, sugar and eggs in a bowl. Beat at medium speed for 2 minutes. Pour into a greased and floured bundt pan. Bake at 325 degrees for 1 hour. Cool completely in the pan on a wire rack. Invert onto a serving plate. Mix the confectioners' sugar and lemon juice in a bowl until smooth. Drizzle over the cake. Yield: 8 to 12 servings.

Gloria J. Snyder, Alpha Delta Phi
Lowry City, Missouri

LEMON BERRY CAKE

1 (2-layer) package
    lemon cake mix
1 cup lemon yogurt
4 eggs

1 (15-ounce) can
    blueberries, drained
Confectioners' sugar

Combine the cake mix, yogurt and eggs and mix well. Beat at medium speed for 2 minutes. Fold in the blueberries. Pour into a greased and floured tube pan. Bake at 350 degrees for 35 to 45 minutes or until the cake tests done. Cool in the pan for 10 minutes. Invert onto a serving plate and cool completely. Dust with confectioners' sugar. Yield: 12 servings.

Margaret L. Wilburn, Laureate Theta Phi
Houston, Texas

LEMON LIME CAKE

1 (2-layer) package
   lemon cake mix
1 (3½-ounce) package
   lemon instant
   pudding mix

1 cup lemon-lime soda
¾ cup vegetable oil
4 eggs
Pineapple Coconut
   Frosting

Combine the cake mix, pudding mix, soda, oil and eggs in a large bowl and mix well. Beat for 2 minutes. Divide the batter evenly among 3 greased and floured 9-inch cake pans. Bake at 350 degrees for 18 to 20 minutes or until the cake tests done. Cool in the pans for 5 minutes. Remove to a wire rack to cool completely. Spread the Pineapple Coconut Frosting between the layers and over the top of the cooled cake. Yield: 12 servings.

PINEAPPLE COCONUT FROSTING

½ cup (1 stick) butter
2 tablespoons
   all-purpose flour
1½ cups sugar

2 eggs
1 (8-ounce) can crushed
   pineapple, drained
1½ cups flaked coconut

Melt the butter in a saucepan over low heat. Whisk in the flour. Add the sugar, eggs, pineapple and coconut and mix well. Cook over low heat for 5 minutes or until the mixture is warmed through, stirring constantly. Bring to a boil. Remove from the heat and cool completely.

Carol Plumb, Preceptor Alpha Epsilon
Edmond, Oklahoma

PECAN LEMON CAKE

1 (2-layer) package
   lemon cake mix
1 cup sour cream
2 cups sugar
Grated zest of 1 lemon

1 egg, beaten
1 teaspoon lemon
   extract
2 cups ground pecans

Prepare and bake the cake mix using the package directions. Combine the sour cream, sugar and lemon zest in a saucepan. Bring to a boil over medium heat, stirring constantly. Place the egg in a small bowl. Add a small amount of the hot mixture into the beaten egg; stir the egg into the hot mixture. Cook for 1 minute, stirring constantly. Cool completely. Stir in the lemon extract and ground pecans. Spread on the cooled cake. Yield: 12 servings.

Greer Neal, Laureate Alpha Nu
Scottsdale, Arizona

KAHLÚA CAKE

2 cups sour cream
4 eggs
¾ cup vegetable oil
⅓ cup Kahlúa
1 (2-layer) package
   devil's food cake mix

1 (4-ounce) package
   chocolate instant
   pudding mix
1 cup (6 ounces)
   chocolate chips

Combine the sour cream, eggs, oil, Kahlúa, cake mix and pudding mix in a bowl and mix well. Stir in the chocolate chips. Pour into a greased bundt pan. Bake at 350 degrees for 1 hour or until a wooden pick inserted in the center comes out clean. Cool in the pan for 10 minutes. Invert onto a serving plate. Yield: 12 servings.

Kathy Simmons, Laureate Beta Beta
Cave Junction, Oregon

KEY LIME ANGEL FOOD CAKE

1 angel food cake
1 (14-ounce) can
   sweetened
   condensed milk
⅓ cup Key lime juice
   (may use lime juice)

1 teaspoon grated
   lime zest
12 ounces whipped
   topping
1 cup sweetened flaked
   coconut

Slice the cake horizontally into 3 layers. Combine the condensed milk, lime juice and lime zest in a bowl and whisk until smooth and thickened. Fold in the whipped topping. Spread between the layers and over the top and side of the cake. Sprinkle with coconut. Garnish with kiwifruit and strawberries if desired. Yield: 16 servings.

Lil Blasko, Laureate Rho
Kindersley, Saskatchewan, Canada

KEY LIME CAKE

1 (2-layer) package
   lemon cake mix
1 (4-ounce) package
   lemon instant
   pudding mix
1 cup water
1 cup vegetable oil

4 eggs
2 tablespoons Key
   lime juice
⅓ cup Key lime juice
2 cups confectioners'
   sugar

Mix the first 5 ingredients and 2 tablespoons lime juice in a bowl. Pour into a greased and floured 9×13-inch cake pan. Bake at 325 degrees for 45 to 55 minutes or until the cake tests done. Cool in the pan for 10 minutes. Pierce the cake with a fork. Mix ⅓ cup lime juice and the confectioners' sugar in a bowl until smooth. Drizzle over the cake. Cool completely in the pan. Yield: 12 servings.

Bonita Jindracek, Laureate Alpha Eta
Fort Lauderdale, Florida

MILKY WAY CAKE

8 (2-ounce) Milky Way Bars	2¹/2 cups all-purpose flour
1 cup (2 sticks) margarine, softened	¹/2 teaspoon baking soda
2 cups sugar	1¹/4 cups buttermilk
4 eggs	1 cup chopped pecans
	Frosting

Combine the candy bars and ¹/2 cup of the margarine in a small saucepan. Melt over low heat, stirring often. Beat the remaining ¹/2 cup margarine and the sugar in a mixing bowl until light and fluffy. Add the eggs and mix well. Combine the flour and baking soda. Add to the batter alternately with the buttermilk. Stir in the candy mixture and the pecans. Pour into a greased and floured tube pan. Bake at 350 degrees for 1 hour and 10 minutes. Cool in the pan for 10 minutes. Invert onto a serving plate. Spread the Frosting on the cooled cake.
Yield: 10 to 12 servings.

FROSTING

2¹/2 cups sugar	1 cup (6 ounces) semisweet chocolate chips
1 cup evaporated milk	
¹/2 cup (1 stick) margarine	1 cup marshmallow cream

Combine the sugar and evaporated milk in a saucepan. Cook to 234 to 240 degrees on a candy thermometer, soft-ball stage, stirring often. Stir in the margarine, chocolate chips and marshmallow cream until smooth.

Sharon Ingram, Laureate Epsilon Theta
St. Petersburg, Florida

NOTTINGHAM CAKE

1 cup sugar	1 tablespoon shortening
1 cup all-purpose flour	2 cups fruit
¹/2 cup milk	1 cup sugar
1 egg	¹/4 cup (¹/2 stick) butter, melted
Dash of salt	
1 teaspoon baking powder	

Combine 1 cup sugar, the flour, milk, egg, salt, baking powder and shortening in a large bowl and mix well. Pour into a greased and floured 9×9-inch cake pan. Combine the fruit, 1 cup sugar and the butter in a bowl and mix well. Spoon over the cake batter. Bake at 350 degrees for 45 minutes. Cool in the pan on a wire rack. Serve with whipped cream or ice cream if desired. Yield: 8 to 10 servings.

Linda Logue, Delta Omega
Archie, Missouri

SWEDISH NUT CAKE

2 cups all-purpose flour	2 cups confectioners' sugar
2 cups sugar	
1¹/2 teaspoons baking soda	¹/2 cup (1 stick) butter or margarine, softened
1 (20-ounce) can crushed pineapple	8 ounces cream cheese, softened
2 eggs, beaten	¹/2 teaspoon vanilla extract
1 teaspoon vanilla extract	1 cup chopped pecans
1 cup pecans	

Combine the flour, sugar and baking soda in a large bowl. Add the pineapple, eggs and 1 teaspoon vanilla and mix well. Stir in 1 cup pecans. Pour into a greased and flour 9×13-inch cake pan. Bake at 350 degrees for 40 to 45 minutes or until the cake tests done. Cool in the pan for 10 minutes. Remove to a wire rack and cool completely. Beat the confectioners' sugar, butter and cream cheese in a bowl until light and fluffy. Add ¹/2 teaspoon vanilla and mix well. Stir in 1 cup pecans. Spread over the cooled cake.
Yield: 16 servings.

Peggy Mead, Preceptor Delta
Moberly, Missouri

OATMEAL CAKE

1 cup quick-cooking oats	1 teaspoon cinnamon
1¹/4 cups boiling water	¹/2 teaspoon salt
1 cup granulated sugar	1 teaspoon baking soda
1 cup packed brown sugar	6 tablespoons butter or margarine, softened
¹/2 cup shortening	³/4 cup packed brown sugar
2 eggs, beaten	
1¹/3 cups cake flour (may use all-purpose flour)	1 cup flaked coconut
	4 teaspoons cream
	¹/2 cup chopped nuts

Place the oats in a small bowl. Add the water. Let stand for 20 minutes. Beat the granulated sugar, 1 cup brown sugar and the shortening in a mixing bowl until light and fluffy. Add the eggs and mix well. Add the cake flour, cinnamon, salt, baking soda and oatmeal mixture and mix well. Pour into a greased and floured 9×9-inch cake pan. Bake at 350 degrees for 35 to 40 minutes or until the cake tests done. Beat the butter and ³/4 cup brown sugar in a bowl until light and fluffy. Add the coconut, cream and nuts and mix well. Spread over the hot cake. Broil until bubbly and light brown. Cool completely in the pan. Yield: 12 servings.

Marjorie Giger, Phi Master
Bellingham, Washington

ORANGE CHIFFON CAKE

1 orange chiffon cake (may use angel food cake)	3 eggs
	1 (20-ounce) can crushed pineapple, drained
1 cup (2 sticks) margarine, softened	2/3 cup chopped pecans
1 1/2 cups sugar	1 (14-ounce) package flaked coconut

Slice the cake horizontally into 3 layers. Beat the margarine and sugar in a bowl until light and fluffy. Add the eggs 1 at a time, mixing well after each addition. Stir in the pineapple, pecans and coconut. Spread the frosting between the layers and over the top and side of the cake. Note: If you are concerned about using raw eggs, use eggs pasteurized in their shells, which are sold at some specialty food stores, or use an equivalent amount of pasteurized egg substitute. Yield: 16 to 20 servings.

Josephine Wilkinson, Alpha Mu Laureate
Waynesboro, Virginia

MANDARIN ORANGE CAKE

1 (2-layer) package yellow cake mix	1 (20-ounce) can crushed pineapple
1 (11-ounce) can mandarin oranges	1 (3-ounce) package vanilla instant pudding mix
4 eggs	
1/2 cup vegetable oil	
8 ounces whipped topping	

Combine the cake mix, oranges, eggs and oil in a bowl and mix well. Pour into 3 greased and floured 8-inch cake pans. Bake at 325 degrees for 15 to 20 minutes or until the cake tests done. Cool in the pans for 10 minutes. Remove to a wire rack to cool completely. Combine the whipped topping, pineapple and pudding mix in a medium bowl and mix well. Spread between the layers and over the top and side of the cake. Yield: 12 servings.

Mildred George, Laureate Zeta
Baton Rouge, Lousiana

ORANGE DATE CAKE

1 teaspoon baking soda	2 cups chopped dates
1 1/3 cups buttermilk	1 cup chopped pecans
1 cup shortening	1 cup orange juice
2 cups granulated sugar	2 cups confectioners' sugar
4 eggs	
4 cups all-purpose flour	2 teaspoons grated orange zest
2 teaspoons grated orange zest	

Dissolve the baking soda in the buttermilk in a small bowl. Beat the shortening and granulated sugar in a large bowl until light and fluffy. Add the eggs 1 at a time, beating well after each addition. Add the flour and mix well. Stir in 2 teaspoons orange zest, the dates and pecans. Pour into a greased and floured tube pan. Bake at 350 degrees for 1 1/2 hours. Pierce the warm cake with a fork. Combine the orange juice, confectioners' sugar and 2 teaspoons orange zest in a bowl and mix until smooth. Pour over the warm cake. Cool completely in the pan. Invert onto a serving plate. Yield: 12 servings.

Molly Patterson, Preceptor Beta Xi
Seminole, Oklahoma

ORANGE SLICE CAKE

1 cup (2 sticks) margarine, softened	3 1/2 cups all-purpose flour
2 cups sugar	1/2 cup buttermilk
4 eggs	1 teaspoon baking soda
4 tablespoons grated orange zest	1 teaspoon vanilla extract
1 pound orange slice candy, chopped	6 ounces frozen orange juice concentrate, thawed
1 cup shredded coconut	
8 ounces chopped dates	
2 cups chopped pecans or walnuts	

Beat the margarine and sugar in a bowl until light and fluffy. Add the eggs 1 at a time, mixing well after each addition. Combine the orange zest, candy, coconut, dates and pecans in a bowl. Add 1/2 cup of the flour and toss to coat. Add to the batter and mix well. Add the remaining 3 cups flour and mix well. Combine the buttermilk and baking soda in a small bowl and mix well. Stir into the batter. Stir in the vanilla. Pour into a greased and floured tube pan. Bake at 300 degrees for 1 3/4 hours. Cool completely in the pan. Invert onto a serving plate. Brush with the orange juice concentrate. Yield: 12 servings.

Joycelynn Arnold, Laureate Iota Eta
Yoakum, Texas

ORANGE JUICE CAKE

1 (2-layer) package yellow cake mix	1 cup orange juice
1/2 cup vegetable oil	1 (4-ounce) box vanilla instant pudding mix
4 eggs	Glaze

Combine the cake mix, oil, eggs, orange juice and pudding mix in a bowl and mix well. Beat at low speed for 2 minutes. Pour into a greased and floured bundt pan. Bake at 350 degrees for 35 to 40 minutes or until the cake tests done. Cool in the pan for 10 minutes. Pierce the cake with a fork. Pour the Glaze over the cake. Cool completely. Invert onto a serving plate. Yield: 12 servings.

GLAZE

1/2 cup (1 stick) butter, softened	1 cup sugar
	3/4 cup orange juice

Bring the butter, sugar and orange juice to a boil in a saucepan over medium heat, stirring frequently.

Jane Johnson, Xi Beta Omega
Hemphill, Texas

ORANGE CAKE

1 cup (2 sticks) margarine, softened	1 cup shredded coconut
2 cups granulated sugar	1 cup all-purpose flour
4 eggs	2 tablespoons plus 1/4 cup orange juice
1/2 cup buttermilk	1 1/2 cups confectioners' sugar
1 teaspoon baking soda	
2 cups all-purpose flour	2 tablespoons grated orange zest
1 cup dates	
1 cup chopped pecans	

Beat the margarine and granulated sugar in a bowl until light and fluffy. Beat in the eggs 1 at a time. Add the buttermilk and mix well. Sift the baking soda and 2 cups flour into the batter and mix well. Combine the dates, pecans, coconut and 1 cup flour in a bowl and toss to coat. Stir in 2 tablespoons orange juice. Add to the batter and mix well. Pour into a greased and floured bundt or tube pan. Bake at 350 degrees for 1 1/2 to 2 hours or until the cake tests done. Pierce the hot cake with a fork. Combine 1/4 cup orange juice, the confectioners' sugar and orange zest in a bowl and mix until smooth. Pour over the cake. Cool completely in the pan. Invert onto a serving plate. Yield: 12 to 16 servings.

Otela Seim, Preceptor Eta
Coram, Montana

PEACH DUMP CAKE

1 (28-ounce) can sliced peaches	1 cup (2 sticks) butter, melted
1 (2-layer) package butter pecan cake mix	1/4 cup chopped pecans

Pour the peaches in a 9×13-inch cake pan. Sprinkle with the cake mix. Drizzle with butter. Sprinkle with pecans. Bake at 350 degrees for 40 minutes. Cool in the pan for 10 minutes. Remove to a wire rack to cool completely. Yield: 12 servings.

Marie Hass, Beta Epsilon
Madison, Wisconsin

PEACH UPSIDE-DOWN CAKE

1/3 cup margarine	1 egg
1/2 cup packed brown sugar	1 teaspoon vanilla extract
1 (29-ounce) can sliced peaches	1 1/4 cups sifted cake flour
1 maraschino cherry	1 1/2 teaspoons baking powder
1/3 cup shortening	
1/2 cup granulated sugar	1/2 teaspoon salt

Melt the margarine in an oven-proof skillet over low heat. Stir in the brown sugar. Drain the peaches, reserving 1/2 cup of the liquid. Arrange the peaches in the brown sugar mixture. Remove from the heat. Place the cherry in the center. Beat the shortening and granulated sugar in a mixing bowl until light and fluffy. Add the egg and vanilla and mix well. Sift the cake flour, baking powder and salt together. Add to the batter alternately with the reserved liquid, mixing well after each addition. Spoon over the peaches in the skillet. Bake at 350 degrees for 45 minutes or until the cake tests done. Cool in the pan for 5 minutes. Invert onto a serving plate. Yield: 12 servings.

Linda K. Morrow, Laureate Gamma Upsilon
Joy, Illinois

PEANUT BUTTER CAKE

1/2 cup (1 stick) butter	1/2 cup milk
1 cup water	1 teaspoon baking soda
1/2 cup peanut butter	1/3 cup milk
1/3 cup vegetable oil	1/2 cup peanut butter
2 cups self-rising flour	1/2 cup (1 stick) butter
1 3/4 cups granulated sugar	1 teaspoon vanilla extract
2 eggs, beaten	3 cups confectioners' sugar
1 teaspoon vanilla extract	

Combine 1/2 cup butter, the water, 1/2 cup peanut butter and the oil in a saucepan. Bring to a boil over low heat, stirring occasionally. Mix the flour, granulated sugar, eggs, 1 teaspoon vanilla, 1/2 cup milk and the baking soda in a bowl. Add the peanut butter mixture and mix well. Pour into a greased 9×13-inch glass cake pan. Bake at 325 degrees for 30 minutes. Cool in the pan for 10 minutes. Remove to a wire rack to cool completely. Combine 1/3 cup milk, 1/2 cup peanut butter and 1/2 cup butter in a saucepan. Bring to a boil over low heat, stirring occasionally. Remove from the heat. Add 1 teaspoon vanilla and the confectioners' sugar and mix until smooth. Spread on the cooled cake. Yield: 12 servings.

Della Marie Foster, Preceptor Beta Psi
Fredericktown, Missouri

PEANUT BUTTER SHEET CAKE

2 cups all-purpose flour	1/2 cup peanut butter
2 cups sugar	1 cup water
1 teaspoon baking soda	1/2 cup buttermilk
1/2 teaspoon salt	2 eggs
1/2 cup shortening	1 teaspoon vanilla
3/4 cup (11/2 sticks)	extract
margarine, softened	Peanut Butter Frosting

Sift the flour, sugar, baking soda and salt into a large bowl. Combine the shortening, margarine, peanut butter and water in a saucepan. Bring to a boil over low heat, stirring occasionally. Add to the dry ingredients and mix well. Add the buttermilk, eggs and vanilla and mix well. Pour into a greased and floured 10×15-inch cake pan. Bake at 350 degrees for 20 minutes. Spread the Peanut Butter Frosting on the hot cake. Cool in the pan. Yield: 20 servings.

PEANUT BUTTER FROSTING

1/2 cup peanut butter	1 (1-pound) package
1/2 cup (1 stick)	confectioners' sugar
margarine	1 teaspoon vanilla
1/3 cup milk	extract

Combine the peanut butter, margarine and milk in a saucepan. Bring to a boil over medium heat, stirring often. Remove from the heat. Add the confectioners' sugar and vanilla and mix until smooth.

Carol Carson, Xi Alpha Omega
Hutchinson, Kansas

PECAN CAKE

2 cups crushed pineapple	1/4 cup (1/2 stick)
2 eggs	margarine, softened
2 cups granulated sugar	8 ounces cream cheese,
2 cups all-purpose flour	softened
2 teaspoons baking	13/4 cups confectioners'
soda	sugar
1 teaspoon vanilla	1 teaspoon vanilla
extract	extract
1/2 cup chopped pecans	1/2 cup chopped pecans

Mix the pineapple, eggs, granulated sugar, flour, baking soda and 1 teaspoon vanilla in a large bowl. Stir in 1/2 cup pecans. Pour into a greased and floured 9×13-inch cake pan. Bake at 350 degrees for 45 minutes. Cool in the pan for 10 minutes. Remove to a wire rack to cool completely. Beat the margarine, cream cheese and confectioners' sugar in a bowl until light and fluffy. Stir in 1 teaspoon vanilla and 1/2 cup pecans. Spread over the cooled cake. Yield: 24 servings.

Margo Kariolich, Alpha Nu Master
Tucson, Arizona

PICNIC CAKE

1/2 cup (1 stick) butter,	1/2 teaspoon salt
softened	1 cup milk
11/2 cups packed light	1 teaspoon vanilla
brown sugar	extract
2 eggs	10 large marshmallows,
21/2 cups all-purpose	halved
flour	1/2 cup light brown sugar
1 tablespoon baking	1/2 cup pecans, chopped
powder	

Beat the butter and 11/2 cups brown sugar in a bowl until light and fluffy. Add the eggs 1 at a time, mixing well after each addition. Sift the flour, baking powder and salt together. Add to the butter mixture alternately with the milk, mixing well after each addition. Add the vanilla and mix well. Pour into a greased and floured 10×10-inch cake pan. Arrange the marshmallows, cut side down, over the batter. Sprinkle with 1/2 cup brown sugar and the pecans. Bake at 350 degrees for 50 minutes. Cool in the pan on a wire rack. Yield: 8 servings.

Susan Moss, Laureate Alpha Chi
Salem, Ohio

PIÑA COLADA CAKE

1 (2-layer) package	6 ounces cream of
yellow cake mix	coconut
1 (14-ounce) sweetened	12 ounces whipped
condensed milk	topping
	7 ounces flaked coconut

Prepare the cake mix using the package directions. Pour into a greased and floured 9×13-inch cake pan. Bake at 350 degrees for 33 to 38 minutes or until the cake tests done. Cool in the pan for 10 minutes. Pierce the cake with a fork. Combine the condensed milk and cream of coconut in a bowl. Pour over the cake. Cool completely. Spread the whipped topping over the cooled cake and sprinkle with coconut. Yield: 12 servings.

Ruth Cook, Epsilon Master
Albuquerque, New Mexico

PINEAPPLE PIÑA COLADA CAKE

1 (8-ounce) can crushed	11/2 cups flaked coconut
pineapple	1 (151/2-ounce) can
1/4 cup vegetable oil	cream of coconut
2 eggs, beaten	12 ounces whipped
1 (2-layer) package	topping
white cake mix	

Drain the pineapple, reserving the juice. Add enough water to the juice to make 11/3 cups and place in a bowl. Add the pineapple, oil, eggs, cake mix and

½ cup of the flaked coconut and mix well. Pour into a greased and floured 9×13-inch cake pan. Bake at 350 degrees for 30 to 35 minutes or until the cake tests done. Remove the pan to a wire rack. Pierce the cake with a fork. Pour the cream of coconut over the hot cake. Cool completely in the pan. Chill until cool. Fold the remaining 1 cup flaked coconut into the whipped topping. Spread over the chilled cake. Yield: 12 to 15 servings.

Cathryn Ren, Xi Kappa Gamma
Galva, Illinois

PINEAPPLE CAKE

1 (2-layer) package yellow cake mix
½ cup (1 stick) butter or margarine
1 (16-ounce) can crushed pineapple
8 ounces whipped topping

Place the cake mix in a large bowl. Cut in the butter until crumbly. Spread the pineapple across a 9×13-inch cake pan. Sprinkle the cake mix over the pineapple. Bake at 350 degrees for 30 minutes. Cool completely in the pan. Serve with whipped topping. Yield: 12 servings.

Lois Reiss, Alpha Tau Master
Sarnia, Ontario, Canada

PINEAPPLE CREAM CAKE

1 (16-ounce) package angel food cake mix
6 ounces pineapple yogurt
12 ounces whipped topping
⅓ cup confectioners' sugar

Prepare and bake the cake mix using the package directions. Invert on a funnel to cool completely. Loosen the cake from the side of the pan with a sharp knife. Invert onto a cake plate. Slice the cake horizontally into 3 layers. Combine the yogurt, whipped topping and confectioners' sugar in a bowl and mix well. Spread between the layers and over the top and side of the cake. Garnish with fruit.
Yield: 14 servings.

Lynn Hillman, Laureate Theta Upsilon
Vista, California

HAWAIIAN PINEAPPLE CAKE

1 (2-layer) package yellow cake mix
8 ounces cream cheese, softened
2 cups milk
2 (3-ounce) packages vanilla instant pudding mix
1 (20-ounce) can crushed pineapple, drained
12 ounces whipped topping
1 (14-ounce) package shredded coconut

Prepare and bake the cake mix using the package directions for a 9×13-inch cake pan. Cool for 10 minutes in the pan. Remove to a wire rack to cool completely. Beat the cream cheese in a bowl until smooth. Add the milk gradually, beating constantly at low speed. Add the pudding mix 1 package at a time, mixing well after each addition. Spread over the cooled cake. Spoon the pineapple over the pudding and spread lightly. Top with an even layer of whipped topping. Sprinkle with the coconut. Chill for several hours before serving. Yield: 12 servings.

Barbara Roy, Laureate Nu
Toms River, New Jersey

PINEAPPLE PLEASURE CAKE

1 (20-ounce) can crushed pineapple
1 (14-ounce) jar pineapple topping
1 (2-layer) package pineapple cake mix
1 cup (2 sticks) butter, sliced thinly
Chopped pecans

Pour the pineapple into a greased and floured 9×13-inch cake pan. Pour the pineapple topping evenly over the top. Sprinkle with the cake mix. Arrange the sliced butter over the cake mix. Sprinkle with pecans. Bake at 325 degrees for 1 hour. Cool in the pan on a wire rack. Yield: 12 servings.

Deborah O'Neill, Theta Psi
Cookeville, Tennessee

PINEAPPLE PUDDING CAKE

1 (2-layer) package yellow cake mix
1 (6-ounce) box vanilla pudding mix
1 (20-ounce) can crushed pineapple
1 tablespoon cornstarch
8 ounces whipped topping
½ to 1 cup shredded coconut
Chopped walnuts

Prepare and bake the cake mix using the package directions for a 9×13-inch cake pan. Cool in the pan for 10 minutes. Remove to a wire rack to cool completely. Prepare the pudding using the package directions. Combine the pineapple and cornstarch in a saucepan. Cook over medium heat until thickened, stirring often. Spoon over the cooled cake. Let stand until set. Spoon the pudding over the pineapple and spread lightly. Cover with whipped topping. Sprinkle with the coconut and walnuts. Chill, covered, until just before serving. Yield: 12 servings.

Gloria Dimmick, Xi Gamma Iota
Orlando, Florida

SWEDISH PINEAPPLE CAKE

2 cups all-purpose flour
2 cups granulated sugar
2 teaspoons baking soda
2 eggs
1 teaspoon vanilla
   extract
1 (20-ounce) can crushed
   pineapple

8 ounces cream cheese,
   softened
1 (1-pound) package
   confectioners' sugar
1/2 cup (1 stick) butter,
   softened
1/2 cup chopped pecans

Mix the flour, granulated sugar, baking soda, eggs, vanilla and pineapple in a bowl. Pour into a greased and floured 11×13-inch cake pan. Bake at 350 degrees for 30 minutes. Cool in the pan for 10 minutes. Remove to a wire rack to cool completely. Beat the cream cheese, confectioners' sugar and butter in a bowl until light and fluffy. Stir in the pecans. Spread over the cooled cake. Yield: 12 to 16 servings.

Patsy Jones, Preceptor Omicron Eta
Navasota, Texas

YELLOW PINEAPPLE CAKE

1 (2-layer) package
   yellow cake mix
1 (3-ounce) package
   vanilla instant
   pudding mix

1 (13-ounce) can crushed
   pineapple, drained
8 ounces whipped
   topping

Prepare and bake the cake mix using the package directions for a 9×13-inch cake pan. Cool in the pan for 10 minutes. Remove to a wire rack to cool completely. Prepare the pudding using the package directions. Spread over the cooled cake. Cover with pineapple. Top with an even layer of whipped topping. Chill until just before serving.
Yield: 12 servings.

Janet Dyke, Preceptor Epsilon Lambda
Wellington, Ohio

PISTACHIO CAKE

1 (2-layer) package
   white cake mix
3 eggs
3/4 cup vegetable oil
1 cup lemon-lime soda
1 (3-ounce) package
   pistachio instant
   pudding mix

1/2 cup chopped walnuts
   or pecans (optional)
1/2 cup shredded coconut
   (optional)
Pistachio Frosting

Combine the cake mix, eggs, oil, soda, and pudding mix in a large bowl and mix well. Stir in the walnuts and coconut. Pour into a greased and floured 9×13-inch cake pan. Bake using the package directions. Cool in the pan for 10 minutes. Remove to a

wire rack to cool completely. Spread the Pistachio Frosting on the cooled cake. Yield: 12 servings.

PISTACHIO FROSTING

1 (3-ounce) package
   pistachio instant
   pudding mix
1 1/2 cups milk

2 packets instant
   whipped topping mix
3 ounces cream cheese,
   softened

Combine the pudding mix, milk, whipped topping mix and cream cheese in a bowl. Beat until of spreading consistency.

Barb Burns, Xi Phi
Council, Iowa

PLUM CAKE

1 cup all-purpose flour
1/2 cup sugar
1/2 teaspoon baking
   powder
1/2 teaspoon salt
1/2 cup milk
1/2 teaspoon vanilla
   extract

3 tablespoons butter,
   melted
2 cups sliced plums
1 cup sugar
1 teaspoon cinnamon
1 cup boiling water

Combine the flour, 1/2 cup sugar, baking powder, salt, milk, vanilla and butter in a bowl and mix well. Pour into a greased and floured 8×8-inch cake pan. Combine the plums, 1 cup sugar and cinnamon in a bowl and toss to coat. Spoon over the batter in an even layer. Top with the water. Bake at 375 degrees for 45 minutes. Cool in the pan for 10 minutes. Remove to a wire rack to cool completely.
Yield: 4 to 6 servings.

Linda Rothrock, Gamma Eta Master
Santa Cruz, California

POPPY SEED BUNDT CAKE

1 (2-layer) package
   yellow cake mix
1 (3-ounce) package
   coconut instant
   pudding mix
1 cup water

1/2 cup vegetable oil
3 eggs
2 tablespoons poppy
   seeds
Confectioners' sugar

Combine the cake mix, pudding mix, water, oil and eggs in a bowl and mix well. Beat for 3 minutes at medium speed. Stir in the poppy seeds. Pour into a greased and floured bundt pan. Bake at 350 degrees for 48 to 52 minutes or until the cake tests done. Cool for 10 minutes in the pan. Invert onto a serving plate. Dust with confectioners' sugar.
Yield: 12 to 15 servings.

Sue Berryman, Laureate Alpha Theta
Wichita, Kansas

APRICOT GINGER POUND CAKE WITH RUM GLAZE

1/3 cup sour cream
1/3 cup milk
1 1/2 cups (3 sticks) unsalted butter, softened
3 cups granulated sugar
7 eggs
3 1/2 cups cake flour
3/4 teaspoon salt
1/2 teaspoon baking powder

1 1/2 teaspoons vanilla extract
1/4 cup chopped candied ginger
1/4 cup chopped dried apricots
2 tablespoons rum
2 tablespoons water
3/4 cup confectioners' sugar

Combine the sour cream and milk in a small bowl and mix well. Beat the butter and granulated sugar in a bowl until light and fluffy. Add the eggs 1 at a time, mixing well after each addition. Combine the flour, salt and baking powder. Add to the batter alternately with the milk mixture, mixing well after each addition. Add the vanilla and mix well. Stir in the ginger and apricots. Pour into a greased and floured bundt pan. Bake at 325 degrees for 55 minutes or until a wooden pick inserted in the center comes out clean. Cool in the pan for 10 minutes. Invert onto a serving plate. Combine the rum, water and confectioners' sugar and mix well. Brush over the cooled cake. Yield: 15 to 20 servings.

Linda Fae Wiedeman, Xi Gamma
Miles City, Montana

BAPTIST POUND CAKE

The secret to this cake is to put it in a cold oven and then turn the heat on.

1/2 cup (1 stick) butter or margarine, softened
1/2 cup shortening
3 cups sugar
5 eggs
Pinch of salt
3 cups all-purpose flour

1/2 teaspoon baking powder
1 cup milk
1 teaspoon vanilla extract
1 tablespoon butternut flavoring

Beat the butter, shortening and sugar in a bowl until light and fluffy. Add the eggs 1 at a time, mixing well after each addition. Sift the salt, flour and baking powder together. Add to the batter alternately with the milk, mixing well after each addition. Add the vanilla and butternut flavoring and mix well. Pour into a greased and floured bundt pan. Place in a cold oven. Bake at 350 degrees for 1 1/4 hours. Cool in the pan for 10 minutes. Invert onto a serving plate. Yield: 24 servings.

Caroline Tate, Laureate Theta
Knoxville, Tennessee

BLUEBERRY POUND CAKE

1 (2-layer) package butter cake mix
3 eggs
1/2 cup vegetable oil
8 ounces cream cheese, softened

1 teaspoon butter flavoring
1 (15-ounce) can blueberries, drained

Mix the cake mix, eggs, oil, cream cheese and butter flavoring in a bowl. Fold in the blueberries. Pour into a greased and floured bundt pan. Bake at 350 degrees for 1 hour. Cool in the pan for 10 minutes. Invert onto a serving plate. Yield: 12 servings.

Judy Ramer, Xi Beta Xi
North Little Rock, Arkansas

BOURBON PECAN POUND CAKE

1 1/2 cups (3 sticks) butter, softened
8 ounces cream cheese, softened
3 cups sugar
6 eggs
3 cups all-purpose flour

1/2 teaspoon salt
1/4 cup bourbon
1 1/2 teaspoons vanilla extract
1 1/2 cups chopped pecans, toasted
Glaze

Beat the butter and cream cheese in a bowl. Add the sugar gradually and beat until light and fluffy. Add the eggs 1 at a time, beating well after each addition. Combine the flour and salt. Add to the butter mixture alternately with the bourbon, mixing well after each addition. Add the vanilla and mix well. Stir in the pecans. Pour into a greased and floured tube pan. Bake at 325 degrees for 1 1/2 hours. Cool in the pan on a wire rack for 15 minutes. Invert onto a serving plate. Drizzle with glaze. Yield: 10 to 12 servings.

GLAZE

2 cups confectioners' sugar
3 tablespoons milk

1 teaspoon vanilla extract

Combine the confectioners' sugar and milk in a bowl and mix until smooth. Stir in the vanilla.

Shirley Welch, Xi Nu Pi
Theodosia, Missouri

*Rosemary Gahr, Laureate Gamma Gamma, Delta, British Columbia, Canada, has an easy recipe for **Blueberry Butter Bundt Cake**. She mixes 1/2 cup vegetable oil, 3 eggs, and 8 ounces softened cream cheese in a bowl. She stirs in 1 package butter cake mix and folds in one drained 15-ounce can blueberries. The batter is poured into a greased and floured bundt pan. It bakes at 325 degrees for 45 minutes.*

BUTTERMILK POUND CAKE

1 cup (2 sticks) butter, softened	1/2 teaspoon salt
1/4 cup shortening	1/4 teaspoon baking powder
3 cups sugar	1 cup buttermilk
5 eggs	1 tablespoon vanilla extract
3 cups all-purpose flour	

Beat the butter, shortening and sugar in a bowl until light and fluffy. Add the eggs 1 at a time, mixing well after each addition. Sift the flour, salt and baking powder together. Add to the batter alternately with the buttermilk, mixing well after each addition. Add the vanilla and mix well. Pour into a greased and floured tube pan. Place in a cold oven. Bake at 325 degrees for 1 1/2 hours or until a wooden pick inserted in the center comes out clean. Cool in the pan for 10 minutes. Invert onto a serving plate. Yield: 16 servings.

Nancy Van Dyke, Xi Alpha Tau
Marietta, Georgia

CHERRY NUT POUND CAKE

1 1/2 cups shortening	3 3/4 cups all-purpose flour
3 cups sugar	3/4 cup milk
6 eggs	1 (5-ounce) jar maraschino cherries, drained and chopped
1/2 teaspoon almond extract	
1/2 teaspoon vanilla extract	Coconut Pecan Frosting

Beat the shortening and sugar in a bowl for 15 minutes. Add the eggs 1 at a time, mixing well after each addition. Add the almond extract and vanilla and mix well. Add the flour and milk alternately, mixing well after each addition. Fold in the cherries. Pour into a greased and floured tube pan. Place in a cold oven. Bake at 275 degrees for 2 hours and 10 minutes or until a wooden pick inserted in the center comes out clean. Cool in the pan for 10 minutes. Invert onto a serving plate. Spread the Coconut Pecan Frosting on the cooled cake. Yield: 16 servings.

COCONUT PECAN FROSTING

8 ounces cream cheese, softened	1 cup shredded coconut
1 (1-pound) package confectioners' sugar	1 cup toasted pecans
1 teaspoon vanilla extract	1 (5-ounce) jar maraschino cherries, drained and chopped
1 teaspoon almond extract	

Beat the cream cheese and confectioners' sugar in a bowl until light and fluffy. Add the vanilla and almond extract and mix well. Stir in the coconut, pecans and cherries.

Carolyn Waters, Xi Psi
Crestview, Florida

CHOCOLATE POUND CAKE

3 cups all-purpose flour	5 eggs
3/4 cup baking cocoa	1 teaspoon vanilla extract
1/2 teaspoon baking powder	1 teaspoon almond extract
1 cup (2 sticks) butter, softened	1 1/4 cups milk
3/4 cup shortening	Glaze
3 cups sugar	

Combine the flour, baking cocoa and baking powder. Beat the butter, shortening and sugar in a bowl until light and fluffy. Add the eggs and mix well. Add the vanilla and almond extract and mix well. Add the dry ingredients alternately with the milk, mixing well after each addition. Pour into a greased and floured bundt pan. Bake at 325 degrees for 1 1/3 hours or until a wooden pick inserted in the center comes out clean. Cool in the pan for 10 minutes. Invert onto a serving plate. Drizzle with the Glaze. Yield: 12 servings.

GLAZE

1/3 cup baking cocoa	Hot water
1 1/2 cups confectioners' sugar	1 teaspoon vanilla extract (optional)
3 tablespoons butter, melted	1 teaspoon almond extract (optional)

Sift the baking cocoa and confectioners' sugar into a bowl. Add the butter and enough water to make a glaze and mix until smooth. Add the vanilla and almond extract and mix well.

Norma Borgmann, Preceptor Delta
Centralia, Illinois

CHOCOLATE CHIP POUND CAKE

1 (2-layer) package butter cake mix	1/4 cup water
3/4 cup vegetable oil	1 cup sour cream
3 eggs	Dash of vanilla extract
1 (3-ounce) box chocolate instant pudding mix	1 cup (6 ounces) chocolate chips

Combine the cake mix, oil and eggs in a bowl and mix well. Add the pudding mix alternately with the water, mixing well after each addition. Add the sour cream and vanilla and mix well. Stir in the chocolate chips. Pour into a greased and floured tube pan. Bake at 350 degrees for 1 hour. Cool in the pan for 10 minutes. Invert onto a serving plate. Yield: 12 servings.

Karen Williams, Xi Gamma Sigma
Van Buren, Arkansas

CREAM CHEESE POUND CAKE

1 cup (2 sticks) butter,
  softened
1/2 cup shortening
3 cups sugar
8 ounces cream cheese,
  softened

3 cups cake flour, sifted
6 eggs
1 teaspoon vanilla
  extract

Beat the butter, shortening and sugar in a bowl until light and fluffy. Add the cream cheese and mix well. Add the flour gradually, mixing well after each addition. Beat in the eggs 1 at a time. Add the vanilla and mix well. Pour into a greased and floured tube pan. Bake at 325 degrees for 80 to 85 minutes or until a wooden pick inserted in the center comes out clean. Cool in the pan for 30 minutes. Invert onto a serving plate. Yield: 12 servings.

Paula Slade, Preceptor Chi
Tallahassee, Florida

CRUNCH POUND CAKE

2 cups all-purpose flour
2 cups sugar
1 cup shortening
6 eggs

1 teaspoon vanilla
  extract
1 teaspoon lemon
  extract

Sift the flour and sugar into a large bowl. Cut in the shortening until crumbly. Add the eggs 1 at a time, mixing well after each addition. Add the vanilla and lemon extract and mix for 15 minutes. Pour into a greased and floured tube pan. Bake at 300 degrees for 60 to 70 minutes or until the cake tests done. Cool in the pan for 10 minutes. Invert onto a serving plate. Yield: 16 servings.

Dari Trout, Rho Alpha
Winfield, Kansas

FIVE-FLAVOR POUND CAKE

1 cup (2 sticks) butter or
  margarine, softened
1/2 cup shortening
3 cups sugar
5 eggs, beaten
3 cups all-purpose flour
1/2 teaspoon baking
  powder
1 cup milk

1 teaspoon each rum
  extract, lemon
  extract, almond
  extract, coconut
  flavoring, butter
  flavoring and
  vanilla extract
Glaze

Beat the butter, shortening and sugar in a bowl until light and fluffy. Add the eggs and mix well. Combine the flour and baking powder. Add to the butter mixture alternately with the milk, mixing well after each addition. Stir in the rum extract, lemon extract, almond extract, coconut flavoring, butter flavoring and vanilla. Spoon into a greased and floured tube pan or a 12-cup bundt pan. Bake at 325 degrees for 1 1/2 hours or until the cake tests done. Drizzle with half the Glaze. Cool in the pan for 10 minutes. Invert onto a serving plate. Drizzle with the remaining Glaze. Freezes well. Yield: 12 servings.

GLAZE

1 cup sugar
1/2 cup water
1 teaspoon vanilla
  extract
1 teaspoon butter
  flavoring
1 teaspoon rum extract

1 teaspoon lemon
  extract
1 teaspoon almond
  extract
1 teaspoon coconut
  flavoring

Combine the sugar, water and flavorings in a saucepan. Bring to a boil over medium heat, stirring occasionally.

Tammy Huckaby, Xi Zeta Lambda
Fort Stockton, Texas

LEMON POUND CAKE

1 1/2 cups sifted
  all-purpose flour
1 teaspoon baking
  powder
3/4 teaspoon salt
1/2 cup (1 stick) unsalted
  butter, melted
1 cup sugar

2 eggs
1/2 cup milk
1/4 cup lemon extract
Grated zest of 2 lemons
1/2 cup almonds, ground
1/3 cup plus 2 tablespoons
  sugar
1/3 cup fresh lemon juice

Sift the flour, baking powder and salt together. Combine the butter and 1 cup sugar in a bowl and mix well. Add the eggs 1 at a time, mixing well after each addition. Add the dry ingredients alternately with the milk, beating constantly on low speed. Add the lemon extract and mix well. Stir in the lemon zest and almonds. Pour into a greased and floured 4×8-inch aluminum loaf pan. Bake at 350 degrees for 65 to 75 minutes or until a wooden pick inserted in the center comes out clean and the top appears cracked. Cool for 2 to 3 minutes. Combine 1/3 cup plus 2 tablespoons sugar and the lemon juice in a saucepan. Cook over low heat until smooth, stirring often. Brush over the warm cake. Cool completely in the pan on a wire rack. Invert onto a serving plate. Freezes well. Yield: 12 to 15 servings.

Jean Sebert, Laureate Alpha Upsilon
Tucson, Arizona

LEMON BLUEBERRY POUND CAKE

1 (2-layer) package yellow cake mix	3 large egg whites
1 cup water	1 large egg
1/3 cup lemon juice	1 cup blueberries
1 teaspoon vanilla extract	1 cup sifted confectioners' sugar
8 ounces cream cheese, softened	4 teaspoons lemon juice

Combine the cake mix, water, 1/3 cup lemon juice, the vanilla, cream cheese, egg whites and egg in a bowl and mix well. Beat at medium speed for 2 minutes. Fold in the blueberries. Pour into a greased and floured 12-cup bundt pan. Bake at 350 degrees for 50 minutes or until a wooden pick inserted in the center comes out clean. Cool in the pan for 10 minutes. Remove to a wire rack to cool completely. Combine the confectioners' sugar and 4 teaspoons lemon juice in a bowl and mix until smooth. Drizzle over the cooled cake. Yield: 16 servings.

Linda Duncan, Preceptor Delta Zeta
Ellinwood, Kansas

KENTUCKY POUND CAKE

1 (20-ounce) can crushed pineapple	2 teaspoons cinnamon
2 1/2 cups self-rising flour	2 teaspoons vanilla extract
1 1/2 cups vegetable oil	1 cup pecans
2 cups granulated sugar	1 cup confectioners' sugar
4 eggs	

Drain the pineapple and reserve the juice. Combine the flour, oil, granulated sugar and eggs in a bowl and mix well. Add the cinnamon and vanilla and mix well. Stir in the pineapple and pecans. Pour into a greased and floured tube pan. Bake at 350 degrees for 1 hour. Cool in the pan for 10 minutes. Invert onto a serving plate. Combine the reserved pineapple juice and confectioners' sugar in a bowl and mix until smooth. Drizzle the glaze over the warm cake. Yield: 12 servings.

Maria Kuhn, Kappa Chi
Woodstock, Georgia

LEMON BUTTERMILK POUND CAKE

1 1/2 cups (3 sticks) butter, softened	1/2 teaspoon baking soda
2 1/2 cups granulated sugar	1 cup buttermilk
4 eggs	1 teaspoon lemon extract
3 1/2 cups cake flour	1/2 cup confectioners' sugar
1/2 teaspoon salt	Juice of 2 lemons

Beat the butter and granulated sugar in a bowl until light and fluffy. Add the eggs 1 at a time, mixing well after each addition. Combine the cake flour, salt and baking soda. Add to the butter mixture alternately with the buttermilk, mixing well after each addition. Add the lemon extract and mix well. Pour into a greased and floured tube pan. Bake at 325 degrees for 1 1/4 hours. Cool in the pan for 10 minutes. Invert onto a serving plate. Combine the confectioners' sugar and lemon juice in a bowl and mix until smooth. Drizzle over the cake. Yield: 12 servings.

Martha Lavallet, Delta Kappa
Daphne, Alabama

LEMON CURD POUND CAKE

1 (2-layer) package yellow cake mix	Grated zest of 1 lemon
1 (11-ounce) jar lemon curd	Juice of 1 lemon
1 cup walnuts, chopped	1 cup confectioners' sugar

Prepare the cake mix using the package instructions, subtracting 1/4 cup water. Stir the lemon curd and walnuts into the batter. Pour into a greased and floured bundt pan. Bake at 350 degrees for 45 to 50 minutes or until the cake tests done. Cool in the pan on a wire rack for 25 minutes. Invert onto a serving plate. Combine the lemon zest, lemon juice and confectioners' sugar in a bowl and mix until smooth. Drizzle over the cake. Yield: 10 to 12 servings.

Jo Rigassio, Eta Nu
Englewood, Florida

LEMON POUND CAKE

1 cup (2 sticks) butter, softened	1 teaspoon lemon extract
3 cups sugar	3 cups all-purpose flour
6 eggs	1/2 teaspoon baking soda
5 tablespoons lemon juice	1/4 teaspoon salt
1 tablespoon grated lemon zest	1 1/4 cups sour cream
	Glaze

Beat the butter and sugar in a bowl until light and fluffy. Add the eggs 1 at a time, mixing well after each addition. Add the lemon juice, lemon zest and lemon extract and mix well. Combine the flour, baking soda and salt. Add to the butter mixture alternately with the sour cream, mixing well after each addition. Pour into a greased and floured tube pan. Bake at 350 degrees for 55 to 60 minutes or until a wooden pick inserted in the center comes out clean. Cool in the pan for 10 minutes. Remove to a wire rack to cool completely. Drizzle the Glaze over the cake. Store in the refrigerator. Yield: 12 to 15 servings.

GLAZE

1/4 cup sour cream
2 tablespoons butter,
softened
2 1/2 cups confectioners'
sugar

3 tablespoons lemon
juice
2 teaspoons grated
lemon zest

Combine the sour cream and butter in a bowl and mix well. Add the confectioners' sugar gradually, mixing well after each addition. Add the lemon juice and lemon zest and mix well.

Pauline Hardman, Alpha Epsilon Master
Ackley, Iowa

LOUISIANA POUND CAKE

1 cup (2 sticks) butter,
softened
2 cups sugar
5 eggs
2 cups all-purpose flour
1/4 teaspoon salt

1 teaspoon lemon
extract
1 teaspoon vanilla
extract
Glaze (optional)

Beat the butter and sugar in a bowl until light and fluffy. Add the eggs and mix well. Add the flour and salt and mix well. Add the lemon extract and vanilla and mix well. Pour into a greased and floured tube pan. Bake at 325 degrees for 1 hour. Cool in the pan for 10 minutes. Invert onto a serving plate. Pour the Glaze over the hot cake. Cool completely.
Yield: 12 servings.

GLAZE

1 cup confectioners'
sugar

2 or 3 tablespoons
lemon juice

Combine the confectioners' sugar and lemon juice in a bowl and mix until smooth.

Lizette L. Pryor, Theta Master
Raleigh, North Carolina

POUND CAKE

1 cup (2 sticks)
margarine, softened
2 cups sugar
2 cups all-purpose flour
1/2 teaspoon salt
5 eggs

1 teaspoon vanilla
extract
1/2 teaspoon lemon
extract
1/2 teaspoon almond
extract

Beat the margarine and sugar in a bowl until light and fluffy. Combine the flour and salt. Add to the margarine mixture alternately with the eggs, mixing well after each addition. Add the vanilla, lemon extract and almond extract and mix well. Pour into a

greased and floured tube or bundt pan. Bake at 300 degrees for 1 hour. Cool in the pan for 20 minutes. Invert onto a serving plate. Serve with fruit and whipped cream if desired. Yield: 12 servings.

Arlene Smith, Laureate Zeta Xi
Austin, Texas

TIRAMISU POUND CAKE

1 pound cake
1/2 cup cold strong coffee
3 tablespoons coffee
liqueur
8 ounces cream cheese,
softened

1/3 cup sugar
2 tablespoons chocolate
syrup
2 tablespoons milk
Crushed English toffee

Slice the pound cake horizontally into 3 layers. Fit the layers in a greased 9×13-inch cake pan. Pierce the cake with a fork. Combine the coffee and 2 tablespoons of the coffee liqueur in a bowl and mix well. Drizzle over the cake. Beat the cream cheese and sugar in a bowl until light and fluffy. Add the chocolate syrup, the remaining 1 tablespoon liqueur and the milk and mix well. Spread over the cake. Chill, covered, for up to 24 hours. Sprinkle with the toffee just before serving. Yield: 12 servings.

Joyce Boor, Theta Master
Great Bend, Kansas

WHISKEY POUND CAKE

2 cups (4 sticks) butter,
softened
2 cups sugar
8 egg yolks, beaten
1/3 cup whiskey
3 cups all-purpose flour,
sifted

4 teaspoons vanilla
extract
8 egg whites
1 cup sugar
1/2 cup chopped pecans
or walnuts

Beat the butter and 2 cups sugar in a bowl until light and fluffy. Add the egg yolks and mix well. Add the whiskey and mix well. Add the flour and vanilla and mix well. Beat the egg whites at low speed in a mixing bowl until foamy. Add 1 cup sugar gradually, beating constantly until stiff peaks form. Fold the egg whites into the batter. Stir in the pecans. Pour into a greased and floured tube pan. Bake at 350 degrees for 1 1/4 to 1 1/2 hours or until the cake tests done. Cool in the pan for 10 minutes. Invert onto a serving plate. Yield: 12 servings.

Grace Powers, Laureate Beta Tau
Elwood, Indiana

PUMPKIN CAKE

2 (15-ounce) cans
  pumpkin
1 (12-ounce) can
  evaporated milk
1 cup sugar
3 eggs
1 teaspoon vanilla
  extract

1 teaspoon cinnamon
1 (2-layer) package
  yellow cake mix
1 cup (2 sticks) butter,
  melted
1½ cups chopped pecans
Cream Cheese Frosting

Line a 9×13-inch cake pan with waxed paper and coat with nonstick cooking spray. Combine the pumpkin, evaporated milk and sugar in a bowl and mix well. Add the eggs, vanilla, cinnamon and cake mix and mix well. Pour into the prepared pan. Drizzle with the butter. Sprinkle with pecans. Bake at 350 degrees for 1 hour or until golden brown. Cool completely in the pan on a wire rack. Invert on a serving plate. Remove the waxed paper. Spread the Cream Cheese Frosting over the cooled cake. Store in the refrigerator. Yield: 18 servings.

CREAM CHEESE FROSTING

8 ounces cream cheese,
  softened
1½ cups confectioners'
  sugar

1 teaspoon vanilla
  extract
12 ounces whipped
  topping

Beat the cream cheese and confectioners' sugar in a bowl until light and fluffy. Add the vanilla and mix well. Fold in the whipped topping.

Anne Handschke, Laureate Chi
Nekoosa, Wisconsin

PUMPKIN CREAM CHEESE CAKE

We have this dessert after wrapping Christmas gifts for our town's needy families.

1 (2-layer) package spice
  cake mix
1 (15-ounce) can
  pumpkin
8 ounces cream cheese,
  softened

3 eggs
⅓ cup orange juice
1 teaspoon cinnamon
¼ cup vegetable oil
¼ cup packed brown
  sugar

Combine the cake mix, pumpkin, cream cheese, eggs and orange juice in a bowl and mix well. Add the cinnamon, oil and brown sugar and mix well. Pour into a greased and floured bundt pan. Bake at 350 degrees for 40 to 45 minutes or until a wooden pick inserted in the center comes out clean. Cool in the pan for 10 minutes. Remove to a wire rack to cool completely. Yield: 24 servings.

Jean Jones, Chi Omega
Buckner, Missouri

PUMPKIN DUMP CAKE

1 (29-ounce) can
  pumpkin
1 (12-ounce) can
  evaporated milk
3 eggs
1 cup sugar
1 teaspoon salt
3 teaspoons pumpkin
  pie spice

1 (2-layer) package
  yellow cake mix
1 cup chopped pecans or
  walnuts
¾ cup (1½ sticks)
  margarine, melted

Combine the pumpkin, evaporated milk, eggs, sugar, salt and pumpkin pie spice in a large bowl and mix well. Pour into a greased and floured 9×13-inch cake pan. Sprinkle with the cake mix and pecans. Drizzle with margarine. Bake at 350 degrees for 1 hour. Cool completely in the pan. Serve with whipped cream if desired. Yield: 12 servings.

Helen Caldwell, Laureate Theta Zeta
Idyllwild, California

❖ PRALINE PUMPKIN CAKE

¾ cup packed brown
  sugar
⅓ cup butter
3 tablespoons heavy
  cream
¾ cup chopped pecans
2 cups all-purpose flour
2 teaspoons pumpkin
  pie spice
2 teaspoons baking
  powder
1 teaspoon baking soda
1 teaspoon salt

4 eggs
1⅔ cups granulated
  sugar
1 cup vegetable oil
2 cups canned pumpkin
¼ teaspoon vanilla
  extract
1¾ cups heavy
  whipping cream
¼ cup confectioners'
  sugar
¼ teaspoon vanilla
  extract

Combine the brown sugar, butter and 3 tablespoons cream in a saucepan. Cook over low heat until the brown sugar dissolves, stirring constantly. Divide between 2 greased 9-inch cake pans and sprinkle with the pecans. Mix the flour, pumpkin pie spice, baking powder, baking soda and salt. Beat the eggs, granulated sugar and oil in a bowl. Beat in the pumpkin and ¼ teaspoon vanilla. Add the dry ingredients and beat just until mixed. Spoon over the praline mixture in the cake pans. Bake at 350 degrees for 30 to 35 minutes or until the cake tests done. Cool in the pans for 5 minutes. Remove to a wire rack to cool completely. Whip 1¾ cups cream in a bowl until soft peaks form. Add the confectioners' sugar and ¼ teaspoon vanilla and whip until stiff peaks form. Place 1 cake layer on a serving plate, praline side up. Spread with two-thirds of the whipped cream mixture. Top with the remaining cake layer, praline side up. Dollop the remaining whipped cream mixture over the top. Chill until ready to serve. Yield: 12 to 14 servings.

Sandra Hatala, Sigma Master
Weirton, West Virginia

RAISIN CAKE

2 cups water	1 teaspoon baking soda
2 cups sugar	1/2 teaspoon allspice
2 cups raisins	1 teaspoon cinnamon
1/2 teaspoon salt	1 cup pecans
1/2 cup shortening	1/2 cup grated apple
3 1/4 cups all-purpose flour	(optional)

Combine the water, sugar, raisins, salt and shortening in a 2-quart saucepan. Bring to a boil over medium heat. Boil for 5 minutes, stirring often. Remove from the heat and cool completely. Sift the flour, baking soda, allspice and cinnamon into a large bowl. Add the raisin mixture and mix well. Stir in the pecans and apple. Pour into a greased and floured bundt pan. Cook for 1 hour. Cool in the pan for 10 minutes. Invert onto a serving plate. Yield: 16 servings.

Yuvonne Martin, Preceptor Gamma Mu
Lubbock, Texas

RASPBERRY CAKE

1 cup miniature marshmallows	2 (10-ounce) packages frozen raspberries, thawed and drained
1 (2-layer) package yellow cake mix	1 (3-ounce) package raspberry gelatin

Place the marshmallows in a 9×13-inch cake pan in an even layer. Prepare the cake mix using the package directions. Pour over the marshmallows. Combine the raspberries and gelatin in a bowl and mix well. Spoon over the cake mix. Bake at 350 degrees for 50 minutes. Cool in the pan for 10 minutes. Remove to a wire rack to cool completely. Serve with ice cream or whipped topping if desired.
Yield: 12 servings.

Rosalie Moore, Preceptor Eta Sigma
Crescent City, California

Marion MacDonald, Preceptor Eta, Thompson, Manitoba, Canada, shared her favorite recipe for **Vanilla Frosting**. *She beats 1 cup margarine and 1 cup sugar in a bowl until light and fluffy. She then combines 2 tablespoons all-purpose flour and 1 cup milk in a saucepan and cooks over low heat until it thickens, stirring often. She lets it cool before adding it to the butter mixture with 1 teaspoon vanilla. She beats the frosting until stiff peaks form.*

RASPBERRY YOGURT CAKE

2 cups sifted all-purpose flour	1 cup packed brown sugar
1 teaspoon baking soda	1 egg
1/2 teaspoon baking powder	1 teaspoon vanilla extract
1/4 teaspoon salt	1 cup raspberry yogurt
1/2 cup (1 stick) butter or margarine, softened	

Sift the flour, baking soda, baking powder and salt together. Beat the butter and brown sugar in a bowl until light and fluffy. Beat in the egg and vanilla. Stir in the dry ingredients alternately with the yogurt just until blended. Spoon into a greased 8-cup tube pan. Bake at 350 degrees for 50 minutes or until the cake tests done. Cool in the pan for 10 minutes. Remove to a wire rack to cool completely. Yield: 10 servings.

Milly Stevens, Preceptor Gamma Epsilon
Aurora, Colorado

RHUBARB CAKE

1 (2-layer) package French vanilla cake mix	1 1/2 cups sugar
	1 teaspoon cinnamon
3 cups chopped rhubarb	1 cup heavy whipping cream

Prepare the cake mix using the package directions. Pour into a greased and floured 9×13-inch cake pan. Combine the rhubarb, sugar and cinnamon in a bowl and mix well. Spoon over the cake mix. Pour the cream over the rhubarb layer. Bake at 350 degrees for 1 hour. Cool in the pan for 10 minutes. Remove to a wire rack to cool completely. Yield: 12 servings.

Marlene Lenz, Laureate Alpha Alpha
Merrill, Wisconsin

RHUBARB DUMP CAKE

6 cups chopped rhubarb	1/2 cup (1 stick) butter, melted
1 (3-ounce) package strawberry gelatin	1/4 cup water
1 cup sugar	Cinnamon to taste
1 (2-layer) package white or yellow cake mix	1/2 cup chopped nuts

Place the rhubarb in a greased 9×13-inch cake pan in an even layer. Sprinkle with the gelatin and sugar. Sprinkle with the cake mix. Combine the butter and water in a small bowl. Drizzle over the cake mix. Sprinkle with cinnamon and nuts. Bake at 350 degrees for 1 hour or until bubbly. Cool completely in the pan on a wire rack. Yield: 12 servings.

Mary Peterson, Xi Alpha Sigma
Burnsville, Minnesota

LUNAR RHUBARB CAKE

1/2 cup (1 stick) butter, softened	1 teaspoon baking soda
1 1/2 cups granulated sugar	1/2 teaspoon salt
1 egg	1 cup buttermilk
1 teaspoon vanilla extract	2 cups chopped rhubarb
2 cups all-purpose flour	1 cup packed brown sugar
	2 teaspoons cinnamon
	1/4 cup (1/2 stick) butter

Beat 1/2 cup butter and the granulated sugar in a bowl until light and fluffy. Add the egg and mix well. Add the vanilla, flour, baking soda, salt and buttermilk and mix well. Stir in the rhubarb. Pour into a greased and floured 9×13-inch cake pan. Combine the brown sugar and cinnamon in a bowl. Cut in 1/4 cup butter until crumbly. Sprinkle over the batter. Bake at 350 degrees for 45 minutes. Cool completely in the pan on a wire rack. Yield: 18 servings.

Madeline Kerr, Laureate Alpha Omicron
Delta, British Columbia, Canada

ITALIAN RUM CAKE

1 cup eggs (about 5 eggs)	1 teaspoon vanilla extract
1 cup sugar	1/2 cup (1 stick) butter, softened
1/2 teaspoon salt	2 tablespoons butter, softened
1 teaspoon vanilla extract	1 cup sifted confectioners' sugar
1 1/4 cups sifted all-purpose flour	1 egg
1/4 cup rum	1 ounce chocolate, melted
3/4 cup sugar	1/2 teaspoon vanilla extract
2 tablespoons cornstarch	
6 egg yolks	
1 1/2 cups milk	

Beat 1 cup eggs in a bowl until thick and pale yellow. Add 1 cup sugar and the salt gradually, mixing well after each addition. Add 1 teaspoon vanilla and mix well. Add the flour 2 tablespoons at a time, mixing well after each addition. Pour into two greased and floured 8-inch cake pans. Bake at 375 degrees for 25 minutes. Cool in the pans for 10 minutes. Remove to a wire rack to cool completely. Slice each layer in half horizontally. Pour the rum over the layers. Combine 3/4 cup sugar and the cornstarch in a saucepan. Add the egg yolks and beat until light and fluffy. Stir in the milk. Cook over medium heat until thickened, stirring constantly. Remove from the heat and stir in 1 teaspoon vanilla. Cool completely. Add 1/2 cup butter and mix well. Spread between the layers of the cake. Beat 2 tablespoons butter and the confectioners' sugar in a bowl until light and fluffy. Add 1 egg and mix well. Add the chocolate and 1/2 teaspoon vanilla and mix well. Spread over the top and side of the cake. Note: If you are concerned about using raw eggs, use eggs pasteurized in their shells, which are sold at some specialty food stores, or use an equivalent amount of pasteurized egg substitute. Yield: 16 servings.

Sylvia Cole, Kappa Master
Knoxville, Iowa

RUM CAKE

1 cup chopped pecans or walnuts	4 eggs
1 (2-layer) package yellow cake mix	1/2 cup cold water
1 (3-ounce) package vanilla instant pudding mix	1/2 cup vegetable oil
	1/2 cup dark rum
	Glaze

Sprinkle the pecans in an even layer in a greased and floured bundt pan. Combine the cake mix, pudding mix, eggs, water, oil and rum in a bowl and mix well. Beat at medium speed for 2 minutes. Pour into the prepared pan. Bake at 325 degrees for 1 hour. Pierce the hot cake with a fork. Drizzle with the Glaze. Cool completely in the pan. Yield: 8 to 12 servings.

GLAZE

1/2 cup (1 stick) butter	1 cup sugar
1/4 cup water	1/2 cup dark rum

Melt the butter in a saucepan over low heat. Stir in the water and sugar. Bring to a boil. Boil for 5 minutes, stirring constantly. Remove from the heat and stir in the rum.

Melissa Greco, Xi Alpha Upsilon
Reno, Nevada

SAUSAGE CAKE

This cake is spicy and different. No one will know there is sausage in it.

1 pound bulk pork sausage	3 cups all-purpose flour
1 1/2 cups packed brown sugar	1 teaspoon ginger
1 1/2 cups granulated sugar	1 teaspoon baking powder
2 eggs	1 teaspoon pumpkin pie spice
1 teaspoon baking soda	1 cup raisins
1 cup cold strong coffee	1 cup chopped nuts

Combine the sausage, brown sugar and granulated sugar in a bowl and mix well. Add the eggs and mix well. Combine the baking soda and coffee in a small bowl. Combine the flour, ginger, baking powder and pumpkin pie spice. Add to the sausage

mixture alternately with the coffee, mixing well after each addition. Stir in the raisins and nuts. Pour into a greased and floured tube pan. Bake at 350 degrees for 1½ hours. Cool in the pan for 10 minutes. Invert onto a serving plate. Store in the refrigerator.
Yield: 16 servings.

Joyce Daugherty, Laureate Chi
Yakima, Washington

SNOW CAKE

1 (2-layer) box yellow or white cake mix
8 ounces light cream cheese, softened
1½ cups skim milk
1 small package sugar-free fat-free vanilla instant pudding mix
1 (20-ounce) can crushed pineapple, drained
9 ounces fat-free whipped topping

Prepare and bake the cake mix using the package directions for a 9×13-inch cake pan. Cool in the pan for 10 minutes. Remove to a wire rack to cool completely. Combine the cream cheese, milk and pudding mix in a bowl and mix well. Spread over the cake. Spoon the pineapple over the cake and spread lightly. Top with an even layer of whipped topping. Yield: 12 to 15 servings.

Barbara E. Downs, Laureate Alpha Gamma
Bella Vista, Arkansas

SPICE CAKE

2 cups all-purpose flour
1 cup sugar
1 teaspoon salt
1 teaspoon baking powder
¾ teaspoon baking soda
¾ teaspoon ground cloves
¾ teaspoon cinnamon
⅔ cup shortening
¾ cup packed brown sugar
1 cup buttermilk or sour milk
3 eggs
Frosting

Combine the flour, sugar, salt, baking powder, baking soda, cloves and cinnamon in a large bowl. Add the shortening, brown sugar and buttermilk and mix well. Beat at medium speed for 2 minutes. Add the eggs and beat for 2 minutes. Pour into a greased and floured 9×13-inch cake pan. Bake at 350 degrees for 35 minutes. Cool in the pan for 10 minutes. Remove to a wire rack to cool completely. Spread the Frosting over the cooled cake. Yield: 12 servings.

FROSTING

⅓ cup (⅔ stick) butter, softened
1 (1-pound) package confectioners' sugar
¼ teaspoon salt
¼ cup milk
1 teaspoon vanilla extract

Beat the butter and confectioners' sugar in a bowl until light and fluffy. Add the salt, milk and vanilla and mix well.

Carolyn Ellis, Xi Delta Theta
Bonham, Texas

STRAWBERRY JAM CAKE

⅔ cup buttermilk
1 teaspoon baking soda
2 cups sifted cake flour
1 teaspoon ground cloves
1 teaspoon allspice
1 teaspoon cinnamon
1 teaspoon nutmeg
¼ teaspoon salt
⅔ cup shortening
1½ cups sugar
4 egg yolks
1 cup strawberry jam
4 egg whites, stiffly beaten
Frosting
1 cup chopped pecans

Combine the buttermilk and baking soda in a small bowl. Sift the cake flour, cloves, allspice, cinnamon, nutmeg and salt together. Beat the shortening and sugar in a bowl until light and fluffy. Add the egg yolks and mix well. Add the jam and mix well. Add the dry ingredients alternately with the buttermilk. Fold in the egg whites. Add the vanilla and mix well. Pour into 2 greased and floured 9-inch cake pans. Bake at 325 degrees for 35 to 40 minutes or until the cake tests done. Cool in the pans for 10 minutes. Remove to a wire rack to cool completely. Spread the Frosting between the layers and across the top and side of the cake. Sprinkle with the pecans. Yield: 16 servings.

FROSTING

1 cup sugar
2 heaping tablespoons flour
1 egg, beaten
1 cup milk
2 tablespoons butter
1 teaspoon vanilla extract

Combine the sugar, flour, egg and milk in a saucepan over medium heat. Cook until the sugar dissolves, stirring often. Remove from the heat. Stir in the butter and vanilla until smooth.

Karen Dryden, Xi Zeta Pi
Adair, Oklahoma

*Shellee Higgs, Laureate Kappa, North Battleford, Saskatchewan, Canada, shares her recipe for foolproof **Seven-Minute Frosting**. She beats 2 egg whites in a bowl until stiff peaks form. She combines 1 cup sugar, 6 tablespoons water, and 1 teaspoon vinegar in a saucepan and cooks over medium heat to 234 to 240 degrees on a candy thermometer, soft-ball stage. She adds this mixture gradually to the egg whites, beating constantly, and spreads the mixture over angel food cake.*

STRAWBERRY CAKE

1 (2-layer) package
   white cake mix
4 eggs
1 (3-ounce) package
   strawberry gelatin
1/2 cup water
1 (10-ounce) package
   frozen strawberries,
   thawed

3/4 cup vegetable oil
1/2 cup (1 stick)
   margarine, softened
1 (1-pound) package
   confectioners' sugar
1 teaspoon vanilla
   extract

Grease a 9×13-inch cake pan and line with waxed paper. Combine the cake mix, eggs, gelatin and water in a bowl and mix well. Add half the strawberries and mix for 1 minute. Add the oil and mix for 1 minute. Pour into the prepared pan. Bake at 350 degrees for 40 to 50 minutes or until the cake tests done. Cool in the pan for 10 minutes. Remove to a wire rack to cool completely. Beat the margarine and confectioners' sugar in a mixing bowl until light and fluffy. Add the vanilla and mix well. Stir in the remaining strawberries. Spread the frosting on the cooled cake. Yield: 16 servings.

Willie Mae Coffman, Iota Master
New Braunfels, Texas

STRAWBERRY REFRIGERATOR CAKE

1 (2-layer) package
   strawberry cake mix
2 (10-ounce) packages
   frozen strawberries,
   thawed

1 (3-ounce) package
   vanilla instant
   pudding mix
1 cup milk
2 cups whipped topping

Prepare the cake mix using the package directions. Pour into a greased and floured 9×13-inch cake pan. Bake at 350 degrees for 35 to 40 minutes or until the cake tests done. Pierce the hot cake with a fork. Purée the strawberries in a blender. Spoon over the cake. Prepare the pudding mix using the package directions, using 1 cup milk. Fold in the whipped topping. Spread over the cake. Garnish with strawberries if desired. Chill for 4 hours or longer before serving. Yield: 16 to 20 servings.

Brenda Smith, Preceptor Alpha Mu
Bessemer, Alabama

STRAWBERRY SODA CAKE

1 (2-layer) box yellow
   cake mix
1 (6-ounce) package
   strawberry gelatin
1 1/2 cups boiling water
1 (12-ounce) can
   strawberry soda

1 (3 1/2-ounce) package
   vanilla instant
   pudding mix
1 1/2 cups milk
8 ounces whipped
   topping

Prepare and bake the cake mix using the package directions for a 9×13-inch cake pan. Pierce the cake with a fork. Combine the gelatin and water in a bowl. Stir in the soda. Spoon over the hot cake. Cool completely in the pan. Combine the pudding mix and milk in a bowl and mix well. Stir in the whipped topping. Spread over the cooled cake. Store in the refrigerator. Yield: 12 servings.

Esther Hobson, Chi Master
Lake Havasu, Arizona

❖ TOBELERONE CAKE

1 (2-layer) package
   yellow cake mix
1 (4-ounce) package
   vanilla instant
   pudding mix
4 eggs
1/2 cup vegetable oil
1/2 cup water

1 cup sour cream
1 (4-ounce) Tobelerone
   bar, chopped
3/4 cup chopped walnuts
   or pecans
3/4 cup chocolate chips
3/4 cup shredded coconut

Combine the cake mix, pudding mix, eggs, oil and water in a large bowl and mix well. Add the sour cream and mix well. Combine the Tobelerone, walnuts, chocolate chips and coconut in a bowl and mix well. Reserve a small amount for garnish. Stir the remainder into the batter. Pour into a greased and floured bundt pan. Bake at 350 degrees for 60 to 70 minutes or until the cake tests done. Cool in the pan for 10 minutes. Invert onto a serving plate. Frost if desired. Sprinkle with the reserved chocolate mixture. Yield: 12 servings.

Dianne Harris-Wakeling, Mu Pi
Virgil, Ontario, Canada

TOMATO SOUP CAKE

This spicy cake tastes great with butter frosting with a hint of lemon.

2 cups all-purpose flour
1/2 teaspoon ground
   cloves
1/2 teaspoon mace
1/2 teaspoon nutmeg
1/2 teaspoon baking
   soda
3 teaspoons baking
   powder

1 cup raisins
2 tablespoons
   shortening
1 cup sugar
1 egg, beaten
1 (11-ounce) can tomato
   soup

Combine the flour, cloves, mace, nutmeg, baking soda, baking powder and raisins. Beat the shortening and sugar in a bowl until light and fluffy. Add the egg and mix well. Add the dry ingredients and mix well. Stir in the tomato soup. Pour into a greased and floured 9×13-inch cake pan. Bake at 350 degrees for

1 hour. Cool in the pan for 10 minutes. Remove to a wire rack to cool completely. Yield: 12 servings.

Valerie Herriges, Preceptor Alpha Epsilon
The Dalles, Oregon

TURTLE CAKE

1 (2-layer) package German chocolate cake mix	1 (14-ounce) can sweetened condensed milk
1/2 cup (1 stick) margarine, softened	1 pound caramel candies
1 1/2 cups water	1 cup pecans
1/2 cup vegetable oil	Frosting

Combine the cake mix, margarine, water, oil and half the condensed milk in a bowl and mix well. Pour half the batter into a greased and floured 9×13-inch cake pan. Bake at 350 degrees for 25 minutes. Combine the candies and the remaining condensed milk in a saucepan over low heat. Cook until smooth, stirring often. Spread over the baked layer. Sprinkle with pecans. Cover with the remaining batter. Bake for 25 to 35 minutes or until the cake tests done. Cool in the pan for 10 minutes. Remove to a wire rack to cool completely. Spread the Frosting on the cooled cake. Yield: 24 servings.

FROSTING

1/2 cup (1 stick) margarine, softened	1 (1-pound) package confectioners' sugar
3 tablespoons baking cocoa	1 teaspoon vanilla extract
6 tablespoons evaporated milk	

Combine the margarine, baking cocoa and evaporated milk in a saucepan. Cook over medium heat until smooth, stirring often. Remove from the heat. Add the confectioners' sugar and vanilla and mix well.

Pamela Ann Austin, Preceptor Beta Lambda
Springdale, Arkansas

WAIT CAKE

1 (2-layer) package butter cake mix	12 ounces shredded coconut
2 cups sugar	1 1/2 cups whipped topping
2 cups sour cream	

Prepare and bake the cake mix using the package directions for two 9-inch cake pans. Cool in the pans for 10 minutes. Remove to a wire rack to cool completely. Slice the layers in half horizontally. Combine the sugar, sour cream and coconut in a bowl and mix well. Reserve 1 cup. Spread the remaining sour cream mixture between the layers of the cake. Combine the reserved sour cream mixture and the whipped topping in a large bowl and mix well. Spread over the top and side of the cake. Chill, covered, until just before serving.
Yield: 12 to 14 servings.

Judy Bruning, Psi Eta
Orrick, Missouri

WALDORF CAKE

1 1/2 cups sugar	2 tablespoons baking cocoa
2 eggs	2 ounces red food coloring
2 cups all-purpose flour	
1 teaspoon vanilla extract	1 teaspoon baking soda
1 cup shortening	1 tablespoon vinegar
1 cup buttermilk	Frosting

Combine the sugar, eggs, flour, vanilla, shortening, buttermilk, baking cocoa and food coloring in a bowl and mix well. Beat at medium speed for 2 minutes. Combine the baking soda and vinegar in a small bowl. Fold into the batter. Pour into a greased and floured 9×13-inch cake pan. Bake at 350 degrees for 35 to 50 minutes or until the cake tests done. Cool in the pan for 10 minutes. Remove to a wire rack to cool completely. Frost the cooled cake. Yield: 16 servings.

FROSTING

1 cup milk	1/2 cup shortening
1/4 cup all-purpose flour	1 cup sugar
1/2 cup (1 stick) margarine, softened	

Combine the milk and flour in a saucepan. Bring to a boil over medium heat, whisking constantly. Cool completely. Beat the margarine, shortening and sugar in a bowl until light and fluffy. Add the milk mixture and mix well.

Kathleen S. Bennett, Laureate Epsilon Kappa
Easton, Pennsylvania

---

*Alta Mae Seiler, Alpha Iota Master, Chico, California, prepares a luscious **Fruit Topping for Angel Food Cake**. She drains one 20-ounce can crushed pineapple and one 16-ounce can pitted cherries and places the fruit in a bowl. She adds 1/2 cup port and lets it stand for several hours to overnight. She whips 1 cup heavy whipping cream and 2 tablespoons sugar in a bowl until stiff peaks form, and folds in 1/2 teaspoon rum flavoring, 1/4 cup currant jelly, and the marinated fruit.*

WHITE SHEET CAKE

This cake is best if you make it one day before you plan to eat it.

1 cup (2 sticks) butter, softened	2 eggs, beaten
1 cup water	1 teaspoon almond extract
2 cups all-purpose flour	1 teaspoon salt
2 cups sugar	1 teaspoon baking soda
1/2 cup sour cream	Walnut Frosting

Combine the butter and water in a large heavy saucepan. Bring to a boil over medium heat, stirring occasionally. Remove from the heat. Stir in the flour, sugar, sour cream, eggs, almond extract, salt and baking soda until smooth. Pour into a greased and floured 10×15-inch baking pan. Bake at 375 degrees for 20 to 22 minutes or until golden brown. Cool in the pan for 20 minutes. Remove to a wire rack to cool. Spread the Walnut Frosting over the warm cake. Yield: 16 to 20 servings.

WALNUT FROSTING

1/2 cup (1 stick) butter, softened	1/2 teaspoon almond extract
1/4 cup milk	1 cup chopped walnuts
41/2 cups confectioners' sugar	

Combine the butter and milk in a saucepan. Bring to a boil over medium heat, stirring occasionally. Remove from the heat. Stir in the confectioners' sugar and almond extract until smooth. Stir in the walnuts.

Jane A. Ross, Iota Master
Carrollton, Missouri

WHITE CAKE WITH FUDGE FROSTING

2 cups all-purpose flour	1 cup cold water
1 cup sugar	1 cup Miracle Whip dressing
11/2 teaspoons baking soda	2 teaspoons vanilla extract
4 tablespoons baking cocoa	Fudge Frosting

Combine the flour, sugar, baking soda and baking cocoa in a bowl. Add the water and Miracle Whip and mix until smooth. Stir in the vanilla. Pour into a greased and floured 7×11-inch cake pan. Bake at 350 degrees for 30 to 35 minutes or until the cake tests done. Cool in the pan for 10 minutes. Remove to a wire rack to cool completely. Spread the Fudge Frosting over the cooled cake. Yield: 16 servings.

FUDGE FROSTING

1 cup sugar	1/4 cup milk
1/4 cup baking cocoa	1 teaspoon vanilla extract
1/4 cup butter or margarine	

Combine the sugar, baking cocoa, butter and milk in a saucepan. Bring to a boil over medium heat, stirring often. Boil for 11/2 minutes, stirring constantly. Remove from the heat and cool completely. Stir in the vanilla. Beat until thickened.

Cindy Layman, Theta Psi
Grove, Oklahoma

WHITE CHOCOLATE CAKE

4 ounces white chocolate	21/2 cups all-purpose flour
1/2 cup boiling water	1 teaspoon baking soda
1 cup (2 sticks) butter, softened	1 teaspoon salt
1 cup sugar	1 cup buttermilk
4 egg yolks	4 egg whites, stiffly beaten
1 teaspoon vanilla extract	1 cup chopped pecans
	1 cup flaked coconut
	Coconut Pecan Frosting

Combine the white chocolate and water in a small bowl and stir until smooth. Beat the butter and sugar in a large bowl until light and fluffy. Add the egg yolks 1 at a time, mixing well after each addition. Add the white chocolate mixture and vanilla and mix well. Sift the flour, baking soda and salt together. Add to the butter mixture alternately with the buttermilk, mixing well after each addition. Fold in the egg whites. Stir in the pecans and coconut. Spoon into a greased and floured 9×13-inch cake pan. Bake at 350 degrees for 25 to 30 minutes or until the cake tests done. Cool in the pan for 10 minutes. Remove to a wire rack to cool completely. Spread the Coconut Pecan Frosting on the cooled cake. Yield: 12 servings.

COCONUT PECAN FROSTING

1 cup evaporated milk	1 teaspoon vanilla extract
1 cup sugar	1 cup chopped pecans
1/4 cup (1/2 stick) butter	1 cup flaked coconut
3 egg yolks	

Combine the evaporated milk, sugar and butter in a saucepan. Bring to a boil over low heat, stirring often. Stir in the egg yolks and vanilla. Cook for 15 minutes, stirring constantly. Remove from the heat. Stir in the pecans and coconut. Beat until thickened.

Janet Singleton, Beta Rho Preceptor
Salem, Indiana

WINE CAKE

1 (2-layer) package yellow cake mix	³/4 cup cream sherry
1 (6-ounce) box vanilla instant pudding mix	³/4 cup vegetable oil
	1 teaspoon nutmeg
4 eggs	Confectioners' sugar for dusting

Combine the cake mix, pudding mix, eggs, sherry, oil and nutmeg in a large bowl and mix well. Pour into a greased and floured tube pan or bundt pan. Bake at 350 degrees for 45 minutes. Cool in the pan for 10 minutes. Invert onto a serving plate. Dust with confectioners' sugar. Yield: 12 servings.

Henrietta Bowen, Laureate Gamma Iota
Springfield, Missouri

YOGURT CAKE

1 (2-layer) package white cake mix	8 ounces whipped topping
8 ounces yogurt (any flavor)	8 ounces yogurt (any flavor)

Prepare the cake mix using the package directions. Stir 8 ounces yogurt into the batter. Pour into a greased and floured 9×13-inch cake pan. Bake at 350 degrees for 30 to 35 minutes or until golden brown. Cool in the pan for 10 minutes. Remove to a wire rack to cool completely. Chill, covered, for 4 hours. Combine the whipped topping and 8 ounces yogurt in a bowl and mix well. Spread on the chilled cake just before serving. Yield: 12 servings.

Wendy Denham, Eta Theta
Tigard, Oregon

ZUCCHINI COCONUT CAKE

3 cups all-purpose flour	1¹/4 cups vegetable oil
2¹/2 teaspoons baking soda	3 teaspoons vanilla extract
¹/4 teaspoon baking powder	1 (11-ounce) can mandarin oranges
1 teaspoon salt	3 eggs
2 cups sugar	2 cups shredded zucchini
1 cup shredded coconut	Cream Cheese Frosting
3 teaspoons cinnamon	¹/2 cup chopped nuts

Combine the flour, baking soda, baking powder, salt, sugar, coconut and cinnamon in a large bowl. Add the oil, vanilla, oranges and eggs and mix well. Stir in the zucchini. Beat for 3 minutes at high speed. Pour into a greased and floured 9×13-inch cake pan. Bake at 350 degrees for 45 to 50 minutes or until a wooden pick inserted in the center comes out clean. Cool in the pan for 10 minutes. Remove to a wire rack to cool completely. Spread the Cream Cheese Frosting over the cooled cake. Sprinkle with the nuts.
Yield: 36 servings.

CREAM CHEESE FROSTING

8 ounces cream cheese, softened	1 teaspoon vanilla extract
2 tablespoons butter, melted	3 cups confectioners' sugar

Beat the cream cheese, butter and vanilla in a bowl until smooth. Add the confectioners' sugar and beat until light and fluffy.

Judy Latta, Delta Eta
Elliot Lake, Ontario, Canada

❖ APPLE CRISP CHEESECAKE

2 cups graham cracker crumbs	1 cup packed brown sugar
1 cup oats	³/4 cup sour cream
¹/3 cup packed brown sugar	1³/4 teaspoons cinnamon
²/3 cup butter or margarine, melted	¹/2 teaspoon nutmeg
	4 eggs
24 ounces cream cheese, softened	2 small apples, peeled and sliced
	Topping

Combine the graham cracker crumbs, oats, ¹/3 cup brown sugar and butter in a bowl and mix well. Press onto the bottom and 1¹/2 inches up the side of a 10-inch springform pan. Chill. Beat the cream cheese, 1 cup brown sugar, sour cream, cinnamon and nutmeg in a large bowl at medium speed for 2 minutes or until smooth. Beat in the eggs 1 at a time. Pour over the prepared crust. Arrange the apple slices over the filling. Sprinkle the Topping evenly over the apples. Bake at 325 degrees for 65 to 75 minutes or until the center is almost set. Remove to a wire rack. Loosen the edge of the cake from the pan with a sharp knife. Cool completely. Chill overnight. Remove the side of the pan. This cheesecake freezes well. Yield: 16 servings.

TOPPING

¹/4 cup rolled oats	1 teaspoon cinnamon
¹/4 cup all-purpose flour	2 tablespoons butter or margarine, softened
¹/4 cup packed brown sugar	

Combine the oats, flour, brown sugar, cinnamon and butter in a bowl and mix until crumbly.

Ellen Osachoff, Laureate Alpha Phi
Delta, British Columbia, Canada

APPLE PECAN CHEESECAKE

16 ounces cream cheese, softened	1/3 cup sugar
1/3 cup sugar	1/2 teaspoon cinnamon
1/2 teaspoon vanilla extract	4 cups thinly sliced peeled Golden Delicious apples
2 eggs	1/2 cup chopped pecans
1 (9-inch) graham cracker pie shell	

Beat the cream cheese, 1/3 cup sugar and the vanilla in a large bowl at medium speed for 2 minutes or until smooth. Beat in the eggs 1 at a time. Pour into the pie shell. Combine 1/3 cup sugar and the cinnamon in a large bowl and mix well. Add the apples and toss gently to coat. Spoon over the filling. Sprinkle with the pecans. Bake at 350 degrees for 1 hour and 10 minutes or until the center is set. Remove to a wire rack to cool completely. Chill. Yield: 8 servings.

Debra Dreiling, Rho Sigma
Gardner, Kansas

BABY CHEESECAKES

Let the kids help make these mini cheesecakes—the portion size is perfect.

16 ounces cream cheese, softened	2 eggs
1 cup sugar	12 vanilla wafers
1 teaspoon vanilla extract	1 (21-ounce) can pie filling (any flavor)

Beat the cream cheese, sugar and vanilla in a large bowl for 2 minutes or until smooth. Beat in the eggs 1 at a time. Place paper liners in 12 muffin cups. Place a vanilla wafer, flat side down, in each cup. Spoon the cream cheese mixture over the wafers. Bake at 350 degrees for 20 minutes or until the centers are almost set. Remove to a wire rack and cool completely. Chill for 4 hours to overnight. Top with the pie filling before serving. Yield: 12 servings.

Melissa Burgin, Xi Gamma Beta
Vidor, Texas

BROWNIE CHEESECAKE SQUARES

1 (20-ounce) package brownie mix	1 teaspoon vanilla extract
32 ounces cream cheese, softened	3 eggs
1 cup sugar	2 ounces semisweet chocolate, melted and cooled
1/2 cup sour cream	

Line a 9×13-inch baking pan with heavy foil, extending the foil 2 inches over the sides of the pan. Coat with nonstick cooking spray. Prepare the brownie mix using the package directions and pour into the prepared pan. Bake at 350 degrees for 15 minutes or until the top is shiny and the center is almost set. Beat the cream cheese, sugar, sour cream and vanilla in a large bowl at medium speed for 3 minutes or until smooth. Beat in the eggs 1 at a time. Pour over the brownie layer. Bake for 40 minutes or until the center is almost set. Remove to a wire rack. Loosen the edge of the cake from the foil. Cool completely. Chill for 4 hours to overnight. Let stand at room temperature for 30 minutes. Lift the cheesecake from the pan, using the foil handles. Drizzle with the chocolate and let stand until the chocolate sets. Cut into squares. Yield: 16 servings.

Carol A. Reed, Laureate Alpha Omega
San Diego, California

BROWNIE CRUST CHEESECAKE

1/2 cup (1 stick) butter	1/2 teaspoon salt
4 ounces unsweetened chocolate	24 ounces cream cheese, softened
1 1/2 cups sugar	3/4 cup sugar
2 eggs	1/2 cup sour cream
1/4 cup milk	1 teaspoon vanilla extract
1 teaspoon vanilla extract	3 eggs
1 cup all-purpose flour	

Melt the butter and chocolate in a large heavy saucepan over low heat, stirring constantly. Cool. Add 1 1/2 cups sugar and mix well. Beat in 2 eggs 1 at a time. Stir in the milk and 1 teaspoon vanilla. Combine the flour and salt. Stir into the chocolate mixture just until blended. Spread in a greased and floured 9-inch springform pan. Bake at 325 degrees for 25 minutes. Beat the cream cheese, 3/4 cup sugar, sour cream and 1 teaspoon vanilla in a large bowl at medium speed for 2 minutes or until smooth. Beat in 3 eggs 1 at a time. Pour over the crust. Bake for 55 to 60 minutes or until the center is almost set. Remove to a wire rack. Loosen the edge of the cake from the pan with a knife. Cool completely. Chill for 4 hours to overnight. Remove the side of the pan. Let stand at room temperature for 30 minutes before serving. Garnish with ice cream topping if desired. Yield: 12 to 16 servings.

Janice K. Jacobson, Lambda Sigma
Centralia, Missouri

2222222222222

CARAMEL APPLE CHEESECAKE

1 (21-ounce) can apple pie filling
1 (9-inch) graham cracker pie shell
16 ounces cream cheese, softened
1/2 cup sugar
1/4 teaspoon vanilla extract
2 eggs
1/4 cup caramel topping
12 pecan halves
2 tablespoons chopped pecans

Reserve 3/4 cup of the pie filling. Spoon the remainder into the pie shell. Beat the cream cheese, sugar and vanilla in a large bowl until smooth. Beat in the eggs 1 at a time. Pour over the pie filling. Bake at 350 degrees for 30 to 35 minutes or until the center is set. Remove to a wire rack and cool to room temperature. Combine the caramel topping and reserved pie filling in a saucepan and warm over medium-low heat for 1 minute or until spreadable. Spread evenly on the cheesecake. Top with the pecan halves and sprinkle with chopped pecans. Chill for 3 hours or longer. Yield: 8 servings.

Jean Poynor, Xi Alpha Nu
Eureka Springs, Arkansas

CHERRY CHEESECAKE

8 ounces cream cheese, softened
1/3 cup sugar
1 cup sour cream
2 teaspoons almond extract
8 ounces whipped topping
1 (9-inch) graham cracker pie shell
1 (21-ounce) can cherry pie filling

Beat the cream cheese, sugar, sour cream and almond extract in a large bowl until smooth. Fold in the whipped topping. Pour into the pie shell. Chill, covered, for 4 hours to overnight. Top with the cherry pie filling just before serving. Yield: 6 to 8 servings.

Joyce Oudendyk, Xi Gamma Phi
Wyoming, Michigan

MARASCHINO CHERRY CHEESECAKE

1 1/3 cups graham cracker crumbs
1/2 cup sugar
1 cup (2 sticks) butter, melted
1 (16-ounce) container soft cream cheese
1/2 cup sugar
3 egg yolks, beaten
1 teaspoon vanilla extract
1/4 teaspoon salt
6 ounces maraschino cherries, drained and chopped
3 egg whites, at room temperature

Mix the graham cracker crumbs, 1/2 cup sugar and the butter in a bowl. Reserve 1/3 cup of the crumbs. Press the remainder onto the bottom of a 9×9-inch baking pan. Beat the cream cheese and 1/2 cup sugar

in a large bowl until smooth. Add the egg yolks, vanilla and salt and mix well. Fold in the cherries. Beat the egg whites in a small bowl until stiff peaks form. Fold into the cream cheese mixture. Pour over the crust. Top with the reserved crumbs. Bake at 350 degrees for 25 to 35 minutes or until set. Remove to a wire rack and cool completely. Chill for 2 hours or longer. Yield: 12 servings.

E. Davine Hébert, Laureate Beta Rho
New Westminster, British Columbia, Canada

CHOCOLATE AMARETTO CHEESECAKE

1 1/4 cups finely crushed chocolate wafer cookies
2 tablespoons sugar
1/4 cup (1/2 stick) butter, melted
16 ounces cream cheese, softened
1/2 cup sugar
2 eggs
2/3 cup sour cream
1 cup (6 ounces) semisweet chocolate chips, melted and cooled
1/3 cup amaretto
1 teaspoon vanilla extract
1/2 teaspoon almond extract

Combine the crushed cookies, 2 tablespoons sugar and the butter in a bowl and mix well. Press onto the bottom and halfway up the side of a 7- or 8-inch springform pan. Chill. Beat the cream cheese and 1/2 cup sugar in a large bowl until smooth. Beat in the eggs 1 at a time. Add the sour cream, chocolate, amaretto, vanilla and almond extract and mix well. Pour over the crust. Bake at 300 degrees for 1 hour or until set. Turn off the oven and let the cheesecake stand in the oven for 1 hour. Remove to a wire rack. Loosen the edge of the cake from the pan with a sharp knife. Cool completely. Chill for at least 24 hours. Remove the side of the pan. Serve with whipped cream if desired. Yield: 12 to 16 servings.

Theresa (Terry) Flesher, Laureate Alpha Alpha
Kingston, Ontario, Canada

*Patti Confer, Preceptor Alpha Upsilon, Tamaqua, Pennsylvania, makes a delicious **Bailey's Irish Cream Cake**. She combines 1 package devil's food cake mix, one 4-ounce package vanilla instant pudding mix, 1 cup sour cream, 4 eggs, and 1 cup Bailey's Irish cream in a bowl and mixes well. She folds in 1 cup chocolate chips and pours the batter into a greased and floured bundt pan. The cake bakes at 350 degrees for 45 minutes. She cools the cake in the pan for 15 minutes, then inverts it onto a serving plate. She mixes 1 container chocolate frosting and 3 tablespoons Bailey's Irish cream in a bowl and spreads it over the top and side of the cake.*

NO-BAKE CHOCOLATE AMARETTO SWIRL CHEESECAKE

20 to 30 chocolate wafer cookies
1 envelope unflavored gelatin
1/2 cup amaretto
16 ounces cream cheese, softened
3/4 cup packed brown sugar
1 cup heavy whipping cream, whipped
6 ounces semi-sweet chocolate, melted and cooled

Line the bottom and side of a 9- or 10-inch spring-form pan with the cookies; chill. Sprinkle the gelatin over the amaretto in a small saucepan and let stand for 5 minutes. Beat the cream cheese and the brown sugar in a large bowl until smooth. Warm the gelatin mixture over low heat for 1 minute or until the gelatin dissolves, stirring constantly. Add to the cream cheese mixture and mix well. Fold in the whipped cream. Reserve 1 cup of the cream cheese mixture. Fold the chocolate into the remaining cream cheese mixture. Reserve 1/2 cup of the chocolate mixture. Pour the remaining chocolate mixture into the pan and spread evenly. Spread the reserved 1 cup plain cream cheese mixture evenly over the chocolate layer. Top with the reserved 1/2 cup chocolate mixture and marbleize with a spatula. Chill for 4 hours to overnight. Remove the side of the pan.
Yield: 12 to 16 servings.

Yvonne Evans, Xi Eta
Burton, New Brunswick, Canada

CARAMEL-TOPPED CHOCOLATE CHEESECAKE

1 1/3 cups finely crushed pecan shortbread cookies
1/4 cup (1/2 stick) butter or margarine, melted
24 ounces cream cheese, softened
3/4 cup granulated sugar
1/4 cup packed brown sugar
1 teaspoon vanilla extract
1/4 cup milk
2 tablespoons all-purpose flour
2 eggs
1 egg yolk
1/2 cup semisweet chocolate chips
1 1/2 teaspoons shortening
1/2 cup coarsely chopped pecans, toasted
2 tablespoons caramel topping

Combine the crushed cookies and butter in a bowl and mix well. Press onto the bottom of a greased 9-inch springform pan. Beat the cream cheese, granulated sugar, brown sugar and vanilla in a large bowl until smooth. Beat in the milk and flour until blended. Beat in the eggs and egg yolk. Pour over the crust. Place the pan on a baking sheet. Bake at 325 degrees for 45 to 50 minutes or until the center is set. Remove to a wire rack and cool for 10 minutes. Loosen the edge of the cake from the pan with a knife. Cool for 1 hour. Chill, covered, for 6 hours to overnight. Remove the side of the pan. Microwave the chocolate chips and shortening in 1-cup glass measure on High for 1 minute or until melted. Stir until smooth. Top the cheesecake with the pecans. Drizzle with the chocolate and the caramel topping. Chill until just before serving.
Yield: 12 to 16 servings.

Marilyn Heffron, Alpha Gamma Delta
Warsaw, Missouri

CHOCOLATE MALT CHEESECAKE

1 cup finely crushed pretzels
1/4 cup sugar
1/3 cup unsalted butter, melted
24 ounces cream cheese, softened
1 (14-ounce) can sweetened condensed milk
4 eggs
1 cup (6 ounces) semisweet chocolate chips, melted and cooled
3/4 cup chocolate malt powder
1 teaspoon vanilla extract

Combine the pretzels, sugar and butter in a bowl and mix well. Press onto the bottom of a 9-inch spring-form pan. Beat the cream cheese in a large bowl until smooth and fluffy. Beat in the condensed milk. Add the eggs, chocolate, malt powder and vanilla and mix well. Pour over the crust. Bake at 300 degrees for 65 minutes or until the center is almost set. Remove to a wire rack. Loosen the edge of the cake from the pan with a knife. Cool completely. Chill for 6 hours to overnight. Remove the side of the pan. Garnish with whipped cream and chocolate shavings or malted milk balls. Yield: 12 to 16 servings.

Carmella Markett, Laureate Gamma Lambda
Downers Grove, Illinois

GERMAN CHOCOLATE CHEESECAKE

1 cup graham cracker crumbs
2 tablespoons sugar
3 tablespoons butter, melted
24 ounces cream cheese, softened
1/2 cup sugar
1/4 cup all-purpose flour
3 eggs
4 ounces German's sweet chocolate, melted
2 teaspoons vanilla extract
1/3 cup evaporated milk
1/3 cup sugar
1/4 cup (1/2 stick) butter
1 egg, beaten
1/2 cup flaked coconut
1/2 cup chopped nuts
1/2 teaspoon vanilla extract

Press a mixture of the graham cracker crumbs, 2 tablespoons sugar and 3 tablespoons butter onto the bottom of an 8-inch springform pan. Bake at 350 degrees for 10 minutes. Beat the cream cheese, 1/2 cup sugar and the flour in a large bowl at medium speed for 2 minutes or until smooth. Beat in 3 eggs 1 at a time. Stir in the chocolate and 2 teaspoons vanilla until blended. Pour over the prepared crust. Bake for 45 to 50 minutes or until set. Remove to a wire rack and cool for 15 minutes. Loosen the edge of the cake from the pan with a sharp knife. Cool for 30 minutes. Remove the side of the pan and cool for 1 hour. Combine the evaporated milk, 1/3 sugar, 1/4 cup butter and 1 egg in a small saucepan. Cook over medium-low heat for 5 minutes or until thickened, stirring constantly. Stir in the coconut, nuts and vanilla. Spread over the cheesecake. Chill for 4 hours or longer.
Yield: 12 to 16 servings.

Lesley Murray, Laureate Eta
Wasilla, Alaska

NO-BAKE CHOCOLATE PEANUT BUTTER CHEESECAKE

1 3/4 cups sugar-free fat-free vanilla yogurt
1 small package sugar-free chocolate instant pudding mix
8 ounces fat-free cream cheese, softened
8 ounces reduced-fat cream cheese, softened
2 tablespoons peanut butter
1 (9-inch) chocolate crumb pie shell

Beat the yogurt and pudding mix in a large bowl until smooth. Add the cream cheeses and peanut butter and beat until blended. Spoon into the pie shell and swirl the top with the back of a spoon. Chill, covered, for 1 hour or until set. Yield: 6 to 8 servings.

Marian Seidlitz, Laureate Rho
Merrill, Wisconsin

*Willie Sloan, Theta Phi, Belton, Texas, shared her recipe for **Dutch Cocoa Cream Cake**. She begins by sifting 2 cups sifted flour, 4 teaspoons baking powder, 1 teaspoon salt, 1 2/3 cups sugar, and 5 tablespoons baking cocoa into a mixing bowl. She adds 2/3 cup shortening and mixes well. She adds 1 1/3 cups evaporated milk, 1/2 cup water, and 1 1/3 teaspoons vanilla extract and mixes for 2 minutes. Finally, she adds 3 eggs and mixes for 2 minutes. She pours the mixture into two greased and floured 9-inch cake pans. The cake is baked at 350 degrees for 30 to 40 minutes. After cooling the layers on a wire rack, she splits them in half horizontally and spreads whipped cream between them. She finishes by spreading milk chocolate frosting over the top and side of the cake.*

LIGHT FRUITY CHEESECAKE

1 1/4 cups graham cracker crumbs
1/4 cup (1/2 stick) butter or margarine, melted
1 small package sugar-free gelatin (any flavor)
2/3 cup boiling water
1 cup fat-free or low-fat cottage cheese
1 (8-ounce) container fat-free cream cheese spread
2 cups light whipped topping
1 cup or more berries or other fruit

Combine the graham cracker crumbs and butter in a bowl and mix well. Press onto the bottom of an 8- or 9-inch springform pan. Combine the gelatin and boiling water in a large bowl. Stir for 2 minutes or until the gelatin dissolves. Cool for 5 minutes. Pour the gelatin, cottage cheese and cheese spread into a blender or food processor. Process until smooth. Pour into the large bowl and fold in the whipped topping. Spread over the crust. Chill for 4 hours or longer. Remove the side of the pan. Top with the berries just before serving. Yield: 8 servings.

Teresa Waddington, Preceptor Delta Gamma
Langley, British Columbia, Canada

IRISH CREAM CHEESECAKE

1 3/4 cups finely crushed chocolate graham crackers
6 tablespoons (3/4 stick) butter, melted
24 ounces cream cheese, softened
1 cup sugar
4 eggs
1/3 to 1/2 cup Irish cream liqueur
1/2 cup (3 ounces) miniature semisweet chocolate chips
1 teaspoon all-purpose flour
1/4 cup miniature semisweet chocolate chips

Combine the graham crumbs and butter in a bowl and mix well. Press onto the bottom and 1 inch up the side of a greased 9-inch springform pan. Beat the cream cheese and sugar in a large bowl until smooth. Beat in the eggs 1 at a time. Stir in the liqueur. Combine 1/2 cup chocolate chips and the flour in a small bowl and toss to coat. Stir into the batter. Pour over the crust. Sprinkle 1/4 cup chocolate chips on top. Bake at 375 degrees for 40 to 50 minutes or until the center is almost set. Remove to a wire rack and cool for 10 minutes. Loosen the edge of the cake from the pan with a sharp knife. Cool completely. Chill for 3 hours or longer. Remove the side of the pan. Garnish with whipped cream and chocolate curls if desired. Yield: 12 to 16 servings.

Anita Brown, Preceptor Xi Zeta
Abilene, Texas

OLD-FASHIONED LEMON CHEESECAKE

2¹/₂ cups finely crushed
    vanilla wafers
¹/₂ cup (1 stick) butter,
    melted
2 (3-ounce) packages
    lemon gelatin
2 cups boiling water
2 (12-ounce) cans
    evaporated milk,
    chilled
16 ounces cream cheese,
    softened
1¹/₂ to 2 cups sugar
4 teaspoons lemon juice
4 teaspoons vanilla
    extract

Combine the vanilla wafer crumbs and butter in a bowl and mix well. Press onto the bottom of a 9×13-inch dish. Combine the gelatin and boiling water in a large bowl. Stir for 2 minutes or until the gelatin dissolves. Cool. Pour the evaporated milk into a large chilled bowl and beat until soft peaks form. Beat the cream cheese and sugar in a bowl until smooth. Add the gelatin mixture, lemon juice and vanilla and mix well. Fold into the whipped evaporated milk. Pour over the crust. Chill for 3 hours or until set. Cut into squares. Yield: 12 to 16 servings.

Martha Hallman, Preceptor Beta Eta
Jackson, Tennessee

LEMONADE CHEESECAKE

³/₄ cup finely crushed
    chocolate graham
    crackers
2 tablespoons butter,
    melted
1 envelope unflavored
    gelatin
¹/₄ cup cold water
8 ounces reduced-fat
    cream cheese,
    softened
8 ounces fat-free cream
    cheese, softened
³/₄ cup sugar or Splenda
1 cup light or fat-free
    sour cream
1 (6-ounce) can frozen
    lemonade
    concentrate, thawed
¹/₄ cup finely crushed
    chocolate graham
    crackers

Combine ³/₄ cup graham crumbs and the butter in a bowl and mix well. Press onto the bottom of an 8-inch nonstick springform pan. Freeze. Soften the gelatin in the water in a 1-cup glass measure. Let stand for 5 minutes. Microwave on High for 40 to 50 seconds or until the gelatin dissolves; stir. Cool. Beat the cream cheeses and sugar in a large bowl until smooth and fluffy. Add the sour cream, lemonade and gelatin and mix well. Pour over the frozen crust. Chill for 4 hours or longer. Remove the side of the pan. Sprinkle with ¹/₄ cup graham crumbs. Garnish with lemon slices if desired. Yield: 8 to 12 servings.

Barbara Roberts, Preceptor Delta Chi
Hays, Kansas

LIGHT AND LUSCIOUS CHEESECAKE

1¹/₄ cups crushed pecans
¹/₄ cup Splenda
1 tablespoon reduced-fat
    margarine, melted
24 ounces reduced-fat
    cream cheese, softened
1 cup Splenda
2 teaspoons vanilla
    extract
1 teaspoon lemon juice
3 eggs
1 ounce semisweet
    chocolate, melted and
    cooled (optional)

Mix the the pecans, ¹/₄ cup Splenda and the margarine in a bowl. Press onto the bottom of a 9-inch springform pan. Bake at 400 degrees for 10 minutes. Cool on a wire rack. Beat the cream cheese, 1 cup Splenda, the vanilla and lemon juice in a bowl until smooth. Beat in the eggs 1 at a time. Pour over the crust. Drizzle with the chocolate and marbelize with a spatula if desired. Bake at 350 degrees for 35 to 45 minutes or until set. Remove to a wire rack. Run a sharp knife around the edge of the pan to loosen. Cool completely. Chill for 4 hours to overnight. Remove the side of the pan. Yield: 8 to 12 servings.

Sandy Malget, Xi Epsilon Rho
Perry, Oklahoma

EASY NO-BAKE CHEESECAKE

8 ounces cream cheese,
    softened
1 (14-ounce) can
    sweetened
    condensed milk
1 teaspoon vanilla
    extract
1 (9-inch) graham
    cracker pie shell
Fresh fruit

Beat the cream cheese in a bowl until smooth and fluffy. Beat in the condensed milk. Add the vanilla and mix well. Pour into the pie shell. Chill, covered, for 3 hours or until set. Top with the fruit just before serving. Yield: 6 to 8 servings.

Joan McCoy, Laureate Delta Kappa
Oakville, Ontario, Canada

NO-BAKE CHEESECAKE

8 ounces cream cheese,
    softened
¹/₃ cup sugar
1 cup sour cream
2 teaspoons vanilla
    extract
8 ounces whipped
    topping
1 (9-inch) graham
    cracker pie shell
Strawberries or
    strawberry pie filling

Beat the cream cheese and sugar in a large bowl until smooth. Add the sour cream and vanilla and mix well. Fold in the whipped topping. Spoon into the pie shell. Chill, covered, for 4 hours or until set. Serve with strawberries. Yield: 8 to 12 servings.

Suzanne E. Veselka, Xi Upsilon Phi
Yoakum, Texas

PEACHES AND CREAM CHEESECAKE

3/4 cup all-purpose flour
1 teaspoon baking
  powder
1/2 teaspoon salt
1 (3-ounce) package
  vanilla pudding mix
3 tablespoons margarine,
  softened
1 egg
1/2 cup milk

1 (15- to 20-ounce) can
  peach slices
8 ounces cream cheese,
  softened
1/2 cup sugar
1 tablespoon sugar
  (optional)
1/2 teaspoon cinnamon
  (optional)

Beat the flour, baking powder, salt, pudding mix, margarine, egg and milk in a large bowl at medium speed for 2 minutes. Pour into a greased deep dish pie plate. Drain the peaches, reserving 3 tablespoons of the syrup. Beat the cream cheese, 1/2 cup sugar and the reserved peach syrup in a large bowl until smooth. Spread over the batter to within 1 inch of the edge. Arrange the peaches in a pinwheel design on top of the cream cheese mixture. Combine 1 tablespoon sugar and the cinnamon in a small bowl and sprinkle over the top. Bake at 350 degrees for 30 to 35 minutes or until set. Remove to a wire rack to cool. Chill. Yield: 8 servings.

Cherry L. Buckley, Iota Iota
Parker, Kansas

PEANUT BUTTER CUP CHEESECAKE

1 1/4 cups graham cracker
  crumbs
1/2 cup finely crushed
  cream-filled
  chocolate sandwich
  cookies
1/4 cup sugar
6 tablespoons (3/4 stick)
  butter, melted
3/4 cup peanut butter

24 ounces cream cheese,
  softened
1 cup sugar
1 cup sour cream
1 1/2 teaspoons vanilla
  extract
3 eggs
1 cup hot fudge topping
16 bite-size peanut
  butter cups

Combine the graham cracker crumbs, crushed cookies, 1/4 cup sugar and the butter in a bowl and mix well. Press onto the bottom and 1 inch up the side of a greased 9-inch springform pan. Place on a baking sheet. Bake at 350 degrees for 7 to 9 minutes. Cool. Microwave the peanut butter in a 2-cup glass measure on High for 30 seconds or until softened. Spread over the crust to within 1 inch of the edge. Beat the cream cheese and 1 cup sugar in a large bowl until smooth. Add the sour cream and vanilla and mix well. Beat in the eggs 1 at a time. Reserve 1 cup of the cream cheese mixture in a medium bowl. Pour the remainder over the crust. Microwave 1/4 cup of the fudge topping in a 1-cup glass measure on High for 30 seconds or until thinned. Fold into the reserved cream cheese mixture. Spoon over the filling and marbleize with a spatula. Place on a baking sheet and bake for 55 to 60 minutes or until the center is almost set. Remove to a wire rack and cool for 10 minutes. Loosen the cake from the pan with a sharp knife. Cool for 1 hour. Microwave the remaining 3/4 cup hot fudge topping in a 1-cup glass measure on High for 30 seconds or until warmed. Spread over the cheesecake. Cut each peanut butter cup into 4 wedges. Arrange on top of the cheesecake. Chill overnight. Remove the side of the pan. Yield: 12 to 16 servings.

Brenda Graham, Xi Rho Lambda
Amarillo, Texas

MINI PEANUT BUTTER CHEESECAKES

1 1/2 cups graham cracker
  crumbs
1/4 cup sugar
1/4 cup (1/2 stick) butter,
  melted
12 bite-size peanut
  butter cups

16 ounces cream cheese,
  softened
1 cup sugar
1/4 cup all-purpose flour
1 teaspoon vanilla or
  almond extract
2 eggs

Combine the graham cracker crumbs, 1/4 cup sugar and butter in a bowl and mix well. Press onto the bottoms of 12 paper-lined muffin cups. Place 1 peanut butter cup over each crust. Beat the cream cheese and sugar in a large bowl until smooth. Add the flour and vanilla and mix well. Beat in the eggs 1 at a time. Spoon into the muffin cups. Bake at 350 degrees for 20 minutes or just until set. Remove to a wire rack and cool completely. Serve at room temperature or chilled. Yield: 12 servings.

Cynthia Albert, Beta Phi
Wilber, Nebraska

*Ruth Ellen Shaffer, Upsilon Master, Lancaster, Ohio, shared her recipe for moist **Pistachio Marble Pudding Cake**. She combines 1 package yellow cake mix, one 4-ounce package pistachio instant pudding mix, 4 eggs, 1 cup water, 1/4 cup canola oil, and 1/2 teaspoon almond extract in a mixing bowl and mixes well. She beats the mixture at medium speed for 4 minutes. She mixes 1 cup of the batter and 1/4 cup chocolate syrup in a small bowl. She pours the pistachio batter into a greased and floured tube pan. She drops the chocolate batter by spoonfuls into the pan and marbleizes with a knife. The cake is baked at 350 degrees for 50 to 55 minutes. It is cooled in the pan for 15 minutes and removed to a wire rack to cool completely. Just before serving, she dusts the cake with confectioners' sugar.*

PINEAPPLE CHEESECAKE SQUARES

This no-crust cheesecake is gluten free.

1 (8-ounce) can crushed pineapple	2 teaspoons vanilla extract
1 cup sugar	16 ounces cream cheese, cut in cubes and softened
1/2 cup milk	
3 eggs	
1/4 cup cornstarch	Cinnamon

Drain the pineapple and reserve the juice. Combine the sugar, reserved pineapple juice, milk, eggs, cornstarch and vanilla in a blender and process for 1 minute or until smooth. Add the cream cheese gradually and blend until smooth. Pour into a greased 9×9-inch baking dish. Spoon the pineapple evenly over the top. Sprinkle with cinnamon. Bake at 300 degrees for 50 to 60 minutes or until set. Remove to a wire rack and cool for 1 hour. Chill. Cut into squares. Yield: 8 to 12 servings.

Tricia Bagley, Laureate Theta Mu
Kingwood, Texas

PRALINE PECAN CHEESECAKE

11/4 cups graham cracker crumbs	1 (5-ounce) can evaporated milk
1/4 cup granulated sugar	1 cup packed brown sugar
1/4 cup finely chopped pecans	2 tablespoons all-purpose flour
Dash of cinnamon	
1/4 cup (1/2 stick) butter, melted	11/2 teaspoons vanilla extract
24 ounces cream cheese, softened	3 eggs
	1 cup pecan halves

Combine the graham cracker crumbs, granulated sugar, chopped pecans, cinnamon and butter in a bowl and mix well. Press onto the bottom of a 9-inch springform pan. Bake at 350 degrees for 10 minutes. Remove to a wire rack. Beat the cream cheese, evaporated milk and brown sugar in a large bowl until smooth. Add the flour and vanilla and mix well. Beat in the eggs 1 at a time. Pour over the crust. Bake for 50 to 55 minutes or until the center is almost set. Remove to a wire rack. Loosen the edge of the cake from the pan with a sharp knife. Cool completely. Arrange the pecan halves on top. Chill for 4 hours to overnight. Remove the side of the pan.
Yield: 12 to 16 servings.

Thelma True Borger, Preceptor Alpha Omega
Mason City, Iowa

❖ PUMPKIN CHOCOLATE CHEESECAKE BARS

11/4 cups graham cracker crumbs	1 cup pumpkin
1/4 cup sugar	1/2 teaspoon vanilla extract
7 tablespoons butter, melted	1/4 teaspoon salt
16 ounces cream cheese, softened	6 ounces milk chocolate, chopped
13/4 cups sugar	2 tablespoons butter
3 eggs	11/4 cups sour cream
1/2 teaspoon pumpkin pie spice	1/4 cup sugar
	Nutmeg

Combine the graham crackers, 1/4 cup sugar and 7 tablespoons butter in a bowl and mix well. Pat into a greased 9×13-inch baking pan. Beat the cream cheese and 13/4 cups sugar in a mixing bowl until light and fluffy. Add the eggs 1 at a time, beating well after each addition. Add the pumpkin pie spice, pumpkin, vanilla and salt and mix well. Place 11/4 cups of the cream cheese mixture into a medium bowl. Melt the chocolate and 2 tablespoons butter in a saucepan over low heat, stirring often. Add to the 11/4 cups cream cheese mixture and mix well. Spread over the unbaked crust. Bake at 325 for 15 minutes. Spread the remaining cream cheese mixture over the baked layer. Bake for 25 to 30 minutes or until set. Cool. Combine the sour cream and 1/4 cup sugar in a bowl and mix well. Spread over the cooled bars. Sprinkle with nutmeg. Chill for 2 hours or longer. Cut into bars. Store in the refrigerator.
Yield: 2 dozen bars.

Jane Owen, Xi Xi
Lynchburg, Virginia

SOPAIPILLA CHEESECAKE

2 (8-count) packages refrigerated crescent rolls	1/2 cup (1 stick) butter or margarine, melted
16 ounces cream cheese, softened	1/2 cup sugar
1 cup sugar	2 to 3 teaspoons cinnamon
1 teaspoon vanilla extract	

Unroll 1 package of the rolls in a 9×13-inch baking pan and press onto the bottom of the pan. Press the seams to seal. Beat the cream cheese, 1 cup sugar and the vanilla in a large bowl until smooth. Spread over the dough. Unroll the second package of the rolls over the cream cheese layer and press the seams to seal. Pour the butter evenly over the top. Combine

1/2 cup sugar and the cinnamon in a small bowl and mix well. Sprinkle over the top. Bake at 350 degrees for 30 to 40 minutes or until set. Remove to a wire rack to cool completely. Yield: 16 to 20 servings.

DeeDee Slone, Pi Iota
Trophy Club, Texas

SOUR CREAM-TOPPED CHEESECAKE

2 cups graham cracker crumbs	**1 cup sugar**
1/2 cup sugar	**1 teaspoon vanilla extract**
1/2 cup (1 stick) butter, melted	**4 eggs**
1 teaspoon cinnamon	**Topping**
24 ounces cream cheese, softened	

Combine the graham cracker crumbs, 1/2 cup sugar, butter and cinnamon in a bowl and mix well. Reserve 2 to 3 tablespoons of the crumb mixture. Press the remainder onto the bottom of a 9-inch springform pan. Beat the cream cheese, 1 cup sugar and the vanilla in a large bowl until smooth. Beat in the eggs 1 at a time. Pour over the crust. Bake at 325 degrees for 50 to 60 minutes or until the center is almost set. Cool for 10 minutes. Spread the Topping over the cheesecake. Sprinkle with the reserved crumbs. Bake at 450 degrees for 5 minutes or until the top is set and golden. Remove to a wire rack. Loosen the edge of the cake from the pan with a sharp knife. Cool completely. Chill for 4 hours to overnight. Remove the side of the pan. Yield: 12 to 16 servings.

TOPPING

2 cups sour cream	**1 tablespoon vanilla extract**
2 tablespoons sugar	

Combine the sour cream, sugar and vanilla in a bowl and mix well.

Helen Askeland, Omicron Eta
Orland, California

UPSIDE-DOWN STRAWBERRY CHEESECAKE

4 ounces cream cheese, softened	**4 ounces whipped topping**
1/4 cup sugar	**1 cup strawberry glaze**
1/2 cup sour cream	**1 (9-inch) graham cracker pie shell**
1 teaspoon vanilla extract	**1 pint strawberries, thinly sliced**

Beat the cream cheese and sugar in a medium bowl until smooth and fluffy. Add the sour cream and

vanilla and mix well. Fold in the whipped topping. Spread half the glaze over the bottom of the pie shell. Layer with the strawberries and the remaining glaze. Spoon the cream cheese mixture over the glaze. Chill, covered, for 4 hours or until set. Garnish with whole strawberries. Yield: 8 servings.

Gail Kunsman, Xi Sigma Omicron
Yuba City, California

SUGAR-FREE CHEESECAKE

1 cup finely crushed sugar-free vanilla wafers	**3/4 cup Splenda**
1/2 cup Splenda	**4 eggs**
1/2 cup (1 stick) butter or margarine, melted	**2 1/2 cups heavy whipping cream**
16 ounces cream cheese, softened	**1 cup sour cream (optional)**

Combine the vanilla wafer crumbs, 1/2 cup Splenda and butter in a bowl and mix well. Press onto the bottom and up the side of an 8-inch springform pan. Beat the cream cheese and 3/4 cup Splenda in a large bowl until smooth. Beat in the eggs 1 at a time. Add the cream gradually, beating until smooth. Strain through a sieve onto the crust. Place the pan on a baking sheet. Bake at 325 degrees for 1 hour or until set. Turn off the oven and let the cheesecake stand in the oven for 1 hour. Remove to a wire rack. Loosen the edge of the cake from the pan with a knife. Cool completely. Chill for 4 hours to overnight. Remove the side of the pan. Top with the sour cream just before serving. Yield: 12 servings.

Joan Mize, Xi
Brandon, Mississippi

Carol Langworth, Theta Beta, Sicamous, British Columbia, Canada, loves making **Orange Cake.** *She combines 1 cup raisins and 1 peeled and quartered orange in a food processor or blender and processes for 30 seconds. She adds 3/4 cup honey, 3/4 cup softened butter, 3/4 cup sour milk, 2 cups all-purpose flour, 1 teaspoon baking soda, and 1 teaspoon baking powder and processes until smooth. She pours the mixture into a greased and floured 9×13-inch cake pan. The cake is baked at 325 degrees for 30 to 35 minutes. As it cools, she combines 1 tablespoon softened butter, 6 ounces softened cream cheese, 1/4 cup honey, 2 teaspoons vanilla extract, and 1/2 cup chopped nuts in a bowl and mixes well. She frosts the cooled cake and garnishes with nuts and orange zest.*

TIRAMISU CHEESECAKE SQUARES

88 vanilla wafers	4 eggs
2 teaspoons instant coffee granules	1 tablespoon instant coffee granules
2 tablespoons hot water	1 tablespoon hot water
32 ounces cream cheese, softened	8 ounces whipped topping
1 cup sugar	2 tablespoons baking cocoa
1 cup sour cream	

Line a 9×13-inch baking pan with heavy foil, extending the foil 2 inches over the sides of the pan. Layer half the vanilla wafers on the bottom of the pan. Dissolve 2 teaspoons instant coffee in 2 tablespoons water in a small bowl. Brush half of the coffee over the wafers, reserving the remainder. Beat the cream cheese and sugar in a large bowl until smooth. Add the sour cream and mix well. Beat in the eggs 1 at a time. Dissolve 1 tablespoon instant coffee in 1 tablespoon water in a small bowl. Place 3¹/₂ cups of the cream cheese mixture in a medium bowl. Stir in the coffee. Pour over the wafers. Layer the remaining wafers over the coffee batter and brush with the reserved coffee. Pour the remaining cream cheese mixture over the wafers. Bake at 325 degrees for 45 to 50 minutes or until the center is almost set. Remove to a wire rack. Loosen the edge of the cake from the foil. Cool completely. Chill for 3 hours to overnight. Lift the cheesecake from the pan using the foil handles. Spread with the whipped topping and dust with the baking cocoa. Cut into squares.
Yield: 16 servings.

Alice Dorene Prior, Laureate Alpha Alpha
Spokane, Washington

EASY VANILLA CHEESECAKE

3/4 cup milk	16 ounces cream cheese, cut into cubes
2 teaspoons vanilla extract	1 cup sour cream
2 eggs	2 tablespoons sugar
1 cup sugar	2 teaspoons vanilla extract
1/2 cup baking mix	

Combine the milk, vanilla, eggs, sugar and baking mix in a blender and process for 15 seconds. Add the cream cheese gradually and process for 2 minutes or until smooth. Pour into a greased 9-inch pie plate. Bake at 350 degrees for 40 to 45 minutes or until the center is puffed and set. Combine the sour cream, sugar and vanilla in a bowl and mix well. Spread on the baked cheesecake. Remove to a wire rack to cool completely. Chill for 3 hours or longer.
Yield: 8 servings.

Joy Ellison, Preceptor Beta Zeta
Greensboro, North Carolina

VANILLA PRALINE CHEESECAKE

66 vanilla wafers	1 teaspoon vanilla extract
1/4 cup sugar	3 eggs
1/4 cup (1/2 stick) butter or margarine, melted	25 caramel candies
24 ounces cream cheese, softened	3 tablespoons milk
1 cup sugar	1/2 cup pecan pieces, toasted
1/2 cup sour cream	

Finely crush 50 of the vanilla wafers and place them in a bowl. Add 1/4 cup sugar and the butter and mix well. Press onto the bottom of a 9-inch springform pan. Line the side of the pan with the remaining 16 wafers, pressing into the crust. Beat the cream cheese and 1 cup sugar in a large bowl at medium speed for 2 minutes or until smooth. Add the sour cream and vanilla and mix well. Beat in the eggs 1 at a time. Pour over the crust. Bake at 325 degrees for 45 to 50 minutes or until the center is almost set. Remove to a wire rack. Loosen the edge of the cheesecake from the pan with a sharp knife. Cool completely. Chill for 4 hours to overnight. Remove the side of the pan. Microwave the caramels and milk in a 1-quart glass measure on High for 1 minute or until melted. Stir well and cool slightly. Pour over the cheesecake. Top with the pecans. Yield: 16 servings.

Pam Gooch, Xi Zeta Iota
Richmond, Missouri

WHITE CHOCOLATE LIME CHEESECAKE

24 to 30 ladyfingers, split	1 envelope unflavored gelatin
16 ounces cream cheese, softened	1/4 cup lime juice
1 cup sugar	2 teaspoons grated lime zest
6 ounces white chocolate, melted and cooled	1 cup heavy whipping cream, whipped

Line the bottom and side of an 8- or 9-inch springform pan with the ladyfingers, rounded sides against the pan. Beat the cream cheese and sugar in a large bowl until smooth and fluffy. Add the white chocolate and mix well. Sprinkle the gelatin over the lime juice in a small saucepan and let stand for 5 minutes. Warm over low heat for 1 minute or until the gelatin dissolves, stirring constantly. Add to the cream cheese mixture and mix well. Fold in the lime zest and whipped cream. Pour into the pan. Chill for 3 hours or until set. Remove the side of the pan. Garnish with strawberries and lime slices if desired.
Yield: 8 to 12 servings.

Mary Brosseau, Preceptor Alpha Rho
Powell River, British Columbia, Canada

Spoonfuls
PUDDINGS, TORTES AND TRIFLES

APRICOT LEMON PUDDING

1 (3¹/₂-ounce) package
    lemon instant
    pudding mix
1 cup apricot nectar
    (apricot juice)
1 cup sour cream

Whisk all the ingredients in a bowl for 2 minutes. Pour into serving dishes and chill until set. Yield: 4 to 6 servings.

Peggy Schulze, Laureate Beta Pi
Clay Center, Kansas

LIGHT BANANA PUDDING

2 large packages fat-free
    sugar-free vanilla
    instant pudding mix
12 ounces fat-free
    whipped topping
1 cup fat-free sour cream
1 (11-ounce) package
    reduced-fat vanilla
    wafers
6 bananas, sliced

Prepare the pudding mix using the package directions. Fold in half the whipped topping and the sour cream. Layer the vanilla wafers and bananas in a 9×13-inch baking pan. Top with the pudding mixture. Spread the remaining whipped topping over the top. Chill, covered, for 2 hours. Yield: 12 servings.

Renée Gillchrest, Preceptor Tau
Marietta, South Carolina

BANANA PUDDING

1 (14-ounce) can
    sweetened
    condensed milk
1¹/₂ cups cold water
1 (3¹/₂-ounce) package
    vanilla instant
    pudding mix
3 cups heavy whipping
    cream
1 (12-ounce) package
    vanilla wafers
4 cups sliced bananas

Combine the condensed milk and water in a bowl. Beat at medium speed for 1 minute. Add the pudding mix and beat for 2 minutes. Chill, covered, for 3 hours or longer. Whip the cream in a mixing bowl. Fold in the pudding mixture. Arrange one-third of the vanilla wafers over the bottom of a large glass serving bowl. Arrange one-third of the bananas over the wafers. Spread one-third of the pudding mixture evenly over the bananas. Repeat the layers two more times. Garnish with additional vanilla wafers or vanilla wafer crumbs. Chill, covered tightly with plastic wrap, for 4 to 8 hours. Yield: 15 servings.

Jane Bronnenberg, Preceptor Alpha Epsilon
Oklahoma City, Oklahoma

RICH BANANA PUDDING

8 ounces cream cheese,
    softened
1 (14-ounce) can
    sweetened
    condensed milk
12 ounces whipped
    topping
1 (6-ounce) package
    French vanilla
    instant pudding mix
2 cups milk
2 (7¹/₄-ounce) packages
    Chessman cookies
6 to 8 bananas, sliced

Beat the cream cheese and condensed milk in a bowl until smooth. Fold in the whipped topping. Whisk the pudding mix and milk in a mixing bowl for 2 minutes. Fold in the cream cheese mixture. Line a serving bowl with half the cookies. Arrange the bananas over the cookies. Pour the pudding mixture over the bananas. Arrange the remaining cookies over the pudding mixture. Chill, covered, for several hours. Yield: 15 servings.

Brenda Campbell, Beta Xi
Scott City, Missouri

ALMOND BREAD PUDDING

1 large loaf French bread, sliced	1 teaspoon almond extract
8 eggs (or 4 eggs and 8 egg whites)	1/4 cup (about 3 ounces) almond paste, cut into very small pieces
1 1/2 cups sugar	1/2 cup chopped almonds
3 cups milk	
2 teaspoons vanilla extract	

Arrange the bread slices in the bottom of a greased 9×13-inch baking dish, placing the smaller slices on the bottom. Whisk the eggs, sugar, milk, vanilla and almond extract in a bowl. Pour evenly over the bread. Sprinkle the almond paste over the top. Press gently with the back of a spoon. Let stand for 10 minutes. Sprinkle with the almonds. Bake at 350 degrees for 35 to 40 minutes or until golden brown and puffed. Remove to a wire rack to cool. Yield: 10 servings.

Jane Dudine, Alpha Zeta
Bethany Beach, Delaware

AMARETTO BREAD PUDDING

1 cup raisins	1 tablespoon vanilla extract
2 tablespoons amaretto	1/2 cup (1 stick) butter
1 loaf French bread	1 cup confectioners' sugar
4 cups milk	1/4 cup amaretto
1/2 cup granulated sugar	
6 eggs, beaten	

Combine the raisins and 2 tablespoons amaretto in a bowl. Cut the bread into 1-inch cubes. Combine the bread and milk in a large bowl. Add the raisin mixture, granulated sugar, eggs and vanilla and mix well. Pour into a greased 9×13-inch baking pan. Bake at 375 degrees for 45 minutes. Poke holes at 1-inch intervals in the top of the pudding with a wooden spoon handle. Combine the butter, confectioners' sugar and 1/4 cup amaretto in a saucepan. Cook until smooth and hot, stirring frequently. Pour over the top of the hot pudding. Yield: 12 servings.

Della R. Webster, Omicron Master
Manhattan, Kansas

DONUT BREAD PUDDING WITH HOT RUM SAUCE

2 dozen glazed donuts	1 egg, lightly beaten
1 (14-ounce) can sweetened condensed milk	1 cup raisins (optional)
	1/2 cup water
1 (20-ounce) can crushed pineapple	1/2 cup packed brown sugar
1 teaspoon vanilla extract	1/4 cup warm water
	Cornstarch
	2 tablespoons rum

Cut the donuts into small pieces and place in a bowl. Add the condensed milk, pineapple, vanilla, egg and raisins and mix well. Pour into a greased 9×13-inch baking pan. Bake at 350 degrees for 45 minutes. Cool in the pan on a wire rack. Combine 1/2 cup water and the brown sugar in a saucepan. Bring to a boil over medium heat, stirring frequently. Mix 1/4 cup water with cornstarch in a small bowl. Add to the boiling sugar mixture. Cook until thickened, stirring constantly. Stir in the rum. Serve hot over the warm pudding. Yield: 12 servings.

Nancy L Crissman, Alpha Tau Master
Castanea, Pennsylvania

❖ PIÑA COLADA BREAD PUDDING WITH COCONUT RUM SAUCE

6 eggs	1 tablespoon vanilla extract
2 egg yolks	1 teaspoon nutmeg
1 cup sugar	1/2 teaspoon salt
2 cups heavy cream	1 cup flaked coconut
1 (14-ounce) can cream of coconut	1 (1 1/2-pound) loaf white bread, cubed
3/4 cup milk	Coconut Rum Sauce
1/4 cup coconut-flavored rum	

Whisk the eggs, egg yolks and sugar in a large bowl. Whisk in the cream, cream of coconut, milk, rum, vanilla, nutmeg and salt. Stir in the coconut. Add the bread and mix well. Pour into a greased 9×13-inch baking dish. Bake at 325 degrees for 1 hour or until the center is firm. Cool slightly in the pan. Drizzle the warm Coconut Rum Sauce over the warm pudding. Yield: 8 servings.

COCONUT RUM SAUCE

1 cup (2 sticks) butter	2 cups flaked coconut, toasted
1/2 cup sugar	
6 tablespoons coconut-flavored rum	

Combine the butter, sugar and rum in a saucepan. Cook over medium heat until smooth, stirring frequently. Stir in the coconut.

Jackie Sanders, Preceptor Gamma Gamma
Petersburg, Virginia

PACIFIC NORTHWEST BREAD PUDDING

6 cups cubed stale French bread	1/2 cup dried cherries
	3 eggs
1/2 cup dried or fresh blueberries	4 cups French vanilla nondairy liquid coffee creamer
1/2 cup thinly sliced apples	Nutmeg

Combine the first 4 ingredients in a large bowl. Beat the eggs in a bowl. Stir in the creamer. Add to the bread mixture and mix well. Pour into a nonstick 9×11-inch baking pan. Sprinkle with nutmeg. Chill, covered, for 2 hours or longer. Bake at 350 degrees for 45 minutes. Remove to a wire rack to cool. Serve with whipped cream or framboise liqueur.
Yield: 8 to 10 servings.

Karen Yong, Xi Beta Zeta
Colbert, Washington

WHITE CHOCOLATE BREAD PUDDING

1 loaf French bread, cut into small cubes	1/2 cup sugar
3 cups heavy cream	2 eggs, beaten
10 ounces white chocolate, chopped	8 egg yolks, beaten
1 cup milk	1/2 cup heavy cream
	8 ounces white chocolate, chopped

Spread the bread cubes on a baking sheet. Bake at 200 degrees until dry. Arrange in a greased 9×13-inch baking dish. Combine 3 cups cream and 10 ounces white chocolate in a double boiler. Cook until smooth, stirring frequently. Remove to a large bowl. Combine the milk, sugar, eggs and egg yolks in a double boiler. Cook until warm, stirring frequently. Stir into the melted chocolate mixture. Drizzle half over the bread in the baking dish. Let stand for 15 minutes. Pour the remaining mixture evenly over the bread. Bake, covered with foil, at 275 degrees for 1 hour. Bake, uncovered, for 15 minutes longer or until golden brown. Remove to a wire rack to cool completely. Chill for 45 minutes. Cut into squares and place on serving plates. Combine 1/2 cup cream and 8 ounces white chocolate in a double boiler. Cook until smooth, stirring frequently. Spoon over the pudding and serve topped with chocolate shavings. Yield: 15 servings.

Jackie Robinson, Kappa Mu
Miami, Oklahoma

STEAMED CARROT PUDDING

This recipe has been in my husband's family for over 70 years and is a Thanksgiving tradition.

1 cup grated peeled carrots	1 cup sugar
1 cup grated peeled potatoes	1 teaspoon salt
1 cup sifted all-purpose flour	1 teaspoon baking soda
1/2 cup (1 stick) butter or margarine, melted	1 teaspoon cinnamon
	1 teaspoon allspice
	1 teaspoon nutmeg
	1 cup raisins
	1/2 cup chopped nuts

Mix the carrots and potatoes in a bowl. Stir in the flour. Add the butter, sugar, salt, baking soda, cinnamon, allspice and nutmeg and mix well. Add the raisins and nuts and mix well. Pour into a greased pudding mold. Cover tightly with foil. Place on a rack in a large saucepan. Add enough boiling water to the saucepan to come halfway to two-thirds up the side of the pudding mold. Cover tightly and let stand for 3 hours. Remove the mold carefully to a wire rack and cool for 10 minutes. Invert onto a serving plate. Serve with whipped cream.
Yield: 6 to 8 servings.

Mary Elizabeth Atkin, Preceptor Gamma Pi
Lincoln City, Oregon

CHERRY PUDDING

1 (16-ounce) can water-packed pitted tart cherries	1 teaspoon butter, softened
1 cup all-purpose flour	1 tablespoon all-purpose flour
1 cup sugar	2/3 cup sugar
1/2 teaspoon baking soda	1 teaspoon butter (optional)
1 egg, beaten	

Drain the cherries, reserving the juice. Mix 1 cup flour, 1 cup sugar and the baking soda in a bowl. Add the egg and 1 teaspoon butter and mix well. Stir in the cherries. Spoon into a greased 8×8-inch baking pan. Bake at 350 degrees for 25 to 30 minutes. Whisk the reserved cherry juice, 1 tablespoon flour, 2/3 cup sugar and 1 teaspoon butter in a saucepan. Cook over medium heat until thickened, stirring constantly. Spoon over the warm pudding. Yield: 6 to 8 servings.

Andrea Marsh, Xi Beta
Columbus, Georgia

CHERRY MOUSSE PUDDING

1 (31/2-ounce) package chocolate instant pudding mix	10 chocolate sandwich cookies, crushed
11/2 cups milk	11/2 cups canned cherry pie filling
8 ounces whipped topping	6 chocolate sandwich cookies, crushed

Whisk the pudding mix and milk in a bowl for 2 minutes. Fold in one-third of the whipped topping and 10 crushed cookies. Spoon half the pudding mixture into a 11/2-quart serving bowl. Spread one-third of the whipped topping over the pudding mixture and top with 1 cup of the pie filling. Spread the remaining pudding mixture over the pie filling. Spread with the remaining whipped topping and top with the remaining pie filling. Sprinkle 6 crushed cookies over the top. Yield: 12 servings.

Madalyn Fae Fazzolari, Laureate Beta Eta
Clackamas, Oregon

BAKED CHERRY PUDDING

2 (16-ounce) cans pitted
   tart cherries
1 cup all-purpose flour
1 teaspoon baking
   powder
1/4 teaspoon salt
1/2 cup sugar

1/4 cup (1/2 stick) butter,
   softened
1 egg
1/2 cup milk
1/2 teaspoon vanilla
   extract
1/2 cup sugar

Drain the cherries, reserving 1 cup juice. Combine the flour, baking powder, salt and 1/2 cup sugar. Beat the butter, egg, milk and vanilla in a bowl for 2 minutes. Add the dry ingredients and beat for 1 minute. Pour into a greased 9×13-inch baking pan. Top with the cherries and sprinkle with 1/2 cup sugar. Heat the reserved cherry juice in a saucepan until hot. Pour evenly over the sugar layer. Bake at 375 degrees for 25 minutes or until golden brown. Cool in the pan for 10 minutes. Serve warm or at room temperature with ice cream or whipped topping.
Yield: 15 to 18 servings.

Coralie Clary, Zeta Master
Mesa, Arizona

HOMEMADE CHOCOLATE PUDDING

3/4 cup sugar
3 heaping tablespoons
   baking cocoa
3 heaping tablespoons
   cornstarch
Dash of salt

2 cups hot milk
1 tablespoon butter or
   margarine
1 teaspoon vanilla
   extract

Mix the sugar, baking cocoa, cornstarch and salt in a saucepan. Stir in the hot milk gradually. Bring to a boil over medium heat, stirring constantly. Boil for 1 to 2 minutes, stirring constantly. Remove from the heat and add the butter and vanilla. Beat for 2 to 3 minutes. Pour into serving dishes. Chill until cold. Serve with a dollop of whipped topping.
Yield: 4 servings.

Charlotte Ballard, Preceptor Lambda
Plattsburg, Missouri

LACTOSE-FREE CHOCOLATE PUDDING

1 cup soft tofu
1/4 cup vegetable oil
1/2 cup Splenda
1/4 cup baking cocoa

1/4 teaspoon salt
11/2 teaspoons vanilla
   extract

Combine the tofu, oil, Splenda, baking cocoa, salt and vanilla in a blender or food processor. Process until smooth and creamy. Pour into serving dishes and chill until cold. Yield: 2 to 4 servings.

Theresa Viola, Pi Iota
Prairie Village, Kansas

BAKED CHOCOLATE PUDDING

1 cup all-purpose flour
2 teaspoons baking
   powder
1/4 teaspoon salt
3/4 cup packed brown
   sugar
1/2 cup milk

2 teaspoons vegetable
   oil or melted butter
1 cup packed brown
   sugar
1/4 cup baking cocoa
13/4 cups hot water

Mix the flour, baking powder, salt and 3/4 cup brown sugar in a bowl. Add the milk and oil and mix well. Spread in a nonstick 7×12-inch baking pan. Combine 1 cup brown sugar, the baking cocoa and water in a bowl and mix well. Pour evenly over the batter in the pan. Bake at 350 degrees for 40 minutes. Cool completely in the pan. Yield: 6 servings.

Lois L. Drobot, Beta Iota
Porcupine Plain, Saskatchewan, Canada

CRANBERRY PUDDING

This recipe can be steamed in the top of a double boiler or can be doubled and baked in a bundt pan set in a pan of hot water at 300 degrees for 2 hours.

2 teaspoons baking soda
1/2 cup water
1/4 cup light corn syrup
1/4 cup molasses
11/2 cups all-purpose
   flour
2 cups fresh or frozen
   cranberries

1/4 cup (1/2 stick) butter
   or margarine
1 cup sugar
1 cup heavy cream
1 teaspoon vanilla
   extract

Dissolve the baking soda in the water in a bowl. Add the corn syrup, molasses, and flour and mix well. Stir in the cranberries. Spoon into a greased pudding mold. Place on a rack in a large saucepan. Add enough boiling water to the saucepan to come halfway to two-thirds up the side of the pudding mold. Cover tightly and let stand for 2 hours. Remove the mold carefully to a wire rack and let stand for 10 minutes. Invert onto a serving plate. Combine the butter, sugar, cream and vanilla in a saucepan. Bring to a slow boil over medium heat, stirring frequently. Serve over the pudding. Yield: 6 servings.

Kathy Clow, Preceptor Eta
Thompson, Manitoba, Canada

CRANBERRY TAPIOCA PUDDING

This is a new way to serve cranberries at Thanksgiving.

2 cups cranberry juice
   cocktail
1/3 cup quick-cooking
   tapioca

1/2 cup sugar
1/2 teaspoon salt
1 cup burgundy

Mix the cranberry juice cocktail, tapioca, sugar and salt in a 3-quart saucepan. Let stand for 5 minutes. Cook over medium heat for 5 minutes or until thickened and beginning to boil, stirring constantly. Add the wine. Cook for 5 minutes, stirring constantly. Spoon into heatproof wine glasses or dessert dishes. Chill, covered, for 2 hours or until cold. Serve with a dollop of whipped topping if desired. Yield: 6 servings.

Mary Lynne Partridge, Xi Gamma
Miles City, Montana

DATE PUDDING

1 cup all-purpose flour	1/2 cup milk
2 teaspoons baking powder	1 cup packed brown sugar
1 cup granulated sugar	2 cups boiling water
Pinch of salt	1 tablespoon butter or margarine
1 cup chopped dates	
1 cup chopped nuts	

Mix the first 4 ingredients in a bowl. Stir in the dates and nuts. Add the milk and mix well. Spoon into a greased 9×13-inch baking pan. Combine the brown sugar, water and butter in a bowl and mix well. Pour evenly over the batter in the pan. Bake at 350 degrees for 30 to 40 minutes. Cool completely in the pan. Serve with whipped cream. Yield: 15 servings.

Shirley Crabtree, Alpha Epsilon Master
Bethany, Missouri

HASTY PUDDING

1 cup all-purpose flour	2/3 cup milk
1/3 cup packed brown sugar	1 cup packed brown sugar
1 tablespoon baking cocoa	1 tablespoon all-purpose flour
1 1/2 teaspoons baking powder	1 tablespoon butter
1/4 teaspoon salt	1/8 teaspoon salt
1 tablespoon butter, softened	2 cups boiling water
1 cup raisins	2 teaspoons vanilla extract

Sift 1 cup flour, 1/3 cup brown sugar, the baking cocoa, baking powder and 1/4 teaspoon salt into a bowl. Stir in the butter and raisins. Add the milk and mix well. Spoon into a greased 8×8×6-inch baking pan. Mix 1 cup brown sugar, 1 tablespoon flour, 1 tablespoon butter and 1/8 teaspoon salt in a bowl. Add the water and mix well. Stir in the vanilla. Pour evenly over the batter. Bake at 375 degrees for 45 minutes. Serve hot with ice cream. Yield: 6 to 8 servings.

Cindy Bazin, Xi Alpha Phi
Stony Plain, Alberta, Canada

INDIAN PUDDING

1/2 cup sugar	2 1/2 to 3 cups milk
1/2 teaspoon cinnamon	3 cups cornflakes
1/4 teaspoon nutmeg	1 tablespoon butter
1/4 teaspoon salt	or margarine,
2 eggs, beaten	cut into pieces
1/4 cup molasses	

Combine the sugar, cinnamon, nutmeg and salt in a bowl. Add the eggs and mix well. Add the molasses and mix well. Stir in the milk gradually. Add the cornflakes and mix well. Spread in a greased baking dish. Dot with butter. Place the baking dish in a larger baking pan. Add enough boiling water to the larger pan to come 2 inches up the side of the baking dish. Bake at 250 degrees for 1 hour, stirring every 15 minutes. Cool for 10 minutes in the pan. Serve warm with whipped cream. Yield: 4 to 6 servings.

Norma J. Reed, Preceptor Gamma
Boscawen, New Hampshire

NEW ENGLAND INDIAN PUDDING

4 cups scalded milk	1 teaspoon salt
5 tablespoons yellow cornmeal	1/2 teaspoon ginger
2 tablespoons butter	1/4 teaspoon cinnamon
1 cup dark molasses	2 eggs, beaten
	1 cup milk

Pour the scalded milk into a double boiler. Stir in the cornmeal slowly. Cook for 15 minutes, stirring frequently. Stir in the butter, molasses, salt, ginger and cinnamon. Stir in the eggs gradually. Cook for 5 minutes, stirring constantly. Pour into a greased 9×13-inch baking dish. Pour the cold milk evenly over the batter in the baking dish. Bake at 350 degrees for 1 hour. Cool in the pan for 10 minutes. Serve warm with vanilla ice cream if desired. Yield: 6 to 8 servings.

Jacqueline V. Perry, Xi Delta Nu
Centerville, Massachusetts

*LouAnn Rochford, Xi Alpha Sigma, North Platte, Nebraska, shares her recipe for **Peachy Angel Food Dessert**. She begins by tearing an angel food cake into bite-size pieces and preparing two 1-ounce envelopes whipped topping mix using the package directions. Having set aside the cake pieces and prepared topping, she beats 6 ounces softened cream cheese in a large mixing bowl and adds 1 cup confectioners' sugar, beating well. The prepared whipped topping is folded in followed by the cake pieces. She stirs gently to coat the cake pieces evenly. Lastly, she spoons the mixture into a 9×13-inch cake pan and tops with 1 can peach pie filling. Chill until serving time.*

❖ BAKED LEMON PUDDING

2 egg whites	2 egg yolks
1/4 teaspoon salt (optional)	2 tablespoons butter, melted
1/2 cup sugar	3 tablespoons all-purpose flour
1 tablespoon grated lemon zest	1/4 cup sugar
5 tablespoons lemon juice	1 cup milk

Beat the eggs whites and salt in a bowl until soft peaks form. Add 1/2 cup sugar gradually and beat until stiff peaks form. Mix the next 4 ingredients in a bowl. Combine the flour and 1/4 cup sugar. Add to the lemon mixture and beat well. Add the milk and mix well. Fold in the egg whites. Pour into a greased 1-quart baking dish. Place the baking dish in a larger baking pan containing 1/2 inch of hot water. Bake at 325 degrees for 1 hour or until golden brown. Cool in the pan for 10 minutes. Serve warm with whipped cream if desired. Yield: 4 to 6 servings.

Penny Holloman, Preceptor Alpha Lambda
Roswell, Georgia

MANGO PUDDING

1 1/2 envelopes unflavored gelatin	1/2 cup cold water
3/4 cup cold water	2 cups fresh or frozen mango chunks, puréed
1/2 cup sugar	
3/4 cup boiling water	1 cup milk

Dissolve the gelatin in 3/4 cup cold water in a bowl. Combine the sugar and 3/4 cup boiling water in a saucepan. Cook over medium heat until the sugar dissolves, stirring frequently. Stir in the gelatin mixture. Remove from the heat and stir in 1/2 cup cold water. Cool completely. Stir in the mango. Stir in the milk. Pour into a serving bowl. Chill, covered, overnight. Yield: 4 to 6 servings.

Doreen McDonald, Xi Alpha Epsilon
Courtenay, British Columbia, Canada

ORANGE PUDDING

2 egg yolks	4 oranges, peeled and cut into bite-size pieces
1/3 cup sugar	
1 tablespoon cornstarch	
2 cups milk	2 egg whites

Beat the egg yolks in a bowl. Stir in the sugar and cornstarch. Heat the milk in a saucepan until warm. Stir in the egg yolk mixture. Cook over medium heat to almost boiling, stirring constantly. Pour over the orange pieces in a bowl. Let stand for 10 minutes. Beat the egg whites in a bowl until stiff peaks form. Fold into the orange mixture. Spoon into a greased

7×9-inch or 8×8-inch baking dish. Bake at 350 degrees for 35 to 40 minutes. Remove to a wire rack to cool. Yield: 6 servings.

Winifred Melvin, Alpha Master
Bangor, Maine

ORANGE RAISIN PUDDING

2 cups all-purpose flour	1 cup sugar
1 teaspoon baking soda	1 egg, beaten
1/8 teaspoon salt	1 cup sour milk
Grated zest of 1 orange	1/2 cup sugar
1 cup raisins, ground	1/2 cup orange juice
2 tablespoons butter, softened	

Sift the flour, baking soda and salt together. Add the orange zest and raisins and mix well. Beat the butter, 1 cup sugar and egg in a bowl until light and fluffy. Beat in the raisin mixture alternately with the sour milk. Spoon into a greased baking dish. Bake at 375 degrees for 1 hour. Remove to a wire rack to cool. Dissolve 1/2 cup sugar in the orange juice in a bowl. Pour evenly over the warm pudding. Serve with whipped cream if desired. Yield: 15 servings.

Martha Shipco, Theta Master
Fairmont, West Virginia

PERSIMMON PUDDING

2 cups all-purpose flour	1 1/2 cups sugar
1/2 teaspoon baking powder	2 cups persimmon pulp
	2 cups milk
1/2 teaspoon baking soda	1 teaspoon vanilla extract
1/2 teaspoon salt	
1 teaspoon cinnamon	1/4 cup (1/2 stick) butter or margarine, melted
2 eggs	

Mix the flour, baking powder, baking soda, salt and cinnamon in a bowl. Beat the eggs and sugar in a bowl. Add the persimmon pulp and mix well. Stir in the dry ingredients alternately with the milk. Stir in the vanilla. Pour the butter into a 9×13-inch baking pan. Add the batter. Bake at 325 degrees for 1 hour. Cool completely in the pan. Serve with whipped cream if desired. Yield: 12 servings.

Phyllis Croslow, Preceptor Delta
Centralia, Illinois

Mary Frances Reynolds, Delta Kappa, Ellisville, Mississippi, prepares **Butter Cream Sauce** *by combining 1/2 cup (1 stick) margarine, 1 cup sugar, 1 small can evaporated milk and 2 egg yolks in the top of a double boiler. She cooks it over simmering water until thickened, stirring constantly. It is served warm over bread pudding.*

PERSIMMON PUDDING WITH LEMON SAUCE

2 cups sugar
2¹/2 cups all-purpose
  flour
2 teaspoons baking soda
¹/2 teaspoon salt
2 teaspoons cinnamon
1 teaspoon ground
  cloves
¹/4 teaspoon nutmeg
1 cup raisins

2 cups chopped nuts
  (optional)
2 cups persimmon pulp
¹/4 cup milk
3 tablespoons butter,
  melted
2 teaspoons vanilla
  extract
Lemon Sauce

Mix the sugar, flour, baking soda, salt, cinnamon, cloves and nutmeg in a bowl. Add the raisins and nuts and mix well. Add the persimmon pulp, milk, butter and vanilla and mix just until combined. Pour into 2 or 3 greased loaf pans. Bake or steam at 300 degrees for 1 to 1¹/2 hours. Cool in the pans for 10 minutes. Remove to a wire rack to cool completely. Drizzle with Lemon Sauce just before serving. Yield: 20 to 30 servings.

LEMON SAUCE

¹/4 cup (¹/2 stick) butter
2 tablespoons
  all-purpose flour
  or cornstarch
1 cup sugar

2 cups boiling water
Grated zest of 1 lemon
Juice of 2 lemons
Juice of 1 small orange

Melt the butter in a saucepan over medium heat. Stir in the flour. Stir in the sugar. Stir in the water gradually. Stir in the lemon zest, lemon juice and orange juice. Cook until thickened, stirring constantly.

Anne Elmore-DeVinny, Laureate Beta Psi
Orlando, Florida

PINEAPPLE PICNIC PUDDING

¹/2 cup (1 stick) butter or
  margarine, softened
1 cup sugar
4 eggs

1 (20-ounce) can crushed
  pineapple
6 slices bread, cubed

Beat the butter and sugar in a bowl until light and fluffy. Add the eggs 1 at a time, beating well after each addition. Add the pineapple and mix well. Fold in the bread cubes. Pour into a greased 1¹/2-quart baking dish. Bake at 350 degrees for 1 hour. Remove to a wire rack to cool. Yield: 6 servings.

Mary Ellen Bradley, Laureate Beta
Landisville, Pennsylvania

LOW-FAT PINEAPPLE YOGURT PUDDING

This makes a great alternative to ice cream when trying to lose weight.

1 (20-ounce) can
  pineapple chunks or
  crushed pineapple
1 large package fat-free
  sugar-free vanilla
  instant pudding mix

4 cups fat-free vanilla
  yogurt

Drain the pineapple, reserving the juice. Whisk the reserved pineapple juice and pudding mix in a bowl. Add the yogurt and mix well. Stir in the pineapple. Chill, covered, for 1 hour. Yield: 4 to 6 servings.

Deirdre Walford, Preceptor Gamma
Pointe Claire, Quebec, Canada

PISTACHIO AND PINEAPPLE PUDDING

1 (3¹/2-ounce) package
  pistachio instant
  pudding mix
1 (20-ounce) can crushed
  pineapple

1 cup miniature
  marshmallows
2 cups whipped topping

Combine the pudding mix, pineapple and marshmallows in a bowl and mix well. Fold in the whipped topping. Chill, covered, for 1 hour or longer. Yield: 6 servings.

Charlotte V. Cronshey, Preceptor Alpha Theta
Huntingtown, Maryland

RED RASPBERRY PUDDING

1 cup all-purpose flour
¹/2 cup sugar
1 teaspoon baking
  powder
1 tablespoon butter

¹/2 cup milk
2 cups raspberries
1 cup hot water or
  raspberry juice
Sugar to taste

Sift the flour, ¹/2 cup sugar and the baking powder into a bowl. Cut in the butter until crumbly. Stir in the milk. Pat into a nonstick 8×8-inch baking pan. Combine the raspberries, water and sugar to taste in a saucepan. Bring to a boil over medium heat, stirring frequently. Pour evenly over the prepared crust. Bake at 350 degrees for 30 to 40 minutes. Remove to a wire rack to cool. Serve with whipped cream if desired. Yield: 9 servings.

Karen Crook, Laureate Alpha Eta
Moses Lake, Washington

CREAMY RICE PUDDING

6 cups milk	1/2 cup raisins or
3/4 cup sugar	maraschino cherries
3/4 cup rice	2 tablespoons rum
1 tablespoon vanilla	(optional)
extract	1/2 cup whipped topping
1/4 teaspoon salt	(optional)

Combine the milk and sugar in a 4-quart saucepan. Bring to a boil over medium heat, stirring occasionally. Stir in the rice. Bring to a boil and reduce the heat to low. Simmer, covered, for 1 hour and 15 minutes or until slightly thickened and very creamy, stirring occasionally. Remove from the heat and stir in the vanilla, salt, raisins and rum. Pour into a bowl and cool slightly. Chill, covered, until cold. Fold in the whipped topping. Yield: 6 servings.

Karen Shultz, Preceptor Omicron Rho
Bedford, Texas

SUGAR-FREE RICE PUDDING

3/4 cup instant rice	3 cups cold low-fat milk
1/2 cup raisins	1/2 teaspoon cinnamon
1 large package sugar-	
free vanilla instant	
pudding mix	

Cook the instant rice using the package directions. Add the raisins and cool completely. Whisk the pudding mix and milk in a bowl for 2 minutes. Add the rice and raisins and mix well. Sprinkle with cinnamon. Chill, covered, until ready to serve. Top with reduced-fat whipped topping if desired. Yield: 6 servings.

Rose Ann Aungst, Xi Eta Psi
Tallmadge, Ohio

SNOW PUDDING WITH RASPBERRY SAUCE

This light dessert goes well with Christmas cookies.

2 envelopes unflavored	1 tablespoon lemon
gelatin	juice
1 cup cold water	1 (20-ounce) package
2 cups heavy whipping	frozen raspberries
cream	1 tablespoon cornstarch
2 cups milk	Sugar to taste
1 cup sugar	

Soften the gelatin in the water in a bowl. Whip the cream in a large bowl until stiff peaks form. Beat in the milk slowly. Beat in 1 cup sugar gradually. Beat in the gelatin mixture and lemon juice. Pour into a serving bowl. Chill, covered, overnight. Combine the raspberries and cornstarch in a saucepan. Cook over medium heat until thickened, stirring frequently. Press through a sieve to remove the seeds. Stir in sugar to taste. Chill, covered, until cold. Serve with the pudding. Yield: 8 to 10 servings.

Linda Davis, Laureate Beta Xi
Marysville, Washington

LEMON SNOW PUDDING

1 1/3 cups water	2 tablespoons water
2/3 cups sugar	3 tablespoons lemon
3 tablespoons	juice
cornstarch	2 egg whites

Combine 1 1/3 cups water and the sugar in a saucepan. Bring to a boil over medium heat, stirring occasionally. Dissolve the cornstarch in 2 tablespoons water in a small bowl. Add to the sugar mixture. Cook for 10 to 15 minutes, stirring frequently. Stir in the lemon juice. Pour into a bowl and cool completely. Beat the egg whites in a bowl until stiff peaks form. Fold into the lemon mixture. Pour into a mold. Chill, covered, overnight. Unmold onto a serving plate and serve with your favorite sauce. Yield: 6 to 8 servings.

Wendy Hart, Laureate Tau
Fort Qu'Appelle, Saskatchewan, Canada

SNOWFLAKE PUDDING

The presentation of this pudding at Christmas is beautiful. It is a light dessert that my family requests every year.

1 envelope unflavored	1 teaspoon almond
gelatin	extract
1 1/4 cups milk	1 1/3 cups flaked coconut
1 cup sugar	Raspberry Sauce or
1/2 teaspoon salt	Lingonberry Sauce
2 cups whipping cream,	
whipped	

Soften the gelatin in 1/4 cup of the milk in a bowl. Bring the remaining 1 cup milk, sugar and salt to a boil in a saucepan. Remove from the heat. Stir in the gelatin. Chill the gelatin mixture in the refrigerator until the consistency of egg whites. Fold in the whipped cream, almond extract and coconut. Chill, covered, until ready to serve. Serve in individual dishes and top with the sauce. Yield: 10 to 12 servings.

RASPBERRY SAUCE

1 (10-ounce) package	1 1/2 teaspoons cornstarch
frozen raspberries	1/4 cup sugar

Combine the raspberries and cornstarch in a saucepan. Cook over medium heat until thickened and clear, stirring frequently. Stir in the sugar. Chill, covered, until serving time.

LINGONBERRY SAUCE

1 cup water
1 cup sugar
Lingonberries

Combine the water and sugar in a saucepan. Bring to a boil. Add the lingonberries.

Linda Dahlquist, Laureate Alpha Gamma
Bella Vista, Arkansas

MICROWAVE VANILLA PUDDING

To make chocolate pudding, increase the sugar to 1 cup and add 2 ounces unsweetened chocolate.

$^2/_3$ cup sugar
$^1/_3$ cup cornstarch
$^1/_4$ teaspoon salt
$^1/_2$ cup milk
$1^1/_2$ cups milk
2 eggs, beaten
2 tablespoons butter
$1^1/_2$ teaspoons vanilla
extract

Mix the sugar, cornstarch, salt and $^1/_2$ cup milk in a microwave-save bowl until smooth. Stir in $1^1/_2$ cups milk. Microwave on High for 5 minutes, stirring frequently. Stir a small amount of the hot mixture into the eggs in a bowl; stir the eggs into the hot mixture. Microwave on High for 45 seconds or to boiling. Stir in the butter and vanilla. Chill, covered, until cold. Yield: 4 to 6 servings.

Karen Parker, Omicron Eta
Chico, California

BANANA TORTE

4 firm bananas, sliced
$^1/_2$ cup lemon juice
$1^1/_2$ cups graham cracker crumbs
$^1/_4$ cup sugar
$^1/_2$ cup (1 stick) butter, melted
1 cup sour cream
1 ($3^1/_2$-ounce) package vanilla instant pudding mix
12 ounces whipped topping
$^1/_3$ cup chopped pecans

Combine the bananas and lemon juice in a bowl and toss well; drain. Combine the graham cracker crumbs, sugar and butter in a bowl and mix until crumbly. Press into the bottom and up the side of a 9-inch springform pan. Beat the sour cream and pudding mix in a bowl at low speed for 2 minutes. Fold in the whipped topping and the bananas. Spoon into the prepared crust. Chill, covered, for up to 6 hours. Loosen from the side of the pan with a sharp knife and remove the side. Sprinkle with the pecans. Yield: 8 to 10 servings.

Darlene Fier, Laureate Gamma Alpha
DeWitt, Iowa

BANANA SPLIT TORTE

2 cups graham cracker crumbs
$^1/_2$ cup (1 stick) butter or margarine, melted
2 eggs
2 cups sifted confectioners' sugar
$^3/_4$ cup ($1^1/_2$ sticks) butter or margarine, softened
1 teaspoon vanilla extract
1 (20-ounce) can crushed pineapple, drained
3 cups sliced bananas
8 ounces whipped topping
$^1/_2$ cup chopped pecans
Chocolate syrup
Maraschino cherries

Combine the graham cracker crumbs and $^1/_2$ cup butter in a bowl and mix until crumbly. Press into the bottom of a nonstick 9×13-inch baking pan. Beat the eggs in a bowl at high speed for 4 minutes or until thick and pale yellow. Add the confectioners' sugar, $^3/_4$ cup butter and the vanilla and beat for 5 minutes. Spread over the prepared crust. Chill for 30 minutes. Spread the pineapple over the butter mixture and top with bananas. Spread the whipped topping evenly over the bananas and sprinkle with pecans. Drizzle with chocolate syrup and top with cherries. Chill, covered, for 6 to 10 hours. Note: If you are concerned about using raw eggs, use eggs pasteurized in their shells, which are sold at some specialty food stores, or use an equivalent amount of pasteurized egg substitute. Yield: 12 servings.

Belinda Whitfield, Xi Gamma Omicron
Martinez, Georgia

BLACK FOREST TORTE

This is my son's favorite cake. I made it for the groom's table at his wedding.

1 (2-layer) package chocolate cake mix
1 container vanilla frosting
8 ounces cream cheese, softened
1 tablespoon lemon juice
1 (21-ounce) can cherry pie filling
1 teaspoon cinnamon

Prepare and bake the cake mix using the package directions for a bundt pan. Cool in the pan for 10 minutes. Remove to a wire rack to cool completely. Slice horizontally into 3 layers. Beat the frosting and cream cheese in a bowl until light and fluffy. Beat in the lemon juice. Mix the pie filling and cinnamon in a bowl. Place the bottom cake layer on a serving plate. Spread with one-third of the cream cheese mixture and one-third of the pie filling. Repeat with the remaining cake layers, cream cheese mixture and pie filling. Chill until set. Yield: 10 to 12 servings.

Delilah Williams, Gamma Master
Columbus, Mississippi

MOCHA BROWNIE TORTE

²/₃ cup hot water
2 tablespoons instant
   coffee granules
1 (15-ounce) package
   brownie mix
2 teaspoons vanilla
   extract

4 egg whites, lightly
   beaten
8 ounces whipped
   topping
1 tablespoon instant
   coffee granules

Combine the hot water and 2 tablespoons coffee granules in a bowl and stir to dissolve. Add the brownie mix, vanilla and egg whites and mix well. Pour into 2 greased 9-inch baking pans. Bake at 325 degrees for 20 minutes. Cool in the pans for 5 minutes. Remove to a wire rack to cool completely. Place the whipped topping in a bowl. Fold in 1 tablespoon coffee granules. Spread between the layers and over the top and side of the cake. Store in the refrigerator. Yield: 12 servings.

Carrie Begemann, Delta Psi
Odessa, Missouri

BUTTER PECAN TORTE

60 butter crackers, finely
   crushed
¹/₂ cup (1 stick) butter or
   margarine, melted
2 (3¹/₂-ounce) packages
   coconut cream
   instant pudding mix

1¹/₂ cups milk
1 quart butter pecan ice
   cream, softened
9 ounces whipped
   topping

Combine the crushed crackers and butter in a bowl and mix until crumbly. Press half the cracker mixture into the bottom of a nonstick 9×13-inch baking pan. Beat the pudding mix and milk in a bowl for 2 minutes. Fold in the ice cream. Spoon over the prepared crust. Spread the whipped topping evenly over the ice cream mixture. Sprinkle with the remaining cracker mixture. Chill, covered, for 8 to 10 hours. Yield: 8 to 10 servings.

Katherine Radford, Xi Gamma Alpha
Waterford, Michigan

CHERRY TORTE

1¹/₂ cups sugar
1 cup all-purpose flour
1 teaspoon baking soda
1 teaspoon cinnamon
1 egg

2 tablespoons
   vegetable oil
2 to 3 cups fresh or
   frozen tart cherries
Chopped nuts (optional)

Mix the sugar, flour, baking soda and cinnamon in a bowl. Add the egg and oil and mix well. Stir in the cherries and nuts. Pour into a nonstick 10×10-inch baking pan. Bake at 350 degrees for 30 minutes or until a wooden pick inserted in the center comes out clean. Cool in the pan for 10 minutes. Remove to a wire rack to cool completely. Serve warm or at room temperature with whipped topping or cream if desired. Yield: 8 servings.

Dawn Morrow, Preceptor Alpha
Spokane, Washington

CHOCOLATE RASPBERRY TORTE

1 (2-layer) package
   chocolate cake mix
Almond-flavored
   liqueur

3 cups heavy whipping
   cream
1 (21-ounce) can
   raspberry pie filling

Prepare and bake the cake mix using the package directions for two 9-inch cake pans. Cool in the pans for 10 minutes. Remove to a wire rack to cool completely. Slice each layer in half horizontally to make a total of 4 layers. Brush the cut side of each layer with almond-flavored liqueur. Whip the cream in a bowl. Fold in the pie filling. Place one cake layer in a 10-inch springform pan and spread with one-fourth of the whipped cream mixture. Top with another cake layer and spread with one-fourth of the whipped cream mixture. Repeat with the remaining ingredients. Chill, covered, until cold. Loosen from the side of the pan with a sharp knife and remove the side. Drizzle with melted chocolate or garnish with shaved chocolate and fresh raspberries if desired. Yield: 12 servings.

Betty Sheppard, Preceptor Beta
Corner Brook, Newfoundland, Canada

CHOCOLATE TRUFFLE TORTE

2²/₃ cups (16 ounces)
   semisweet chocolate
   chips
1 cup (2 sticks) unsalted
   butter

6 eggs
1 (10-ounce) package
   frozen raspberries,
   thawed
Whipped cream

Combine the chocolate chips and butter in a microwave-safe bowl. Microwave on Medium until smooth, stirring occasionally. Beat the eggs in a double boiler for 10 minutes or until thickened and doubled in volume. Fold the eggs into the chocolate mixture. Line an 11-inch springform pan with waxed paper and butter the waxed paper. Pour the chocolate mixture into the prepared pan. Bake at 425 degrees for 5 minutes. Cover the pan with foil. Bake for 10 minutes longer. Cool completely in the pan. Chill, covered, until cold. Loosen from the side of the pan with a sharp knife and remove the side. Purée the raspberries in a blender or food processor.

Spoon the raspberry purée onto serving plates and top each with a slice of the torte. Top with whipped cream. Yield: 12 to 16 servings.

Priscilla Culkowski, Xi Zeta Iota
Williamsburg, Virginia

DATE CHOCOLATE CHIP TORTE

1 cup chopped dates
1 teaspoon baking soda
1¼ cups boiling water
  or hot coffee
³/4 cup (1½ sticks)
  butter, softened
1 cup sugar
2 eggs
1½ cups all-purpose
  flour

1 teaspoon vanilla
  extract
1 teaspoon cinnamon
½ teaspoon salt
½ cup sugar
½ cup chopped nuts
½ cup (3 ounces)
  chocolate chips

Mix the dates and baking soda in a bowl. Add the water and let stand until cool. Beat the butter and 1 cup sugar in a large bowl until light and fluffy. Add the eggs, flour, vanilla, cinnamon and salt and mix gently. Fold in the date mixture. Pour into a nonstick 9×13-inch baking pan. Mix ¹/2 cup sugar, the nuts and chocolate chips in a bowl. Sprinkle over the batter in the pan. Bake at 350 degrees for 35 to 40 minutes or until a wooden pick inserted in the center comes out clean. Cool in the pan for 10 minutes. Remove to a wire rack to cool. Serve warm or chilled with whipped topping. Yield: 15 servings.

Virginia R. Panko, Laureate Beta Theta
St. Catharines, Ontario, Canada

WALNUT CHOCOLATE TORTE

4 extra-large eggs
³/4 cup sugar
1 cup walnuts
1 teaspoon vanilla
  extract
2 tablespoons
  all-purpose flour

2½ teaspoons baking
  powder
2 tablespoons baking
  cocoa
1½ cups heavy
  whipping cream
³/4 cup chocolate syrup

Process the eggs in a blender for a few seconds. Add the sugar, walnuts, vanilla, flour, baking powder and baking cocoa and process at high speed for 1 minute. Pour into a greased and floured 9- or 10-inch cake pan. Bake at 350 degrees for 30 minutes or until a wooden pick inserted in the center comes out clean. Cool in the pan for 10 minutes. Remove to a wire rack to cool completely. Whip the cream and chocolate syrup in a bowl until stiff peaks form. Spread over the top and side of the cake. Yield: 8 to 10 servings.

Trudy Richard, Preceptor Mu Sigma
Borrego Springs, California

DOUBLE CHOCOLATE TORTE

1 (15-ounce) package
  fudge brownie mix
1 cup (6 ounces)
  semisweet chocolate
  chips, melted

½ cup (1 stick) butter,
  softened
1 (21-ounce) can cherry
  pie filling (optional)
2 cups whipped topping
Chocolate sprinkles

Prepare the brownie mix using the package directions. Spread in a greased 9-inch cake pan. Bake at 350 degrees for 38 to 42 minutes or until the center springs back when lightly touched. Cool in the pan for 10 minutes. Invert onto a serving plate and cool completely. Combine the chocolate and butter in a bowl and mix until smooth. Spread over the cooled cake. Chill until set. Spread the pie filling over the top. Serve with whipped topping and chocolate sprinkles. Yield: 9 to 12 servings.

Mary Jo Schoech, Gamma Theta
Russell, Kansas

COFFEE TORTE

1 pound cake, thinly
  sliced
1 cup strong coffee
16 ounces cream cheese,
  softened

½ cup sugar
2 tablespoons almond-
  flavored liqueur
2 cups whipped topping
1 teaspoon baking cocoa

Arrange half the pound cake over the bottom of a 9×13-inch baking pan. Drizzle with half the coffee. Beat the cream cheese, sugar and liqueur in a bowl until light and fluffy. Fold in the whipped topping. Spread half the cream cheese mixture over the pound cake in the pan. Arrange the remaining cake slices over the top and drizzle with the remaining coffee. Spread with the remaining cream cheese mixture. Sprinkle with baking cocoa. Chill, covered, for several hours to overnight. Yield: 12 to 16 servings.

Barbara Kennedy, Laureate Lambda
Ft. Pierce, Florida

---

*Judith A. Nicholas, Laureste Gamma Delta, Lexington, Missouri, prepares **Tropical Twinkie Delight** by cutting one 10-count box Twinkie snack cakes lengthwise and arranging them cut side up in a single layer in a 9×13-inch baking dish. She prepares two 3½-ounce packages vanilla instant pudding mix using the package directions and pours it over the Twinkies. She combines one 15-ounce can drained crushed pineapple, 2 sliced bananas, and 8 ounces whipped topping in a bowl and spreads it over the pudding. The dessert is completed with a sprinkling of nut topping and then chilled, covered, until cold.*

PINEAPPLE LEMON TORTE

This torte is a refreshing and simple dessert to make. It is light, cool, and wonderful on hot summer nights.

1 (6-ounce) package
  lemon instant
  pudding mix
1 (20-ounce) can crushed
  pineapple
2 cups whipping cream,
  whipped

1 angel food cake
1 (8- or 11-ounce)
  can mandarin
  oranges, drained
  and patted dry

Combine the pudding mix and pineapple in a bowl and mix well. Fold in the whipped cream. Slice the angel food cake into layers. Spread the pudding mixture between the layers. Arrange the mandarin oranges on the top. Yield: 8 to 10 servings.

Jo Ann Addington, Beta Lambda Master
Lancaster, California

ITALIAN RASPBERRY TORTE

1¼ cups all-purpose
  flour
½ teaspoon baking
  powder
½ teaspoon baking soda
¼ teaspoon salt
⅔ cup sugar
½ cup sour cream
½ cup (1 stick) butter,
  melted
2 eggs

½ teaspoon vanilla
  extract
¼ teaspoon almond
  extract
8 ounces cream cheese,
  softened
¼ cup sugar
¼ cup sour cream
¼ teaspoon almond
  extract
2 cups raspberries

Combine the flour, baking powder, baking soda and salt. Combine ⅔ cup sugar and ½ cup sour cream in a bowl and mix well. Stir in the butter. Add the eggs, vanilla and ¼ teaspoon almond extract and mix well. Add the dry ingredients and stir just until combined. Pour into a greased 9-inch springform pan. Bake at 350 degrees for 15 minutes. Beat the cream cheese and ¼ cup sugar in a bowl until smooth. Beat in ¼ cup sour cream and ¼ teaspoon almond extract. Spread carefully over the baked layer. Bake for 20 to 25 minutes or until the top is set and the edge is golden brown. Cool in the pan on a wire rack. Arrange the raspberries on top of the cake and cool for 40 minutes. Loosen from the side of the pan with a sharp knife and remove the side of the pan. Chill, covered, until cold. Garnish with mint sprigs. Yield: 12 to 16 servings.

Jan Meredith, Laureate Beta Gamma
Fredericksburg, Virginia

RED-LETTER DAY TORTE

2 cups sifted all-purpose
  flour
1 teaspoon salt
1 cup shortening
1 egg, lightly beaten
2 (14½-ounce) cans
  pitted tart cherries
¾ cup sugar
3 tablespoons quick-
  cooking tapioca
3 egg yolks, beaten

½ teaspoon red food
  coloring
2 teaspoons lemon juice
3 egg whites
1 teaspoon vanilla
  extract
¼ teaspoon cream
  of tartar
Dash of salt
¾ cup sugar
1 cup chopped walnuts

Sift the flour and 1 teaspoon salt into a bowl. Cut in the shortening until crumbly. Add the egg and stir until a soft dough forms. Pat into a greased 7×11-inch baking pan. Bake at 425 degrees for 20 minutes. Cool in the pan on a wire rack. Drain the cherries, reserving 1 cup of juice. Mix the reserved juice, ¾ cup sugar, the tapioca, egg yolks and food coloring in a saucepan. Let stand for at least 5 minutes. Bring to a boil over medium heat, stirring constantly. Remove from the heat and stir in the cherries and lemon juice. Cool completely. Pour evenly over the baked crust. Beat the egg whites, vanilla, cream of tartar and salt in a bowl until soft peaks form. Add ¾ cup sugar gradually and beat until stiff peaks form. Fold in the walnuts. Spread evenly over the cherry mixture. Bake at 350 degrees for 17 to 20 minutes or until light brown. Remove to a wire rack to cool.
Yield: 9 to 12 servings.

Kay Johnson, Omega Preceptor
Cynthiana, Kentucky

STRAWBERRY CHEESECAKE TORTE

1 small package sugar-
  free strawberry
  gelatin
½ cup boiling water
¼ cup seedless
  strawberry jam
1 loaf pound cake or
  loaf angel food cake
8 ounces fat-free cream
  cheese, softened
⅓ cup fat-free milk

2 tablespoons lemon
  juice
3 cups fat-free whipped
  topping
1 (3½-ounce) package
  cheesecake or vanilla
  instant pudding mix
1 cup strawberries
1 kiwifruit, halved
  and sliced

Dissolve the gelatin in the water in a bowl. Add the jam and stir until smooth. Place the cake on a plate. Pierce with a fork. Brush the cake with the gelatin mixture. Chill for 10 minutes. Beat the cream cheese, milk and lemon juice in a bowl until smooth. Add the whipped topping and pudding mix and whisk well. Trim the edges of the cake and cut lengthwise into 3 equal slices. Lay one slice on a serving plate and spread with one-third of the cream cheese mixture. Repeat the layers two more times. Arrange the strawberries and kiwifruit over the top. Yield: 12 servings.

Gwyn Bacot, Xi Alpha Phi
Natchez, Mississippi

TIRAMISU TOFFEE TORTE

1 (2-layer) package white cake mix	2 cups heavy whipping cream
1¼ cups strong coffee, at room temperature	⅓ cup chocolate syrup
4 egg whites	2 teaspoons vanilla extract
5 (1½-ounce) chocolate-covered toffee bars, chopped	6 tablespoons strong brewed coffee, at room temperature
4 ounces cream cheese, softened	1 (1½-ounce) chocolate-covered toffee bar, chopped
⅔ cup sugar	

Line two 9-inch cake pans with waxed paper and grease the waxed paper. Beat the cake mix, 1 cup of the coffee and the egg whites in a bowl at low speed until moistened. Beat at high speed for 2 minutes. Fold in 4 candy bars. Pour into the prepared pans. Bake at 350 degrees for 25 to 30 minutes or until a wooden pick inserted in the center comes out clean. Cool in the pans for 10 minutes. Remove to a wire rack to cool completely. Slice each layer in half horizontally to make a total of 4 layers. Beat the cream cheese and sugar in a chilled bowl until light and fluffy. Add the cream, chocolate syrup, ¼ cup of the coffee and vanilla. Beat at high speed for 5 minutes or until light and fluffy. Place one cake layer on a serving plate and drizzle with 2 tablespoons of the remaining coffee. Spread with ¾ cup of the cream cheese mixture. Repeat the layers two more times. Top with the remaining cake layer and spread the remaining cream cheese mixture over the top and side of the cake. Chill, covered, overnight. Sprinkle with 1 candy bar. Yield: 12 to 14 servings.

Jenny Poole, Preceptor Mu
Lexington, Kentucky

---

*Debbie Ficken, Alpha Delta Rho, Chillicothe, Missouri, makes a luscious **Brandy Sauce** to serve over bread pudding. She starts by combining 12 eggs, 1 cup sugar, 1 teaspoon vanilla extract, 1 cup (2 sticks) melted butter and 2 cups milk in a double boiler over medium heat. She cooks the mixture until it thickens to the consistency of pudding, stirring constantly. She stirs in 1 cup brandy and cooks the mixture for 2 minutes longer, stirring constantly. She stores the sauce in an airtight container in the refrigerator.*

WALNUT TORTE

11 egg whites	1 cup (2 sticks) unsalted butter, softened
Pinch of salt	3 cups confectioners' sugar
¾ cup granulated sugar	1 egg yolk
1 cup finely chopped walnuts	2 tablespoons baking cocoa
¼ cup dry bread crumbs	1 tablespoon instant coffee granules
¼ heaping cup all-purpose flour	1 teaspoon lemon juice
1 teaspoon baking powder	1 egg white
1 teaspoon vanilla extract	

Beat the egg whites and salt in a bowl until soft peaks form. Add the granulated sugar gradually and beat until stiff peaks form. Combine the walnuts, bread crumbs, flour, baking powder and vanilla in a large bowl and mix well. Fold in the egg whites. Spoon into 2 greased and floured 8-inch cake pans. Bake at 350 degrees for 30 minutes or until a wooden pick inserted in the center comes out clean. Cool in the pans for 5 minutes. Remove to a wire rack to cool completely. Beat the butter, confectioner's sugar, egg yolk, baking cocoa, coffee granules and lemon juice in a bowl until light and fluffy. Beat 1 egg white in a small bowl until stiff peaks form. Fold into the butter mixture. Spread the frosting between the layers and over the top and side of the cooled cake. Note: If you are concerned about using raw eggs, use eggs pasteurized in their shells, which are sold at some specialty food stores, or use an equivalent amount of pasteurized egg yolk and pasteurized egg white. Yield: 16 servings.

Stella Sinclair, Theta Chi
Delaware, Ontario, Canada

APRICOT NECTAR TRIFLE

½ cup cornstarch	1 angel food cake, torn into pieces
1 cup sugar	8 ounces whipped topping
46 ounces apricot nectar (apricot juice)	Chopped nuts

Mix the cornstarch and sugar in a saucepan. Whisk in the apricot nectar. Bring to a boil over medium heat, stirring constantly. Cook until thickened, stirring constantly. Remove from the heat and cool completely. Arrange the cake pieces in a 9×13-inch baking pan. Pour the apricot mixture evenly over the cake. Chill, covered, for 2 to 3 hours. Spread the whipped topping evenly over the cake mixture. Sprinkle with nuts. Chill, covered, overnight. Yield: 12 to 15 servings.

Karen Martin, Preceptor Gamma Upsilon
Hotchkiss, Colorado

ANGEL BERRY TRIFLE

Try using other fruits in this light dessert.

1½ cups milk	2 teaspoons vanilla
1 small package fat-free	extract
sugar-free vanilla	12 ounces light whipped
instant pudding mix	topping
1 cup fat-free vanilla	1 angel food cake, cut
yogurt	into 1-inch cubes
6 ounces light cream	2 cups raspberries
cheese, softened	2 cups blackberries
½ cup reduced-fat	2 cups blueberries
sour cream	

Whisk the milk and pudding mix in a bowl for 2 minutes. Beat the yogurt, cream cheese, sour cream and vanilla in a large bowl until smooth. Fold in the pudding and 1 cup of the whipped topping. Arrange one-third of the cake pieces across the bottom of a trifle bowl. Pour one-third of the pudding mixture evenly over the cake. Sprinkle with one-third of the raspberries, one-third of the blackberries and one-third of the blueberries. Spread half of the remaining whipped topping over the berries. Repeat the layers two more times, eliminating the whipped topping from the last layer. Chill, covered, until just before serving. Yield: 14 servings.

Eugenia Richardson, Iota Master
Calgary, Alberta, Canada

BERRY ALMOND TRIFLE

This colorful and light dessert is approved by the American Heart Association.

1 (16-ounce) package	1 teaspoon vanilla
frozen unsweetened	extract
blueberries	⅓ cup confectioners'
1 (12-ounce) package	sugar
frozen unsweetened	1 large package fat-free
raspberries	sugar-free vanilla
½ cup granulated sugar	instant pudding mix
¼ cup water	8 ounces fat-free or low-
2½ tablespoons	fat whipped topping
cornstarch	1 angel food cake, torn
¼ teaspoon almond	into small pieces
extract	½ cup sliced almonds,
2 cups fat-free or low-	toasted
fat plain yogurt	

Mix the blueberries, raspberries, granulated sugar, water and cornstarch in a skillet until the cornstarch dissolves. Bring to a boil over medium-high heat, stirring frequently. Remove the blueberries and raspberries with a slotted spoon to a bowl. Reduce

the heat to medium. Cook for 1 minute or until thickened, stirring constantly. Add to the berries. Stir in the almond extract. Cool for 30 minutes. Whisk the yogurt and vanilla in a large bowl. Whisk in the confectioners' sugar and pudding mix. Fold in the whipped topping. Arrange one-third of the cake over the bottom of a trifle bowl. Pour one-third of the yogurt mixture evenly over the cake. Top with one-third of the berry mixture. Repeat the layers. Top with the remaining cake and spread the remaining yogurt mixture evenly over the top. Refrigerate the remaining berry mixture in a sealed container. Chill the trifle, tightly covered, for 8 hours or longer. Top with the remaining berry mixture and sprinkle with the almonds just before serving. Yield: 24 servings.

Pauline M. DiPasquale, Laureate Beta Eta
Portland, Oregon

BLACK FOREST TRIFLE

1 (21-ounce) can cherry	1 angel food cake, torn
pie filling	into large pieces
2 cups low-fat cherry	1 (12-ounce) jar
yogurt	chocolate topping
8 ounces light whipped	Chopped almonds
topping	

Combine the pie filling and yogurt in a bowl and mix well. Fold in the whipped topping. Alternate layers of cake, yogurt mixture and chocolate sauce in a trifle bowl, making at least 3 layers and ending with the yogurt mixture. Sprinkle with almonds. Chill, covered, until just before serving. Garnish with additional whipped topping, chocolate shavings or maraschino cherries. Yield: 12 servings.

Joyce Fred, Alpha Iota Master
Springfield, Illinois

BROWNIE TRIFLE

1 (19½-ounce) package	1 small package fat-free
brownie mix	sugar-free chocolate
½ cup vegetable oil	instant pudding mix
¼ cup water	2 cups skim milk
½ cup egg substitute	1 cup (6 ounces) toffee
1 tablespoon instant	bits
coffee granules	16 ounces whipped
	topping

Combine the brownie mix, oil, water and egg substitute in a bowl and mix well. Stir in the coffee granules. Bake using the package directions for a 9×13-inch baking pan. Cool completely in the pan on a wire rack. Cut into 1-inch squares. Whisk the pudding mix and milk in a bowl for 2 minutes.

Arrange half of the brownies over the bottom of a trifle bowl. Pour half the pudding evenly over the brownies. Reserve 2 tablespoons of the toffee bits. Sprinkle half the remaining toffee bits over the pudding layer in the trifle bowl and spread with half the whipped topping. Repeat the layers. Sprinkle with the reserved toffee bits. Chill, covered, for 4 hours or longer. Yield: 20 servings.

Fayan Rochowiak, Preceptor Iota
Independence, Missouri

BROWNIE TOFFEE TRIFLE

1 (19¹/2-ounce) package chewy brownie mix	**2¹/4 cups milk**
¹/2 cup chopped nuts (optional)	**16 ounces whipped topping**
1 (6-ounce) package chocolate instant pudding mix	**4 to 6 (1¹/2-ounce) chocolate-covered toffee bars, chopped**

Prepare the brownie mix using the package directions, stirring the nuts into the batter. Bake using the package directions for a 9×13-inch baking pan. Cool completely in the pan on a wire rack. Cut into squares. Whisk the pudding mix and milk in a bowl for 2 minutes. Fold in 1 cup of the whipped topping. Alternate layers of the brownies, pudding, the remaining whipped topping and candy in a trifle bowl, making 2 layers. Chill, covered, for 4 to 6 hours. Yield: 20 to 24 servings.

Donna Fagg, Theta Gamma
Arkansas City, Kansas

CHOCOLATE ANGEL FOOD SNOWBALL

12 ounces German's sweet chocolate	**4 egg whites**
3 tablespoons confectioners' sugar	**2 angel food cakes, cut into ¹/2-inch slices**
3 tablespoons water	**2 cups heavy whipping cream**
4 egg yolks, beaten	**2 teaspoons granulated sugar**
1 teaspoon vanilla extract	**1 teaspoon vanilla extract**
Dash of salt	

Melt the chocolate in a double boiler. Pour into a large bowl and cool completely. Beat in the confectioners' sugar, water, egg yolks, 1 teaspoon vanilla and salt. Beat the egg whites in a bowl until stiff peaks form. Fold into the chocolate mixture. Line a waxed paper-lined bowl with cake slices. Spread some of the chocolate mixture over the cake. Alternate cake slices and the chocolate mixture to fill the bowl. Chill, covered, overnight. Invert onto a serving plate. Whip the cream, granulated sugar and 1 teaspoon vanilla in a bowl until stiff peaks form. Spread over the cake. Note: If you are concerned about using raw eggs, use eggs pasteurized in their shells, which are sold at some specialty food stores, or use an equivalent amount of pasteurized egg yolk and pasteurized egg white. Yield: 12 to 14 servings.

Lois Swanson, Alpha Iota Master
Ellisville, Missouri

CHOCOLATE BERRY TRIFLE

1 (6-ounce) package vanilla instant pudding mix	**Fresh or frozen strawberries or raspberries**
1 (2-layer) package devil's food cake mix	**Hot fudge sauce**
	16 ounces light whipped topping

Prepare the pudding mix using the package directions. Chill, covered. Prepare and bake the cake mix using the package directions for a 9×13-inch baking dish. Cool completely in the pan on a wire rack. Cut into bite-size pieces. Arrange half the cake pieces over the bottom of a trifle bowl. Pour half the pudding over the cake. Top with berries and drizzle with hot fudge sauce. Spread with half the whipped topping. Repeat the layers. Drizzle hot fudge sauce over the top. Chill, covered, until ready to serve. Yield: 10 to 12 servings.

Margaret Lutz, Xi Gamma Phi
Wyoming, Michigan

CHOCOLATE COFFEE TRIFLE

1 (4-ounce) package chocolate pudding mix	**4 cups heavy whipping cream, whipped**
1 (2-layer) package chocolate fudge cake mix	**6 (1¹/2-ounce) chocolate-covered toffee bars, chopped**
	¹/2 cup strong coffee, at room temperature

Prepare the pudding mix using the package directions; cool. Prepare and bake the cake mix using the package directions for a 9×13-inch baking pan. Cool in the pan for 10 minutes. Remove to a wire rack to cool completely. Crumble the cooled cake. Alternate layers of cake, pudding, whipped cream, candy and coffee in a trifle bowl, making 3 layers. Chill, covered, for up to 24 hours. Yield: 10 to 12 servings.

Barb McCrinole, Theta Eta
Merville, British Columbia, Canada

CHOCOLATE RASPBERRY TRIFLE

1/4 cup reduced-sugar
   raspberry jam
1 angel food cake, cut
   into 1-inch cubes
2 cups prepared
   chocolate instant
   pudding

2 cups raspberries
8 ounces whipped
   topping
1 tablespoon chocolate
   syrup

Microwave the jam in a small microwave-safe bowl for 30 seconds or until melted. Arrange one-fourth of the cake cubes over the bottom of a trifle bowl. Drizzle with 1 tablespoon jam and 1/2 cup pudding. Sprinkle with 1/2 cup raspberries. Cover with one-fourth of the whipped topping. Repeat the layers two more times. Top with the remaining cake, pudding and 1/4 cup raspberries. Spread with the remaining whipped topping and sprinkle with the remaining raspberries. Drizzle with the remaining jam and the chocolate syrup. Chill, covered, for 2 hours or longer. Yield: 12 servings.

Jenny Lane, Xi Eta Sigma
Gowrie, Iowa

CHOCOLATE STRAWBERRY TRIFLE

2 (31/2-ounce) packages
   white chocolate
   instant pudding mix
3 cups milk
12 ounces whipped
   topping
1 (10-ounce) package
   frozen sliced
   strawberries, thawed

1 angel food cake,
   cut into cubes
2 cups fresh
   strawberries, sliced
Confectioners' sugar
Chopped nuts

Whisk the pudding mix and milk in a large bowl for 2 minutes. Fold in the whipped topping, 10 ounces strawberries and the cake. Spoon into a trifle bowl or 9×13-inch baking dish. Chill, covered, until cold. Top with the fresh strawberries, dust with confectioners' sugar and sprinkle with nuts just before serving. Yield: 12 servings.

Georgia Maneke, Pi Master
Godfrey, Illinois

CHOCOLATE TOFFEE TRIFLE

1 (2-layer) package
   chocolate cake mix
1/4 cup coffee-flavored
   liqueur
1 (6-ounce) package
   chocolate instant
   pudding mix

18 ounces whipped
   topping
4 large chocolate-
   covered toffee bars,
   chopped

Prepare the cake mix using the package directions, substituting the coffee liqueur for water. Bake using the package directions for a 9×13-inch baking pan. Cool in the pan for 10 minutes. Remove to a wire rack to cool completely. Cut into cubes. Prepare the pudding mix using the package directions. Alternate layers of cake, pudding, whipped topping and crushed candy in a trifle bowl, ending with whipped topping and crushed candy. Chill, covered, until ready to serve. Yield: 8 to 10 servings.

Lee Theobald, Laureate Epsilon Omega
Bradenton, Florida

DEATH BY CHOCOLATE

1 (2-layer) package
   devil's food cake mix
3/4 to 1 cup Irish cream
   liqueur
4 (23/4-ounce) packages
   milk chocolate
   instant mousse mix

4 cups heavy whipping
   cream, whipped
6 (11/2-ounce) chocolate-
   covered toffee bars,
   chopped

Prepare and bake the cake mix using the package directions for a 9×13-inch baking pan. Cool in the pan for 10 minutes. Remove to a wire rack to cool completely. Cut into very small squares in the pan and loosen from the pan. Drizzle the liqueur evenly over the cake in the pan. Let stand for several hours or longer. Prepare the chocolate mousse using the package directions. Alternate layers of cake, mousse, whipped cream and crushed candy in a trifle bowl, making 3 layers. Chill, covered, until ready to serve. Yield: 20 servings.

Angela Ficken, Xi Alpha Omicron
Glenwood, Iowa

FRUIT COCKTAIL TRIFLE

1/2 angel food cake,
   cut into cubes
3 tablespoons sherry
1 (14-ounce) can fruit
   cocktail, drained

1 (16-ounce) can Devon
   cream or vanilla
   custard
2 cups heavy whipping
   cream, whipped

Arrange the cake cubes over the bottom of a trifle bowl. Drizzle the sherry over the cake. Top with the fruit cocktail. Spread the Devon cream evenly over the fruit. Top with an even layer of whipped cream. Chill, covered, until ready to serve. Yield: 6 servings.

Elaine Dinel, Delta Eta
Elliot Lake, Ontario, Canada

HOLIDAY TRIFLE

1 (2-layer) white
  cake mix
2 (6-ounce) packages
  vanilla pudding mix
2 (16-ounce) packages
  frozen raspberries,
  thawed

2 to 4 tablespoons
  sherry (optional)
Whipped cream

Prepare and bake the cake mix using the package directions for a 9×13-inch baking pan. Cool in the pan for 15 minutes. Remove to a wire rack to cool completely. Slice horizontally into 4 layers. Prepare the pudding mix using the package directions; cool slightly. Fit 1 cake layer into the bottom of a trifle bowl. Drizzle 2 to 4 tablespoons of raspberries over the cake. Pour 1 cup of the pudding over the raspberries and drizzle with a small amount of sherry. Continue layering, ending with raspberries on top. Chill, covered, overnight. Serve with whipped cream. Yield: 18 servings.

Marion C. Webster, Iota Rho
Gananoque, Ontario, Canada

PEACH POUND CAKE TRIFLE

1 (6-ounce) package
  vanilla instant
  pudding mix
1/4 cup sour cream

3/4 cup whipped topping
1 pound cake
6 cups sliced peaches

Prepare the pudding mix using the package directions. Fold in the sour cream and whipped topping. Cut the pound cake into into 1/2-inch slices. Arrange half the slices in the bottom of a straight-sided 3-quart serving dish. Top with half the peaches. Pour half the pudding mixture over the peaches. Repeat the layers. Chill, covered, until cold. Garnish with chopped pecans if desired. Serves 10 to 12.

Betty Fielding, Preceptor Lambda
Ely, Nevada

PINEAPPLE ANGEL FOOD TRIFLE

1 (16-ounce) can
  pineapple tidbits
2 (3 1/2-ounce) packages
  vanilla instant
  pudding mix
3 cups milk

1 cup sour cream
1 angel food cake, cut
  into 1-inch cubes
8 ounces whipped
  topping (optional)

Drain the pineapple, reserving 1 cup juice. Mix the pudding mix, milk and 1/2 cup of the reserved pineapple juice in a bowl. Beat at low speed for 2 minutes or until thickened. Fold in the sour cream and pine-

apple. Arrange one-third of the cake cubes in the bottom of a 16-cup glass bowl. Drizzle with 2 to 3 tablespoons of the pineapple juice. Spread one-third of the pudding over the top. Repeat the layers 2 more times. Chill, covered for 3 hours or longer. Spread the whipped topping over the top. Garnish with pineapple slices and serve. Yield: 12 servings.

Jane Ellen Hiller, Laureate Epsilon
Laurel, Delaware

PUMPKIN BREEZE DESSERT

2 (3 1/2-ounce) packages
  fat-free French
  vanilla instant
  pudding mix
3 cups skim milk
1 tablespoon pumpkin
  pie spice
1 (15-ounce) can
  pumpkin

1 (14-ounce) can
  fat-free sweetened
  condensed milk
1 prepared pumpkin
  spice cake or carrot
  cake, thinly sliced
12 to 16 ounces fat-free
  whipped topping
Additional pumpkin
  pie spice

Whisk the pudding mix and milk in a large bowl until smooth. Add 1 tablespoon pumpkin pie spice, the pumpkin and condensed milk and mix well. Let the pudding mixture stand for 15 minutes. Layer the cake slices, pudding and whipped topping one-third at a time in a round glass bowl, ending with the whipped topping. Sprinkle the top with additional pumpkin pie spice to add color. Chill in the refrigerator until serving time. Yield: 12 servings.

Brenda Singleton, Laureate Phi
Walnut Ridge, Arkansas

RASPBERRY ANGEL FOOD TRIFLE

1 (3 1/2-ounce) package
  French vanilla
  instant pudding mix
1 cup milk
8 ounces whipped
  topping

1 angel food cake, torn
  into bite-size pieces
2 cups raspberries
Whipped cream

Whisk the pudding mix and milk in a bowl for 2 minutes. Fold in the whipped topping. Arrange half the cake cubes over the bottom of a trifle bowl. Spread half the pudding mixture over the cake. Sprinkle with half the raspberries and cover with whipped cream. Repeat the layers. Yield: 6 to 8 servings.

Joan Pauly, Laureate Rho
Duncan, South Carolina

SHERRY TRIFLE

12 ounces dry sponge
   cake or pound cake
24 dry ladyfingers
1/2 cup sherry
4 egg yolks
1/2 cup sugar
1 (2-inch) vanilla bean,
   split

3/4 cup sherry
1 tablespoon
   all-purpose flour
4 egg whites
1 (8-ounce) jar seedless
   raspberry jam or
   currant jelly

Cut the cake into 1-inch slices. Fit half the cake slices into the bottom of a trifle bowl. Fit the ladyfingers upright around the edge of the bowl. Drizzle 1/2 cup sherry over the cake and ladyfingers in the trifle bowl. Combine the egg yolks, sugar, vanilla bean and 3/4 cup sherry in a double boiler and mix well. Cook over simmering water until warm. Stir in the flour. Cook until the mixture coats the back of a spoon, stirring constantly. Remove the vanilla bean. Remove the cooked custard to a bowl and cool. Beat the egg whites in a bowl until stiff peaks form. Fold into the cooled custard. Pour half the custard into the trifle bowl. Spread the remaining cake slices with some of the jam and arrange over the custard layer. Pour the remaining custard evenly over the top. Dollop the remaining jam over the custard. Draw a wooden pick through the jam to make a star pattern on top of the custard. Chill, covered. Serve at room temperature. Yield: 12 to 16 servings.

Jeanine Puskas, Preceptor Zeta Nu
Cathedral City, California

STRAWBERRY CREAM TRIFLE

1 (3-ounce) package
   strawberry gelatin
1 cup boiling water
1 cup strawberry yogurt
4 cups sliced strawberries

6 tablespoons sugar
2 cups heavy whipping
   cream, whipped
1 angel food cake,
   cut into 1-inch pieces

Dissolve the gelatin in the water in a large bowl. Chill until the consistency of unbeaten egg whites. Beat until frothy. Fold in the yogurt. Sprinkle the sugar over the strawberries in a bowl and let stand for a few minutes. Stir into the gelatin mixture. Fold in the whipped cream. Fold in the cake. Spoon into a 9×13-inch baking pan. Chill, covered, for 3 hours or longer. Serve garnished with whole strawberries and whipped cream. Yield: 12 servings.

Dona Garrison, Alpha Iota Master
Chico, California

STRAWBERRY POUND CAKE TRIFLE

1 (3 1/2-ounce) package
   vanilla instant
   pudding mix
1 cup milk
1 cup sour cream
Confectioners' sugar

1 quart strawberries,
   sliced
1 pound cake, cut into
   1/4-inch slices
Sherry
Whipped topping

Process the first 3 ingredients in a food processor for a few seconds. Sprinkle confectioners' sugar over the strawberries in a bowl. Drizzle the pound cake slices with sherry. Alternate layers of pound cake, pudding mixture and strawberries in a trifle bowl. Spread with whipped topping. Yield: 6 servings.

Deanna Culbertson, Gamma Upsilon
Phillipsburg, Kansas

ANGEL FOOD STRAWBERRY TRIFLE

1 (6-ounce) package
   strawberry gelatin
2 cups boiling water
2 (10-ounce) packages
   frozen sliced
   strawberries,
   thawed

12 ounces whipped
   topping
2 (3-ounce) packages
   vanilla instant
   pudding mix, prepared
1 angel food cake, torn
   into bite-size pieces

Dissolve the gelatin in the water in a bowl. Stir in the strawberries. Fold the whipped topping into the pudding. Alternate layers of cake, the gelatin mixture and pudding mixture in a 4-quart glass bowl, making 4 layers. Chill until cold. Yield: 12 to 15 servings.

Roberta Lyons, Preceptor Nu
Frederick, Maryland

TWINKIE SURPRISE

1 (10-count) box
   Twinkie snack cakes
5 bananas, sliced
1 (6-ounce) package
   vanilla instant
   pudding mix
2 3/4 cups milk

1 (6-ounce) package
   chocolate instant
   pudding mix
2 3/4 cups milk
16 ounces whipped
   topping
Toffee bits

Cut the Twinkies lengthwise. Arrange, cut side up, in a single layer in a 9×13-inch baking dish. Top with the bananas. Whisk the vanilla pudding mix and 2 3/4 cups milk in a bowl for 2 minutes. Pour over the bananas. Whisk the chocolate pudding mix and 2 3/4 cups milk in a bowl for 2 minutes. Pour over the vanilla pudding. Spread the whipped topping over the chocolate pudding. Cover and chill. Sprinkle with toffee bits just before serving. Yield: 12 to 15 servings.

Judy Tompkins, Kappa
Emery, South Dakota

Cookie Jar
COOKIES AND BARS

ALMOND COOKIES

3 tablespoons
  butter, softened
1/2 cup sugar
1/2 teaspoon vanilla
  extract
1/4 teaspoon almond
  extract
3 egg whites
1/3 cup all-purpose flour
1/2 cup sliced almonds

Beat the butter and sugar in a bowl until light and fluffy. Add the vanilla, almond extract and egg whites and mix well. Add the flour and mix well. Stir in the almonds. Drop by scant tablespoonfuls onto a greased cookie sheet and shape into ovals. Bake at 350 degrees for 5 to 8 minutes or until golden brown. Cool on the cookie sheet for 1 minute. Remove to a wire rack to cool completely. Yield: 2 dozen cookies.

M. Fournier, Xi Alpha Epsilon
Comox, British Columbia, Canada

ALMOND BUTTER STICKS

1 cup (2 sticks)
  butter, softened
8 ounces cream
  cheese, softened
2 1/4 cups all-purpose
  flour
2 teaspoons baking
  powder
1/8 teaspoon salt
1 1/2 cups sugar
4 1/2 teaspoons almond
  extract

Beat the butter and cream cheese in a bowl until light and fluffy. Add the flour, baking powder and salt and mix well. Knead on a floured surface until smooth. Combine the sugar and almond extract in a bowl and mix well. Divide the dough in half. Roll 1 portion into an 8×14-inch rectangle. Sprinkle with 3 to 4 tablespoons of the sugar mixture. Fold one end of the dough over the center. Fold the other end of the dough over to make 3 layers. Repeat rolling, sprinkling and folding 2 times. Roll into an 8×14-inch rectangle. Cut into 1 1/2×3-inch strips. Place on an ungreased cookie sheet. Bake at 400 degrees for 8 to 10 minutes or until light brown. Cool on the cookie sheet for 1 minute. Remove to a wire rack to cool completely. Yield: 5 dozen cookies.

Kathy Young, Laureate Beta Beta
Cave Junction, Oregon

APPLESAUCE RAISIN COOKIES

This recipe is approved for diabetics.

1 cup all-purpose flour
1 cup whole wheat
  flour
2 1/2 cups rolled or
  quick-cooking oats
1 tablespoon baking
  powder
1 teaspoon baking soda
1 1/2 teaspoons cinnamon
1/2 teaspoon nutmeg
1/2 teaspoon allspice
1/4 teaspoon cream
  of tartar
1 package (3 tablespoons)
  Butter Buds
2/3 cup Sugar Twin Brown
  Sugar or Splenda
  Brown Sugar Blend
1/2 cup raisins
2 eggs
2 2/3 cups unsweetened
  applesauce
1/2 cup water
1 tablespoon vanilla
  extract
1/2 cup chopped nuts

Combine the first 12 ingredients in a mixing bowl. Beat in the eggs, applesauce, water and vanilla, mixing well. Add the flour mixture and mix well. Stir in the nuts. Drop by tablespoonfuls onto a greased cookie sheet. Bake at 375 degrees for 15 minutes. Cool on the cookie sheet for 1 minute. Remove to a wire rack to cool completely. Yield: 4 dozen cookies.

Betty West, Laureate Omicron
Pahrump, Nevada

CHERRY COCONUT BUTTON COOKIES

3/4 cup (1 1/2 sticks)
  butter or margarine,
  softened
1 cup packed
  brown sugar
1 egg
1 teaspoon vanilla
  extract

2 cups all-purpose flour
1 teaspoon baking soda
1/4 teaspoon salt
1/2 cup chopped pecans
1/2 cup chopped
  maraschino cherries
1/2 cup shredded coconut

Beat the butter and brown sugar in a bowl until light and fluffy. Add the egg, vanilla, flour, baking soda and salt and mix well. Stir in the pecans, cherries and coconut. Drop by rounded teaspoonfuls onto a greased cookie sheet. Bake at 375 degrees for 10 to 12 minutes or until firm. Cool on the cookie sheet for 1 minute. Remove to a wire rack to cool completely. Yield: 4 dozen cookies.

Linda Bilbra Nelson
Roanoke, Virginia

FROSTED BANANA COOKIES

3/4 cup shortening
3/4 cup packed brown
  sugar
1 egg
1/2 teaspoon vanilla
  extract

2 bananas, mashed
1 teaspoon baking soda
1/4 teaspoon salt
2 cups all-purpose flour
Frosting

Beat the shortening and brown sugar in a bowl until light and fluffy. Add the egg, vanilla and bananas and mix well. Add the baking soda, salt and flour and mix well. Drop by teaspoonfuls onto a greased cookie sheet. Bake at 350 degrees for 8 to 10 minutes or until light brown. Cool on the cookie sheet for 1 minute. Remove to a wire rack to cool completely. Frost the cooled cookies. Yield: 3 dozen cookies.

FROSTING

3 tablespoons milk
  (or 4 tablespoons
  cream)
6 tablespoons brown
  sugar

1/2 teaspoon vanilla
  extract
4 tablespoons butter
1/2 to 3/4 pound
  confectioners' sugar

Combine the milk, brown sugar, vanilla and butter in a saucepan. Bring to a boil over medium heat, stirring often. Remove from the heat and add enough confectioners' sugar to make of spreading consistency, stirring until smooth.

Sandi Davison, Alpha Gamma Master
Kansas City, Missouri

DOUBLE CHOCOLATE BISCOTTI

These are wonderful spread with Camembert and served with your favorite wine or after dinner drink.

2 cups all-purpose flour
1/2 cup baking cocoa
1/2 teaspoon baking soda
1/2 teaspoon salt
1/2 cup (1 stick) unsalted
  butter, softened
1 cup sugar
2 large eggs

1/2 cup (3 ounces)
  semisweet chocolate
  chips
1/2 cup (3 ounces)
  chocolate-covered
  espresso beans
1 egg white, lightly
  beaten

Sift the flour, baking cocoa, baking soda and salt together. Beat the butter and sugar in a mixing bowl until light and fluffy. Add the eggs and mix well. Add the flour mixture gradually, mixing well after each addition. Stir in the chocolate chips and espresso beans. Divide the dough in half. Shape each portion into 2-inch wide log. Place 2 inches apart on a cookie sheet. Brush the logs with the egg white. Bake at 325 degrees for 30 minutes or until set. Cool on the cookie sheet for 15 minutes. Remove to a cutting board. Cut diagonally with a serrated knife into 1/2-inch slices. Arrange the slices on a cookie sheet. Bake at 350 degrees for 15 minutes or until slightly dry. Remove to a wire rack to cool completely. Yield: 3 dozen biscotti.

Erin A. Lollis, Preceptor Mu Sigma
Borrego Springs, California

BUTTERFINGER COOKIES

1/2 cup (1 stick)
  butter, softened
3/4 cup granulated sugar
2/3 cup packed
  brown sugar
2 egg whites
1 1/4 cups chunky
  peanut butter

1 1/2 teaspoons vanilla
  extract
1 cup all-purpose flour
1/2 teaspoon baking soda
1/4 teaspoon salt
5 Butterfinger candy
  bars, chopped

Beat the butter, granulated sugar and brown sugar in a bowl until light and fluffy. Add the egg whites and mix well. Add the peanut butter and vanilla and mix well. Add the flour, baking soda and salt and mix well. Stir in the candy bars. Shape into 1 1/2 inch balls and place on a greased cookie sheet. Bake at 350 degrees for 10 to 12 minutes or until golden brown. Cool on the cookie sheet for 1 minute. Remove to a wire rack to cool completely. Yield: 4 dozen cookies.

Betty Randol, Laureate Delta Epsilon
Independence, Missouri

BUTTERSCOTCH COOKIES

1/2 cup (1 stick) unsalted butter, melted	2 eggs
1/4 cup packed brown sugar	1 tablespoon baking cocoa
1 (2-layer) package yellow cake mix	1 cup (6 ounces) butterscotch chips
	1/2 cup chopped walnuts

Mix the first 5 ingredients in a bowl. Stir in the butterscotch chips and walnuts. Drop by tablespoonfuls onto a greased cookie sheet. Bake at 350 degrees for 13 minutes. Cool on the cookie sheet for 1 minute. Remove to a wire rack to cool completely. Yield: 2 dozen cookies.

Barbara Greinke, Preceptor Alpha
Lenexa, Kansas

CARAMEL ACORNS

2 1/2 cups all-purpose flour	3/4 cup packed brown sugar
1 teaspoon baking powder	1/3 cup ground pecans
1 cup (2 sticks) butter	1/2 pound caramel candies
1 teaspoon vanilla extract	2 tablespoons water
	1 3/4 cups ground pecans

Sift the flour and baking powder together. Combine the butter, vanilla, brown sugar and 1/3 cup pecans in a 2-quart saucepan. Cook over medium heat until the butter melts, stirring often. Add the flour mixture and mix well. Shape into balls and place on an ungreased cookie sheet. Flatten with a spoon and pinch one end to form a point. Bake at 350 degrees for 8 to 10 minutes or until light brown. Cool on the cookie sheet for 1 minute. Remove to a wire rack to cool completely. Heat the caramel candies and water in a saucepan over low heat until the candies are melted, stirring constantly. Place 1 3/4 cups pecans in a shallow dish. Dip the flat end of each cookie into the caramel and coat with the ground pecans. Place on waxed paper. Let stand until firm. Yield: 2 dozen cookies.

Margaret Gebhardt, Alpha Epsilon
Minneapolis, Minnesota

CARROT COOKIES

1 cup shortening	2 teaspoons baking powder
3/4 cup granulated sugar	1/2 teaspoon salt
2 eggs	3/4 cup shredded coconut
1 cup mashed cooked carrots	Orange Butter Frosting
2 cups all-purpose flour	

Beat the shortening and sugar in a bowl until light and fluffy. Add the eggs and carrots and mix well.

Add the flour, baking powder and salt and mix well. Stir in the coconut. Drop by teaspoonfuls onto a greased cookie sheet. Bake at 400 degrees for 8 to 10 minutes or until firm. Cool on the cookie sheet for 1 minute. Remove to a wire rack to cool completely. Frost the cookies. Yield: 3 to 4 dozen cookies.

ORANGE BUTTER FROSTING

3 tablespoons margarine, softened	2 teaspoons grated orange zest
1 1/2 cups confectioners' sugar	1 tablespoon orange juice

Beat the margarine and confectioners' sugar in a bowl until light and fluffy. Add the orange zest and orange juice and mix well.

Barbara Riley, Laureate Beta Tau
Anderson, Indiana

CHERRY WINK COOKIES

3/4 cup shortening	1 teaspoon baking powder
1 cup sugar	1/2 teaspoon salt
2 eggs	1 cup chopped walnuts
2 teaspoons milk	1 cup dates
1 teaspoon vanilla extract	1/3 cup maraschino cherries
2 1/2 cups all-purpose flour	2 1/2 cups crushed cornflakes
1/2 teaspoon baking soda	

Beat the shortening and sugar in a bowl until light and fluffy. Add the eggs, milk and vanilla and mix well. Sift the flour, baking soda, baking powder and salt together. Add to the shortening mixture gradually, mixing well after each addition. Stir in the walnuts, dates and cherries. Shape by teaspoonfuls into balls. Roll in the crushed cornflakes. Place on a greased cookie sheet. Bake at 375 degrees for 10 to 12 minutes or until firm. Cool on the cookie sheet for 1 minute. Remove to a wire rack to cool completely. Yield: 3 dozen cookies.

Barbara Lyons, Laureate Kappa
Zephyr Hills, Florida

JoAnne Hoffer, Laureate Theta Omega, Sunnyvale, California, likes to prepare **Caramel Graham Cookies** *with ingredients she always has on hand. She lines two baking sheets with 28 graham crackers and sprinkles them with 1 cup sliced almonds. She combines 1 1/2 cups butter and 3/4 cup packed brown sugar in a saucepan, brings the mixture to a boil over medium heat, and boils for 2 minutes, stirring often. She pours the hot mixture over the graham crackers and bakes them at 350 degrees for 10 minutes.*

CHOCOLATE CHIP COOKIES

1/2 cup (1 stick)
  margarine, softened
1/2 cup shortening
1 1/2 cups packed
  brown sugar
1 1/2 cups granulated
  sugar
3/4 cup vegetable oil
4 eggs
2 teaspoons vanilla
  extract
4 3/4 cups all-purpose
  flour

2 teaspoons baking
  powder
1 1/2 teaspoons salt
1 1/2 teaspoons
  baking soda
1 cup (6 ounces)
  miniature "M & M's"
  Chocolate Candies
3/4 cup Grape-Nuts
  cereal
2/3 cup chopped walnuts

Beat the margarine, shortening, brown sugar and granulated sugar in a bowl until light and fluffy. Beat in the oil, eggs and vanilla. Add the flour, baking powder, salt, and baking soda and mix well. Stir in the chocolate candies, cereal and walnuts. Drop by tablespoonfuls 2 inches apart onto a cookie sheet. Bake at 375 degrees for 10 minutes or until light brown. Do not overbake. Cool on the cookie sheet for 1 minute. Remove to a wire rack to cool completely. Yield: 5 dozen cookies.

Debbie Stormont, Gamma Upsilon
Phillipsburg, Kansas

NUTTY CHOCOLATE CHIP COOKIES

1 cup (2 sticks) unsalted
  butter, softened
3/4 cup granulated sugar
3/4 cup packed
  brown sugar
2 eggs
1 tablespoon vanilla
  extract
2 1/2 cups sifted
  unbleached flour
1 teaspoon baking soda

1 teaspoon salt
7 ounces macadamia
  nuts, chopped
1 cup walnuts, chopped
1 cup pecans, chopped
2 cups (12 ounces) milk
  chocolate chips
2 cups (12 ounces)
  miniature semisweet
  chocolate chips

Beat the butter, granulated sugar and brown sugar in a bowl until light and fluffy. Add the eggs and vanilla and mix well. Add the flour, baking soda and salt and mix well. Stir in the macadamia nuts, walnuts, pecans, milk chocolate chips and semisweet chocolate chips. Drop by teaspoonfuls onto an ungreased cookie sheet. Bake at 375 degrees for 10 to 12 minutes or until light brown. Cool on the cookie sheet for 1 minute. Remove to a wire rack to cool completely. Yield: 10 dozen cookies.

Yvonne Campbell
Grants Pass, Oregon

CHOCOLATE CHIP PUDDING COOKIES

2 1/4 cups all-purpose
  flour
1 teaspoon baking soda
1 cup (2 sticks) butter or
  margarine, softened
1/4 cup granulated sugar
3/4 cup packed
  brown sugar
1 teaspoon vanilla
  extract

2 eggs
1 (4-ounce) package
  French vanilla
  instant pudding mix
2 cups (12 ounces)
  chocolate chips
1 cup chopped nuts
  (optional)

Combine the flour and baking soda. Beat the butter, granulated sugar and brown sugar in a bowl until light and fluffy. Add the vanilla, eggs and pudding mix and mix well. Add the flour mixture gradually, mixing well after each addition. Stir in the chocolate chips and nuts. Drop by rounded teaspoonfuls 2 inches apart onto an ungreased baking sheet. Bake at 375 degrees for 8 to 10 minutes or until light brown. Cool on the cookie sheete for 1 minute. Remove to a wire rack to cool completely. Yield: 7 dozen.

Florence Wheeler, Alpha Delta Rho
Chillicothe, Missouri

CHOCOLATE CRACKLES

1 cup (6 ounces)
  semisweet chocolate
  chips, melted
1 cup packed brown
  sugar
1/3 cup vegetable oil
2 eggs
1 teaspoon vanilla
  extract

1 cup all-purpose flour
1 teaspoon baking
  powder
1/4 teaspoon salt
1/2 cup chopped nuts
1/2 cup (or more)
  confectioners' sugar

Combine the chocolate, brown sugar and oil in a bowl and mix well. Add the eggs 1 at a time, mixing well after each addition. Beat in the vanilla. Combine the flour, baking powder and salt. Add to the chocolate mixture and mix well. Stir in the nuts. Chill, covered, for 2 hours or longer. Drop teaspoonfuls of dough into the confectioners' sugar and roll to coat. Place 2 inches apart on a greased cookie sheet. Bake at 350 degrees for 10 to 12 minutes or until firm. Cool on the cookie sheet for 1 minute. Remove to a wire rack to cool completely. Coat with confectioners' sugar again if desired. Yield: 4 dozen cookies.

Colleen Kohler, Alpha Iota Master
St. Louis, Missouri

CHOCOLATE CRACKLETOPS

2 cups all-purpose flour	1/2 cup (1 stick) butter or
2 teaspoons baking	margarine
powder	4 ounces unsweetened
4 eggs, lightly beaten	chocolate, chopped
2 teaspoons vanilla	1 3/4 cups miniature
extract	"M & M's" Chocolate
2 cups sugar	Candies
	Additional sugar

Combine the flour and baking powder. Combine the eggs and vanilla in a small bowl. Combine 2 cups sugar, the butter and chocolate in a 2-quart saucepan. Cook over low heat until smooth, stirring constantly. Stir a small amount of the hot mixture into the egg mixture; stir the egg mixture into the hot mixture. Add the flour mixture and mix well. Wrap in plastic wrap. Chill for 1 hour. Stir in the chocolate candies. Chill, wrapped, for 1 hour. Shape into 1-inch balls. Roll in sugar. Place 2 inches apart on a foil-lined cookie sheet. Bake at 350 degrees for 10 to 12 minutes or until light brown. Do not overbake. Cool on the cookie sheet for 1 minute. Remove to a wire rack to cool completely. Yield: 5 dozen cookies.

Melissa Ragon, Mu
Sutherlin, Oregon

CHOCOLATE SURPRISE COOKIES

2 3/4 cups all-purpose	2 eggs
flour	1 teaspoon vanilla
3/4 cup baking cocoa	extract
1/2 teaspoon baking	1/2 cup chopped pecans
powder	1 tablespoon granulated
1/2 teaspoon baking soda	sugar
1 cup (2 sticks) butter,	1/2 cup chopped pecans
softened	9 ounces Rolo candies
1 1/2 cups packed light	3 ounces white almond
brown sugar	bark candy, melted
1/2 cup granulated sugar	

Combine the flour, baking cocoa, baking powder and baking soda. Beat the butter, brown sugar and 1/2 cup granulated sugar in a bowl until light and fluffy. Add the eggs and vanilla and mix well. Add the flour mixture gradually, mixing well after each addition. Stir in 1/2 cup pecans. Wrap in plastic wrap. Chill for 30 minutes or until firm. Combine 1 tablespoon granulated sugar and 1/2 cup pecans in a shallow dish. Shape dough by tablespoonfuls around 1 piece Rolo candy, covering the candy completely. Press one side of the cookie into the pecan mixture. Place nut side up 3 inches apart on a cookie sheet. Bake at 375 degrees for 10 to 12 minutes or until set and slightly cracked. Cool on the cookie sheet for 1 minute. Remove to a wire rack to cool completely. Drizzle with the almond bark. Place on waxed paper. Let stand until firm. Yield: 3 1/2 to 4 dozen cookies.

Sandy Helms, Laureate Beta
Longview, Washington

❖ WHITE CHOCOLATE MACADAMIA NUT COOKIES

1/2 cup (1 stick) butter or	2 cups all-purpose flour
margarine, softened	1/2 teaspoon salt
1/2 cup shortening	1 teaspoon baking soda
3/4 cup packed brown	7 ounces macadamia
sugar	nuts, chopped
1/2 cup granulated sugar	16 ounces white
1 egg	chocolate, chopped
1 1/2 teaspoons vanilla	
extract	

Beat the butter, shortening, brown sugar and granulated sugar in a bowl until light and fluffy. Add the egg and vanilla and mix well. Combine the flour, salt and baking soda. Add gradually to the butter mixture, mixing well after each addition. Stir in the nuts and white chocolate. Drop by teaspoonfuls 2 inches apart onto a greased cookie sheet. Bake at 350 degrees for 8 to 10 minutes or until light brown. Cool on the cookie sheet for 1 minute. Remove to a wire rack to cool completely. Yield: 5 dozen cookies.

Beverly Morgan, Laureate Tau
Anderson, Indiana

CHOCOLATE TOFFEE COOKIES

I experimented with a basic chocolate chip cookie recipe and came up with this cookie.

2 1/4 cups all-purpose	3/4 cup packed brown
flour	sugar
1/2 cup baking cocoa	1 teaspoon vanilla
1 teaspoon baking soda	extract
1 teaspoon salt	2 eggs
1 cup (2 sticks) butter or	2 cups (12 ounces)
margarine, softened	English toffee bits
3/4 cup granulated sugar	

Combine the flour, baking cocoa, baking soda and salt. Beat the butter, granulated sugar and brown sugar in a bowl until light and fluffy. Add the vanilla and eggs and mix well. Add the flour mixture and mix well. Stir in the toffee bits. Drop by rounded tablespoonfuls onto a greased cookie sheet. Bake at 350 degrees for 12 to 15 minutes or until firm. Cool on the cookie sheet for 1 minute. Remove to a wire rack to cool completely. Yield: 2 dozen cookies.

Melanie Payne, Preceptor Delta Tau
Gladstone, Missouri

CHOCOLATE WHOPPERS

2 ounces unsweetened chocolate
6 ounces semisweet chocolate
6 tablespoons butter
1/4 cup all-purpose flour
1/4 teaspoon baking powder
1/2 teaspoon salt
3/4 cup sugar
2 eggs
2 teaspoons instant coffee granules
2 teaspoons vanilla extract
1 cup (6 ounces) semisweet chocolate chips
1 cup chopped walnuts
1 cup chopped pecans, toasted

Combine the unsweetened chocolate, semisweet chocolate and butter in a small saucepan. Cook over low heat until smooth, stirring constantly. Sift the flour, baking powder and salt together. Combine the sugar, eggs, instant coffee and vanilla in a large bowl and mix for 2 minutes. Add the chocolate mixture and dry ingredients and mix well. Stir in the chocolate chips, walnuts and pecans. Drop by rounded tablespoonfuls onto a foil-lined cookie sheet. Bake at 350 degrees for 17 minutes. Do not overbake. Cool on the cookie sheet for 1 minute. Remove to a wire rack to cool completely. Yield: 15 large cookies.

Barbara Polodna, Zeta Sigma
Fairfield Bay, Arkansas

CITRUS COOKIES

3/4 cup (1 1/2 sticks) plus 1 tablespoon butter, softened
1/2 cup granulated sugar
1/2 cup confectioners' sugar
1 teaspoon each grated lemon zest, grated orange zest and grated lime zest
2 tablespoons lime juice
1/2 teaspoon vanilla extract
2 cups all-purpose flour
1/4 teaspoon baking soda
1/4 teaspoon salt
1/2 cup colored sugar (yellow, orange or green)
2 cups confectioners' sugar
1 tablespoon lemon juice
2 tablespoons orange juice
1/2 teaspoon vanilla extract

Beat the butter, granulated sugar and 1/2 cup confectioners' sugar in a bowl until light and fluffy. Add the lemon zest, orange zest, lime zest, lime juice and 1/2 teaspoon vanilla and mix well. Add the flour, baking soda and salt and mix well. Divide the dough in half. Shape each portion into an 8-inch log. Chill, tightly wrapped, for 4 hours to overnight. Cut into 1/4-inch slices. Place 2 inches apart on a cookie sheet. Sprinkle with colored sugar. Bake at 350 degrees for 10 to 12 minutes or until golden brown. Cool on the cookie sheet for 1 minute. Remove to a wire rack to cool completely. Combine the remaining ingredients in a medium bowl and mix until smooth. Spoon the frosting into a pastry tube fitted with a plain tip. Draw a circle inside the cookie. Pipe three lines so that the cookie resembles a sliced citrus fruit (or sliced pie). Let stand until firm.
Yield: 2 dozen cookies.

Jill McCormick, Preceptor Delta Beta
Leonard, Michigan

COCOA DROP COOKIES

1/2 cup shortening
1 cup sugar
1 egg
1 3/4 cups all-purpose flour
1/2 teaspoon baking soda
1/2 teaspoon salt
1/2 cup baking cocoa
3/4 cup buttermilk (or sour milk)
1 teaspoon vanilla extract
Chocolate Frosting
1 cup chopped walnuts (optional)

Beat the shortening and sugar in a bowl until light and fluffy. Add the egg and mix well. Combine the flour, baking soda, salt and baking cocoa in a large bowl. Add to the shortening mixture and mix well. Add the buttermilk and the vanilla extract and mix well. Wrap in plastic wrap. Chill for 1 hour. Drop by rounded teaspoonfuls 2 inches apart onto a cookie sheet. Bake at 400 degrees for 8 to 10 minutes or until set. Cool on the cookie sheet for 1 minute. Remove to a wire rack to cool completely. Dip cookies in the chocolate frosting. Coat with walnuts and place on waxed paper. Let stand until firm.
Yield: 3 dozen cookies.

CHOCOLATE FROSTING

1 tablespoon butter
1 ounce unsweetened chocolate
1 cup confectioners' sugar

Combine the butter, chocolate and confectioners' sugar in a saucepan. Cook over low heat until smooth, stirring constantly. Add enough warm water to make of spreading consistency.

Connie Robison, Epsilon Master
Doniphan, Nebraska

*Cindy Bingheim, Psi Pi, Mazon, Illinois, prepares moist **Fudgy Brownies** with a few additions to store-bought brownie mix. She prepares the brownies using the package directions. She stirs in 1 cup sour cream and 1 cup chocolate chips and pours the mixture into a 9×13-inch baking pan. The brownies are baked at 350 degrees for 35 minutes and cooled before cut into squares.*

ESPRESSO DELIGHTS

These are great with coffee.

1 cup (2 sticks) butter, softened	1 teaspoon vanilla extract
2/3 cup sifted confectioners' sugar	1 ounce semisweet chocolate, chopped
2 cups all-purpose flour	Additional confectioners' sugar for sprinkling
1 tablespoon instant espresso	
1/2 teaspoon cinnamon	

Beat the butter and confectioners' sugar in a bowl until light and fluffy. Add the flour, espresso, cinnamon and vanilla and mix well. Stir in the chocolate. Shape by tablespoonfuls into crescents on an ungreased cookie sheet. Flatten slightly with a glass. Bake at 325 degrees for 15 minutes. Sprinkle with confectioners' sugar. Cool on the cookie sheet for 1 minute. Remove to a wire rack to cool completely. Yield: 3 dozen cookies.

Marilyn A. Williams, XP
Athens, Ohio

CHRISTMAS FRUIT COOKIES

These cookies get better with age if stored in an airtight container.

3 cups all-purpose flour	4 pounds candied pineapple, chopped
3 teaspoons baking soda	1 pound golden raisins
1 teaspoon cinnamon	1/2 cup (1 stick) butter, softened
1 teaspoon ground cloves	1 cup packed brown sugar
1 teaspoon allspice	2/3 cup bourbon
1 pound candied cherries, chopped	4 eggs
2 pounds pecans, chopped	3 tablespoons milk

Sift the flour, baking soda, cinnamon, cloves and allspice together. Combine the candied cherries, pecans, candied pineapple and raisins in a large bowl. Add 1 cup of the flour mixture and toss to coat. Beat the butter and brown sugar in a bowl until light and fluffy. Add the bourbon, eggs and milk and mix well. Add the remaining flour mixture and mix well. Stir in the fruit mixture. Wrap in plastic wrap. Chill for 2 hours or longer. Drop by teaspoonfuls onto a cookie sheet. Bake at 300 degrees for 20 to 25 minutes or until firm. Cool on the cookie sheet for 1 minute. Remove to a wire rack to cool completely. Yield: 15 dozen cookies.

Gladys Crouch, Preceptor Lambda Delta
Kilgore, Texas

SOUR CREAM FRUIT DROPS

2 1/2 cups all-purpose flour	1/2 cup granulated sugar
1/2 teaspoon baking soda	2 eggs
1 teaspoon salt	1 cup sour cream
1 teaspoon cinnamon	1 teaspoon vanilla extract
1/4 teaspoon ground cloves	1 cup chopped dates
1/2 cup (1 stick) butter or margarine, softened	1 cup glacé cherries
1 cup packed brown sugar	1 cup chopped nuts
	2 cups raisins
	1 tablespoon grated orange zest

Combine the flour, baking soda, salt, cinnamon and cloves. Beat the butter, brown sugar and granulated sugar in a bowl until light and fluffy. Add the eggs, sour cream and vanilla and mix well. Combine the dates, cherries, nuts, raisins, and orange zest in a large bowl. Add 1/2 cup of the dry ingredients and toss to coat. Add the remaining dry ingredients to the butter mixture and mix well. Stir in the fruit. Drop by rounded teaspoonfuls 2 inches apart onto a greased cookie sheet. Bake at 375 degrees for 10 to 12 minutes or until golden brown. Cool on the cookie sheet for 1 minute. Remove to a wire rack to cool completely. Yield: 5 dozen cookies.

K. Joanne Hamilton, Preceptor Omicron
Fruitvale, British Columbia, Canada

SPICY GINGERSNAPS

These cookies improve with age.

3/4 cup (1 1/2 sticks) butter, softened	1 teaspoon ginger
1 cup sugar	1 teaspoon ground cloves
1/4 cup molasses	1 teaspoon cream of tartar
1 egg, beaten	Additional sugar for rolling
2 cups all-purpose flour	
2 teaspoons baking soda	
1 teaspoon cinnamon	

Beat the butter and sugar in a bowl until light and fluffy. Add the molasses and egg and mix well. Add the flour, baking soda, cinnamon, ginger, cloves and cream of tartar and mix well. Shape into balls. Roll in sugar. Place 2 inches apart on a greased cookie sheet. Bake at 350 degrees for 12 to 14 minutes or until firm. Cool on the cookie sheet for 1 minute. Remove to a wire rack to cool completely. Yield: 6 dozen cookies.

Kathy Standrige, Preceptor Alpha Psi
Clarksville, Arkansas

GINGERSNAPS

1 cup (2 sticks) margarine, softened	4 cups all-purpose flour
2 cups sugar	2 teaspoons ginger
2 eggs	1 teaspoon baking soda
1 cup molasses	1 teaspoon salt

Beat the margarine and sugar in a bowl until light and fluffy. Add the eggs and molasses and mix well. Add the flour, ginger, baking soda and salt and mix well. Shape into 1-inch balls. Place on a greased cookie sheet. Bake at 350 degrees for 10 to 12 minutes or until firm. Cool on the cookie sheet for 1 minute. Remove to a wire rack to cool completely. Yield: 4 dozen cookies.

Lois Scott, Laureate Alpha Phi
Brantford, Ontario, Canada

GUMDROP COOKIES

This is a family tradition at Christmas.

1/2 cup shortening	2 1/2 cups all-purpose flour
1 cup sugar	2 teaspoons baking powder
1 egg	1/4 cup milk
1/2 teaspoon salt	1 cup chopped gumdrops
1/2 teaspoon vanilla extract	Cream for brushing
1/2 teaspoon lemon extract	

Cream the shortening and sugar in a bowl until light and fluffy. Add the egg and mix well. Add the salt, vanilla and lemon extract and mix well. Sift the flour and baking powder together. Add to the shortening mixture with the milk and mix well. Stir in the gumdrops. Drop by spoonfuls onto a greased cookie sheet. Flatten slightly with a glass and brush with cream. Bake at 400 degrees for 10 minutes or until light brown. Cool on the cookie sheet for 1 minute. Remove to a wire rack to cool completely. Yield: 2 dozen cookies.

Debbie A. Collins, Kappa Kappa
Meriden, Kansas

HIGH FIBER NO-BAKE COOKIES

3 cups rolled oats	1 cup shredded coconut
1 cup Kellogg's All-Bran Buds Cereal	1 cup nuts
6 tablespoons baking cocoa	1/2 cup (1 stick) margarine
	1 3/4 cups sugar
	1/2 cup milk

Combine the oats, bran cereal, baking cocoa, coconut and nuts in a large bowl and mix well. Combine the margarine, sugar and milk in a saucepan. Bring to a boil over medium heat, stirring often. Boil for 3 minutes, stirring constantly. Add to the dry ingredients and mix well. Drop by spoonfuls onto waxed paper. Let stand until firm. Yield: 3 dozen cookies.

Susanna T. Scott, Laureate Gamma Iota
Comox, British Columbia, Canada

ITALIAN COOKIES

3 eggs	2 cups sifted all-purpose flour
Pinch of salt	Extra light olive oil for deep frying
3 tablespoons sugar	Confectioners' sugar
1 tablespoon vanilla extract	

Beat the eggs, salt, sugar and vanilla in a mixing bowl. Add the flour and mix well. Knead on a floured surface until smooth. Roll very thin. Cut as desired. Drop into 375-degree oil. Fry for 1 minute. Remove with a slotted spoon. Drain on paper towels. Dust with confectioners' sugar. Yield: 3 dozen cookies.

Christina Figueroa, Beta Zeta Master
Costa Mesa, California

LEMON DROPS

1/2 cup shortening	1/3 cup milk
1/2 cup (1 stick) butter, softened	1 tablespoon grated lemon zest
1 cup all-purpose flour	1 cup all-purpose flour
3/4 cup sugar	Cream Cheese Frosting

Beat the shortening and butter in a bowl until light and fluffy. Add 1 cup flour and mix well. Add the sugar, milk and lemon zest and mix well. Add 1 cup flour and mix well. Drop by rounded teaspoonfuls 2 inches apart onto an ungreased cookie sheet. Bake at 375 degrees for 10 minutes or until light brown. Cool on the cookie sheet for 1 minute. Remove to a wire rack to cool completely. Frost the cooled cookies. Yield: 4 dozen cookies.

CREAM CHEESE FROSTING

4 ounces cream cheese, softened	2 tablespoons lemon juice
1/4 cup (1/2 stick) butter, softened	2 1/4 to 2 1/2 cups confectioners' sugar
1 cup confectioners' sugar	2 drops yellow food coloring (optional)

Beat the cream cheese, butter and 1 cup confectioners' sugar in a bowl until light and fluffy. Stir in the lemon juice. Add enough confectioners' sugar to make of spreading consistency, about 2 1/4 cups, and mix until smooth. Stir in the food coloring.

Vicky Laws, Chi Omicron
Naperville, Illinois

LEMON GINGER COOKIES

3/4 cup (1 1/2 sticks) margarine, softened	2 teaspoons baking soda
1 cup packed brown sugar	1/2 teaspoon salt
1 egg	3 teaspoons ginger
1/4 cup molasses	1 teaspoon cinnamon
1 tablespoon grated lemon zest	2 1/4 cups all-purpose flour
	Granulated sugar for rolling

Beat the margarine and brown sugar in a bowl until light and fluffy. Add the egg, molasses and lemon zest and mix well. Add the baking soda, salt, ginger, cinnamon and flour and mix well. Shape into balls. Roll in granulated sugar and place on a cookie sheet. Bake at 350 degrees for 10 minutes, or just until set. Cool on the cookie sheet for 1 minute. Remove to a wire rack to cool completely. Yield: 4 dozen cookies.

FloyDeen Leetch, Preceptor Lambda Alpha
Gravois Mills, Missouri

JAM DAINTIES

3/4 cup (1 1/2 sticks) butter, softened	1 tablespoon hot water
1/2 cup packed brown sugar	Pinch of salt
2 eggs, beaten	1 teaspoon vanilla extract
1 teaspoon baking powder	2 cups all-purpose flour
	1 cup jam (any flavor)

Beat the butter and brown sugar in a bowl until light and fluffy. Add the eggs and mix well. Dissolve the baking powder in hot water in a small bowl. Add to the butter mixture and mix well. Add the salt, vanilla and flour and mix well. Shape into balls and place on a cookie sheet. Flatten slightly with a glass. Bake at 350 degrees for 15 to 18 minutes or until light brown. Cool on the cookie sheet for 5 minutes. Spread jam to taste over the flat side of one cookie. Top with the flat side of another cookie. Yield: 1 dozen cookies.

Elaine Dewalt, Zeta Master
Saskatoon, Saskatchewan, Canada

COCONUT MACAROONS

3 cups shredded coconut	2 egg whites, stiffly beaten
1 teaspoon almond extract	1 teaspoon cream of tartar
1/8 teaspoon salt	
2/3 cup sweetened condensed milk	

Combine the coconut, almond extract and salt in a bowl and mix well. Stir in the sweetened condensed milk to form a thick paste. Fold in the egg whites and

cream of tartar with a spatula. Drop by teaspoonfuls 2 inches apart onto a greased cookie sheet. Bake at 350 degrees for 8 minutes or until light brown. Cool on the cookie sheet for 1 minute. Remove to a wire rack to cool completely. Yield: 4 dozen macaroons.

Beverley Neff, Rho Master
South Charleston, West Virginia

CHOCOLATE-DIPPED COCONUT MACAROONS

3/4 cup sugar	3 egg whites, stiffly beaten
2 1/2 cups flaked sweetened coconut	4 ounces semisweet chocolate, melted

Combine the sugar and coconut in a bowl and mix well. Fold in the egg whites with a spatula. Drop by tablespoonfuls 2 inches apart onto a parchment-paper lined cookie sheet. Bake at 350 degrees for 12 to 15 minutes or until golden brown. Cool completely on the cookie sheet. Dip the cookies into the melted chocolate and place on waxed paper. Let stand until firm. Yield: 2 dozen macaroons.

Catherine Cox, Laureate Rho
Kindersley, Saskatchewan, Canada

OATMEAL MACAROONS

1/3 cup maple syrup	2 egg whites, stiffly beaten
1 cup rolled oats	
1/2 cup shredded coconut	

Combine the syrup and oats in a bowl and mix well. Stir in the coconut. Fold in the egg whites with a spatula. Drop by teaspoonfuls onto a greased cookie sheet. Bake at 350 degrees for 15 minutes. Cool on the cookie sheet for 1 minute. Remove to a wire rack to cool completely. Yield: 2 dozen macaroons.

Marilyn Borras, Preceptor Alpha Zeta
Stafford, Virginia

PECAN MACAROONS

2 egg whites	2 cups pecan halves
1 3/4 cups packed brown sugar	

Beat the egg whites in a bowl until soft peaks form. Add the brown sugar gradually, beating until stiff peaks form. Fold in the pecans. Drop by tablespoonfuls onto a cookie sheet. Bake at 275 degrees for 30 minutes or until light brown. Cool completely on the cookie sheet. Yield: 1 dozen macaroons.

Toni V. Sweeney, Preceptor Omicron Alpha
Laguna Niguel, California

NO-BAKE PEANUT BUTTER COOKIES

1½ cups sugar	2 teaspoons vanilla
½ cup milk	extract
¼ cup maple syrup	2 cups quick-cooking
½ cup peanut butter	oats

Combine the sugar, milk and maple syrup in a saucepan. Bring to a boil over medium heat, stirring often. Boil for 3 minutes, stirring constantly. Remove from the heat and stir in the peanut butter and vanilla. Stir in the oats. Drop by rounded teaspoonfuls onto waxed paper. Let stand for 2 hours or until firm. Yield: 2 dozen cookies.

Sheila Woodard, Laureate Delta Mu
Milford, Ohio

CHOCOLATE CHIP MERINGUE COOKIES

4 egg whites, at room	½ teaspoon vanilla
temperature	extract
¼ teaspoon cream	2 cups (12 ounces)
of tartar	chocolate chips
¾ cup sugar	

Beat the egg whites and cream of tartar in a medium bowl until soft peaks form. Add the sugar gradually, beating until stiff peaks form. Beat in the vanilla. Fold in the chocolate chips. Drop by teaspoonfuls onto a greased and floured cookie sheet. Bake at 200 degrees for 1¾ hours. Cool on the cookie sheet for 1 minute. Remove to waxed paper to cool completely. Yield: 3 dozen cookies.

Jean Van Stelten, Epsilon Master
Manchester, New Hampshire

GLAZED CHOCOLATE MERINGUE COOKIES

3 egg whites	½ cup (3 ounces)
¾ teaspoon vanilla	semisweet chocolate
extract	chips (optional)
¾ cup sugar	1 tablespoon shortening
¾ cup baking cocoa,	(optional)
sifted	

Beat the egg whites and vanilla in a bowl until soft peaks form. Add the sugar gradually, beating until stiff peaks form. Fold in the baking cocoa. Place the dough in a pastry tube fitted with a star tip. Press onto a parchment paper-lined cookie sheet. Bake at 300 degrees for 35 to 40 minutes or until light brown. Cool on the cookie sheet for 1 minute. Remove to a wire rack to cool completely. Cook the chocolate chips and shortening in a saucepan over low heat until smooth, stirring frequently. Dip the cookies into the melted chocolate and place on waxed paper. Let stand until firm. Yield: 3 dozen cookies.

Carol J. Harper, Alpha Delta Phi
Lowry City, Missouri

❖ COFFEE MELTAWAYS

4 egg whites, at room	½ teaspoon instant
temperature	coffee
½ teaspoon cream	1 cup sugar
of tartar	

Beat the egg whites, cream of tartar and coffee until soft peaks form. Add the sugar 1 tablespoon at a time, beating until stiff peaks form. Drop by teaspoonfuls onto a parchment paper-lined cookie sheet. Bake at 250 degrees for 1 hour. Turn off the oven and leave cookies for 8 hours. Cool completely on the cookie sheet. Yield: 3 dozen cookies.

Colette Culver, Preceptor Iota
Eugene, Oregon

MOLASSES COOKIES

¼ cup shortening	¼ teaspoon salt
1 cup sugar	1 teaspoon cinnamon
2 eggs	1½ teaspoons baking
3 tablespoons molasses	soda
4 cups all-purpose flour	1 teaspoon ginger
1 teaspoon ground	Additional sugar
cloves	for rolling

Beat the shortening and sugar in a bowl until light and fluffy. Add the eggs and molasses and mix well. Add the flour, cloves, salt, cinnamon, baking soda and ginger and mix well. Shape into 1-inch balls. Roll in sugar. Bake at 350 degrees for 9 to 10 minutes or until firm. Cool on the cookie sheet for 1 minute. Remove to wire racks to cool completely.
Yield: 4 dozen cookies.

Lexie Foster, Laureate Theta Epsilon
San Marcos, California

❖ MOLASSES STRIPS

¾ cup vegetable oil	½ teaspoon salt
1 cup sugar	½ teaspoon cinnamon
1 egg	¼ teaspoon ginger
¼ cup molasses	¼ teaspoon ground
2 cups all-purpose flour	cloves
2 teaspoons baking soda	

Combine the oil, sugar, egg and molasses in a bowl and mix well. Sift the flour, baking soda, salt, cinnamon, ginger and cloves together. Add to the oil mixture and mix well. Divide the dough into 6 equal portions. Roll each portion into a $^1/_4$ to $^1/_2$-inch thick strip on a floured surface. Place strips 3 inches apart on an ungreased cookie sheet. Bake at 350 degrees for 8 to 10 minutes or until golden brown. Cool for 4 minutes on the cookie sheet. Cut into strips. Yield: 4 dozen strips.

Sheila Simmons, Xi Beta Xi
Othello, Washington

OATMEAL COOKIES

1 cup shortening	2 eggs, beaten
1 cup granulated sugar	1$^1/_2$ cups self-rising flour
1 cup packed brown sugar	3 cups quick-cooking oats
1 teaspoon vanilla extract	1 cup pecans, chopped

Beat the shortening, granulated sugar and brown sugar in a bowl until light and fluffy. Add the vanilla and eggs and mix well. Add the flour and mix well. Stir in the oats and pecans. Shape into 1-inch balls and place on a greased cookie sheet. Bake at 350 degrees for 10 to 12 minutes or until light brown. Cool on the cookie sheet for 1 minute. Remove to a wire rack to cool completely.
Yield: 5 to 6 dozen cookies.

Syble Lamons, Preceptor Alpha Mu
McCalla, Alabama

OATMEAL COCONUT COOKIES

1 cup (2 sticks) butter, softened	1 teaspoon baking powder
1 cup granulated sugar	1 teaspoon baking soda
1 cup packed light brown sugar	$^1/_2$ teaspoon salt
2 eggs, lightly beaten	3 cups quick-cooking oats
2 teaspoons vanilla extract	1 cup shredded coconut
2 tablespoons water	1 cup (6 ounces) semisweet chocolate chips
2 cups all-purpose flour	

Beat the butter, granulated sugar and brown sugar in a bowl until light and fluffy. Add the eggs and vanilla and mix well. For soft cookies, add 2 tablespoons water and mix well. Sift the flour, baking powder, baking soda and salt together. Add to the butter mixture gradually, mixing well after each addition. Stir in the oats, coconut and chocolate chips. Drop by teaspoonfuls onto a greased cookie sheet. Bake at 350 degrees for 8 to 12 minutes or until light brown. Cool on the cookie sheet for 1 minute. Remove to a wire rack to cool completely. Yield: 3 to 4 dozen cookies.

Jeanne M. Myers, Beta Alpha
Jefferson, Iowa

OATMEAL CRISPIES

1 cup shortening	1$^1/_2$ cups all-purpose flour
1 cup packed brown sugar	1 teaspoon salt
1 cup granulated sugar	1 teaspoon baking soda
2 eggs, beaten	3 cups quick-cooking oats
1 teaspoon vanilla extract	1$^1/_2$ cups chopped walnuts

Beat the shortening, brown sugar and granulated sugar in a bowl until light and fluffy. Add the eggs and vanilla and mix well. Sift the flour, salt and baking soda together. Add to the shortening mixture and mix well. Stir in the oats and walnuts. Shape into a log. Chill, tightly wrapped, overnight. Cut into $^1/_4$-inch slices and place on an ungreased cookie sheet. Bake at 350 degrees for 10 minutes. Cool on the cookie sheet for 1 minute. Remove to a wire rack to cool completely. Yield: 5 dozen cookies.

G. Ann Bedinghaus, Alpha Gamma Master
Hutchinson, Kansas

SWEDISH OATMEAL COOKIES

I won an award for this recipe in the Pillsbury Bake Off more than forty years ago.

$^1/_2$ cup shortening	1$^1/_2$ cups quick-cooking oats
$^1/_2$ cup granulated sugar	$^1/_3$ cup granulated sugar
$^1/_2$ cup packed brown sugar	1 teaspoon light corn syrup
1 egg	$^1/_4$ cup ($^1/_2$ stick) butter
$^1/_2$ teaspoon vanilla extract	$^1/_4$ teaspoon almond extract
$^3/_4$ cup all-purpose flour	$^1/_3$ cup sliced almonds
$^1/_2$ teaspoon salt	
$^1/_2$ teaspoon baking soda	

Beat the shortening, $^1/_2$ cup granulated sugar and brown sugar in a bowl until light and fluffy. Add the egg and vanilla and mix well. Combine the flour, salt, baking soda and oats. Add to the shortening mixture and mix well. Drop by teaspoonfuls onto an ungreased cookie sheet. Bake at 350 degrees for 8 minutes. Combine $^1/_3$ cup sugar, the butter and corn syrup in a saucepan. Bring to a boil over medium heat, stirring often. Remove from the heat and stir in the almond extract. Stir in the almonds. Spoon $^1/_2$ teaspoon of the almond mixture into the center of each cookie, pressing lightly. Bake 6 to 8 minutes longer or until brown. Cool on the cookie sheet for 1 minute. Remove to a wire rack to cool completely.
Yield: 3 dozen cookies.

Irma Kaufman, Laureate Beta Sigma
Sun City Center, Florida

SCOTTISH OATCAKES

4 cups all-purpose flour	2 teaspoons baking soda
1¹/2 cups granulated sugar	6 cups rolled oats
2 tablespoons brown sugar	2 cups shortening
2 teaspoons salt	¹/2 cup (1 stick) butter, softened
	1 cup cold water

Sift the flour, granulated sugar, brown sugar, salt and baking soda into a large bowl. Stir in the oats. Add the shortening and butter and mix just until combined. Add the water and mix with your hands for 1 minute. Roll ¹/4 to ¹/2-inch thick on a floured surface. Cut as desired. Bake at 350 degrees for 8 to 10 minutes or until light brown. Cool on the cookie sheet for 1 minute. Remove to a wire rack to cool completely. Yield: 4 dozen cookies.

Martha Cormier, Xi Lambda
Amherst, Nova Scotia, Canada

FROSTED SUGAR COOKIES

¹/2 cup (1 stick) butter or margarine, softened	¹/4 teaspoon salt
¹/4 cup packed brown sugar	1 egg white
1 egg yolk	¹/2 cup chopped nuts
¹/2 teaspoon vanilla extract	1 container vanilla or cream cheese frosting
1 cup all-purpose flour	"M & M's" Peanut Chocolate Candies for garnish

Beat the butter and brown sugar in a bowl until light and fluffy. Stir in the egg yolk and vanilla. Sift the flour and salt together. Add to the butter mixture and mix well. Chill, covered, for 1 hour. Shape into balls. Dip in egg white and roll in nuts. Place on a cookie sheet. Bake at 350 degrees for 5 minutes. Make an indentation in each cookie with the back of your thumb. Bake for 5 to 7 minutes longer. Cool on the cookie sheet for 2 minutes. Remove to a wire rack to cool completely. Frost the cookies and garnish with the candies. Yield: 1¹/2 dozen cookies.

Georgine Wasley, Preceptor Nu Delta
Nevada City, California

SOFT SUGAR COOKIES

1 cup (2 sticks) butter, softened	1 teaspoon vanilla extract
¹/4 cup granulated sugar	1 teaspoon baking soda
³/4 cup packed brown sugar	2¹/4 cups all-purpose flour
1 (4-ounce) package vanilla instant pudding mix	1 cup (6 ounces) miniature chocolate chips
2 eggs	

Beat the butter, granulated sugar and brown sugar in a bowl until light and fluffy. Add the pudding mix, eggs and vanilla and mix well. Add the baking soda and flour and mix well. Stir in the chocolate chips. Drop by teaspoonfuls onto a greased cookie sheet. Bake at 350 degrees for 8 to 10 minutes or until light brown. Cool on the cookie sheet for 1 minute. Remove to a wire rack to cool completely. Yield: 4 to 5 dozen cookies.

Ruth Ellen Smith, Gamma Lambda
Chariton, Iowa

PEANUT BUTTER SANDWICH COOKIES

1 cup (2 sticks) margarine, softened	2 teaspoons baking soda
1 cup granulated sugar	Additional granulated sugar
1 cup packed brown sugar	¹/4 cup chunky peanut butter
2 eggs, beaten	1 teaspoon vanilla extract
1 cup chunky peanut butter	2 tablespoons milk
1 teaspoon vanilla extract	3 cups sifted confectioners' sugar
3 cups all-purpose flour	

Beat the margarine, granulated sugar and brown sugar in a bowl until light and fluffy. Add the eggs, 1 cup peanut butter and 1 teaspoon vanilla and mix well. Combine the flour and baking soda. Add to the margarine mixture and mix well. Shape into 1¹/4-inch balls and place 2 inches apart on an ungreased cookie sheet. Flatten with a fork dipped in granulated sugar to form a crosshatch design. Bake at 350 degrees for 6 to 8 minutes or until light brown. Cool on the cookie sheet for 1 minute. Remove to a wire rack to cool completely. Combine the ¹/4 cup peanut butter, 1 teaspoon vanilla extract, milk and confectioners' sugar in a bowl and mix until smooth. Add more milk if the filling seems too thick. Spread filling to taste over the bottom of one cookie. Top with another cookie. Yield: 2¹/2 dozen cookies.

Darice Todd, Gamma Pi
Kirksville, Missouri

PECAN FINGERS

1 cup (2 sticks) butter, softened	1 tablespoon water
¹/4 cup confectioners' sugar	2 cups all-purpose flour
¹/4 teaspoon salt	2 cups ground pecans
1 teaspoon vanilla extract	Additional confectioners' sugar for sprinkling

Beat the butter and 1/4 cup confectioners' sugar in a bowl until light and fluffy. Add the salt, vanilla, water, flour and pecans and mix well. Shape by spoonfuls into crescents on a cookie sheet. Bake at 350 degrees for 15 minutes. Cool on the cookie sheet for 1 minute. Remove to a wire rack to cool completely. Sprinkle with confectioners' sugar.
Yield: 3 to 4 dozen cookies.

Joyce Keller, Laureate Epsilon Theta
Pinellas Park, Florida

PERSIMMON COOKIES

2 teaspoons baking soda	1 teaspoon ground
2 cups persimmon pulp	cloves
1 cup shortening	1 teaspoon cinnamon
2 cups sugar	1 teaspoon nutmeg
2 eggs, beaten	2 cups raisins
4 cups all-purpose flour	2 cups chopped walnuts
1 teaspoon salt	

Combine the baking soda and persimmon pulp in a bowl and mix well. Let stand for several minutes until thickened. Beat the shortening and sugar in a bowl until light and fluffy. Add the eggs and the persimmon mixture and mix well. Sift the flour, salt, cloves, cinnamon and nutmeg together. Add to the persimmon mixture and mix well. Stir in the raisins and walnuts. Drop by teaspoonfuls onto a greased cookie sheet. Bake at 350 degrees for 12 to 15 minutes. Cool on the cookie sheet for 1 minute. Remove to a wire rack to cool completely. Yield: 5 dozen cookies.

R. Louise Dibble, Xi Rho Iota
Redding, California

PINEAPPLE COOKIES

1 cup shortening	4 cups all-purpose flour
1 cup packed brown	1/4 teaspoon salt
sugar	1 teaspoon baking soda
1 cup granulated sugar	1 (20-ounce) can crushed
2 eggs, beaten	pineapple, drained
1 teaspoon vanilla	
extract	

Beat the shortening, brown sugar and granulated sugar in a bowl until light and fluffy. Add the eggs and vanilla and mix well. Add the flour, salt and baking soda and mix well. Stir in the pineapple. Drop by spoonfuls onto a greased baking sheet. Bake at 350 degrees for 12 to 15 minutes or until golden brown. Cool on the cookie sheet for 1 minute. Remove to a wire rack to cool completely.
Yield: 3 to 4 dozen cookies.

Shirley Peterson, Laureate Kappa
Beatrice, Nebraska

POTATO CHIP COOKIES

2 cups (4 sticks)	1 cup crushed potato
butter or margarine,	chips
softened	1 cup (6 ounces) white
1 cup sugar	chocolate chips
3 cups all-purpose flour	1 cup chopped
1 teaspoon almond	macadamia nuts
extract	

Beat the butter and sugar in a mixing bowl until light and fluffy. Add the flour and almond extract and mix well. Stir in the potato chips, white chocolate chips and macadamia nuts. Drop by teaspoonfuls 2 inches apart on an ungreased cookie sheet. Bake at 350 degrees for 15 minutes. Cool on the cookie sheet for 1 minute. Remove to a wire rack to cool completely. Yield: 3 dozen cookies.

Pauline B. Chiorgno, Beta Lambda Master
Corpus Christi, Texas

PUMPKIN CHOCOLATE CHIP COOKIES

1 1/2 cups (3 sticks)	4 cups all-purpose flour
butter, softened	2 teaspoons baking soda
2 cups packed brown	2 teaspoons cinnamon
sugar	1 teaspoon salt
1 cup granulated sugar	2 cups quick-cooking
1 (15-ounce) can	oats
pumpkin	2 cups (12 ounces)
1 egg	chocolate chips
1 teaspoon vanilla	
extract	

Beat the butter, brown sugar and granulated sugar in a bowl until light and fluffy. Add the pumpkin, egg and vanilla and mix well. Add the flour, baking soda, cinnamon and salt and mix well. Stir in the oats and chocolate chips. Drop by tablespoonfuls 2 inches apart onto a cookie sheet. Bake at 350 degrees for 10 to 12 minutes. Cool on the cookie sheet for 1 minute. Remove to a wire rack to cool completely. Yield: 10 dozen cookies.

Margaret Love, Beta Pi Master
Santa Barbara, California

*Marylee Clark, Laureate Zeta Upsilon, Modesto, California, uses lemon cake mix to make her easy **Lemon Drop Cookies**. She combines the cake mix, 2 cups whipped topping and 1 egg in a bowl and mixes well. She shapes the dough by teaspoonfuls into balls, rolls them in confectioners' sugar, and arranges them on a greased cookie sheet. The cookies are baked at 350 degrees for 12 to 15 minutes or until firm.*

PUMPKIN RAISIN COOKIES

1 (14-ounce) package
   Pillsbury Pumpkin
   Quick Bread mix
1/2 cup raisins
1/4 cup candied ginger

1/2 cup (1 stick) butter or
   margarine, melted
1 egg
1/4 cup sugar
1 teaspoon cinnamon

Combine the bread mix, raisins and candied ginger in a bowl and mix well. Add the butter and egg and mix well. Mixture may be slightly crumbly. Combine the sugar and cinnamon in a small bowl and mix well. Shape the dough into 1½-inch balls. Roll in the cinnamon-sugar. Place 2 inches apart on an ungreased cookie sheet. Bake at 350 degrees for 12 to 15 minutes or until firm. Cool on the cookie sheet for 1 minute. Remove to a wire rack to cool completely. Yield: 1½ dozen cookies.

Evelyn Smith, Theta Master
Great Bend, Kansas

JUMBO RAISIN COOKIES

2 cups raisins
1 cup water
1 teaspoon vanilla
   extract
1 cup (2 sticks) butter or
   margarine, softened
2 cups sugar
3 eggs
4 cups all-purpose flour

1 teaspoon cinnamon
1 teaspoon baking soda
1 teaspoon baking
   powder
1/2 teaspoon salt
1/4 teaspoon allspice or
   ground cloves
1/4 teaspoon nutmeg

Combine the raisins and water in a saucepan. Cook over medium heat for 3 minutes, stirring occasionally. Cool completely. Stir in the vanilla. Beat the butter and sugar in a bowl until light and fluffy. Beat in the eggs. Sift the remaining ingredients together. Add to the butter mixture and mix well. Stir in the raisin mixture. Drop by spoonfuls onto a greased cookie sheet. Bake at 350 degrees for 10 minutes. Cool on the cookie sheet for 1 minute. Remove to a wire rack to cool completely. Yield: 7 dozen cookies.

Delores D. Roberts, Preceptor Beta
Butte, Montana

RAISIN PUFF COOKIES

1 cup water
1½ cups raisins
1 cup (2 sticks) butter,
   softened
1½ cups sugar
1 teaspoon vanilla
   extract

2 eggs
3½ cups all-purpose
   flour
1 teaspoon baking soda
1/2 teaspoon salt
1/2 cup sugar
1 teaspoon cinnamon

Combine the water and raisins in a saucepan. Cook over medium heat until the water has been absorbed, stirring occasionally. Cool completely. Beat the butter and 1½ cups sugar in a bowl until light and fluffy. Add the vanilla and eggs and mix well. Add the flour, baking soda and salt and mix well. Stir in the raisin mixture. Mix 1/2 cup sugar and cinnamon in a bowl. Shape the dough into 1-inch balls. Roll in the cinnamon-sugar and place on an ungreased cookie sheet. Bake at 375 degrees for 8 minutes. Cool on the cookie sheet for 1 minute. Remove to a wire rack to cool completely. Yield: 5 to 6 dozen cookies.

Debbie A. Collins, Kappa Kappa
Meriden, Kansas

SPICED RAISIN COOKIES

1 cup shortening
1½ cups packed
   brown sugar
3 eggs
2 teaspoons vanilla
   extract
3 cups all-purpose flour
1 teaspoon baking soda
1 teaspoon salt

1 teaspoon cinnamon
1/2 teaspoon ground
   cloves
2 cups raisins
1 cup chopped nuts
3 cups confectioners'
   sugar
1/4 cup water

Beat the shortening and brown sugar in a bowl until light and fluffy. Stir in the eggs and 1 teaspoon of the vanilla. Combine the next 5 ingredients. Add to the shortening mixture and mix well. Stir in the raisins and nuts. Chill, wrapped in plastic wrap, for 1 hour or longer. Drop by teaspoonfuls onto a greased cookie sheet. Bake at 350 degrees for 8 to 10 minutes or until light brown. Cool on the cookie sheet for 1 minute. Remove to a wire rack to cool completely. Mix the confectioners' sugar, water, and the remaining vanilla in a bowl until smooth. Place the cookies on waxed paper. Drizzle the glaze over the cookies. Let stand until firm. Yield: 6 to 10 dozen cookies.

Dorothy (Betty) Mullis, Xi Theta Upsilon
Tampa, Florida

RUGELACH

1 pint vanilla ice cream,
   softened
2 cups (4 sticks) butter
   or margarine,
   softened
4 cups all-purpose flour

2 jars apricot jam or
   preserves
2 cups raisins
1 pound chopped
   walnuts
Sugar for sprinkling

Combine the softened ice cream and butter in a bowl and mix well. Add the flour 1 cup at a time, mixing well after each addition. Roll into nine 12-inch circles on a floured surface and cut each circle into 8 slices (like a pizza). Spoon 1/4 teaspoon jam over the wide end of each slice. Top with 3 or 4 raisins and 1/2 teaspoon walnuts. Roll toward the point of the slice to enclose the filling. Sprinkle with sugar. Bake at 375 degrees for 20 minutes. Cool on the cookie sheet for 1 minute. Remove to a wire rack to cool completely. Yield: 6 dozen cookies.

Karen Pesta, Eta
Florence, South Carolina

HONEY SAND TARTS

1/2 cup (1 stick) butter or margarine, melted	1/4 teaspoon almond extract
1 1/2 cups enriched flour, sifted	2 tablespoons honey
1 teaspoon vanilla extract	1/2 cup chopped nuts Confectioners' sugar for sprinkling

Combine the butter, flour, vanilla, almond extract and honey in a bowl and mix well. Stir in the nuts. Shape into balls and place on a cookie sheet. Bake at 400 degrees for 8 to 10 minutes or until golden brown. Sprinkle with confectioners' sugar. Cool on the cookie sheet for 1 minute. Remove to a wire rack to cool completely. Sprinkle with confectioners' sugar a second time. Yield: 4 dozen cookies.

Linda Jo Cottros, Xi Theta Sigma
Frederickstown, Missouri

CRANBERRY PECAN SHORTBREAD COOKIES

1 cup all-purpose flour	3/4 cup (1 1/2 sticks) butter, softened
1/2 cup cornstarch	
1/2 cup confectioners' sugar	1/2 cup dried cranberries
	1/2 cup chopped pecans

Combine the flour, cornstarch and confectioners' sugar in a large bowl. Add the butter and mix well. Knead until a smooth dough forms. Stir in the cranberries and pecans. Divide the dough in half. Shape each portion into a 1 1/2-inch wide log. Chill, tightly wrapped, until firm. Cut into 1/4-inch slices. Place on an ungreased cookie sheet. Bake at 375 degrees for 10 minutes or until light brown. Cool on the cookie sheet for 1 minute. Remove to a wire rack to cool completely. Yield: 2 dozen cookies.

Brenda Mueller, Laureate Alpha Alpha
Merrill, Wisconsin

SHORTBREAD COOKIES

1 cup (2 sticks) butter, softened	1/2 teaspoon lemon extract
1/2 cup sugar	2 1/2 cups sifted all-purpose flour

Beat the butter and sugar in a bowl until light and fluffy. Add the lemon extract and mix well. Add the flour in 3 batches, mixing well after each addition. The dough will be stiff. Knead the dough in the bowl for 10 to 15 minutes or until smooth. Wrap in waxed paper and chill for several hours or until firm. Roll into a 9×11-inch rectangle on a floured surface and cut as desired. Place on a cookie sheet. Bake at 300 degrees for 25 minutes or until firm and golden brown. Cool on the cookie sheet for 1 minute. Remove to a wire rack to cool completely. Yield: 2 dozen cookies.

Heather Cioffi, Delta Beta Nu
Northridge, California

SNOWBALLS

1 cup (2 sticks) butter, softened	2 1/4 cups all-purpose flour
1/2 cup confectioners' sugar	1/4 teaspoon salt
1 teaspoon vanilla extract	1 cup walnuts, ground Additional confectioners' sugar for sprinkling

Beat the butter and confectioners' sugar in a bowl until light and fluffy. Add the vanilla and mix well. Add the flour, salt and walnuts and mix well. Shape into 1-inch balls. Place 1 inch apart on an ungreased cookie sheet. Bake at 400 degrees for 10 minutes or until set but not brown. Sprinkle with confectioners' sugar. Remove to a wire rack to cool completely. Sprinkle with confectioners' sugar a second time. Yield: 3 to 4 dozen cookies.

Janet Falk, Nu Xi
Linwood, Kansas

SOPAIPILLAS

1 3/4 cups all-purpose flour	2 tablespoons shortening
2 teaspoons baking powder	1 quart vegetable oil for deep frying
1 teaspoon salt	Confectioners' sugar or honey
2/3 cup water	

Combine the flour, baking powder and salt in a large bowl. Add the water gradually, mixing well after each addition. Add the shortening and mix well. Knead the dough on a floured surface for 5 minutes. Divide into 3 equal portions. Roll each portion 1/8-inch thick. Cut into circles. Drop into 350-degree oil. Fry for 2 to 3 minutes or until golden brown. Remove with a slotted spoon. Drain on paper towels. Dust with confectioners' sugar or drizzle with honey. Yield: 1 dozen cookies.

Barbara Brooks, Laureate Epsilon Theta
Palm Harbor, Florida

NO-ROLL SUGAR COOKIES

1 cup (2 sticks) butter or margarine, softened	1/4 teaspoon lemon extract
1 cup confectioners' sugar	2 1/2 cups all-purpose flour
1/4 cup granulated sugar	1 teaspoon baking soda
1 egg	1 teaspoon cream of tartar
1 teaspoon vanilla extract	Additional granulated sugar

Beat the butter, confectioners' sugar and granulated sugar in a bowl until light and fluffy. Add the egg, vanilla and lemon extract and mix well. Add the flour, baking soda and cream of tartar and mix well. Drop by teaspoonfuls onto a greased cookie sheet. Flatten with a glass dipped in granulated sugar. Bake at 350 degrees for 15 minutes. Cool on the cookie sheet for 1 minute. Remove to a wire rack to cool completely. Yield: 3 dozen cookies.

Sarah Collins, Preceptor Gamma Eta
New Hampton, Iowa

TEA TIME PECAN TASSIES

3 ounces cream cheese, softened	3/4 cup packed brown sugar
1/2 cup (1 stick) butter or margarine, softened	1 egg
1 cup all-purpose flour	1 teaspoon vanilla extract
1 tablespoon butter, softened	Dash of salt
	3/4 cup chopped pecans

Beat the cream cheese and 1/2 cup butter in a bowl until light and fluffy. Add the flour and mix well. Shape into 24 balls. Press over the bottoms and sides of greased miniature muffin cups. Cream 1 tablespoon butter and the brown sugar in a medium bowl until light and fluffy. Add the egg, vanilla and salt and mix well. Stir in the pecans. Spoon 1 teaspoonful of the mixture over each muffin cup. Bake at 350 degrees for 30 minutes. Cool in the pan. Yield: 2 dozen tassies.

Ina Garrison, Preceptor Beta Pi
Concordia, Kansas

WEDDING COOKIES

1 cup (2 sticks) margarine, softened	2 teaspoons vanilla extract
1/3 cup sugar	2 cups all-purpose flour
2 teaspoons water	1 cup chopped pecans

Beat the margarine and sugar in a bowl until light and fluffy. Add the water and vanilla and mix well. Add the flour and mix well. Stir in the pecans. Shape into balls. Place onto a cookie sheet. Bake at 325 degrees for 20 minutes. Sprinkle with confectioners' sugar. Cool on the cookie sheet for 1 minute. Remove to a wire rack to cool completely. Yield: 3 dozen cookies.

Anita C. Gay, Theta Lambda
Zebulon, North Carolina

WHOOPIE PIES

1 cup shortening	4 cups all-purpose flour
2 cups sugar	1 cup baking cocoa
2 egg yolks	2 teaspoons salt
2 teaspoons vanilla extract	2 teaspoons baking soda
1 cup sour milk	1 cup hot water
	Vanilla Filling

Beat the shortening and sugar in a bowl until light and fluffy. Add the egg yolks, vanilla extract and sour milk and mix well. Sift the flour, baking cocoa and salt into the bowl and mix well. Stir in the baking soda and water. Drop by spoonfuls onto a greased cookie sheet. Bake at 400 degrees for 8 minutes. Cool on the cookie sheet for 1 minute. Remove to a wire rack to cool completely. Spread Vanilla Filling to taste across the flat side of one cookie. Top with the flat side of another cookie. Yield: 4 dozen cookies.

VANILLA FILLING

2 egg whites, stiffly beaten	4 tablespoons milk
2 tablespoons vanilla extract	4 cups confectioners' sugar
4 tablespoons all-purpose flour	1 cup shortening

Combine the egg whites, vanilla extract, flour, milk and 2 cups of the confectioners' sugar and mix until smooth. Add the remaining 2 cups confectioners' sugar and the shortening and mix well.

Connie Aguilera, Preceptor Eta
Wichita, Kansas

ZUCCHINI OATMEAL COOKIES

1/2 cup (1 stick) butter, softened	1/2 teaspoon cinnamon
3/4 cup honey	1/4 teaspoon ground cloves
1 egg	1/4 teaspoon nutmeg
2 cups whole wheat flour	1 cup rolled oats
1 teaspoon baking soda	1 cup raisins
	1 cup grated zucchini

Beat the butter and honey in a bowl until light and fluffy. Add the egg and mix well. Add a mixture of the next 5 ingredients gradually, mixing well after each addition. Stir in the oats, raisins and zucchini. Drop by teaspoonfuls onto a greased cookie sheet.

Flatten with a fork. Bake at 375 degrees for 10 to 12 minutes or until firm. Cool on the cookie sheet for 1 minute. Remove to a wire rack to cool completely. Yield: 5 dozen cookies.

Carol Rott, Delta Eta
Elliot Lake, Ontario, Canada

SWISS ALMOND BARS

2 eggs	1 teaspoon almond
3/4 cup sugar	extract
1/2 cup all-purpose flour	1/2 cup sliced almonds
1/2 cup (1 stick) butter, melted	

Beat the eggs in a bowl until thick and pale yellow. Stir in the sugar and flour. Stir in the butter and almond extract. Spread in a greased 8×8-inch baking pan. Sprinkle with the almonds. Bake at 350 degrees for 15 minutes. Cool slightly. Cut into bars while warm. Let stand until cool. Yield: 1 dozen bars.

Ann-Francis Butts, Iota Master
Burlington, Connecticut

APPLE SQUARES

3 eggs	3 cups all-purpose flour
2 cups sugar	1 teaspoon baking soda
1 cup vegetable oil	1 teaspoon salt
2 teaspoons vanilla extract	1 cup chopped nuts
	3 cups chopped apples

Mix the eggs, sugar and oil in a bowl. Stir in the vanilla. Add the flour, baking soda and salt and mix well. Stir in the nuts and apples. Spread in a greased and floured 10×15-inch baking pan. Bake at 350 degrees for 30 to 45 minutes or until light brown. Cool. Cut into squares. Yield: 2 dozen bars.

Carole Goldinger, Preceptor Delta Nu
Butler, Pennsylvania

DANISH APPLE BARS

2 1/2 cups all-purpose flour	1 cup granulated sugar
1 teaspoon salt	2 tablespoons cinnamon
1 cup shortening	1 egg white, stiffly beaten
2/3 cups milk	2 cups confectioners' sugar
1 egg yolk	1 teaspoon water
1 cup quick-cooking oats	1 teaspoon vanilla extract
5 apples, peeled and sliced	

Combine the flour and salt in a bowl. Cut in the shortening until crumbly. Add the milk and egg yolk and mix just until moistened. Divide the dough in half. Roll 1 portion into a 9×13-inch rectangle on a floured surface. Place on a baking sheet. Sprinkle with oats, apples, granulated sugar and cinnamon, leaving a 1/2-inch edge. Roll out the other portion of dough into a 9×13-inch rectangle and place over the apple layer. Seal the edges. Spread the egg white over the top. Bake at 400 degrees for 20 to 25 minutes or until light brown. Mix the confectioners' sugar, water and vanilla in a bowl until smooth. Drizzle over the warm baked layer. Cut into bars. Yield: 2 dozen bars.

Janet Cherni, Xi Epsilon
Sheridan, Wyoming

MOCK BABY RUTH BARS

2/3 cup margarine, melted	4 cups rolled oats
1 cup packed brown sugar	2 cups (12 ounces) milk chocolate chips
1/4 cup light corn syrup	1 cup (6 ounces) butterscotch chips
1/4 cup chunky peanut butter	2/3 cup chunky peanut butter
1 teaspoon vanilla extract	1 cup salted peanuts

Mix the margarine, brown sugar and corn syrup in a large bowl. Add 1/4 cup peanut butter and the vanilla and mix well. Stir in the oats. Pat into a greased 9×13-inch baking pan. Bake at 375 degrees for 12 minutes. Combine the chocolate chips and butterscotch chips in a saucepan. Melt over low heat, stirring constantly. Add 2/3 cup peanut butter and mix well. Stir in the peanuts. Spread over the baked layer. Cool. Cut into bars. Yield: 1 to 2 dozen bars.

Roberta Lyons, Preceptor Nu
Frederick, Maryland

BLACK-BOTTOM BANANA BARS

1/2 cup (1 stick) butter, softened	1 1/2 cups all-purpose flour
1 cup sugar	1 teaspoon baking powder
1 egg	1 teaspoon baking soda
1 teaspoon vanilla extract	1/2 teaspoon salt
1 1/2 cups mashed bananas	1/4 cup baking cocoa

Beat the butter and sugar in a bowl until light and fluffy. Add the egg and vanilla and mix well. Stir in the bananas. Add the flour, baking powder, baking soda and salt and mix well. Spread half the batter in a greased 9×13-inch baking pan. Add the baking cocoa to the remaining batter and mix well. Spoon into the pan and swirl with a knife to marbleize. Bake at 350 degrees for 25 minutes. Cool. Cut into bars. Yield: 1 to 2 dozen bars.

Rita Ackerman, Preceptor Beta Beta
Colfax, Washington

BUTTER BARS

1 (2-layer) package yellow cake mix	2 eggs
1 egg	1 1/2 teaspoons vanilla extract
1/2 cup (1 stick) butter, melted	1 (1-pound) package confectioners' sugar
8 ounces cream cheese, softened	1/4 cup (1/2 stick) butter, melted

Mix the cake mix, egg and 1/2 cup melted butter in a bowl. Spread in a greased 9×13-inch baking pan. Beat the cream cheese in a large bowl until smooth. Add 2 eggs and the vanilla and mix well. Beat in the confectioners' sugar. Add 1/4 cup butter and mix well. Spoon over the cake mix in the pan. Bake at 350 degrees for 45 minutes. Cool. Cut into bars. Yield: 1 to 2 dozen bars.

Jenny Lynn Varner Hatter, Gamma Chi
Cynthiana, Kentucky

❖ BUTTER PECAN TURTLE BARS

2 cups all-purpose flour	1/2 cup packed light brown sugar
3/4 cup packed light brown sugar	2/3 cup butter
1/2 cup (1 stick) butter, softened	1 1/2 cups (9 ounces) milk chocolate chips
1 1/2 cups pecan halves	

Combine the flour, 3/4 cup brown sugar and 1/2 cup butter in a bowl and mix until crumbly. Pat into a foil-lined 9×13-inch baking pan. Sprinkle with the pecans. Combine 1/2 cup brown sugar and 2/3 cup butter in a saucepan. Bring to a boil over medium heat, stirring constantly. Boil for 1 minute, stirring constantly. Drizzle over the pecans. Bake at 350 degrees for 18 to 20 minutes or until the topping is bubbly. Sprinkle with chocolate chips. Spread the chocolate as it melts. Cool. Cut into bars. Yield: 1 to 2 dozen bars.

Eleanor Strecker, Beta Master
Billings, Montana

BLACK FOREST BROWNIES

1/2 cup (1 stick) butter, softened	1/3 cup baking cocoa
1 cup granulated sugar	1/4 teaspoon salt
2 eggs	8 ounces cream cheese, softened
1 teaspoon vanilla extract	1 cup confectioners' sugar
1/2 cup all-purpose flour	1 cup whipped topping
1/4 teaspoon baking powder	1 (21-ounce) can cherry pie filling

Beat the butter and granulated sugar in a bowl until light and fluffy. Add the eggs and vanilla and mix well. Add the flour, baking powder, baking cocoa and salt and mix well. Spread in a greased springform pan. Bake at 350 degrees for 25 minutes. Cool on a wire rack. Beat the cream cheese and confectioners' sugar in a large bowl until light and fluffy. Fold in the whipped topping. Spread over the baked layer. Top with the pie filling. Chill, covered, until just before serving. Yield: 10 servings.

Penny Davis, Pi Pi
Ames, Iowa

BROWNIES

My mother-in-law, Mildred, created this recipe in World War II during sugar rationing. She entered it in the Oklahoma State Pecan Show until she won silver trays for each grandchild.

1/2 cup shortening	2 teaspoons baking powder
1/2 cup baking cocoa	
2 eggs	1 teaspoon vanilla extract
2 cups maple syrup	
2 cups all-purpose flour	1 cup chopped pecans
1/3 cup sugar	Chocolate Fudge Frosting
1/2 teaspoon salt	

Combine the shortening and the baking cocoa in a saucepan. Cook over low heat until the shortening melts, stirring often. Beat the eggs in a mixing bowl. Add the maple syrup and mix well. Sift the flour, sugar, salt and baking powder together. Add to the syrup mixture and mix well. Add the chocolate mixture and mix well. Stir in the vanilla. Fold in the pecans. Spread in a greased 12×16-inch baking pan. Bake at 350 degrees for 30 minutes. Cool. Frost with the Chocolate Fudge Frosting and cut into squares. Yield: 3 dozen brownies.

CHOCOLATE FUDGE FROSTING

1 (1-pound) package confectioners' sugar	1/4 cup baking cocoa
1/2 cup (1 stick) margarine	1/4 cup milk
	1 teaspoon vanilla extract

Place the confectioners' sugar in a large bowl. Melt the margarine in a saucepan over medium heat. Add the baking cocoa and milk. Bring to a boil, stirring often. Remove from the heat. Stir in the vanilla. Pour into the confectioners' sugar and mix until smooth.

Claudine Ripley, Preceptor Kappa Mu
Vernon, Texas

BLACK WALNUT BROWNIES

3/4 cup all-purpose flour
1/4 teaspoon baking soda
3/4 cup sugar
1/3 cup butter or margarine, softened
2 tablespoons water

2 cups (12 ounces) chocolate chips
1 teaspoon vanilla extract
2 eggs
1/2 cup chopped black walnuts

Combine the flour and baking soda. Combine the sugar, butter and water in a small saucepan. Bring to a boil over medium heat, stirring often. Remove from the heat and stir in 1 cup of the chocolate chips and the vanilla until smooth. Cool completely. Place in a bowl. Add the eggs 1 at a time, mixing well after each addition. Add the flour mixture gradually, mixing well after each addition. Stir in the remaining chocolate chips and the walnuts. Spread in a greased 9×9-inch baking pan. Bake at 325 degrees for 30 to 35 minutes or until the brownies pull from the sides of the pan. Cool. Cut into squares. Yield: 16 brownies.

Mary Ellen Sayers, Chi Omega
Buckner, Missouri

BUTTERSCOTCH BROWNIES

1/2 cup (1 stick) butter or margarine
2 cups packed light brown sugar
2 eggs
1 teaspoon vanilla extract

2 cups all-purpose flour
1/4 teaspoon salt
2 tablespoons baking powder
2 cups shredded coconut (optional)
1/2 cup chopped nuts

Combine the butter and brown sugar in a saucepan. Bring to a boil over low heat, stirring often. Cool. Beat in the eggs 1 at a time. Stir in the vanilla. Sift the flour, salt and baking powder together. Add to the batter and mix well. Stir in the coconut and nuts. Spread in a greased 9×9-inch baking pan. Bake at 350 degrees for 25 to 35 minutes or until the brownies pull from the sides of the pan. Cut into bars while warm. Let stand until cool. Yield: 8 or 9 brownies.

Carol Greene, Laureate Delta Epsilon
Brandon, Florida

CHOCOLATE PEANUT BUTTER BROWNIES

1 (20-ounce) package brownie mix, sifted
1 teaspoon vanilla extract
3 cups confectioners' sugar
1 cup peanut butter

1/2 cup (1 stick) margarine, softened
4 to 6 tablespoons milk
2 ounces semisweet chocolate
2 tablespoons margarine

Prepare the brownies using the package directions. Stir in the vanilla. Bake the brownies using the package directions for chewy brownies. Cool. Combine the confectioners' sugar, peanut butter and 1/2 cup margarine in a bowl and mix until smooth. Stir in enough milk to make of spreading consistency. Frost the cooled brownies. Combine the chocolate and 2 tablespoons margarine in a saucepan. Cook over low heat until smooth, stirring often. Drizzle over the frosted brownies. Chill. Cut into squares.
Yield: 15 brownies.

Diane L. Pruett, Preceptor Alpha Upsilon
Tamaqua, Pennsylvania

DOUBLE CHOCOLATE BROWNIES

1 1/2 cups (9 ounces) semisweet chocolate chips
1/2 cup (1 stick) butter or margarine
1 (14-ounce) can sweetened condensed milk

2 eggs
1 1/4 cups all-purpose flour
1 teaspoon baking powder
1/4 teaspoon salt
1 cup (6 ounces) white chocolate chips

Melt the semisweet chocolate chips and butter in a saucepan over low heat, stirring often. Remove from the heat. Stir in the condensed milk. Add the eggs 1 at a time, mixing well after each addition. Mix in the flour, baking powder and salt. Fold in the white chocolate chips. Pour into a greased 9×13-inch baking pan. Bake at 350 degrees for 25 minutes. Cool. Cut into squares. Yield: 30 brownies.

Vicky Williams, Laureate Alpha Beta
Campbell River, British Columbia, Canada

TRIPLE CHOCOLATE COFFEE BROWNIES

1 (20-ounce) package brownie mix
1 egg, beaten
1/4 cup vegetable oil
1/4 cup coffee liqueur or strong coffee
1/4 cup strong coffee
3/4 cup (4 1/2 ounces) milk chocolate chips

3/4 cup (4 1/2 ounces) white chocolate chips
1/2 cup (3 ounces) semisweet chocolate chips
1/2 cup chopped walnuts or pecans

Combine the brownie mix, egg, oil, coffee liqueur and coffee in a bowl and mix well. Stir in the remaining ingredients. Spread in a greased 9×13-inch baking pan. Bake at 350 degrees for 30 minutes. Cool on a wire rack. Cut into bars. Yield: 36 brownies.

Kathleen Mitchell, Laureate Alpha Rho
Rochester, New York

MARSHMALLOW BROWNIES

1/2 cup (1 stick) margarine, softened	1/2 teaspoon baking powder
2 cups sugar	1/4 teaspoon salt
4 eggs	4 tablespoons baking cocoa
1/2 cup vegetable oil	1 cup chopped walnuts
2 teaspoons vanilla extract	1 cup miniature marshmallows
1 1/2 cups all-purpose flour	Chocolate Frosting

Beat the margarine and sugar in a bowl until light and fluffy. Add the eggs, oil and vanilla and mix well. Add the flour, baking powder, salt and baking cocoa and mix well. Stir in the walnuts. Spread in a greased 9×13-inch pan. Bake at 350 degrees for 30 to 40 minutes or until the brownies pull from the side of the pan. Top with the miniature marshmallows. Bake for 3 to 4 minutes or until the marshmallows are soft. Cool. Frost the brownies. Cut into squares.
Yield: 2 dozen brownies.

CHOCOLATE FROSTING

1/4 cup water	1 teaspoon vanilla extract
1/2 cup packed brown sugar	1 1/2 cups confectioners' sugar
2 ounces chocolate	
3 tablespoons margarine	

Combine the water, brown sugar and chocolate in a saucepan. Bring to a boil over medium heat, stirring often. Boil for 3 minutes, stirring constantly Add 3 tablespoons margarine and the vanilla and stir until smooth. Cool. Add the confectioners' sugar and mix until smooth.

Jo Prusha, Preceptor Gamma
Omaha Nebraska

LIGHT BROWNIES

1 (20-ounce) package fat-free brownie mix	1 teaspoon vanilla extract
6 ounces low-fat vanilla yogurt	1 cup confectioners' sugar
1/3 cup light butter, softened	1/2 cup (3 ounces) semisweet chocolate chips, melted
1/2 teaspoon skim milk	

Prepare the brownie mix using the package directions, using yogurt. Spread in a foil-lined 8-inch baking pan. Bake at 350 degrees for 28 minutes or until a wooden pick inserted in the center comes out clean. Cool on a wire rack. Combine the butter, milk and vanilla in a bowl and mix until smooth. Add the confectioners' sugar and mix until thickened. Gradually add the chocolate, mixing well after each addition. Spread over the cooled brownies. Cut into squares. Yield: 16 brownies.

Anita Wilson, Omega Master
Mansfield, Ohio

MOIST BROWNIES

1/2 cup (1 stick) butter, softened	4 eggs
1 cup sugar	1 cup all-purpose flour
16 ounces chocolate syrup	1 cup chopped pecans
	Chocolate Frosting

Beat the butter and sugar in a bowl until light and fluffy. Add the chocolate syrup and eggs and mix well. Add the flour and mix well. Stir in the pecans. Spread in a 9×13-inch baking pan. Bake at 350 degrees for 25 minutes. Cool for 15 minutes. Pour the Chocolate Frosting over the cooled brownies. Cut into squares. Yield: 2 dozen brownies.

CHOCOLATE FROSTING

1 1/2 cups sugar	1 cup (6 ounces) chocolate chips
6 tablespoons milk	
6 tablespoons butter	

Combine the sugar, milk and butter in a saucepan. Bring to a boil over low heat, stirring often. Boil for 1 minute, stirring constantly. Remove from the heat and stir in chocolate chips until smooth.

Debra Bulloch, Xi Beta Rho
Stuttgart, Arkansas

PEPPERMINT BROWNIES

1 cup (2 sticks) butter	3 3/4 cups sugar
8 ounces unsweetened chocolate, chopped	1/2 teaspoon salt
4 teaspoons instant coffee granules	1/2 teaspoon almond extract
1 tablespoon boiling water	1 2/3 cups all-purpose flour
5 eggs	2 cups chopped walnuts
2 teaspoons vanilla extract	44 "fun-size" York Peppermint Pattie candies

Place the butter and chocolate in a microwave-safe bowl. Microwave, loosely covered, on High for 2 minutes or until melted, stirring every 30 seconds. Cool. Combine the coffee and water in a mixing bowl. Add the eggs, vanilla, sugar, salt and almond extract. Beat at high speed for 3 to 4 minutes or until fluffy. Add the chocolate mixture and flour and mix well. Stir in the walnuts. Spread half of the batter in a greased foil-lined 9×9-inch pan over half the candies. Repeat the layering with the remaining batter and candies in another 9×9-inch pan. Bake at

425 degrees for 25 minutes. Cool. Chill for 6 hours before serving. Cut into squares. Yield: 2 dozen brownies.

Jean Holeczy, Exemplar Preceptor
Spring Hill, Kansas

ZEBRA BROWNIES

1 (20-ounce) package brownie mix	3/4 cup confectioners' sugar
8 ounces cream cheese, softened	3/4 cup milk
	1 (2-layer) package white cake mix

Prepare the brownies using the package directions. Spread in a greased 12×15-inch baking pan. Beat the cream cheese in a bowl for 30 seconds. Add the confectioners' sugar and milk and mix until smooth. Add the cake mix and mix well. Spoon over the brownie layer. Swirl with a knife to marbleize. Bake at 350 degrees for 25 minutes. Cool. Cut into squares. Yield: 2 dozen brownies.

Melody Malek, Beta Chi
Independence, Iowa

BUTTERFINGER BARS

1 cup (2 sticks) butter, softened	4 cups quick-cooking oats
1 cup packed brown sugar	1 cup (6 ounces) chocolate chips
1/2 cup granulated sugar	3/4 cup peanut butter

Beat the butter, brown sugar and granulated sugar in a bowl until light and fluffy. Stir in the oats. Pat into a 9×13-inch baking pan. Bake at 350 degrees for 15 minutes. Cool. Combine the chocolate chips and peanut butter in a saucepan. Cook over low heat until smooth, stirring often. Spread over the baked layer. Cut into bars. Yield: 16 bars.

Bonnie J. Hula, Xi Omicron
Clarksville, Arkansas

CARAMEL SQUARES

1/2 cup (1 stick) margarine, softened	1 1/2 cups all-purpose flour
1/2 cup packed brown sugar	2 teaspoons baking powder
2 egg yolks	1/2 cup chopped walnuts
1 teaspoon vanilla extract	2 egg whites
	1 cup packed brown sugar

Beat the margarine and 1/2 cup brown sugar in a bowl until light and fluffy. Add the egg yolks and vanilla and mix well. Sift the flour and baking powder together. Add to the margarine mixture and mix well.

Spread in a greased 9×9-inch baking pan. Sprinkle with the walnuts. Beat the egg whites until stiff peaks form. Stir in 1 cup brown sugar. Spread over the unbaked squares. Bake at 325 degrees for 25 minutes. Cut into squares while warm. Yield: 16 squares.

Mary Colton, Xi Eta Kappa
Arden, Ontario, Canada

CARROT BARS

I had a kidney transplant ten years ago and became a diabetic. I made these bars for a special Thanksgiving when I had the donor's family at my place to celebrate life.

3 eggs	2 1/2 cups all-purpose flour
1 cup sugar	1/4 cup Splenda
1/2 cup vegetable oil	2 teaspoons baking soda
3 (4-ounce) jars baby food carrots	1 1/2 teaspoons cinnamon
1 teaspoon vanilla extract	1/2 cup drained crushed pineapple
	1/2 cup chopped walnuts

Combine the eggs, sugar, oil, carrots and vanilla in a bowl and mix well. Add the flour, Splenda, baking soda and cinnamon and mix well. Stir in the pineapple and walnuts. Spread in a greased 11×15-inch baking pan. Bake at 350 degrees for 25 to 30 minutes or until firm. Cool. Cut into bars. Yield: 2 dozen bars.

Carolyn H. Schott, Preceptor Beta Gamma
Scottsdale, Arizona

CHOCOLATE CARAMEL BARS

2 cups all-purpose flour	2 cups (12 ounces) semisweet chocolate chips
2 cups quick-cooking oats	
1 1/2 cups packed brown sugar	1 cup chopped pecans or walnuts
1 teaspoon baking soda	1 (23-ounce) jar caramel topping
1/2 teaspoon salt	
1 1/2 cups (3 sticks) butter or margarine	1/4 cup all-purpose flour

Mix 2 cups flour, the oats, brown sugar, baking soda and salt in a bowl. Cut in the butter until crumbly. Divide in half. Pat 1 portion into a greased 9×13-inch baking pan. Bake at 350 degrees for 15 minutes. Sprinkle with chocolate chips and pecans. Whisk the caramel topping and 1/4 cup flour in a bowl until smooth. Drizzle over the baked layer. Sprinkle with the remaining crumb mixture. Bake for 18 to 20 minutes or until golden brown. Cool on a wire rack for 2 hours. Cut into bars. Yield: 2 dozen bars.

Verla R. Rosequist, Eta Master
Midvale, Utah

CHOCOLATE CHIP CHEESECAKE BARS

3/4 cup shortening
3/4 cup granulated sugar
1/3 cup packed brown
    sugar
1 egg
1 1/2 teaspoons vanilla
    extract
1 1/2 cups all-purpose
    flour
1 teaspoon salt
3/4 teaspoon baking soda

1 1/2 cups (9 ounces)
    miniature
    chocolate chips
3/4 cup chopped pecans
16 ounces cream cheese,
    softened
3/4 cup granulated sugar
2 eggs
1 teaspoon vanilla
    extract

Beat the shortening, 3/4 cup granulated sugar and the brown sugar in a bowl until light and fluffy. Add 1 egg and 1 1/2 teaspoons vanilla and mix well. Add the flour, salt and baking soda and mix well. Stir in the chocolate chips and pecans. Reserve 1/3 of the mixture. Spread the remaining mixture in a greased 9×13-inch baking pan. Bake at 350 degrees for 8 minutes. Beat the cream cheese and 3/4 cup granulated sugar in a bowl until smooth. Add 2 eggs and 1 teaspoon vanilla and mix well. Spread over the baked layer. Drop the reserved mixture by teaspoonfuls over the cream cheese layer. Bake for 35 to 40 minutes or until golden brown. Cool on a wire rack. Cut into bars. Store, covered, in the refrigerator. Yield: 3 dozen bars.

Carol Zeiss, Preceptor Delta Tau
St. Peters, Missouri

TOFFEE CHEESECAKE BARS

1 1/4 cups all-purpose
    flour
1 cup confectioners'
    sugar
1/2 cup baking cocoa
1/4 teaspoon baking soda
3/4 cup (1 1/2 sticks) butter
    or margarine
8 ounces cream cheese,
    softened

1 (14-ounce) can
    sweetened
    condensed milk
2 eggs
1 teaspoon vanilla
    extract
1 1/2 cups (9 ounces)
    English toffee bits

Combine the first 4 ingredients in a large bowl. Cut in the butter until crumbly. Pat into an ungreased 9×13-inch baking pan. Bake at 350 degrees for 15 minutes. Beat the cream cheese in a bowl until fluffy. Add the condensed milk, eggs and vanilla and mix well. Stir in 1 cup of the toffee bits. Spread the mixture over the warm baked layer. Bake for 25 minutes or until set. Cool for 15 minutes. Sprinkle with the remaining toffee bits. Chill, covered, until just before serving. Yield: 3 dozen bars.

Lora Alexander, Omicron Theta
Memphis, Missouri

CHOCOLATE CHERRY BARS

This was the first cake my mother let me make, and then it was the first cake I let my daughters make.

1 (2-layer) package
    fudge cake mix
1 (21-ounce) can cherry
    pie filling
1 teaspoon almond
    extract
2 eggs, beaten

1 cup sugar
5 tablespoons butter
1/3 cup milk
1 cup (6 ounces)
    semisweet chocolate
    chips

Mix the first 4 ingredients in a bowl until smooth. Pour into a greased 9×13-inch baking pan. Bake at 350 degrees for 25 to 30 minutes or until the bars test done. Combine the sugar, butter and milk in a saucepan. Bring to a boil over medium heat, stirring constantly. Boil for 1 minute, stirring constantly. Remove from the heat. Stir in the chocolate chips until smooth. Pour over the baked layer. Cool. Cut into bars. Yield: 2 dozen bars.

Polly Wagner, Xi Chi
Louisville, Kentucky

CHOCOLATE OATMEAL BARS

2 cups quick-cooking
    oats
1/2 cup (1 stick) butter,
    melted
1/4 cup corn syrup

1/2 cup packed brown
    sugar
1 cup (6 ounces)
    chocolate chips

Combine the oats, butter, corn syrup and brown sugar in a bowl and mix well. Pat into a greased 9×9-inch microwave-safe pan. Microwave on High for 2 minutes. Rotate 1/4 turn and microwave on High for 2 minutes longer. Sprinkle with chocolate chips. Microwave on Medium-Low for 6 minutes or until chocolate chips are soft. Spread the chocolate evenly. Chill for 30 minutes or longer. Cut into bars. Yield: 1 dozen bars.

Cathy Aubrey, Laureate Psi
Youngstown, New York

CHOCOLATE RASPBERRY CRUMB BARS

1 cup (2 sticks) butter,
    softened
2 cups all-purpose flour
1/2 cup packed light
    brown sugar
1/4 teaspoon salt
1 cup (6 ounces)
    chocolate chips

1 1/4 cups condensed milk
1/2 cup chopped nuts
    (optional)
1/3 cup seedless
    raspberry jam
1 cup (6 ounces)
    chocolate chips

Beat the butter in a bowl until light and fluffy. Add the flour, brown sugar and salt and mix until crumbly. Pat 1 1/4 cups of the mixture into a 9×13-inch baking pan. Bake at 350 degrees for 10 to 12 minutes or until golden brown. Combine 1 cup chocolate chips and the condensed milk in a saucepan. Cook over low heat until smooth, stirring often. Pour evenly over the baked layer. Combine the remaining crumb mixture and nuts in a bowl and mix well. Sprinkle over the bars. Drop the raspberry jam by teaspoonfuls over the crumb mixture. Sprinkle with 1 cup chocolate chips. Bake 25 to 30 minutes or until firm. Cool. Cut into bars. Yield: 3 dozen bars.

Mary A. Courten, Beta Epsilon Master
North Fort Myers, Florida

CHOCOLATE CHIP BARS

2/3 cup shortening	*2 1/2 teaspoons baking*
2 1/2 cups packed brown	*powder*
sugar	*2 cups (12 ounces)*
4 eggs	*semisweet*
2 1/2 cups flour, sifted	*chocolate chips*

Beat the shortening and brown sugar in a bowl until light and fluffy. Add the eggs and mix well. Combine the flour and baking powder. Add to the shortening mixture gradually, mixing well after each addition. Stir in the chocolate chips. Spread in a greased 9×13-inch baking pan. Bake at 350 degrees for 30 to 35 minutes or until bars test done. Cool. Cut into bars. Yield: 2 dozen bars.

Pamela Howe, Mu Psi
Dearborn, Missouri

CHOCOLATE CHIP RASPBERRY BARS

1 1/2 cups all-purpose	*1/4 cup milk*
flour	*1/4 teaspoon vanilla*
1/2 cup sugar	*extract*
1/2 teaspoon baking	*3/4 cup raspberry*
powder	*preserves*
1/2 teaspoon salt	*1 cup (6 ounces)*
1/2 cup (1 stick) butter or	*semisweet*
margarine, softened	*chocolate chips*
1 egg, beaten	

Combine the flour, sugar, baking powder and salt in a bowl. Cut in the butter until crumbly. Add the egg, milk and vanilla and mix well. Reserve 1/2 cup. Spread the remainder in a greased 9×13-inch baking pan. Spoon the preserves over the top and spread lightly. Sprinkle with the chocolate chips. Drop the reserved batter by 1/2 teaspoonfuls over the chocolate chips. Bake at 400 degrees for 25 minutes. Cool on a wire rack. Cut into bars. Yield: 3 dozen bars.

Ruth Townsend, Laureate Lambda
Lower Sackville, Nova Scotia, Canada

CRISPY CHOCOLATE TREATS

1/2 cup (1 stick) butter	*1 cup confectioners'*
2 cups (12 ounces) milk	*sugar*
chocolate chips	*1 teaspoon vanilla*
1/2 cup light corn syrup	*extract*
	5 cups crisp rice cereal

Melt the butter and chocolate chips in a saucepan over low heat, stirring often. Stir in the corn syrup, confectioners' sugar and vanilla until smooth. Stir in the crisp rice cereal. Pat into a greased 9×13-inch baking pan. Chill, covered, for 1 hour or longer. Cut into bars. Yield: 2 to 3 dozen bars.

Toni Lindsey, Preceptor Gamma Phi
Amarillo, Texas

CHRISTMAS BARS

1 cup all-purpose flour	*1/2 teaspoon baking*
1/2 cup (1 stick) butter or	*powder*
margarine, softened	*1/4 teaspoon salt*
3 tablespoons	*1 teaspoon vanilla*
confectioners' sugar	*extract*
2 eggs, slightly beaten	*2/3 cup chopped nuts*
1 cup granulated sugar	*1/2 cup shredded coconut*
1/4 cup all-purpose	*1/2 cup chopped*
flour	*maraschino cherries*

Combine 1 cup flour, the butter and confectioners' sugar in a bowl and mix until smooth. Spread in an ungreased 8×8-inch baking pan. Bake at 350 degrees for 25 minutes. Combine the eggs, granulated sugar, 1/4 cup flour, baking powder, salt and vanilla in a bowl and mix well. Stir in the nuts, coconut and cherries. Spread over the baked layer. Bake 25 minutes. Cool. Cut into bars. Yield: 1 dozen bars.

Patricia Forbes, Preceptor Beta Sigma
Niagara Falls, New York

NO-BAKE COCONUT BARS

2 wrappers graham	*1/2 cup milk*
crackers	*1 cup shredded coconut*
1 cup packed brown	*1 cup graham cracker*
sugar	*crumbs*
1/2 cup (1 stick) butter,	
softened	

Place a single layer of graham crackers across the bottom of a 9×13-inch baking pan. Combine the next 5 ingredients in a saucepan. Cook over low heat for 10 minutes, stirring often. Spoon over the graham cracker layer. Top with a single layer of graham crackers. Yield: 2 dozen bars.

Karla J. Grant, Preceptor Alpha Upsilon
Hayden, Idaho

COCONUT SQUARES

6 tablespoons butter, softened	2 eggs, slightly beaten
1/4 cup granulated sugar	1 cup packed brown sugar
1/4 teaspoon salt	2 tablespoons all-purpose flour
1 cup all-purpose flour	1/2 teaspoon salt
1 teaspoon vanilla extract	1 cup flaked coconut

Beat the butter and granulated sugar in a bowl until light and fluffy. Add 1/4 teaspoon salt and 1 cup flour and mix well. Spread in a 9×9-inch baking pan. Bake at 350 degrees for 15 minutes. Combine the vanilla and eggs in a mixing bowl and mix well. Combine the brown sugar, 2 tablespoons flour and 1/2 teaspoon salt. Add to the egg mixture gradually, mixing well after each addition. Stir in the coconut. Spread over the baked layer. Bake for 20 minutes or until squares test done. Cool. Cut into squares. Yield: 16 squares.

Carolyn Jewel Hancock, Preceptor Beta Pi
Yorktown, Indiana

COFFEE BARS

1 1/2 cups packed brown sugar	3 cups all-purpose flour
2 eggs	1 teaspoon baking powder
1 teaspoon vanilla extract	1 cup (6 ounces) chocolate chips
1 cup vegetable oil	1/2 cup chopped nuts
1 cup strong coffee	Chocolate Frosting
1 teaspoon baking soda	

Combine the brown sugar, eggs, vanilla, oil and coffee in a bowl and mix well. Add the baking soda, flour and baking powder and mix well. Stir in the chocolate chips and nuts. Spread in a greased 11×15-inch baking pan. Bake at 350 degrees for 20 to 25 minutes or until golden brown. Cool. Frost and cut into bars. Yield: 18 bars.

CHOCOLATE FROSTING

1 1/2 cups granulated sugar	6 tablespoons milk
6 tablespoons margarine, softened	1/2 cup (3 ounces) chocolate chips

Combine the sugar, margarine and milk in a saucepan. Bring to a boil over low heat, stirring often. Boil for 30 seconds, stirring constantly. Add the chocolate chips and stir until smooth.

Susan L. Hodge, Delta Master
Rapid City, South Dakota

COCONUT CHOCOLATE BARS

1/2 cup (1 stick) butter or margarine, melted	1 cup (6 ounces) butterscotch chips
1 1/2 cups graham cracker crumbs	1 1/3 cups flaked coconut
1 cup (6 ounces) semisweet chocolate chips	1/2 cup chopped walnuts
	1 (14-ounce) can sweetened condensed milk

Combine the butter and graham cracker crumbs in a bowl and mix well. Pat into an ungreased 9×13-inch baking pan. Sprinkle with chocolate chips, butterscotch chips, coconut and walnuts. Pour the condensed milk over the top. Bake at 350 degrees for 30 minutes. Cool. Cut into bars. Yield: 3 dozen bars.

Diana R. Hobbs, Alpha Gamma Master
St. Petersburg, Florida

FRUIT COCKTAIL BARS

2 eggs	1/2 teaspoon salt
1 1/2 cups sugar	1/2 teaspoon vanilla extract
1 (16-ounce) can fruit cocktail	1 1/2 cups shredded coconut
2 1/4 cups all-purpose flour	1/2 cup chopped nuts
1 1/2 teaspoons baking soda	Glaze

Beat the eggs and sugar in a bowl until fluffy. Add the fruit cocktail, flour, baking soda, salt and vanilla and mix well. Spread in a 10×15-inch baking pan. Sprinkle with coconut and nuts. Bake at 350 degrees for 20 to 25 minutes or until firm. Drizzle the Glaze over the warm baked layer. Cut into bars. Yield: 2 dozen bars.

GLAZE

3/4 cup sugar	1/2 teaspoon vanilla extract
1/4 cup evaporated milk	1/2 cup chopped walnuts
1/2 cup (1 stick butter)	

Bring the first 4 ingredients to a boil in a saucepan over medium heat, stirring often. Cook for 2 minutes. Remove from heat and stir in the walnuts. Cool.

Judy Studybaker, Omicron Eta
Orland, California

Gloria Snyder, Alpha Delta Phi, Lowry City, Missouri, shared her secret recipe for **Flourless Peanut Butter Cookies.** *She mixes 1 cup peanut butter, 1 cup sugar, 1 egg and 1 teaspoon vanilla in a bowl. She drops the dough by teaspoonfuls onto a cookie sheet and flattens with the bottom of a glass dipped in sugar. The cookies are baked at 350 degrees for 15 to 18 minutes.*

FRUIT CAKE BARS

3/4 cup (1 1/2 sticks) butter
  or margarine,
  softened
3/4 cup packed brown
  sugar
3 eggs
1 tablespoon vanilla
  extract

1 1/2 cups all-purpose
  flour
3 cups chopped walnuts
2 cups date halves
1 1/2 cups chopped
  candied pineapple
1 3/4 cups halved red and
  green maraschino
  cherries

Beat the butter and brown sugar in a bowl until light and fluffy. Add the eggs 1 at a time, mixing well after each addition. Add the vanilla and flour and mix well. Stir in the walnuts and dates. Spread in a greased and floured 10×15-inch baking pan. Sprinkle with candied pineapple and cherries, pressing lightly into the batter. Bake at 325 degrees for 40 to 50 minutes or until light brown. Cool. Cut into bars. Yield: 8 dozen bars.

Dorothy J. Cline, Laureate Alpha Nu
Pharr, Texas

COCONUT FUDGE SQUARES

I have always loved Mounds candy bars. These bars have a very similar taste.

1 cup (2 sticks) butter or
  margarine, softened
1 1/2 cups sugar
3 eggs
1 teaspoon vanilla
  extract
1 cup all-purpose flour

1/4 cup baking cocoa
1/2 cup chopped walnuts
1 (14-ounce) can
  sweetened
  condensed milk
1 cup shredded coconut
Fudge Frosting

Beat the butter and sugar in a bowl until light and fluffy. Add the eggs and vanilla and mix well. Combine the flour and baking cocoa. Add to the butter mixture and mix well. Stir in the walnuts. Spread in a greased 9×13-inch baking pan. Bake at 350 degrees for 30 minutes or until the squares test done. Combine the condensed milk and coconut in a bowl and mix well. Spread evenly over the baked layer. Bake for 20 minutes or until the coconut is light brown. Frost while warm. Chill, covered, for 1 hour or longer. Cut into bars. Yield: 4 dozen bars.

FUDGE FROSTING

2 cups confectioners'
  sugar
1/4 cup baking cocoa
5 tablespoons
  evaporated milk

2 tablespoons butter or
  margarine, melted
1/2 teaspoon vanilla
  extract

Combine the confectioners' sugar, baking cocoa, evaporated milk, butter and vanilla in a bowl and mix until smooth.

Sarah P. Coon, Xi Omicron Lambda
Blythe, California

LEMON BARS

1 egg
1/3 cup butter or
  margarine, softened
1 (2-layer) package
  lemon cake mix
1 cup raisins
2 eggs

1 cup granulated sugar
1/2 teaspoon baking
  powder
1/4 teaspoon salt
1/4 cup lemon juice
Confectioners' sugar
  for sprinkling

Combine 1 egg, the butter, cake mix and raisins in a bowl and mix until crumbly. Reserve 1 cup. Pat the remaining mixture into a greased 9×13-inch baking pan. Bake at 350 degrees for 12 to 15 minutes or until light brown. Combine 2 eggs, the sugar, baking powder, salt and lemon juice in a bowl and mix until light and fluffy. Spread over the warm baked crust. Sprinkle with the reserved crumb mixture. Bake for 15 minutes or until golden brown. Sprinkle with confectioners' sugar. Cool. Cut into bars. Yield: 3 dozen bars.

Juanita Bean, Theta Master
Sparks, Nevada

LEMON CREAM CHEESE BARS

1 1/4 cups all-purpose
  flour
1/2 cup rolled oats
1/2 cup packed brown
  sugar
1/4 teaspoon salt
1/2 cup (1 stick) butter
8 ounces cream cheese,
  softened

1/3 cup granulated sugar
1 egg
2 teaspoons grated
  lemon zest
1 tablespoon lemon
  juice
1/4 cup milk

Combine the flour, oats, brown sugar and salt in a bowl. Cut in the butter until crumbly. Pat half of the mixture into an ungreased 8×8-inch baking pan. Combine the cream cheese, granulated sugar, egg, lemon zest, lemon juice and milk in a mixing bowl and mix until smooth. Spread over the prepared crust. Top with the reserved crumb mixture. Bake at 350 degrees for 30 to 35 minutes or until light brown. Cool. Cut into bars. Store in the refrigerator. Yield: 1 dozen bars.

Pat Scharch, Beta Epsilon
Madison, Wisconsin

LEMON SQUARES

1 cup (2 sticks) butter, softened	1 tablespoon grated lemon zest
1/2 cup confectioners' sugar	6 tablespoons lemon juice
2 1/2 cups all-purpose flour	1 teaspoon baking powder
4 eggs	Additional confectioners' sugar for sprinkling
2 cups granulated sugar	

Beat the butter and confectioners' sugar in a bowl until light and fluffy. Add 2 cups of the flour and mix well. Spread in a greased 9×13-inch baking pan. Bake at 350 degrees for 20 minutes. Beat the eggs in a bowl. Gradually add the granulated sugar, mixing well after each addition. Add the lemon zest, lemon juice, the remaining 1/2 cup flour and the baking powder and mix well. Spread over the baked layer. Bake for 20 minutes. Sprinkle with confectioners' sugar. Cool. Cut into squares. Yield: 2 dozen squares.

Linda M. McBride, Preceptor Mu Sigma
Borrego Springs, California

LEMON-CRANBERRY COCONUT SQUARES

If using frozen cranberries, do not thaw before baking.

1 1/2 cups all-purpose flour	1/4 teaspoon salt
1/2 cup confectioners' sugar	6 eggs
2/3 cup unsalted butter, cut into pieces	2 1/2 cups granulated sugar
3/4 cup all-purpose flour	1 cup lemon juice
1 teaspoon baking powder	1 1/2 cups sweetened shredded coconut
	2 cups fresh or frozen cranberries

Combine 1 1/2 cups flour and the confectioners' sugar in a bowl. Cut in the butter until crumbly. Pat into a greased 9×13-inch baking dish. Bake at 350 degrees for 15 to 20 minutes or until edges are golden brown. Combine 3/4 cup flour, the baking powder and the salt. Beat the eggs in a large bowl. Add the granulated sugar gradually, mixing well after each addition. Add the lemon juice and flour mixture and mix well. Stir in the coconut and cranberries. Spread over the baked layer. Bake for 35 to 40 minutes or until firm. Cool. Cut into squares. Will keep in the refrigerator for up to 3 days or in the freezer for up to 1 month. Yield: 2 dozen squares.

Ruth Stevens, Laureate Alpha Iota
Parksville, British Columbia, Canada

NO-BAKE ORANGE BALLS

1/2 cup (1 stick) margarine	1 tablespoon orange extract
1 (6-ounce) container frozen orange juice concentrate	3 cups crushed vanilla wafers
1 (1-pound) package confectioners' sugar	3/4 cup chopped pecans
	1 (1-pound) package flaked coconut

Combine the margarine and orange juice concentrate in a saucepan. Cook over medium heat until smooth, stirring often. Remove to a mixing bowl. Add the confectioners' sugar and orange extract and mix well. Stir in the vanilla wafers and pecans. Cool for 5 minutes. Shape by teaspoonfuls into balls. Roll in coconut. Let stand for 1 hour. Yield: 3 to 4 dozen cookies.

Nona G. Taylor, Xi Sigma
Houston, Texas

CRISPY PEANUT BARS

1/2 cup (1 stick) butter, softened	3 cups miniature marshmallows
2/3 cup packed brown sugar	2/3 cup light corn syrup
2 egg yolks (or 1 egg)	1/4 cup (1/2 stick) butter
1 1/2 cups all-purpose flour	2 teaspoons vanilla extract
1/2 teaspoon baking powder	2 cups (12 ounces) peanut butter chips
1/2 teaspoon salt	2 cups crisp rice cereal
1/2 teaspoon baking soda	2 cups salted peanuts

Beat 1/2 cup butter and the brown sugar in a bowl until light and fluffy. Add the egg yolks and mix well. Add the next 4 ingredients and mix well. Spread in a 9×13-inch baking pan. Bake at 350 degrees for 2 minutes. Sprinkle with marshmallows. Bake for 2 minutes. Combine the corn syrup, 1/4 cup butter, vanilla and peanut butter chips in a microwave-safe bowl. Microwave on High for 1 minute. Stir until smooth. Stir in the crisp rice cereal and peanuts. Spread over the baked layer. Press lightly. Chill, covered, until just before serving. Cut into bars. Yield: 3 dozen bars.

Donna McMichael, Preceptor
Douglas, Wyoming

---

*Jane Lindstrom, Xi Epsilon, Sheridan, Wyoming, prepares easy **Angel Lemon Bars**. She mixes 1 box angel food cake mix and one 21-ounce can lemon pie filling in a bowl. The mixture is spread in a 10×15-inch baking pan and baked at 350 degrees for 25 minutes. She cools the baked layer, frosts it with a container of cream cheese frosting, and cuts it into bars.*

CRISPY PEANUT BUTTER AND CHOCOLATE SQUARES

1/2 cup (1 stick) margarine
1 cup sugar
1 cup light corn syrup
1 cup peanut butter

8 to 10 cups crisp rice cereal
2 cups (12 ounces) milk chocolate chips

Melt the margarine in a large saucepan over medium heat. Add the sugar and corn syrup and cook until the sugar dissolves, stirring constantly. Stir in the peanut butter. Remove from heat. Stir in the crisp rice cereal. Pat into a greased 9×13-inch baking pan. Sprinkle with chocolate chips. Bake at 300 degrees for 2 minutes. Spread the melted chocolate chips evenly. Cool for 2 hours or longer. Cut into squares. Yield: 2 dozen squares.

Mary Kay Henry, Laureate Gamma Alpha
Randolph, Kansas

O'HENRY BARS

4 cups rolled oats
1 cup packed brown sugar
1 cup (2 sticks) margarine, softened

1/2 cup light corn syrup
1 cup (6 ounces) chocolate chips
3/4 cup chunky peanut butter

Combine the oats, brown sugar, margarine and corn syrup in a bowl and mix well. Pat into a 9×13-inch baking pan. Bake at 350 degrees for 10 to 15 minutes or until light brown. Cool. Melt the chocolate chips and peanut butter in a saucepan over low heat, stirring often. Spread over the baked layer. Chill, covered, until just before serving. Cut into bars. Yield: 2 dozen bars.

Michelle Dinger, Beta Chi
Independence, Iowa

OATMEAL FUDGE BARS

3/4 cup (1 1/2 sticks) margarine, softened
2 cups packed brown sugar
2 eggs
2 teaspoons vanilla extract
2 1/2 cups baking mix
3 cups rolled oats

2 cups (12 ounces) chocolate chips
1 cup sweetened condensed milk
2 tablespoons margarine
1/2 teaspoon salt
2 teaspoons vanilla extract
1 cup chopped nuts

Beat 3/4 cup margarine and the brown sugar in a bowl until light and fluffy. Add the eggs and 2 teaspoons vanilla and mix well. Add the baking mix and mix well. Stir in the oats. Reserve 1/3 of the mixture. Pat the remaining mixture into a 10×15-inch baking pan.

Combine the chocolate chips, condensed milk, 2 tablespoons margarine and salt in a saucepan. Cook over low heat until smooth, stirring often. Stir in 2 teaspoons vanilla. Spread over the unbaked layer. Sprinkle with nuts. Drop the reserved mixture by teaspoonfuls over the chocolate. Cool. Cut into bars. Yield: 2 dozen bars.

Karen Dailey, Preceptor Beta Upsilon
Franklin, Pennsylvania

ORANGE CARAMEL SQUARES

1 1/2 cups packed brown sugar
2 eggs
1 1/3 cups sifted all-purpose flour
2/3 cup orange slices

2/3 cup chopped pecans
Grated zest of 1 orange
2/3 cup sifted confectioners' sugar
2 tablespoons cream

Beat the brown sugar and eggs at high speed in a bowl for 3 minutes. Add the flour and mix well. Fold in the orange slices and pecans. Spread in a greased 10×15-inch baking pan. Bake at 350 degrees for 30 to 35 minutes or until golden brown and firm. Combine the orange zest, confectioners' sugar and cream in a bowl and mix until smooth. Spread over the warm layer. Cool. Cut into squares. Yield: 50 squares.

Eunice Whitman, Laureate Epsilon Sigma
Niceville, Florida

PEANUT BUTTER SQUARES

For chewier squares, use chunky peanut butter.

3/4 cup (1 1/2 sticks) margarine, softened
1 cup packed brown sugar
1/3 cup peanut butter
2 cups all-purpose flour

1 teaspoon vanilla extract
1 egg
1/2 cup peanut butter
1 cup (6 ounces) chocolate chips

Beat the margarine and brown sugar in a bowl until light and fluffy. Add 1/3 cup peanut butter, the vanilla and egg and mix well. Add the flour and mix well. Spread in a greased 9×13-inch baking pan. Bake at 350 degrees for 15 to 20 minutes or until firm. Combine 1/2 cup peanut butter and the chocolate chips in a saucepan. Cook over low heat until smooth, stirring constantly. Spread over the warm baked layer. Cool. Cut into squares. Yield: 1 to 2 dozen squares.

Christine Parks, Zeta
Gloucester, Ontario, Canada

CRUNCHY PEANUT BUTTER SQUARES

1/2 cup packed brown sugar	1 teaspoon vanilla extract
1/2 cup light corn syrup	2 cups cornflakes
1 cup chunky peanut butter	1 cup crisp rice cereal Frosting

Combine the brown sugar, corn syrup and peanut butter in a saucepan and mix well. Cook over low heat until smooth, stirring often. Remove from the heat. Stir in the vanilla. Combine the peanut butter mixture, cornflakes and cereal in a large bowl and mix well. Pat into a greased 8×8-inch baking pan. Chill for 10 minutes. Spread with the Frosting. Chill until just before serving. Cut into squares.
Yield: 1 dozen squares.

FROSTING

1/2 cup packed brown sugar	1 tablespoon butter
3 tablespoons milk	1 cup confectioners' sugar

Combine the brown sugar, milk and butter in a saucepan. Bring to a boil over medium heat, stirring often. Cool completely. Stir in the confectioners' sugar until smooth.

Marna Hobson, Delta Eta
Elliot Lake, Ontario, Canada

PECAN SQUARES

2 cups all-purpose flour	1/2 cup granulated sugar
1/4 cup granulated sugar	2 tablespoons all-purpose flour
1/4 teaspoon salt	1/2 teaspoon salt
1 cup (2 sticks) butter or margarine	2 eggs, beaten
2 tablespoons white vinegar	3/4 cup evaporated milk
11/2 cups packed dark brown sugar	1/2 teaspoon vanilla extract
	21/2 cups chopped pecans

Combine 2 cups flour, 1/4 cup granulated sugar and 1/4 teaspoon salt in a large bowl. Cut in the butter until crumbly. Add the vinegar and mix well. Pat into a 10×15-inch baking pan. Combine the dark brown sugar, 1/2 cup granulated sugar, 2 tablespoons flour, 1/2 teaspoon salt, eggs, evaporated milk and vanilla in a bowl and mix well. Stir in the pecans. Spread over the unbaked layer. Bake at 350 degrees on the middle rack for 30 to 35 minutes or until caramel colored. Cool. Cut into squares. Yield: 2 dozen squares.

Carol Ward, Iota Beta
Medicine Lodge, Kansas

TOFFEE PECAN SQUARES

1 (2-layer) package yellow cake mix	1 (14-ounce) can sweetened condensed milk
1 egg	1 egg
1/2 cup (1 stick) margarine, softened	1 cup chopped pecans
1 teaspoon vanilla extract	1/2 cup (3 ounces) English toffee bits

Combine the cake mix, 1 egg and the margarine in a bowl and mix well. Pat into a greased 9×13-inch baking pan. Combine the vanilla, condensed milk and egg in a medium bowl and mix well. Stir in the pecans and toffee bits. Spread over the unbaked layer. Bake at 350 degrees for 25 to 30 minutes or until firm. Cool. Cut into squares. Yield: 1 dozen squares.

Betty A. Hayes, Xi Nu Tau
Laurie, Missouri

PINEAPPLE SQUARES

6 tablespoons butter, softened	1 teaspoon baking powder
1/2 cup granulated sugar	1 (20-ounce) can crushed pineapple, drained
3 egg yolks	3 egg whites
1 teaspoon vanilla extract	1 cup packed brown sugar
11/2 cups all-purpose flour	2 cups shredded coconut

Beat the butter and granulated sugar in a bowl until light and fluffy. Add the egg yolks and vanilla and mix well. Add the flour and baking powder and mix well. Spread in an 8×8-inch baking pan. Top with the pineapple. Beat the egg whites in a bowl until soft peaks form. Add the brown sugar gradually, beating until stiff peaks form. Fold in the coconut. Spread over the pineapple. Bake at 375 degrees for 25 minutes. Cool. Cut into squares. Yield: 1 dozen squares.

Cynthia Strayer, Preceptor Iota Theta
Titusville, Florida

CHEWY PUMPKIN BARS

1 (2-layer) package carrot cake mix	1 cup canned pumpkin
1 egg	1/2 cup sugar
1/2 cup (1 stick) butter, melted	2 eggs
	1/2 cup chopped pecans

Combine 1/3 of the cake mix, 1 egg and the butter in a bowl and mix well. Spread in a greased 9×13-inch baking pan. Bake at 350 degrees for 15 minutes. Combine the remaining cake mix, pumpkin, sugar and 2 eggs in a large bowl and mix well. Spread over the warm baked layer. Sprinkle with the pecans. Bake for 15 to 20 minutes or until firm. Cool. Cut into bars. Store in the refrigerator. Yield: 2 dozen bars.

Brenda J. Tebeau, Laureate Gamma Epsilon
Wentzville, Missouri

FROSTED PUMPKIN BARS

4 eggs	1 teaspoon salt
2 cups sugar	2 teaspoons baking soda
1 cup vegetable oil	2 teaspoons cinnamon
2 cups canned pumpkin	Cream Cheese Frosting
2 cups all-purpose flour	

Combine the eggs, sugar and oil in a large bowl and mix well. Add the pumpkin and mix well. Sift the flour, salt, baking soda and cinnamon into the bowl. Pour into a greased and floured 10×15-inch baking pan. Bake at 350 degrees for 20 to 25 minutes or until firm. Cool. Frost with the Cream Cheese Frosting. Cut into bars. Yield: 2 dozen bars.

CREAM CHEESE FROSTING

1/4 cup (1/2 stick) margarine, softened	1 1/2 cups confectioners' sugar
3 ounces cream cheese, softened	1 teaspoon vanilla extract

Beat the margarine, cream cheese and confectioners' sugar in a bowl until light and fluffy. Add the vanilla and mix well.

Michele Hackney, Xi Alpha Omega
Round Rock, Texas

RASPBERRY BARS

1 cup (2 sticks) butter, melted	16 ounces cream cheese, softened
2 cups all-purpose flour	2 cups confectioners' sugar
2 tablespoons granulated sugar	2 teaspoons vanilla extract
1 (6-ounce) package raspberry gelatin	1/2 teaspoon salt (optional)
2 1/2 cups boiling water	2 cups whipped topping
1/2 cup granulated sugar	
2 (10-ounce) packages frozen raspberries, thawed and drained	

Combine the butter, flour and 2 tablespoons granulated sugar in a bowl and mix well. Pat into a 9×13-inch baking pan. Bake at 300 degrees for 15 minutes. Cool. Combine the gelatin, water and 1/2 cup granulated sugar and stir until dissolved. Stir in the raspberries. Chill, covered, until nearly firm. Beat the cream cheese and confectioners' sugar in a mixing bowl until light and fluffy. Add the vanilla and salt and mix well. Fold in the whipped topping.

Spread over the cooled crust. Spoon the raspberry mixture over the top. Chill for 2 hours or longer. Cut into bars. Yield: 1 dozen bars.

Audrey J. Higgens
Bangor, Maine

ROCKY ROAD BLONDIES

2 1/2 cups all-purpose flour	4 teaspoons vanilla extract
1/2 teaspoon salt	3 cups miniature marshmallows
1 cup (2 sticks) unsalted butter, softened	6 ounces semisweet chocolate, chopped
2 cups packed brown sugar	1/2 cup chopped pecans
4 eggs	1 small jar caramel or chocolate topping

Combine the flour and salt. Beat the butter and brown sugar in a mixing bowl until light and fluffy. Add the eggs 1 at a time, mixing well after each addition. Add the vanilla and mix well. Add the flour mixture gradually, mixing well after each addition. Stir in 1 cup of the marshmallows and the chocolate. Pour into 2 greased 8×8-inch baking pans. Sprinkle with the pecans. Bake at 350 degrees for 15 minutes. Sprinkle with the remaining 2 cups marshmallows. Bake 25 to 30 minutes until the marshmallows start to melt and blondies test done. Cool. Cut into squares. Drizzle with caramel sauce just before serving. Yield: 3 dozen squares.

Barbara Glazer, Xi Gamma Iota
Waterloo, Ontario, Canada

S'MORES BARS

1/2 cup (1 stick) unsalted butter, melted	2 cups miniature marshmallows
2 cups graham cracker crumbs	2/3 cup (4 ounces) semisweet chocolate chips
1 1/2 cups (9 ounces) milk chocolate chips	
1 (14-ounce) can sweetened condensed milk	

Mix the butter and graham cracker crumbs in a bowl. Pat into a 9×9-inch baking pan. Sprinkle with milk chocolate chips. Top with the condensed milk. Bake at 350 degrees for 30 minutes or until golden brown and bubbly. Cool slightly on a wire rack. Sprinkle with the marshmallows. Broil for 15 to 20 seconds or until the marshmallows are light brown. Sprinkle with the semisweet chocolate chips. Cool for 15 minutes or longer. Cut into bars. Yield: 16 bars.

Debbie Sethaler, Alpha Zeta Theta
O'Fallon, Missouri

SCANDINAVIAN KRINGLER

1 cup all-purpose flour
1/2 cup (1 stick) butter
2 tablespoons ice water
1 cup water
1/2 cup (1 stick) butter, softened
1 cup all-purpose flour
3 eggs
1/2 teaspoon almond extract
1 cup confectioners' sugar
1 tablespoon butter, softened
2 to 3 tablespoons milk
1/2 teaspoon almond extract
Sliced almonds for sprinkling

Place 1 cup flour in a medium bowl. Cut in 1/2 cup butter until crumbly. Sprinkle with 2 tablespoons water. Mash with a fork until a soft dough forms. Pat into an ungreased 9×13-inch baking pan. Combine 1 cup water and 1/2 cup butter in a saucepan. Bring to a boil over medium heat, stirring often. Remove from the heat and stir in 1 cup flour. Add the eggs 1 at a time, mixing well after each addition. Stir in 1/2 teaspoon almond extract. Spread over the unbaked crust, leaving 3/4-inch edge. Bake at 350 degrees for 50 to 60 minutes or until brown and puffy. Cool. Combine the confectioners' sugar, 1 tablespoon butter and the milk in a bowl and mix until light and fluffy. Stir in the almond extract. Spread over the baked layer. Sprinkle with almonds. Cut into squares. Yield: 1 dozen squares.

Joan Brode, Xi Rho
North Vancouver, British Columbia, Canada

CHOCOLATE SWEET MARIE BARS

1/2 cup peanut butter
1/2 cup packed brown sugar
1/2 cup corn syrup
1 tablespoon butter
1/2 teaspoon vanilla extract
3 cups crisp rice cereal
3/4 cup Spanish peanuts
3/4 cup (4 1/2 ounces) chocolate chips, melted
3/4 cup (4 1/2 ounces) butterscotch chips, melted

Combine the peanut butter, brown sugar, corn syrup and butter in a saucepan. Cook over low heat until smooth, stirring often. Remove from the heat. Stir in the vanilla, crisp rice cereal and peanuts. Pat into an ungreased 9×9-inch baking pan. Combine the chocolate chips and butterscotch chips in a bowl and mix well. Spread over the peanut butter mixture. Chill. Cut into bars. Yield: 1 dozen bars.

Jeannette Sears, Laureate Alpha Pi
Barrie, Ontario, Canada

SWEET MARIE BARS

1/2 cup packed brown sugar
1/2 cup peanut butter
1/2 cup corn syrup
1 tablespoon butter
1/2 teaspoon vanilla extract
2 cups crisp rice cereal
1/2 cup salted peanuts

Combine the brown sugar, peanut butter and corn syrup in a saucepan. Cook over low heat until smooth, stirring often. Remove from the heat. Stir in the butter, vanilla, crisp rice cereal and peanuts. Pat into a greased 8×8-inch pan. Cool. Cut into bars. Yield: 2 dozen bars.

Wendy Horton, Xi Epsilon Theta
Port Perry, Ontario, Canada

TOFFEE BARS

My daughter has entered these bars into her 4-H project for the past three years and has won a blue ribbon each time!

1 cup (2 sticks) butter, softened
1 cup packed light brown sugar
1 egg yolk
1 teaspoon vanilla extract
1 cup all-purpose flour
1/4 teaspoon salt
9 ounces milk chocolate, melted
Chopped pecans for sprinkling

Beat the butter and brown sugar in a bowl until light and fluffy. Add the egg yolk and vanilla and mix well. Add the flour and salt and mix well. Pat into a greased 9×13-inch baking pan. Bake at 350 degrees for 20 minutes. Spread the melted chocolate over the baked layer. Sprinkle with pecans. Chill until firm. Cut into bars. Yield: 4 to 5 dozen bars.

Donetta Birzer, Beta Pi
Lyons, Kansas

WALNUT COOKIE SQUARES

2 eggs
2 teaspoons vanilla extract
2 cups packed brown sugar
1 cup all-purpose flour
1/2 teaspoon baking soda
1/2 teaspoon salt
1 cup chopped walnuts

Combine the eggs, vanilla and brown sugar in a bowl and stir until combined. Combine the flour, baking soda and salt. Add to the egg mixture gradually, stirring well after each addition. Stir in the walnuts. Spread in a greased 9×13-inch baking pan. Bake at 350 degrees for 25 minutes. Cut into squares while warm. Yield: 2 dozen squares.

Florine Blair, Omicron Eta
Orland, California

Sweet Tooth
CANDY AND CONFECTIONS

BOURBON BALLS

3 cups crushed vanilla
  wafers
1¹/₂ tablespoons baking
  cocoa

3 tablespoons corn syrup
¹/₂ cup bourbon
1 cup chopped pecans
Confectioners' sugar

Combine the vanilla wafers, baking cocoa, corn syrup, bourbon and pecans in a bowl and mix well. Shape by teaspoonfuls into balls. Roll in confectioners' sugar. Yield: 48 servings.

Cindy Montalbano-Johns, Laureate Iota
Raleigh, North Carolina

BUCKEYES

¹/₂ cup (1 stick)
  margarine, softened
1¹/₂ cups peanut butter
1 (1-pound) package
  confectioners' sugar

1 teaspoon vanilla
  extract
2 cups (12 ounces)
  chocolate chips
2 ounces paraffin wax

Combine the margarine, peanut butter, confectioners' sugar and vanilla in a bowl and mix well. Shape into walnut-size balls. Melt the chocolate chips and paraffin in a double boiler, stirring occasionally. Dip the peanut butter balls in the chocolate mixture, leaving a small circle of peanut butter exposed at the top. Place the balls on waxed paper. Let stand until firm. Store in an airtight container in the refrigerator. Yield: 3 to 4 dozen buckeyes.

Beverly Robichaud, Delta Master
Las Vegas, Nevada

BUTTERSCOTCH CLUSTERS

24 ounces (4 cups)
  butterscotch chips,
  melted

¹/₂ cup peanut butter
5 cups cornflakes

Combine the butterscotch chips and peanut butter in a large bowl and mix well. Fold in the cornflakes. Drop by spoonfuls onto waxed paper. Let stand until firm. Yield: 48 servings.

Sharon Grammer, Xi Gamma Alpha
Waterford, Michigan

CAKE BALLS

1 (2-layer) package
  chocolate cake mix
¹/₂ cup baking cocoa
¹/₂ cup confectioners'
  sugar
¹/₂ cup preserves
  (any flavor)

¹/₂ cup (1 stick) butter
1 teaspoon vanilla
  extract
1 (12-ounce) package
  chocolate almond
  bark

Prepare and bake the cake mix using the package directions. Crumble the cooled cake into a large bowl. Combine the next 5 ingredients in a saucepan. Cook over medium heat until smooth, stirring frequently. Pour over the crumbled cake and mix well. Shape into balls. Melt the chocolate bark in a double boiler. Dip the cake balls in the melted chocolate and place on waxed paper. Let stand until firm. Yield: 18 servings.

Jane Moyer, Xi Zeta Rho
Lamar, Missouri

CAPTAIN CRUNCH CANDY

2 pounds almond bark, melted
3 tablespoons peanut butter
1 (15-ounce) box Cap'n Crunch Cereal
1 (16-ounce) jar dry-roasted peanuts

Combine the almond bark and peanut butter in a bowl and stir until smooth. Add the cereal and peanuts and mix well. Spread the mixture over 2 foil-lined baking sheets. Let stand until firm. Break into pieces. Yield: 24 servings.

Connie Berry, Beta
Terre Haute, Indiana

NUTTY CARAMELS

1 cup heavy cream
2 cups sugar
1³/4 cups light corn syrup
1 cup (2 sticks) butter
1/8 teaspoon salt
1 cup heavy cream
1 cup chopped nuts

Combine 1 cup cream, the sugar, corn syrup, butter and salt in a saucepan. Cook over medium heat for 30 minutes, stirring occasionally. Stir in 1 cup heavy cream and the nuts. Cook to 240 to 248 degrees on a candy thermometer, firm-ball stage, stirring constantly. Pour into a greased 9×13-inch baking pan. Let stand until firm. Cut into squares and wrap each piece in waxed paper. Yield: 2 pounds.

Karen Andler, Preceptor Gamma Iota
Colorado Springs, Colorado

HONEYCOMB CARAMELS

1/3 teaspoon cream of tartar
1 teaspoon hot water
4 cups packed brown sugar
2 cups heavy cream
6 tablespoons butter
16 ounces comb honey
4 ounces unsweetened chocolate
2 teaspoons vanilla extract
2 cups chopped nuts (optional)

Dissolve the cream of tartar in the hot water in a small bowl. Combine the brown sugar and cream in a saucepan. Bring to a boil over medium heat, stirring frequently. Stir in the cream of tartar mixture, butter, honey and chocolate. Cook to 240 to 248 degrees on a candy thermometer, firm-ball stage, stirring occasionally. Remove from the heat and stir in the vanilla and nuts. Pour into a buttered baking pan. Let stand until firm. Cut into squares. Yield: 3 pounds.

Barbara Miller, Preceptor Gamma Iota
Colorado Springs, Colorado

MICROWAVE CARAMELS

1 cup (2 sticks) butter
2¼ cups packed brown sugar
1 (14-ounce) can sweetened condensed milk
1 cup light corn syrup
1 teaspoon vanilla extract
1/2 cup chopped nuts (optional)

Combine the butter, brown sugar, condensed milk and corn syrup in a large microwave-safe bowl. Microwave on High for 5 minute; stir. Microwave on High for 5 minutes. Beat well with a wooden spoon. Microwave on High for 7 minutes. Beat well with a wooden spoon. Stir in the vanilla and nuts. Pour into a buttered 7×11-inch baking dish. Let stand until firm. Cut into squares and wrap each piece in waxed paper. Yield: 2 pounds.

Kathryn Erickson, Preceptor Alpha Sigma
Russell, Iowa

CARAMEL TURTLES

1 cup small pecan halves
36 caramel candies
1/2 cup melted milk chocolate chips

Arrange the pecan halves, flat side down, in clusters of 2 on a greased baking sheet. Top each cluster with a caramel. Bake at 325 degrees for 4 to 5 minutes or until the caramels soften. Press each caramel with a buttered spatula to flatten. Remove the clusters to waxed paper. Drizzle with chocolate. Let stand until firm. Yield: 3 dozen turtles.

Virginia Lee Gilliam, Laureate Beta Beta
Cave Junction, Oregon

TRIPLE CHOCOLATE FANTASY

1 pound white almond bark, chopped
1 pound chocolate almond bark, chopped
2 cups (12 ounces) semisweet chocolate chips
4 ounces German's sweet chocolate, chopped
3 cups lightly toasted chopped pecans

Place the white almond bark, chocolate almond bark, chocolate chips and sweet chocolate in a slow cooker. Cook, covered, on High for 1 hour; do not stir. Cook, covered, on Low for 1 hour, stirring every 15 minutes. Stir in the pecans. Drop by spoonfuls onto waxed paper. Let stand until firm. Store in an airtight container. Yield: 4 to 5 dozen chocolates.

Beth Koester, Preceptor Delta
Centralia, Illinois

CHOCOLATE AND NUT TOFFEE CRACKERS

This recipe is very easy and tastes just like toffee. Try using white chocolate or butterscotch chips instead of chocolate chips.

Saltine crackers	2 cups (12 ounces)
1 cup (2 sticks) butter	chocolate chips
3/4 cup packed brown sugar	1 cup chopped nuts

Fit the crackers in a single layer in a nonstick 10×15-inch baking pan. Combine the butter and brown sugar in a saucepan. Bring to a boil over medium heat, stirring frequently. Boil for 3 minutes, stirring constantly. Pour evenly over the crackers. Sprinkle with the chocolate chips. Bake at 400 degrees for 4 minutes. Spread the melted chocolate evenly with a knife or spatula. Sprinkle with the nuts. Cool slightly and cut into squares. Yield: 5 dozen crackers.

Annie Cavalli, Xi Master
Pueblo, Colorado

CHOCOLATE LOGS

2 cups (12 ounces) chocolate chips	1/4 teaspoon salt
2/3 cup evaporated milk	4 1/2 cups confectioners' sugar
1 tablespoon vanilla extract	1 cup chopped walnuts (optional)

Cook the chocolate chips with the evaporated milk in a saucepan over medium heat until smooth, stirring often. Remove from the heat and stir in the remaining ingredients. Spoon onto waxed paper and cover with a sheet of waxed paper. Chill for 1 hour. Shape into 2 logs and wrap in waxed paper. Chill until firm. Slice just before serving. Yield: 2 dozen slices.

Sandy Guthrie, Alpha Alpha Master
Wheeling, West Virginia

CHOCOLATE PEANUT BUTTER CANDY

2 (12-ounce) packages chocolate creme drops	1 (18-ounce) jar chunky peanut butter
1/2 cup (1 stick) butter or margarine	

Melt the chocolate creme drops and butter in a microwave-safe on High bowl in the microwave, stirring occasionally. Add the peanut butter and mix well. Pour into a buttered 9×13-inch baking pan. Let stand until firm. Cut into squares.
Yield: 4 dozen squares.

Jo Ann Hunter, Preceptor Epsilon
Nashville, Tennessee

CHOCOLATE PEANUT BUTTER BALLS

1 (13 1/2-ounce) package graham cracker crumbs	2 cups (12 ounces) chocolate chips
1 (1-pound) package confectioners' sugar	2 cups (12 ounces) butterscotch chips
1 1/2 cups peanut butter	2 ounces paraffin wax

Combine the graham cracker crumbs, confectioners' sugar and peanut butter in a bowl and mix well. Shape into balls. Melt the chocolate chips, butterscotch chips and paraffin in a double boiler, stirring occasionally. Dip the peanut butter balls in the melted chocolate and place on waxed paper. Let stand until firm. Yield: 5 to 6 dozen balls.

Dena Hammye, Preceptor Gamma Delta
Lakeland, Florida

SLOW-COOKER CHOCOLATE PEANUT CLUSTERS

1 (16-ounce) jar each salted peanuts and dry-roasted peanuts	4 ounces German's sweet chocolate, chopped
2 pounds white chocolate, chopped	2 cups (12 ounces) chocolate chips

Place the salted peanuts and dry-roasted peanuts in a slow cooker. Top with the white chocolate, sweet chocolate and chocolate chips. Cook, covered, on Low for 2 hours; do not stir. Cool slightly and mix well. Drop by spoonfuls onto waxed paper. Let stand until firm. Yield: 8 dozen clusters.

Mary Rudolph, Xi Epsilon Psi
Paducah, Kentucky

COCONUT BONBONS

1 (14-ounce) package flaked coconut	2 cups (12 ounces) chocolate chips
1 (14-ounce) can sweetened condensed milk	1 1/3 ounces paraffin wax

Combine the coconut and condensed milk in a bowl and mix well. Shape into 1-inch balls. Arrange on a greased and floured baking sheet. Bake at 250 degrees for 25 minutes or until golden brown. Melt the chocolate chips and paraffin in a double boiler, stirring occasionally. Dip the hot coconut balls in the melted chocolate and place on waxed paper. Let stand until firm. Yield: 3 to 4 dozen bonbons.

Barbara J. Craig, Preceptor Epsilon
Gary, Indiana

COCONUT CHOCOLATE DROPS

1 cup (6 ounces) semisweet chocolate chips	1 cup (6 ounces) milk chocolate chips
	8 ounces shredded coconut, toasted

Combine the semisweet chocolate chips and milk chocolate chips in a saucepan. Cook over low heat until smooth, stirring often. Remove from the heat and stir in the coconut. Drop by spoonfuls onto waxed paper. Let stand until firm. Yield: 20 servings.

Debby Chesterman, Beta Gamma
Nebraska City, Nebraska

DATE BALLS

1 (1-pound) package confectioners' sugar	1 (8-ounce) package dates, cut into halves
1 cup granulated sugar	1 egg
1/2 cup (1 stick) butter	2 cups crisp rice cereal
1/2 cup chopped pecans	

Place the confectioners' sugar in a bowl. Combine the granulated sugar, butter, pecans, dates and egg in a heavy saucepan. Cook over medium heat for 12 minutes, stirring constantly. Remove from the heat. Stir in the crisp rice cereal. Drop by spoonfuls into the confectioners' sugar. Shape into balls and place on waxed paper. Let stand until firm. Yield: 48 servings.

Lillian Taylor, Xi Beta Sigma
Natchitoches, Lousiana

DATE ROLL CANDY

3 cups sugar	1/2 teaspoon salt
2 tablespoons butter	11/2 cups chopped dates
1 cup milk	1 cup chopped nuts

Combine the sugar, butter, milk and salt in a saucepan. Cook over medium heat until the sugar dissolves, stirring constantly. Stir in the dates and nuts. Cook to 234 to 240 degrees on a candy thermometer, soft-ball stage, stirring constantly. Remove from the heat and cool to room temperature. Beat until very thick. Spoon onto a wet dish towel and shape into a log. Roll up in the towel and chill until firm. Slice just before serving. Yield: 12 servings.

Jeannine Bewley, Nu Master
Amarillo, Texas

CLASSIC DIVINITY

21/2 cups sugar	1 teaspoon vanilla extract
1/2 cup light corn syrup	
1/2 cup water	1 cup chopped nuts (optional)
2 egg whites	

Mix the sugar, corn syrup and water in a saucepan. Bring to a boil, stirring constantly. Cook to 234 to 240 degrees on a candy thermometer, soft-ball stage. Beat the egg whites in a bowl until stiff peaks form. Add the hot syrup gradually, beating constantly. Stir in the vanilla. Beat by hand for 15 minutes. Stir in the nuts. Drop by teaspoonfuls quickly onto waxed paper. Let stand until firm. Yield: 30 pieces.

Ann Levingston, Theta Chi
Steinhatchee, Florida

MAGIC DIVINITY

3 cups sugar	1 envelope unflavored gelatin
3/4 cup light corn syrup	
3/4 cup hot water	1 teaspoon vanilla extract
Dash of salt	
2 egg whites, at room temperature	1 cup chopped nuts

Combine the sugar, corn syrup, water and salt in a saucepan and mix well. Bring to a boil, stirring constantly. Cook to 252 degrees on a candy thermometer, hard-ball stage. Beat the egg whites in a bowl until stiff peaks form. Beat in the gelatin gradually. Add the hot syrup gradually, beating constantly. Beat at high speed until thick and no longer glossy. Stir in the vanilla and nuts. Pour into a buttered dish. Let stand until firm. Cut into squares. Yield: 30 squares.

Anita Thetford, Laureate Theta Theta
Hurst, Texas

NEVER-FAIL DIVINITY

With this recipe, I can now serve a pretty plate of delicious divinity during the holidays and nobody knows (or didn't) that it wasn't made with egg whites. It's creamy and never sugary.

3 cups sugar	1 teaspoon vanilla extract
2/3 cup water	
1/4 teaspoon salt	3 cups pecans, coarsely chopped
2 (7-ounce) jars marshmallow creme	

Mix the sugar, water and salt in a saucepan. Bring to a boil, stirring constantly. Cook to 238 degrees on a candy thermometer, soft-ball stage. Remove from the heat and stir in the remaining ingredients. Beat until thick and no longer glossy. Pour into a lightly buttered 9×13-inch baking pan. Let stand until firm. Cut into squares. Yield: 9 to 10 dozen squares.

Myrt Mortimore, Laureate Delta Psi
San Angelo, Texas

BUTTER PECAN FUDGE

1/2 cup (1 stick) butter	*1 teaspoon vanilla*
1/2 cup granulated sugar	*extract*
1/2 cup packed brown	*2 cups confectioners'*
sugar	*sugar*
1/2 cup heavy cream	*1 cup pecans halves,*
1/8 teaspoon salt	*toasted and chopped*

Combine the butter, granulated sugar, brown sugar, cream and salt in a large heavy saucepan. Bring to a boil over medium heat, stirring occasionally. Boil for 5 minutes, stirring constantly. Remove from the heat and stir in the vanilla. Add the confectioners' sugar and stir until smooth. Stir in the pecans. Pour into a buttered 8×8-inch baking pan. Let stand until firm. Cut into 1-inch squares. Store in an airtight container in the refrigerator. Yield: 1 1/4 pounds.

Marjorie Buckner, Beta Kappa Master
Welland, Ontario, Canada

CHOCOLATE PECAN FUDGE

3 (4 1/2-ounce) milk	*1/4 cup (1/2 stick)*
chocolate bars,	*margarine*
chopped	*1 teaspoon vanilla*
2 cups (12 ounces)	*extract*
chocolate chips	*4 1/2 cups sugar*
1 (7-ounce) jar	*1 (12-ounce) can*
marshmallow creme	*evaporated milk*
4 cups chopped pecans	

Combine the milk chocolate, chocolate chips, marshmallow creme, pecans, margarine and vanilla in a large bowl. Combine the sugar and evaporated milk in a saucepan. Bring to a boil, stirring frequently. Boil for exactly 6 minutes; the mixture will turn light brown. Add to the chocolate mixture and stir until smooth. Pour onto a greased 10×15-inch baking sheet. Let stand until firm. Cut into squares. Yield: 5 dozen squares.

Vera Patricia Hall, Beta Lambda
Stafford, Texas

EASY FUDGE

2 cups (12 ounces)	*1 (7-ounce) jar*
semisweet	*marshmallow creme*
chocolate chips	*2 tablespoons butter*
12 ounces German's	*1 (12-ounce) can*
sweet chocolate,	*evaporated milk*
chopped	*4 1/2 cups sugar*

Combine the chocolate chips, sweet chocolate and marshmallow creme in a large bowl. Melt the butter in a saucepan. Stir in the evaporated milk and sugar. Bring to a boil, stirring frequently. Boil for 5 minutes, stirring constantly. Pour over the chocolate mixture.

Stir until smooth. Pour into a greased 9×13-inch baking pan. Chill until firm. Cut into squares. Yield: 9 dozen squares.

Gail Archambeau
Hot Springs, South Dakota

FIVE-POUND FUDGE

4 1/2 cups sugar	*4 (4 1/2-ounce) milk*
1/2 cup (1 stick) butter	*chocolate bars,*
1 (12-ounce) can	*chopped*
evaporated milk	*1 (14-ounce) jar*
3 cups (18 ounces)	*marshmallow creme*
chocolate chips	*1 cup chopped nuts*

Line a 9×13-inch baking pan with foil and butter the foil. Bring the sugar, butter and evaporated milk to a boil in a saucepan or in a microwave-safe bowl in the microwave, stirring occasionally. Boil for 4 1/2 minutes, stirring frequently. Add the chocolate chips, milk chocolate and marshmallow creme and stir until smooth. Stir in the nuts. Pour into the prepared pan. Let stand until firm. Cut into squares. Yield: 4 to 5 dozen squares.

Ja Lynn Bruno, Lambda Upsilon
Pleasant Hill, Missouri

GRANOLA FUDGE CLUSTERS

This makes a great gift. Combine the cereal and nuts and pour into a canning jar. Top with a piece of foil and then add the chocolate chips and butterscotch chips. Top with a decorative lid and attach the recipe.

1 cup (6 ounces)	*1 1/4 cups granola cereal*
chocolate chips	*1 cup chopped walnuts*
1 cup (6 ounces)	
butterscotch chips	

Melt the chocolate chips and butterscotch chips in a saucepan over low heat, stirring occasionally. Remove from the heat and stir in the cereal and walnuts. Drop by tablespoonfuls onto waxed paper. Let stand until firm. Yield: about 4 dozen clusters.

Virginia Morgan, Theta Master
Aurora, Nebraska

Rowena Bienvenu, Xi Beta Sigma, Natchitoches, Louisiana, shares her recipe for **Pecan Rolls**. *She crushes one 14-ounce package vanilla wafers and chops 4 cups pecans. They are then combined in a large bowl. One 14-ounce can condensed milk is stirred in gradually until the mixture is moistened. She dips her hands in cold water and roll portions of the wafer mixture into logs. The logs are chilled thoroughly then cut into about 100 slices.*

HOLIDAY FUDGE

2 cups (12 ounces) semisweet chocolate chips	1 cup chopped pecans or walnuts
1 (14-ounce) can sweetened condensed milk	1/4 cup mixed candied fruit, chopped

Line a 5×9-inch loaf pan with waxed paper, allowing the waxed paper to extend over the edges of the pan. Lightly butter the waxed paper. Melt the chocolate chips in a double boiler, stirring occasionally. Add the sweetened condensed milk, pecans and candied fruit and mix well. Pour into the prepared pan. Chill until firm. Lift out of the pan by the waxed paper edges and place on a cutting board. Remove the waxed paper and cut into squares. Yield: 32 squares.

Sarah M. Stephens, Tau Master
Austin, Texas

PEANUT CHOCOLATE FUDGE

2 cups (12 ounces) chocolate chips	1 (10-ounce) package miniature marshmallows
2 cups (12 ounces) butterscotch chips	1 (10-ounce) can mixed nuts
1 cup peanut butter	

Combine the chocolate chips and butterscotch chips in a microwave-safe bowl. Microwave on Medium until melted, stirring occasionally. Add the peanut butter, marshmallows and nuts and mix well. Spread in a nonstick baking pan or drop by spoonfuls onto waxed paper. Let stand until firm. Cut into squares if in a pan. Yield: 4 dozen candies.

Crystal Westphalen, Beta Omega
Scottsbluff, Nebraska

ROCKY ROAD FUDGE

2 cups (12 ounces) semisweet chocolate chips	1 (10-ounce) package miniature marshmallows
1/2 cup (1 stick) butter or margarine	Confectioners' sugar

Combine the chocolate chips and butter in a saucepan. Cook over low heat until smooth, stirring occasionally. Remove from the heat and cool slightly. Stir in the marshmallows. Shape into 3 logs on separate sheets of waxed paper. Roll up in the waxed paper and chill until firm. Unwrap and roll the logs in confectioners' sugar. Slice. The logs freeze well. Yield: 2 dozen slices.

Laura Sutton, Eta Epsilon
Albuquerque, New Mexico

QUICK AND EASY ROCKY ROAD FUDGE

2 cups (12 ounces) semisweet chocolate chips	1 teaspoon vanilla extract
1 (14-ounce) can sweetened condensed milk	1 (2-ounce) package nut topping
	1 cup miniature marshmallows

Combine the chocolate chips and condensed milk in a saucepan. Cook over low heat until smooth, stirring constantly. Remove from the heat and stir in the vanilla and nut topping. Add the marshmallows and mix well. Spread in a buttered baking dish. Chill for 1 hour or until set. Cut into squares. Yield: 2 dozen squares.

Janet Zornig, Preceptor Nu Chi
Flournoy, California

TEN-MINUTE FUDGE

This is very easy and children enjoy making it.

3 cups (18 ounces) semisweet chocolate chips	Dash of salt
	1 1/2 teaspoons vanilla extract
1 (14-ounce) can sweetened condensed milk	1/2 to 1 cup chopped nuts (optional)

Line a 9×9-inch baking pan with foil and butter the foil. Melt the chocolate chips, condensed milk and salt in a microwave-safe bowl in the microwave or in a heavy saucepan over medium heat, stirring occasionally. Stir in the vanilla and nuts. Pour into the prepared pan. Chill for 2 hours or until firm. Invert the fudge onto a cutting board and remove the foil. Cut into squares. Store in an airtight container in the refrigerator. Yield: 2 pounds.

Neldalea Dotray, Laureate Gamma Pi
Greenville, Illinois

VELVEETA PEANUT BUTTER FUDGE

8 ounces Velveeta cheese, cubed	3/4 cup (1 1/2 sticks) butter
2 (1-pound) packages confectioners' sugar	1 teaspoon vanilla extract
	1 cup peanut butter

Melt the cheese, confectioners' sugar and butter in a microwave-safe bowl in the microwave, stirring occasionally. Stir in the vanilla and peanut butter. Cool slightly. Knead in the bowl. Pat into a greased 9×13-inch baking pan. Chill until firm. Cut into squares. Yield: 4 to 5 dozen squares.

Frances Buck, Epsilon Alpha
Mesquite, Texas

VELVEETA FUDGE

2 cups (4 sticks) butter
1 pound Velveeta cheese,
   cubed
1 tablespoon vanilla
   extract

4 (1-pound) packages
   confectioners' sugar
1 cup baking cocoa
1 pound chopped nuts
   (optional)

Melt the butter, cheese and vanilla in a large saucepan over medium heat, stirring frequently. Stir in the confectioners' sugar and baking cocoa. Cook until smooth and creamy, stirring constantly; do not boil. Remove from the heat and stir in the nuts. Pour evenly into a buttered 11×13-inch baking pan. Chill until firm. Cut into squares. Yield: 12 dozen squares.

Ronda Pratt, Xi Mu
Peoria, Arizona

FOUR-STEP DECADENT WHITE FUDGE

2 cups (12 ounces) white
   chocolate chips
8 ounces cream cheese,
   softened
4 cups confectioners'
   sugar

1½ teaspoons vanilla
   extract
1 cup chopped pecans or
   other nuts

Melt the white chocolate chips in a double boiler, stirring until smooth. Beat the cream cheese, confectioners' sugar and vanilla in a bowl until light and fluffy. Add the melted chocolate and mix well. Stir in the pecans. Pour into a greased 8×8-inch baking pan. Chill until firm. Cut into 1-inch squares.
Yield: 64 squares.

Kristie Sturrock, Preceptor Beta Gamma
Jacksonville, Texas

WHITE DIVINITY FUDGE

1 (2-pound) package
   white or chocolate
   almond bark
8 ounces cream cheese,
   softened

3 tablespoons
   margarine, softened
1 cup chopped pecans or
   other nuts

Melt the almond bark in a microwave-safe bowl in the microwave, stirring occasionally. Add the cream cheese and margarine and beat for 8 minutes or until fluffy and no longer glossy. Stir in the pecans. Pour into a buttered 9×13-inch baking dish. Chill until firm. Cut into squares. Yield: about 4 dozen squares.

Mary Lee Bishop, Alpha Lambda Master
Cape Girardeau, Missouri

HONEY CANDY

2 cups sugar
1 cup honey

1 cup heavy cream

Combine the sugar, honey and cream in a saucepan. Cook over medium heat to 300 to 310 degrees on a candy thermometer, hard-crack stage, stirring constantly. Pour into a buttered pie plate and let stand until cool enough to handle. Pull the candy with buttered fingers until stiff and light. Stretch into long strips on a work surface. Score with a sharp knife at 1-inch intervals. Let stand until firm. Break the candy into 1-inch pieces. Yield: 4 dozen pieces.

Jacqueline L. Nichols, Alpha Delta Phi
Lowry City, Missouri

TOFFEE CRACKERS

40 saltine crackers
1 cup (2 sticks) butter
¾ cup packed brown
   sugar

2 cups (12 ounces)
   chocolate chips

Fit the crackers in a single layer in a foil-lined 10×15-inch baking pan. Combine the butter and brown sugar in a saucepan. Bring to a boil over medium-high heat, stirring frequently. Boil for 5 minutes, stirring constantly. Pour evenly over the crackers. Bake at 400 degrees for 5 minutes. Sprinkle with the chocolate chips. Bake for 1 minute longer. Spread the melted chocolate evenly with a knife or spatula. Chill, covered, overnight. Peel off the foil and break into small pieces. Yield: 8 dozen pieces.

Carolyn Court, Preceptor Nu
Frederick, Maryland

IRISH CREAM BALLS

3 cups crushed vanilla
   wafers
1 cup chopped pecans
¾ cup confectioners'
   sugar
½ cup Irish cream
   liqueur

3 tablespoons light
   corn syrup
1½ teaspoons baking
   cocoa
1 cup confectioners'
   sugar

Mix the vanilla wafers, pecans, ¾ cup confectioners' sugar, liqueur, corn syrup and baking cocoa in a bowl. Let stand for 5 minutes. Shape into 1-inch balls. Spread 1 cup confectioners' sugar in a shallow dish. Roll the balls in the confectioners' sugar and place on a wire rack. Let stand for 1 hour. Roll the balls in the confectioners' sugar again. Store in an airtight container. Yield: 3 dozen balls.

Cinda Dowell, Alpha Epsilon Alpha
Odessa, Missouri

QUICK AND EASY MACAROONS

1/2 cup (1 stick) butter, melted
4 cups pecans, chopped
2 (1-pound) packages confectioners' sugar
1 2/3 cups flaked coconut
1 teaspoon vanilla extract
1 (14-ounce) can sweetened condensed milk
2 cups (12 ounces) chocolate chips
2 tablespoons shortening

Pour the butter over the pecans in a large bowl. Add the confectioners' sugar, coconut, vanilla and sweetened condensed milk and mix well. Chill, covered, for 1 hour. Shape into marble-size balls and place on a platter. Freeze until firm. Melt the chocolate chips and shortening in a double boiler, stirring occasionally. Dip the coconut balls in the melted chocolate and place on waxed paper. Let stand until firm. These freeze well. Yield: 8 to 10 dozen balls.

Pam Klasing, Preceptor Nu Alpha
San Antonio, Texas

BUTTER MINTS

These are nice to make for weddings and you can tint the mints to match the color of the bridesmaid's dresses.

5 cups confectioners' sugar
1/4 cup (1/2 stick) butter, softened
1/2 teaspoon mint extract
3 tablespoons boiling water
Food coloring

Combine the confectioners' sugar, butter, mint extract and water in a bowl and mix well. Stir in food coloring to achieve desired tint. Fill small candy molds with the mint mixture and unmold onto waxed paper. Let stand until firm. Store in an airtight container. Yield: 6 to 8 dozen mints.

Kathleen Radcliffe, Alpha Master
Lancaster, Pennsylvania

CHOCOLATE MINTS

1 cup (6 ounces) chocolate chips
1 teaspoon butter or margarine
1/2 teaspoon peppermint extract

Melt the chocolate chips, butter and peppermint extract in a heavy saucepan over low heat, stirring occasionally. Drop by scant teaspoonfuls onto waxed paper. Let stand until firm. Yield: about 5 dozen mints.

Nancy Gienow, Xi Mu
Edmonton, Alberta, Canada

SPICED NUTS

1 egg white
1 teaspoon water
1/4 teaspoon salt (optional)
1/2 cup sugar
1/2 teaspoon cinnamon
1 pound assorted nuts

Beat the egg white, water and salt in a bowl until frothy. Mix the sugar and cinnamon in a bowl. Add to the egg white mixture and mix well. Add the nuts and stir to coat. Spread over a nonstick baking sheet. Bake at 225 degrees for 1 hour, stirring every 15 minutes. Remove to a wire rack to cool completely. Store in an airtight container. Yield: 16 servings.

Mary Kathryn Hinton, Laureate Alpha Nu
Rochester, New York

SALTED NUT SQUARES

2 1/2 tablespoons butter or margarine
2 cups (12 ounces) peanut butter chips
1 (14-ounce) can sweetened condensed milk
2 cups miniature marshmallows
1 (16-ounce) jar salted peanuts

Melt the butter and peanut butter chips in a microwave-safe bowl in the microwave, stirring occasionally. Stir in the sweetened condensed milk. Add the marshmallows and mix well. Place half the peanuts in an even layer in a nonstick 9×13-inch baking pan. Top evenly with the marshmallow mixture and press lightly. Sprinkle with the remaining peanuts and press lightly. Let stand until firm. Cut into squares. Yield: 6 to 8 dozen squares.

Sue Gechter, Preceptor Beta Psi
Dodge City, Kansas

OREO DROPS

1 (18-ounce) package double-stuffed cream-filled chocolate sandwich cookies, crushed
8 ounces cream cheese, softened
8 ounces white chocolate, melted

Combine the crushed cookies and the cream cheese in a bowl and mix well. Shape by tablespoonfuls into balls. Coat with white chocolate and place on waxed paper. Let stand until firm. Yield: 24 servings.

Marti Thruston, Preceptor Lambda Iota
Jefferson City, Missouri

PEANUT BUTTER BALLS

2 cups peanut butter
2 cups (4 sticks) butter,
  melted
3 (1-pound) packages
  confectioners' sugar

1 teaspoon vanilla
  extract
24 ounces chocolate,
  melted

Combine the peanut butter, butter, confectioners' sugar and vanilla in a bowl and mix well. Shape into 1-inch balls and place on a baking sheet. Freeze until firm. Coat the frozen balls with the melted chocolate and place on waxed paper. Let stand until firm. Freeze until just before serving. Yield: 72 servings.

Robin Cannon, Kappa Upsilon
Bonaire, Georgia

PEANUT BUTTER PINWHEELS

1 cup (2 sticks) butter,
  softened
2 (1-pound) packages
  confectioners' sugar

1 teaspoon vanilla
  extract
Peanut butter

Beat the butter and half the confectioners' sugar in a bowl until smooth. Beat in enough of the remaining confectioner's sugar to form a mixture stiff enough to roll out. Roll to 1/4-inch thick on a work surface dusted with confectioners' sugar. Spread with a thin layer of peanut butter. Roll to enclose the filling and cut in half. Stretch each half to form a 1-inch-wide log. Cut into 1/2-inch slices and place on a platter. Chill until firm. Yield: 3 to 4 dozen slices.

Cathy Teter, Xi Epsilon Gamma
Edinburgh, Indiana

PEANUT BUTTER TREATS

1 cup light corn
  syrup or honey
1 cup peanut butter
1 1/2 cups dry milk
  powder

1 cup confectioner's
  sugar
1 1/2 cups graham cracker
  crumbs or finely
  chopped nuts

Combine the corn syrup and peanut butter in a bowl and mix well. Stir in the dry milk and confectioners' sugar gradually and mix until smooth. Shape into 1-inch wide logs and roll in the graham cracker crumbs. Slice into 1-inch pieces.
Yield: 4 dozen candies.

Cheryol Miller, Xi Lambda Gamma
Mansfield, Ohio

CRANBERRY NUT CANDY

1 (24-ounce) package
  vanilla almond bark,
  chopped
1/2 cup pecans

1/2 cup almonds
1/2 cup peanuts
1/2 cup sweetened dried
  cranberries

Melt the almond bark in a microwave-safe bowl in the microwave, stirring occasionally. Add the pecans, almonds, peanuts and dried cranberries and mix well. Spread over waxed paper. Let stand until firm. Break into pieces. Yield: 4 dozen candies.

B. J. Francis, Laureate Theta Mu
Kingwood, Texas

SUGAR-COATED PEANUTS

1 cup sugar
1/2 cup water

2 cups raw peanuts

Mix the sugar and water in a large cast-iron skillet. Stir in the peanuts. Cook over medium heat until all the liquid is absorbed, stirring constantly. Spread over a nonstick baking sheet. Bake at 300 degrees for 30 minutes, stirring often. Yield: 10 servings.

Jackie Ann Nelson, Xi Theta Chi
Chesapeake, Virginia

MOCK PEANUT BRITTLE

My first-grade teacher shared this recipe over 25 years ago and I've loved it ever since.

1 cup light corn syrup
1 cup sugar

1 cup peanut butter
8 cups cornflakes

Combine the corn syrup and sugar in a saucepan. Bring to a boil over medium heat, stirring occasionally. Remove from the heat and stir in the peanut butter until smooth. Pour over the cornflakes in a large bowl and mix well. Spread gently in a greased 9×13-inch baking pan. Let stand until firm. Cut into squares. Yield: 4 dozen squares.

Shannon Harms, Alpha Zeta
Los Alamos, New Mexico

Amber Vines, Beta Iota Theta, Lake Jackson, Texas, shared her simple recipe for Mock Bonbons. She crushes 1 package chocolate sandwich cookies and mixes the crumbs with 8 ounces softened cream cheese in a bowl. She shapes the mixture into a ball, wraps it in plastic wrap, and chills for 45 minutes or longer. She melts 1 package chocolate almond bark in a saucepan over low heat, shapes the cream cheese mixture into 1-inch balls, and coats them with the almond bark. The bonbons stand on waxed paper until firm.

MICROWAVE PEANUT BRITTLE

1 cup sugar	1 tablespoon butter or
1/2 cup light corn	margarine
syrup	1 teaspoon vanilla
1 1/2 cups raw peanuts	extract
1/4 teaspoon salt	1 teaspoon baking soda

Combine the sugar, corn syrup, peanuts and salt in a 3-quart microwave-safe bowl. Microwave on High for 7 1/2 to 9 1/2 minutes or until golden brown. Stir in the butter and vanilla. Microwave on High for 1 minute or to 300 to 310 degrees on a candy thermometer, hard-crack stage. Stir in the baking soda. Pour onto a well greased baking sheet and spread the mixture thinly. Let stand until firm. Break into pieces. Yield: 1 pound.

Wilma N. Bledsoe, Laureate Mu
Hot Springs. Arkansas

PEANUT CLUSTERS

2 cups (12 ounces)	2 teaspoons shortening
peanut butter chips	2 cups peanuts
or chocolate chips	

Combine the peanut butter chips and shortening in a microwave-safe bowl. Microwave on High for 1 minute and stir well. Microwave on High for 15 seconds or until smooth. Add the peanuts and mix well. Spoon into paper-lined miniature muffin cups. Chill for 1 hour. Yield: 2 to 2 1/2 dozen clusters.

Kandee Graham, Alpha Lambda Master
Hershey, Pennsylvania

❖ CHOCOLATE PEANUT CLUSTERS

1 (24-ounce) package	1 cup (6 ounces) milk
white almond bark,	chocolate chips
chopped	2 cups (12 ounces)
4 ounces German's	semisweet chocolate
sweet chocolate,	chips
chopped	1 (16-ounce) jar unsalted
	roasted peanuts

Place the white almond bark, sweet chocolate, milk chocolate chips and semisweet chocolate chips in a slow cooker. Cook, covered, on Low for 2 hours; do not stir during cooking. Stir until smooth. Stir in the peanuts. Drop by teaspoonfuls onto waxed paper. Chill until firm. Store in an airtight container in the refrigerator. Yield: 8 to 9 dozen clusters.

Sylvia Carpenter, Xi Alpha Omega
Murfreesboro, Tennessee

PECAN BARK

24 graham crackers	1 cup packed brown
1 cup chopped pecans	sugar
1 cup (2 sticks) unsalted	
butter	

Fit the graham crackers in a single layer in a foil-lined 10×15-inch baking pan. Sprinkle evenly with the pecans. Melt the butter in a saucepan. Stir in the brown sugar. Bring to a boil over medium heat, stirring frequently. Boil for 1 minute, stirring constantly. Pour evenly over the crackers and pecans. Bake at 350 degrees for 10 minutes. Place immediately in the freezer and freeze for 1 hour. Break into pieces. Store in an airtight container. Yield: 6 to 7 dozen pieces.

Rosemary Weart, Laureate Delta Xi
Needles, California

MICROWAVE PECAN BRITTLE

1 cup pecan halves	1 teaspoon butter
1 cup sugar	1 teaspoon vanilla
1/2 cup light corn syrup	extract
1/2 teaspoon salt	1 teaspoon baking soda

Combine the pecans, sugar, corn syrup and salt in a microwave-safe 1 1/2-quart bowl or 8-cup glass measuring cup and mix well. Microwave on High for 4 minutes; stir well. Microwave on High for 4 minutes. Stir in the butter and vanilla. Microwave on High for 2 minutes. Add the baking soda and stir gently until light and foamy. Pour onto a greased baking sheet. Cool for 30 minutes to 1 hour. Break gently into pieces. Store in an airtight container. Yield: 1 pound.

Carol Brodt Kettler, Preceptor Epsilon Lambda
Pearland, Texas

SUGARED PECANS

These are great to have around during the holidays. My daughter gives them as teachers' gifts.

2 cups sugar	2 tablespoons water
2 teaspoons cinnamon	2 pounds pecan halves
2 egg whites	

Mix the sugar and cinnamon in a bowl. Whisk the egg whites and water in a large bowl until foamy. Stir in the pecans. Add the sugar mixture and toss to coat. Spread over a nonstick baking sheet. Bake at 250 degrees for 1 hour, stirring every 15 minutes. Remove to a wire rack to cool completely.
Yield: 32 servings.

Elisha Betchan, Alpha Tau Delta
Rockdale, Texas

EASY PRALINES

1 (1-pound) package   **2 tablespoons margarine**
  brown sugar   **2 cups pecans**
1 cup heavy cream

Combine the brown sugar and cream in a microwave-safe bowl. Microwave on High for 7 minutes; stir well. Microwave on High for 7 minutes. Stir in the margarine and pecans. Microwave on High for 2 minutes. Drop by spoonfuls onto buttered waxed paper. Let stand until firm. Yield: 2 pounds.

Dolores Fritz, Delta Lambda Master
Houston, Texas

POTATO CHIP CANDY

2 cups each (12 ounces   **1¹/2 cups unsalted**
  each) chocolate chips,   **peanuts**
  peanut butter chips   **1¹/2 cups crushed**
  and butterscotch chips   **potato chips**

Melt the chocolate chips, peanut butter chips and butterscotch chips in a large microwave-safe bowl in the microwave or in a double boiler. Stir until smooth. Add the peanuts and potato chips and mix well. Drop by teaspoonfuls onto waxed paper or into small paper baking cups. Let stand until firm. Yield: 6 dozen candies.

Carla Dawson-Parniak, Laureate Alpha Omega
Sault Ste. Marie, Ontario, Canada

PRETZEL CANDY

2 cups (12 ounces) milk   **2 tablespoons peanut**
  chocolate chips   **butter**
2 cups (12 ounces)   **2 cups crushed pretzels**
  peanut butter chips

Melt the chocolate chips, peanut butter chips and peanut butter in a microwave-safe bowl in the microwave, stirring occasionally. Add the pretzels and mix well. Spread in a greased foil-lined 9×13-inch baking pan. Chill until firm. Cut into squares or break into pieces. Yield: 9 dozen squares.

Nela Manning, Tau Master
Washington, Pennsylvania

---

*Ann Lipps, Preceptor Theta, Williamson, West Virginia, contributed her unique recipe for **Chinese Chews**. She places 1 cup each chocolate chips and butterscotch chips in a microwave-proof dish, Microwaves for 2 minutes on High, and stirs the chips until smooth. She stirs in one 8-ounce can chow mein noodles and 1 cup peanuts. She drops the mixture by teaspoonfuls onto waxed paper and chills until firm.*

HARD ROCK CANDY

Flavoring oils are more concentrated than extracts and can be found in the baking aisle or where candy-making supplies are sold.

2 cups granulated sugar   **¹/2 teaspoon wintergreen,**
³/4 cup light corn syrup   **peppermint, butter**
1 cup water   **rum or anise**
¹/2 teaspoon salt   **flavoring oil**
Red or green food   **1 cup confectioners'**
  coloring   **sugar**

Cook the first 4 ingredients in a large heavy saucepan over high heat to 300 to 310 degrees on a candy thermometer, hard-crack stage, stirring constantly. Remove from the heat and stir in enough food coloring to achieve the desired tint and the flavoring oil. Sprinkle confectioners' sugar over a large cutting board. Pour the hot sugar mixture evenly over the board. Cut quickly into bite-size pieces with a sharp knife or let stand until firm and break into pieces. Place the candy and 1 up confectioners' sugar a sealable plastic bag. Shake to coat. Yield: 1¹/2 pounds.

Patricia A. Siron, Laureate Gamma Mu
Mexico, Missouri

RUM BALLS

3 cups vanilla wafer   **1¹/3 cups sweetened**
  crumbs   **condensed milk**
1 cup chopped walnuts   **Confectioners' sugar**
¹/4 cup rum

Combine the vanilla wafer crumbs and walnuts in a bowl and mix well. Add the rum and sweetened condensed milk and mix well. Chill for 1 hour. Shape into 1-inch balls and coat in confectioners' sugar. Store in an airtight container in the refrigerator or freezer. Yield: 4 dozen balls.

Joann Templeton, Laureate Gamma
Pickering, Ontario, Canada

PECAN RUM BALLS

1 (11-ounce) package   **¹/2 cup light corn syrup**
  chocolate or vanilla   **¹/4 cup rum**
  wafers, crushed   **¹/2 cup confectioners'**
1¹/2 cups finely chopped   **sugar**
  pecans

Combine the crushed wafers and pecans in a bowl. Stir in the corn syrup and the rum. Shape into 1-inch balls. Roll in confectioners' sugar. Yield: 48 servings.

Inga Goebel, Zeta Master
Havre, Montana

SALTINE CRACKER CANDY

1 package saltine crackers
1 cup (2 sticks) margarine
1 cup sugar
1 cup (6 ounces) peanut butter chips
1 cup (6 ounces) chocolate chips

Fit the crackers closely together in a single layer in the center of a foil-lined baking sheet. Combine the margarine and sugar in a saucepan. Bring to a boil over medium heat, stirring frequently. Boil for 3 minutes, stirring constantly. Pour evenly over the crackers. Bake at 400 degrees for 5 to 7 minutes or until light brown. Sprinkle with the peanut butter chips and chocolate chips and spread evenly with a knife or spatula. Chill for 1 to 2 hours. Break into pieces. Yield: 6 to 7 dozen pieces.

Sharon Donahue, Laureate Alpha Alpha
Wausau, Wisconsin

ENGLISH TOFFEE

3/4 cup chopped almonds
1 cup (2 sticks) butter
1 cup sugar
2 cups (12 ounces) chocolate chips
1/4 cup chopped almonds

Place 3/4 cup chopped almonds in a buttered 8×10-inch baking pan. Combine the butter and sugar in a saucepan. Cook over high heat until caramel colored, stirring constantly. Pour evenly over the almonds in the pan. Sprinkle with the chocolate chips and let stand for a few minutes. Spread the melted chocolate evenly with the back of a spoon or a spatula and sprinkle with 1/4 cup chopped almonds. Let stand until firm. Break into pieces. Yield: 1 1/2 pounds.

Billie Porter, Preceptor Iota Beta
Camarillo, California

TREE BARK

Saltine crackers
1 cup (2 sticks) butter
1 cup packed dark brown sugar
1 1/3 cups (8 ounces) chocolate chips
Chopped almonds or pecans

Fit the crackers closely together in a single layer in a nonstick 10×15-inch baking pan. Combine the butter and brown sugar in a saucepan. Bring to a boil, stirring frequently. Boil for 3 minutes, stirring constantly. Pour evenly over the crackers. Bake at 350 degrees for 5 minutes. Sprinkle with the chocolate chips. Let stand for 5 minutes. Spread the melted chocolate evenly with a knife or spatula. Sprinkle with the almonds. Chill for 1 hour. Break into pieces. Yield: 6 to 7 dozen pieces.

Kerstin Landwer, Omicron Mu
Joplin, Missouri

WHITE CHOCOLATE PARTY MIX

16 cups popped popcorn
3 cups frosted toasted oat cereal
1 1/2 cup pecan halves
1 (10-ounce) package pretzel sticks
1 (10-ounce) package toffee bits
1 (14-ounce) package "M & M's" Chocolate Candies
4 cups (24 ounces) vanilla or white chocolate chips
2 tablespoons vegetable oil

Combine the popcorn, cereal, pecans, pretzels, toffee bits and candy in a very large bowl and mix well. Melt the vanilla chips and oil in a microwave-safe bowl in the microwave. Stir until smooth. Pour over the popcorn mixture and toss to coat. Spread onto baking sheets. Let stand until firm. Store in an airtight container. Yield: 9 1/2 quarts.

Debbie Wolfe, Alpha Beta Master
Farmington, West Virginia

WHITE CHOCOLATE PEANUT CRUNCH

1 (18-ounce) box graham cracker cereal
1 (10-ounce) package pretzel sticks
1 (16-ounce) jar dry-roasted peanuts
1 (24-ounce) package white almond bark, chopped

Combine the cereal, pretzels and peanuts in a large bowl and mix well. Melt the almond bark in a microwave-safe bowl in the microwave according to package directions. Stir until smooth. Pour over the cereal mixture and mix well. Spread over waxed paper. Let stand until firm. Break into pieces. Store in an airtight container for up to 3 weeks. Yield: 25 to 30 servings.

Jo Ann Kidd, Xi Alpha Xi
Bessemer, Alabama

❖ WHITE CHOCOLATE POPCORN CRUNCH

14 cups popped popcorn
2 cups roasted cashews or pecans
3 cups melted white chocolate

Combine the popcorn and cashews in a large bowl and toss well. Add the white chocolate and stir gently until well coated. Spread in a waxed paper-lined 10×15-inch baking pan. Chill for 30 minutes or until the coating hardens. Cut into squares or break into pieces. Store in an airtight container for up to one week. Yield: 8 dozen squares.

Eugenia Richardson, Iota Master
Calgary, Alberta, Canada

The Icebox

FROZEN TREATS

ANGEL FOOD CAKE ROLL

1 (16-ounce) package
   angel food cake mix
5 teaspoons
   confectioners' sugar
1 small package
   sugar-free vanilla
   instant pudding mix
1 cup reduced-fat
   strawberry yogurt
3 drops red food
   coloring (optional)
8 ounces reduced-fat
   whipped topping

Prepare the cake mix using the package directions. Pour into a waxed paper-lined 10×15-inch baking pan. Bake at 350 degrees for 15 to 20 minutes or until the cake springs back when lightly touched. Cool in the pan for 5 minutes. Dust a clean kitchen towel lightly with the confectioners' sugar. Invert the cake onto the towel. Remove the waxed paper. Roll the warm cake in the towel as for a jelly roll from the short side and place on a wire rack to cool. Whisk the pudding mix, yogurt and food coloring together in a bowl. Fold in the whipped topping. Unroll the cooled cake carefully and remove the towel. Spread the filling within 1 inch of the edge and reroll. Wrap in plastic wrap and freeze. Remove the cake from the freezer 30 minutes before serving. Yield: 8 servings.

Becky Castellari, Preceptor Delta
Centralia, Illinois

*Jacqueline Nichols, Alpha Delta Phi, Lowry City, Missouri, makes a refreshing **Apple Milkshake** with just a few ingredients. For two milkshakes, she combines 2 cups vanilla ice cream with 1 cup apple juice and 1/4 teaspoon cinnamon in a blender and processes for 20 seconds or until smooth.*

APPLE CRISP PARFAITS

This was included in a collection of recipes from my cousin when I was married.

1 cup rolled oats
1/2 cup packed
   brown sugar
1/4 cup (1/2 stick)
   butter, melted
1 (21-ounce) can apple
   pie filling
1/4 teaspoon cinnamon
1 quart vanilla
   ice cream

Combine the oats, brown sugar and butter in an 8×8-inch baking pan and stir well. Bake at 350 degrees for 10 minutes. Cool in the pan and crumble. Combine the pie filling and cinnamon in a small bowl and mix well. Layer the ice cream, apple filling and oat mixture in parfait glasses. Yield: 8 servings.

Linda Ball, Xi Zeta Pi
Pryor, Oklahoma

EASY BANANAS FOSTER

1/4 cup packed
   brown sugar
3 tablespoons rum
3 tablespoons butter,
   cut into small pieces
3 firm bananas, sliced
1/2 teaspoon cinnamon
Vanilla ice cream

Sprinkle the brown sugar in the bottom of a 9×9-inch baking pan. Sprinkle with rum and dot with butter. Layer with the bananas and sprinkle with cinnamon. Bake, loosely covered, at 400 degrees for 15 minutes or until bubbly around the edge. Stir gently and spoon over vanilla ice cream just before serving. Yield: 4 servings.

Donna Dietrich, Preceptor Alpha Gamma
Yankton, South Dakota

OLD-FASHIONED BANANA SPLIT

This is a wonderful recipe to make ahead and have on hand. The chocolate sauce is to-die-for and makes a great topping for ice cream.

1 wrapper graham crackers, crushed	1/2 cup (1 stick) butter
3 bananas, halved lengthwise	2 cups confectioners' sugar
1/2 gallon Neapolitan ice cream	1 (12-ounce) can evaporated milk
1 cup chopped walnuts	1 teaspoon vanilla extract
1 cup (6 ounces) semisweet chocolate chips	2 cups heavy whipping cream

Sprinkle the graham cracker crumbs in the bottom of an 11×15-inch dish, reserving about 1/4 cup. Arrange the bananas over the crumbs. Slice the ice cream block into thick pieces and arrange over the bananas. Sprinkle with the walnuts. Freeze, covered, until firm. Melt the chocolate chips and butter in a small saucepan over low heat, stirring often. Stir in the confectioners' sugar and evaporated milk. Cook until thick and smooth, stirring constantly. Stir in the vanilla. Cool to room temperature. Pour over the walnut layer. Whip the cream in a mixing bowl and spread over the chocolate layer. Sprinkle with the reserved graham cracker crumbs. Freeze until firm. Remove from the freezer a few minutes before serving. Cut into squares. Yield: 18 servings.

Carol Pfalzgraf, Gamma Nu
Wellington, Kansas

BLIZZARD

1/4 cup (1/2 stick) butter	2 tablespoons milk
3 tablespoons peanut butter	1 1/2 teaspoons vanilla extract
1 1/4 cups crushed chocolate sandwich cookies	16 ounces whipped topping
8 ounces cream cheese, softened	1/4 cup crushed chocolate sandwich cookies
1/2 cup sugar	1/4 cup chocolate topping
1/2 cup peanut butter	1/4 cup butterscotch topping
2 eggs	

Melt the butter and 3 tablespoons peanut butter in the microwave in a microwave-proof bowl. Stir in 1 1/4 cups cookie crumbs. Press onto the bottom of a 9×13-inch dish. Beat the cream cheese, sugar, 1/2 cup peanut butter, eggs, milk and vanilla in a large mixing bowl until thick and smooth. Fold in the whipped topping. Spread over the cookie crumb layer. Sprinkle with 1/4 cup cookie crumbs. Swirl the chocolate

and butterscotch toppings over the top. Freeze for 12 hours. Remove from the freezer 15 to 20 minutes before serving. Cut into squares. Note: If you are concerned about using raw eggs, use eggs pasteurized in their shells, which are sold at some specialty food stores, or use an equivalent amount of pasteurized egg substitute. Yield: 10 servings.

Sally J. King, Beta Eta Master
Nepean, Ontario, Canada

BUTTER BRICKLE FROZEN DELIGHT

1 1/4 cups graham cracker crumbs	3/4 cup chopped pecans
1/3 cup butter, melted	8 ounces cream cheese, softened
1/4 cup granulated sugar	1 (14-ounce) can sweetened condensed milk
1 cup all-purpose flour	
3/4 cup quick-cooking oats	12 ounces whipped topping
1/4 cup packed brown sugar	1 (12-ounce) jar caramel topping
1/2 cup (1 stick) butter, melted	

Combine the graham cracker crumbs, 1/3 cup butter and the granulated sugar in a bowl and mix well. Press in the bottom of a 9-inch springform pan. Bake at 350 degrees for 6 minutes. Cool completely. Combine the flour, oats, brown sugar, 1/2 cup butter and the pecans in a large bowl and mix well. Pat lightly onto a baking sheet. Bake at 400 degrees for 10 to 15 minutes or until light brown. Crumble while hot; cool completely. Beat the cream cheese in a large bowl until smooth. Beat in the condensed milk. Fold in the whipped topping. Layer half the cream cheese mixture, half the oat crumbles and half the caramel topping over the crust. Repeat the layers. Freeze until firm. Remove the pan side and serve cold. Yield: 12 servings.

Michelle Doyle, Xi Omega
Worland, Wyoming

FROZEN CHERRY DESSERT

1 (21-ounce) can cherry pie filling	8 ounces whipped topping
1 (14-ounce) can sweetened condensed milk	2 cups miniature marshmallows

Combine the pie filling and condensed milk in a bowl and mix well. Fold in the whipped topping and marshmallows. Pour into an 8×12-inch glass dish. Freeze until firm. Yield: 6 to 8 servings.

Debbi Newcomer, Xi Theta Beta
Oak Grove, Missouri

CHOCOLATE CHIP CREAMSICLE CAKE

1 (11-ounce) package
  prepared miniature
  brownies, cut in half
  horizontally
1 quart chocolate chip
  ice cream, softened

1 quart orange sherbet,
  softened
8 ounces whipped
  topping
Chocolate curls
  (optional)

Line an 8-inch springform pan with plastic wrap, leaving a 2-inch overhang. Press half the brownie pieces onto the bottom of the prepared pan to form a crust. Chop the remaining brownie pieces coarsely. Spread the chocolate chip ice cream over the crust and top with the chopped brownies. Freeze for 1 hour or until firm. Spread the sherbet over the top. Freeze until firm. Remove the side of the pan. Invert onto a serving plate and remove the bottom of the pan and the plastic wrap. Spread with the whipped topping and garnish with chocolate curls. Serve immediately or freeze until just before serving. Yield: 12 servings.

Marge Smalyga, Xi Theta
Fonthill, Ontario, Canada

FROZEN CHOCOLATE MOUSSE

2 cups heavy
  whipping cream
1/4 cup almond-
  chocolate or coffee
  liqueur

1/2 cup chocolate syrup
Crushed cookies or
  chopped nuts
  (optional)
Raspberry Sauce

Whip the cream in a chilled large mixing bowl until stiff peaks form. Fold in the liqueur and chocolate syrup with a rubber spatula. Spread in an ungreased 9×9-inch dish. Freeze, covered, for at least 4 hours and up to 3 months. Cut into squares. Garnish with crushed cookies or nuts and serve with Raspberry Sauce. Yield: 9 servings.

RASPBERRY SAUCE

1 package frozen
  raspberries, thawed
  and drained

3 tablespoons sugar
2 teaspoons cornstarch

Combine the raspberries, sugar and cornstarch in a saucepan. Cook over medium heat until thickened, stirring constantly. Boil for 1 minute longer, stirring constantly. Press through a fine sieve to remove the seeds if desired.

Norma Gilmore, Laureate Alpha Chi
Pittsburg, Kansas

ROLLED ICE CREAM CAKE

1 (16-ounce) package
  angel food cake mix

1/2 gallon ice cream,
  softened (any flavor)

Prepare and bake the cake mix using the package directions for a large sheet cake pan. Cool in the pan for 5 minutes. Dust a clean kitchen towel lightly with confectioners' sugar. Invert the cake onto the towel. Roll the warm cake in the towel as for a jelly roll from the short side. Chill for 8 to 10 hours. Unroll the cake carefully and remove the towel. Spread with the ice cream to the edge and reroll. Wrap in foil and freeze until firm. Yield: 8 to 10 servings.

Jan Pringle, Theta Gamma
Arkansas City, Kansas

ICE CREAM CAKE

This is a beautiful tall cake that is impressive to serve. I won a holiday dessert contest with this recipe.

1 large angel food cake
1 cup half-and-half
1/2 cup sugar
4 egg yolks,
  lightly beaten
2 tablespoons cornstarch

2 tablespoons water
1 cup heavy
  whipping cream
Red and green
  maraschino cherries
Chopped walnuts

Slice the cake horizontally into 3 layers. Combine the half-and-half, sugar, egg yolks, cornstarch and water in a saucepan and mix well. Place the pan over simmering water. Cook until thickened, stirring often. Cool to room temperature. Whip the cream in a mixing bowl until stiff peaks form. Fold into the half-and-half mixture. Spread between the layers and over the top and side of the cake. Top with maraschino cherries and walnuts. Freeze until firm. Remove from the freezer 30 minutes before serving. Yield: 10 servings.

Dottie Twyford, Alpha Iota Master
Springfield, Illinois

LEMONADE CAKE

Serve this pretty cake at your next ladies' gathering. My sorority sisters all love it.

1 angel food cake
1 (6-ounce) can frozen
  pink lemonade,
  partially frozen

1 quart vanilla ice cream,
  softened
2 cups heavy whipping
  cream
Sugar to taste

Slice the cake horizontally into 3 layers. Combine the lemonade and ice cream in a large bowl and mix well. Spread between the cake layers. Whip the cream in a mixing bowl until stiff peaks form, gradually adding sugar to taste. Spread over the top and side of the cake. Freeze until firm. Remove from the refrigerator just before serving. Yield: 10 to 12 servings.

Beth Menefee, Xi Beta Alpha
Artesia, New Mexico

RAINBOW CAKE

When we were in the Air Force, a friend on the base shared this recipe. We especially enjoyed it on summer days.

1 large angel food cake
1 (3-ounce) package
   strawberry gelatin
1 (3-ounce) package
   lime gelatin
1 (3-ounce) package
   orange gelatin
2 (10-ounce) packages
   frozen strawberries,
   thawed and drained

1 quart vanilla
   ice cream, softened
1 (10-ounce) package
   frozen blueberries,
   thawed and drained
2 (11-ounce) cans
   mandarin oranges,
   drained

Divide the cake into 3 equal portions. Tear each portion into bite-size pieces and place in 3 bowls. Pour one flavor of gelatin in each bowl and toss to coat. Arrange the strawberry cake pieces in the bottom of an ungreased tube or bundt cake pan. Cover with the strawberries. Top with ⅓ of the ice cream. Layer the lime cake pieces, blueberries, ⅓ of the ice cream, orange cake pieces, mandarin oranges and the remaining ice cream. Freeze, covered, until firm. Invert onto a serving plate. Yield: 12 servings.

Kam Boles, Xi Omega
Highlands Ranch, Colorado

CHOCOLATE COCONUT DESSERT

1 cup (6 ounces)
   semisweet
   chocolate chips
1 (12-ounce) can
   evaporated milk
5 cups miniature
   marshmallows

6 tablespoons butter
1⅓ cups flaked coconut
2 cups crisp rice cereal,
   crushed
1 cup chopped nuts
½ gallon vanilla
   ice cream

Combine the chocolate chips and evaporated milk in a small saucepan over low heat. Bring to a boil, stirring constantly. Simmer for 4 minutes or until thick. Add the marshmallows and stir until smooth. Cool completely. Melt the butter in a skillet and stir in the coconut. Cook over medium heat until lightly browned, stirring constantly. Add the cereal and nuts. Spread 3 cups of the cereal mixture in a 9×13-inch dish. Cut the block of ice cream lengthwise into two halves; cut each half into 12 slices. Arrange 12 ice cream slices over the cereal layer. Spread half the chocolate sauce over the top. Layer with the remaining ice cream slices, chocolate sauce and cereal mixture. Freeze until firm. Remove from the freezer 5 to 10 minutes before serving. Yield: 16 servings.

Rhea Roantree, Preceptor
Gananoque, Ontario, Canada

COCONUT SHERBET DELIGHT

1 (16-ounce) package
   macaroons,
   coarsely crumbled
1½ cups chopped pecans
   or walnuts

18 ounces whipped
   topping
2 quarts sherbet,
   softened (any flavor)

Combine the macaroon crumbs and pecans in a large bowl and mix well. Fold in the whipped topping. Spread half the mixture across the bottom of a 9×13-inch dish. Freeze until firm. Spread the sherbet over the frozen layer. Freeze until firm. Top with the remaining whipped topping mixture and freeze until ready to serve. Yield: 15 servings.

Shirley Slater, Theta Master
Great Bend, Kansas

FROZEN CRANBERRY AND PINEAPPLE SQUARES

1 (14-ounce) can
   sweetened
   condensed milk
¼ cup lemon juice
1 (20-ounce) can crushed
   pineapple, drained
1 (16-ounce) can whole
   cranberry sauce

2 cups miniature
   marshmallows
½ cup chopped pecans
Red food coloring
   (optional)
8 ounces whipped
   topping

Mix the condensed milk and lemon juice in a bowl. Stir in the next 5 ingredients. Fold in the whipped topping. Spoon into a 9×13-inch dish. Freeze until firm. Cut into squares. Yield: 12 to 16 servings.

Mildred Sharp, Kappa Master
McClave, Colorado

FROZEN CRANBERRY BANANA SALAD

1 (20-ounce) can
   pineapple tidbits
5 firm bananas
1 (16-ounce) can whole-
   berry cranberry sauce

½ cup sugar
½ cup chopped walnuts
12 ounces whipped
   topping

Drain the pineapple, reserving the juice. Cut the bananas lengthwise and slice into bite-size pieces. Combine the bananas and reserved pineapple juice in a medium bowl. Mix the cranberry sauce and sugar in a large bowl. Drain the bananas. Add to the cranberry mixture and mix well. Stir in the pineapple and walnuts. Fold in the whipped topping. Spoon into a 9×13-inch dish. Freeze until firm. Remove from the freezer 15 to 20 minutes before serving. Cut into squares. Yield: 12 to 16 servings.

Carolyn P. Rice, Gamma Master
Vero Beach, Florida

DRUMSTICK DESSERT

1½ cups graham
   cracker crumbs
½ cup chopped
   unsalted peanuts
¼ cup (½ stick)
   butter, melted
2 tablespoons
   peanut butter
8 ounces cream cheese,
   softened

½ cup sugar
½ cup peanut butter
1 teaspoon vanilla
   extract
3 eggs
12 ounces whipped
   topping
8 teaspoons chocolate
   syrup

Combine the graham cracker crumbs, peanuts, butter and 2 tablespoons peanut butter in a bowl and mix well. Press onto the bottom of a 9×13-inch dish, reserving a small amount for garnish. Combine the cream cheese, sugar, ½ cup peanut butter and vanilla in a large bowl and mix well. Add the eggs 1 at a time, beating well after each addition. Fold in the whipped topping. Spread over the crumb layer. Drizzle with the chocolate syrup and swirl with a knife to marbleize. Sprinkle with the reserved crumb mixture. Freeze until firm. Remove from the freezer 1 hour before serving. Note: If you are concerned about using raw eggs, use eggs pasteurized in their shells or use an equivalent amount of pasteurized egg substitute. Yield: 10 servings.

Arlene Wagner, Mu
Santa Monica, California

FROZEN FRUIT CUPS

2 cups sour cream, or
   1 cup sour cream and
   1 cup plain yogurt
2 tablespoons lemon
   juice
¾ cup sugar
⅛ teaspoon salt

1 (8-ounce) can crushed
   pineapple, drained
¼ cup chopped
   maraschino cherries
3 bananas, chopped
¼ cup chopped pecans

Combine the sour cream, lemon juice, sugar and salt in a large bowl and mix well. Stir in the pineapple, cherries, bananas and pecans. Spoon into paper-lined muffin cups. Freeze until firm. Store in plastic freezer bags. Yield: 18 fruit cups.

Beverly Moore, Preceptor Alpha Beta
Horn Lake, Mississippi

FRUIT FREEZIES

Try the recipe with different fruit combinations, such as watermelon and strawberries, or pears and blackberries.

1 can peaches, drained
1 cup raspberries

1 tablespoon honey
1 teaspoon lemon juice

Process the peaches in a blender until smooth. Add the raspberries, honey and lemon juice and process until smooth. Pour into a 10×15-inch pan and freeze until almost firm. Cut into wedges or scoop with a melon baller to serve. Yield: 5 to 6 servings.

Annette Thivierge, Xi Iota
Lewiston, Idaho

FROZEN FRUIT SALAD

8 ounces cream cheese,
   softened
¾ cup sugar
3 large bananas, chopped
1 (20-ounce) can crushed
   pineapple, drained

1 (16-ounce) package
   frozen strawberries,
   thawed and drained
12 ounces whipped
   topping

Beat the cream cheese and sugar in a large bowl until light and fluffy. Fold in the bananas, pineapple, strawberries and whipped topping. Spoon into a 9×13-inch dish. Freeze until firm. Remove from the freezer 30 minutes before serving. Yield: 8 to 10 servings.

Lynnette Robinson, Preceptor Lambda Iota
New Bloomfield, Missouri

MILK CHOCOLATE ALMOND DELIGHT

1½ cups graham
   cracker crumbs
¼ cup sugar
¼ cup (½ stick) butter
   or margarine,
   melted
20 large marshmallows
½ cup milk

1 (7-ounce) bar milk
   chocolate with
   almonds, chopped
9 ounces whipped
   topping
1 (10-ounce) package
   frozen strawberries,
   thawed and puréed

Combine the graham cracker crumbs, sugar and butter in a bowl and mix well. Press onto the bottom of a foil-lined 8×8-inch dish. Combine the marshmallows and milk in a saucepan over simmering water, stirring constantly until smooth. Remove from the heat. Add the chocolate and stir until smooth. Cool completely. Fold in 2¼ cups of the whipped topping. Spread over the prepared crust. Freeze, covered, for 1 hour. Place the remaining whipped topping in a bowl. Fold in ½ cup of the strawberry purée. Spread over the chocolate layer. Freeze, covered, for several hours. Cut into squares. Spoon a small amount of the remaining strawberry purée over each serving. Yield: 9 to 12 servings.

Marilou Martell, Laureate Beta Phi
Mountlake Terrace, Washington

ICE CREAM BARS

2 cups Honey Nut Chex cereal, crushed	1/2 cup chopped walnuts
1 cup flaked coconut	1/2 cup (1 stick) butter, melted
3/4 cup packed brown sugar	1/2 gallon French vanilla ice cream, softened

Combine the cereal, coconut, brown sugar, walnuts and butter in a large bowl and mix well. Press onto the bottom of a greased 9×13-inch dish, reserving a a small amount for garnish. Spread the ice cream over the top and sprinkle with the reserved cereal mixture. Freeze until firm. Cut into bars.
Yield: 10 servings.

Jane St. Germain, Xi Theta Alpha
Stoney Creek, Ontario, Canada

COOKIES AND CREAM DELIGHT

When I made this for a family birthday party, my chocolate-loving son-in-law said that it was the best chocolate cake he'd ever eaten.

2 cups crushed chocolate sandwich cookies	1 (12-ounce) can evaporated milk
1/2 cup (1 stick) butter or margarine, melted	1/2 cup (1 stick) butter or margarine
1/2 cup granulated sugar	1 teaspoon vanilla extract
1/2 gallon chocolate, coffee, or vanilla ice cream, softened	1 1/2 cups salted peanuts
2 cups confectioners' sugar	8 ounces whipped topping
2/3 cup (4 ounces) semisweet chocolate chips	1/2 cup crushed chocolate sandwich cookies

Combine 2 cups cookie crumbs, 1/2 cup melted butter and the granulated sugar in a bowl and mix well. Press onto the bottom of an ungreased 9×13-inch dish. Freeze for 15 minutes. Spread the ice cream over the prepared crust. Freeze for 3 hours or until firm. Combine the confectioners' sugar, chocolate chips, evaporated milk and 1/2 cup butter in a saucepan. Cook over medium heat, stirring often. Bring to a boil. Lower the heat and simmer for 8 minutes, stirring occasionally. Remove from the heat and stir in the vanilla. Cool completely. Spoon over the ice cream layer and sprinkle with peanuts. Freeze until firm. Spread the whipped topping over the top and sprinkle with 1/2 cup cookie crumbs. Freeze, tightly covered, for at least 3 hours before serving.
Yield: 12 to 16 servings.

Mary Ann Engelmann, Psi Mu
Pembroke Pines, Florida

COCONUT ALMOND ICE CREAM DESSERT

2 cups graham cracker crumbs	1 (14-ounce) can sweetened condensed milk
1/2 cup (1 stick) butter, melted	Shredded coconut, toasted
8 ounces cream cheese, softened	Sliced almonds, toasted
24 ounces whipped topping	

Combine the graham cracker crumbs and butter in a small bowl and mix well. Press onto the bottom of large springform pan. Combine the cream cheese, whipped topping and condensed milk in a mixing bowl and beat until smooth. Spread over the crumb layer. Sprinkle with coconut and almonds. Freeze until firm. Remove from the freezer 5 minutes before serving. Yield: 12 to 15 servings.

Hilda G. MacLaughlan, Laureate Lambda
Lower Sackville, Nova Scotia, Canada

BUTTER PECAN ICE CREAM DESSERT

1 cup graham cracker crumbs	2 (3-ounce) packages vanilla instant pudding mix
1 cup crushed soda crackers	1/2 gallon butter pecan ice cream, softened
1/2 cup (1 stick) butter, melted	8 ounces whipped topping
1 1/2 cups milk	

Combine the graham cracker crumbs, crushed soda crackers and butter in a bowl and mix well. Press onto the bottom of a 9×13-inch baking dish. Bake at 350 degrees for 10 minutes. Cool completely. Combine the pudding mix and milk in a large bowl and mix well. Stir in the ice cream. Spread over the cooled crust and cover with whipped topping. Chill in the refrigerator if serving the same day or freeze for later use. Yield: 16 to 20 servings.

Evelyn Ickes, Laureate Delta Rho
Alliance, Ohio

CARAMEL PECAN ICE CREAM DESSERT

1 3/4 cups all-purpose flour	1 cup (2 sticks) butter, melted
1 cup chopped pecans	1 1/2 cups caramel topping
1 cup packed brown sugar	1/2 gallon vanilla or butterscotch ripple ice cream, softened
1 cup rolled oats	

Combine the flour, pecans, brown sugar and oats in a bowl. Stir in the butter and mix well. Spread on a large baking sheet with sides. Bake at 400 degrees for

15 minutes or just until golden, stirring occasionally. Cool completely. Press half the crumb mixture onto the bottom of a 9×13-inch dish. Drizzle with half the caramel topping. Spread the ice cream over the caramel. Sprinkle with the remaining crumb mixture and drizzle with the remaining caramel topping. Freeze, covered, until firm. Cut into squares. Yield: 10 to 12 servings.

Patricia Wilson, Xi Alpha Mu
Belleville, Ontario, Canada

CHOCOLATE CINNAMON ICE CREAM

My Indiana chapter did an ice cream project that got me interested in recipes that don't require an ice cream maker.

4 egg yolks
1/4 cup light corn syrup
4 ounces semisweet
 chocolate, melted

1 cup heavy whipping
 cream, whipped
1/2 teaspoon cinnamon

Beat the egg yolks lightly in a saucepan. Stir in the corn syrup and melted chocolate. Place over simmering water. Cook until thickened, stirring occasionally. Cool. Fold in the whipped cream and cinnamon. Pour into a freezer container and freeze until firm. Yield: 1 1/4 pints.

Sharon Rutherford, Alpha Omicron Theta
Cleburne, Texas

COCONUT ICE CREAM DESSERT

2 cups vanilla
 wafer crumbs
1/2 cup (1 stick) butter,
 melted
3 tablespoons sugar
2 (3-ounce) packages
 coconut instant
 pudding mix
1 1/2 cups milk

1 quart vanilla ice
 cream, softened
8 ounces whipped
 topping
3/4 cup vanilla
 wafer crumbs
1 cup chopped nuts
1/2 cup chopped
 maraschino cherries

Combine 2 cups vanilla wafer crumbs, the butter and sugar in a bowl and mix well. Pat onto the bottom of a 9×13-inch dish. Combine the pudding mix and milk in a large bowl and mix well. Stir in the ice cream. Spread over the prepared crust. Cover with whipped topping. Sprinkle with 3/4 cup vanilla wafer crumbs, the nuts and cherries. Freeze until firm. Remove from the freezer just before serving. Yield: 15 servings.

Dorothy Miles, Laureate Alpha Rho
Cape Girardeau, Missouri

CRUNCHY ICE CREAM DESSERT

3 cups crisp rice cereal
1 cup packed
 brown sugar
1 cup shredded coconut
1 (3-ounce) bag sliced
 almonds

1/2 cup (1 stick) butter,
 melted
1/2 gallon chocolate
 ripple ice cream

Combine the rice cereal, brown sugar, coconut, almonds and butter in a large bowl and mix well. Spread evenly across a greased baking sheet. Bake at 300 degrees for 20 minutes. Cool completely. Press half the cereal mixture onto the bottom of a greased 9×13-inch dish. Slice the block of ice cream into serving-size pieces and arrange over the cereal layer. Top with the remaining cereal mixture. Freeze until firm. Yield: 10 to 12 servings.

Shirley Balasko, Preceptor Beta Phi
Centennial, Colorado

RAINBOW ICE CREAM MOLD

1/2 gallon vanilla ice
 cream, softened
1 pint orange sherbet

1 pint lime sherbet
1 pint lemon sherbet

Spread 1 cup of the vanilla ice cream over the bottom of a bundt pan. Scoop the orange, lime and lemon sherbets into golf ball-size balls. Place 1/3 of the balls over the vanilla ice cream layer. Continue laying the ice cream and sherbet balls 1/3 at a time, pressing firmly on each layer and ending with the ice cream. Smooth the top. Freeze, covered, until just before serving. Dip the mold in warm water and invert onto a serving plate. Yield: 15 to 20 servings.

Diane Summerfield, Xi Alpha Gamma Lambda
Corsicana, Texas

OLD-FASHIONED VANILLA ICE CREAM

4 eggs
2 1/2 cups sugar
2 tablespoons vanilla
 extract

4 cups half-and-half
1/4 teaspoon salt
5 cups (about) milk

Beat the eggs in a mixing bowl until foamy. Add the sugar gradually, beating until thickened. Beat in the vanilla, half-and-half and salt. Pour into an ice cream freezer container; add milk to the fill line and stir well. Freeze using the manufacturer's directions. Serve with strawberries or other toppings. Note: If you are concerned about using raw eggs, use eggs pasteurized in their shells or use an equivalent amount of pasteurized egg substitute. Yield: 4 quarts.

Janice Carter, Xi Gamma Epsilon
Mohave Valley, Arizona

❖ RASPBERRY ICE CREAM DESSERT

2 cups crisp rice cereal
1 cup packed
    brown sugar
1 cup shredded coconut
1 cup chopped walnuts
1/2 cup (1 stick) butter,
    melted

1/2 gallon vanilla ice
    cream, softened
2 (10-ounce) bags frozen
    raspberries
2 tablespoons
    granulated sugar

Combine the cereal, brown sugar, coconut, walnuts and butter in a large bowl and mix well. Press half the cereal mixture onto the bottom of a 9×13-inch dish. Spread the ice cream evenly over the cereal layer. Top with the remaining cereal mixture. Freeze until firm. Cut into squares. Combine the raspberries and sugar in a saucepan. Cook over low heat until warm, adding a little cornstarch dissolved in water to thicken if necessary. You can use fresh raspberries instead of the raspberry sauce. Yield: 15 servings.

Kimberly Pague, Delta Alpha Nu
Orange, California

TOFFEE ICE CREAM SANDWICH DESSERT

12 ice cream sandwiches
8 ounces whipped
    topping

1 jar caramel topping
1/3 cup (2 ounces)
    toffee bits

Line a 9×12-inch dish with the ice cream sandwiches. Cover with whipped topping. Drizzle with caramel topping, Sprinkle with toffee bits. Freeze until firm. Yield: 6 to 8 servings.

Bonna Goode, Laureate Upsilon
Utica, Kentucky

ICE CREAM SANDWICH DESSERT

12 ice cream
    sandwiches
6 ounces caramel
    topping

6 ounces chocolate
    topping
8 ounces whipped
    topping

Line a 9×13-inch dish with the ice cream sandwiches. Drizzle with the caramel and chocolate toppings. Cover with the whipped topping. Drizzle with additional caramel topping if desired. Freeze until firm. Yield: 20 servings.

Carole Smock, Preceptor Alpha Epsilon
Bowling Green, Kentucky

MALTED MILK BALL DESSERT

1 small package
    malted milk balls,
    crushed

12 ounces whipped
    topping
12 ice cream sandwiches

Combine 3/4 of the malted milk balls with the whipped topping in a bowl and mix well. Line a 9×13-inch dish with the ice cream sand-wiches, cutting them lengthwise to fit. Top with the whipped topping mixture. Sprinkle with the remaining crushed malted milk balls. Freeze, covered, until firm. Yield: 12 to 15 servings.

Cathy Gilliland, Alpha Kappa
Rose Hill, Iowa

FROZEN KOOL-AID DESSERT

This is such a tasty dessert that no one will believe that it's made with Kool-Aid. And with so many flavors to choose from, you can make it to suit individual tastes.

1 envelope Kool-Aid
    drink mix
    (any flavor)
1 cup sugar

2 cups milk
1 cup heavy whipping
    cream

Combine the drink mix, sugar and milk in a bowl and stir until the drink mix and sugar dissolve. Pour into a freezer container and freeze for 1 hour or until slushy. Whip the cream in a mixing bowl until stiff peaks form. Add the slushy mixture and beat just until combined. Pour into the freezer container and freeze for 2 hours or until firm. Yield: 6 to 8 servings.

Gina Marie Aleo, Laureate Epsilon Zeta
Wilkes-Barre, Pennsylvania

FLORENTINE LEMON CREAM

We have an abundance of lemons here in Napa, and this recipe is a good way to use them up.

4 or 5 Meyer lemons
    (about 1 cup juice)
2 cups sugar
1 cup milk

2 cups nonfat
    half-and-half
1 cup heavy whipping
    cream

Grate the lemon zest. Juice the lemons. Combine the zest, sugar, milk and half-and-half in a large saucepan. Cook over low heat just until the sugar dissolves, stirring often. Do not boil. Pour into a stainless steel bowl. Chill, covered, for 1 hour or longer. Stir the lemon juice slowly into the chilled milk mixture. Whip the cream in a mixing bowl until stiff peaks form. Fold into the lemon mixture. Freeze for 5 hours or longer, stirring occasionally during the first few hours. Scoop the lemon cream into individual serving dishes and garnish with curls of lemon zest or mint sprigs. Yield: 8 to 10 servings.

Wendy Bennett, Xi Pi Rho
Napa, California

ICED LEMON CREAM

1 cup heavy whipping
  cream
1³/4 cups sugar

2 cups milk
Juice of 2 lemons
Grated zest of 2 lemons

Whip the cream in a chilled mixing bowl until soft peaks form. Stir in the sugar, milk, lemon juice and zest. Pour into a 5-cup container. Freeze, covered, for 6 hours. Spoon the mixture into a food processor and process until smooth. Pour into a serving dish or ramekins and freeze until firm. Yield: 10 servings.

Claire Swinhoe, Preceptor Beta
Los Alamos, New Mexico

FRESH LEMON FREEZE

This dessert is especially refreshing after a heavy meal.

6 large lemons
2 cups half-and-half
1 cup sugar

1¹/2 tablespoons grated
  lemon zest

Cut off the top third of the lemons. Scoop out the pulp. Strain to obtain ¹/2 cup juice. Combine the half-and-half and sugar in a bowl and mix until the sugar dissolves. Add the lemon juice and zest and mix well. Pour into a loaf pan and freeze for 2 to 3 hours. Spoon the frozen mixture into a mixing bowl and beat until smooth. Spoon into the hollow lemons. Place the filled lemons upright in a tray and freeze until firm. Yield: 6 servings.

Carol Darlington, Nu Eta
Asbury, Missouri

LIME GRANITA

3 cups water
³/4 cup sugar
¹/2 cup lime juice

1 teaspoon (or more)
  grated lime zest

Combine the water, sugar, lime juice and lime zest in a saucepan. Cook over medium heat, stirring occasionally. Bring to a gentle boil. Pour into a 9×13-inch dish. Freeze for 2 hours, stirring the mixture every 30 minutes. Spoon the frozen mixture into a plastic container and store in the freezer. Fluff with a fork and spoon into martini glasses. Garnish with a twist of lime. Yield: 6 to 8 servings.

Kris Weishaupt, Preceptor Omicron
Trail, British Columbia, Canada

"MELON" SURPRISE

1 quart lime sherbet,
  softened
¹/2 gallon strawberry ice
  cream, softened

1 cup (6 ounces)
  miniature
  chocolate chips

Spread the sherbet across a large round plastic bowl, forming a 1-inch thick shell. Freeze until firm. Combine the ice cream and chocolate chips in a bowl and mix well. Spoon into the sherbet shell. Freeze, covered, until firm. Invert onto a serving plate and slice. Yield: 8 servings.

Dottie Smith, Xi Epsilon
New Smyrna Beach, Florida

ORANGE BOMBE

Try varying this recipe with your own favorite flavors of sherbet and ice cream.

¹/2 cup raisins
¹/2 cup brandy
1 pint orange sherbet,
  softened

1 quart vanilla
  ice cream, softened

Combine the raisins and brandy in a small bowl. Let stand, covered, at room temperature for 1 to 3 days. Spread the sherbet across a 6-cup bowl or round mold, forming a thick shell. Freeze until firm. Drain the raisins. Place in a bowl with the ice cream and mix well. Pack into the center of the mold. Freeze, covered with foil, until firm. Unmold onto a serving plate. Slice and pour 1 or more spoonfuls of brandy over each serving. Yield: 6 to 8 servings.

Lettice Thompson, Rho Master
Victoria, British Columbia, Canada

DECADENT PEANUT BUTTER DESSERT

1 cup graham cracker
  crumbs
¹/4 cup (¹/2 stick) butter,
  melted
³/4 cup chunky peanut
  butter

4 ounces white
  chocolate
¹/2 gallon vanilla ice
  cream, softened

Combine the graham cracker crumbs and butter in a small bowl and mix well. Press onto the bottom of a 9×9-inch dish, reserving a small amount for garnish. Place the peanut butter and white chocolate in a microwave-safe dish. Microwave on Medium for 2¹/2 minutes, stirring once or twice. Reserve 2 tablespoons. Pour the remaining peanut butter mixture into a bowl. Add the ice cream and mix until smooth. Spoon over the prepared crust and freeze until firm. Drizzle with the reserved peanut butter mixture and sprinkle with the reserved crumb topping. Yield: 6 to 8 servings.

Marie Glaves, Beta Kappa Master
Dunnville, Ontario, Canada

PEANUT BUTTER AND CHOCOLATE RIBBON DESSERT

This is a great way to enjoy the taste of peanut butter and chocolate without having to turn on my oven in the summer.

8 peanut butter
   sandwich cookies,
   crushed
2 tablespoons butter,
   melted
8 ounces cream cheese,
   softened
1/2 cup peanut butter
1/2 cup sugar

2 teaspoons vanilla
   extract
12 ounces whipped
   topping
2 ounces semisweet
   chocolate, melted
4 peanut butter
   sandwich cookies,
   crushed

Combine 8 crushed cookies and the butter in a bowl and mix well. Press onto the bottom of a foil-lined 5×9-inch loaf pan. Combine the cream cheese, peanut butter, sugar and vanilla in a mixing bowl and beat until smooth. Fold in 3 cups of the whipped topping. Combine half the cream cheese mixture with the melted chocolate in a small bowl and mix well. Layer half the remaining cream cheese mixture, the chocolate mixture and the remaining cream cheese mixture over the prepared crust. Freeze for 4 hours or until firm. Invert onto a tray and remove the foil. Invert again onto a serving plate. Top with the remaining whipped topping. Sprinkle with 4 crushed cookies. Yield: 12 servings.

Kelly Smolek, Zeta Chi
Idaville, Indiana

FROZEN PEPPERMINT DELIGHT

I serve this pretty, festive dessert for Christmas. Both adults and children ask for seconds.

1 (14-ounce) package
   chocolate sandwich
   cookies, crushed
1/2 cup (1 stick) butter,
   melted
1 gallon peppermint
   ice cream, softened

12 ounces whipped
   topping
1 (12-ounce) jar hot
   fudge topping,
   warmed
Crushed peppermint
   candy

Combine the crushed cookies and butter in a bowl and mix well. Press onto the bottom of an ungreased 9×13-inch dish. Layer the ice cream and whipped topping over the crumb layer. Freeze, covered, for up to 2 months. Drizzle with the hot fudge topping and sprinkle with peppermint candy.
Yield: 12 to 15 servings.

Pat Ward, Laureate Delta Kappa
Oakville, Ontario, Canada

CHEESECAKE PIE

1/4 cup (1/2 stick)
   margarine
1 (7-ounce) package
   shredded coconut
1 1/2 cups chopped pecans
1 (14-ounce) can
   sweetened
   condensed milk

8 ounces cream cheese,
   softened
16 ounces whipped
   topping
2 graham cracker pie
   shells
1 or 2 jars caramel
   topping

Melt the margarine in a large skillet over medium-high heat. Stir in the coconut and pecans. Cook until browned, stirring constantly. Combine the sweetened condensed milk and cream cheese in a mixing bowl and beat until smooth. Fold in the whipped topping. Spoon 1/4 of the cream cheese mixture into each of the pie shells. Sprinkle each with 1/4 of the toasted coconut and pecans. Top with the desired amount of caramel topping. Repeat the layers. Freeze for 4 hours or longer. Remove from the freezer 10 to 15 minutes before serving. Yield: 12 to 16 servings.

Angie Torbett, Iota Sigma
Englewood, Tennessee

CHOCOLATE MINT PIE

15 chocolate mint
   sandwich cookies,
   crushed
1 quart coffee ice cream,
   softened

1/2 cup (3 ounces)
   semisweet
   chocolate chips
3 tablespoons heavy
   whipping cream or
   condensed milk

Press the cookie crumbs onto the bottom and up the side of a greased 9-inch pie plate. Bake at 350 degrees for 10 minutes. Cool completely. Spread the ice cream over the crumb layer. Freeze, covered, with wax paper, until firm. Melt the chocolate chips in a small saucepan over low heat and stir in the cream. Spread over the ice cream layer. Freeze until firm. Remove from the freezer just before serving. Yield: 8 servings.

Elizabeth Bateman, Xi Eta Rho
Hampton, Ontario, Canada

CRUNCHY ICE CREAM PIE

The crunchy coconut base gives this dessert a different taste. I served this at a family gathering instead of a birthday cake and it was a hit.

3/4 cup (1 1/2 sticks)
   butter, softened
3/4 cup packed brown
   sugar
1 cup chopped pecans

3 cups cornflakes,
   lightly crushed
1 cup shredded coconut
1 quart vanilla ice
   cream, softened

Beat the butter and brown sugar in a bowl until light and fluffy. Stir in the pecans, cornflakes and coconut. Press 2/3 of the cornflake mixture onto the bottom and up the side of a 9-inch pie plate. Spread the ice cream over the cornflake layer. Sprinkle with the remaining cornflake mixture. Freeze until firm. Yield: 8 servings.

Marina Cram, Xi Zeta
Brandon, Manitoba, Canada

FROZEN CREAM PIE

I make several of these pies at one time and keep them on hand in my freezer. There is always one to pull out when company drops by or to take to friends and family gatherings.

8 ounces cream cheese, softened
1 (14-ounce) can sweetened condensed milk
8 ounces whipped topping
1 graham cracker pie shell
1 jar caramel topping
1 cup toasted shredded coconut
1 cup toasted chopped pecans

Combine the cream cheese and condensed milk in a mixing bowl and mix well. Fold in the whipped topping. Spoon half the mixture into the pie shell. Drizzle with the desired amount of caramel topping. Sprinkle with half the coconut and half the pecans. Repeat the layers. Freeze, covered, until firm. Serve frozen. Yield: 8 servings.

Trina Jackson, Beta Eta
Hamlin, West Virginia

LEMON FREEZER PIE

1 (3-ounce) package sugar-free instant vanilla pudding mix
1 cup milk (2% or less)
8 ounces fat-free cream cheese, softened
1 envelope sugar-free lemonade drink mix
8 ounces fat-free whipped topping
10 sugar-free lemon sandwich cookies, crushed
1 low-fat graham cracker pie shell

Whisk the pudding mix and milk together in a bowl. Combine the cream cheese and drink mix in a mixing bowl and beat until smooth. Beat in the pudding mixture. Fold in 1/3 of the whipped topping. Fold in the cookie crumbs, reserving a small amount for garnish. Fold in the remaining whipped topping. Spoon into the pie shell and sprinkle with the reserved cookie crumbs. Freeze for 3 hours. Remove from the freezer 15 minutes before serving.
Yield: 6 to 8 servings.

Shirley Arseneau, Preceptor Delta Upsilon
Huber Heights, Ohio

MUDSLIDE PIE

1 1/2 quarts vanilla ice cream, softened
2 ounces Kahlúa
1 baked (9-inch) pie shell
Chocolate syrup
Whipped topping

Combine the ice cream and Kahlúa in a bowl and mix well. Spoon into the pie shell. Drizzle with chocolate syrup. Freeze until firm. Serve with whipped topping. Yield: 6 to 8 servings.

Celia Mendieta, Preceptor Epsilon
Cache, Oklahoma

ORANGE ICE CREAM PIE

1/2 cup sweetened orange drink mix
1/2 cup warm water
1 pint vanilla ice cream, softened
8 ounces whipped topping
1 (9-inch) graham cracker pie shell

Dissolve the drink mix in the water in a large bowl. Stir in the ice cream. Fold in the whipped topping. Pour into the pie shell and freeze until firm. Store in the freezer for up to 2 months. Yield: 8 servings.

Gloria Nolan, Preceptor Omicron Sigma
Flower Mound, Texas

FROZEN PEANUT BUTTER PIE

8 ounces whipped topping
1 (9-inch) graham cracker pie shell
1/2 cup chunky peanut butter
1 cup cold milk
1 (3-ounce) package vanilla instant pudding mix

Spread 1 cup of the whipped topping in the pie shell. Freeze for 10 minutes. Beat the peanut butter in a bowl. Add the milk gradually, beating well after each addition. Add the pudding mix and beat on low for 1 to 2 minutes. Fold in the remaining whipped topping. Spoon into the pie shell. Freeze for 4 hours or until firm. Garnish with whipped cream and chopped nuts if desired. Yield: 8 servings.

Chrissy John, Beta
Terre Haute, Indiana

---

*Virginia M. Lee, Laureate Eta Nu, Houston, Texas, makes a fast **Frozen Amaretto** by combining amaretto and softened French vanilla ice cream. She mixes 1 1/2 ounces of the liqueur with 2 scoops ice cream in a bowl. She spoons the mixture into large martini glasses and freezes until set. Just before serving, she adds a pirouline cookie to each glass.*

RASPBERRY SQUARES

1/2 cup (1 stick) margarine, softened	*1 cup boiling water*
1 cup all-purpose flour	*1 (14-ounce) package frozen raspberries*
2 tablespoons granulated or brown sugar	*32 large marshmallows*
1 (3-ounce) package raspberry gelatin	*1/2 cup milk*
	1 cup whipped cream

Combine the margarine, flour and sugar in a bowl and mix well. Press onto the bottom of a 9×9-inch baking dish. Bake at 350 degrees for 10 minutes. Cool completely and freeze until firm. Combine the gelatin, water and frozen raspberries in a large bowl and stir until syrupy. Pour over the frozen base. Microwave the marshmallows and milk in a microwave-proof dish, stirring occasionally until melted. Cool completely. Fold in the whipped cream. Spread over the raspberry layer. Freeze until firm. Cut into squares. Yield: 9 to 10 servings.

Isobel Burnstad, Alpha Sigma Master
Langley, British Columbia, Canada

SNICKER PIE

1/2 gallon fat-free vanilla ice cream, softened	*8 ounces fat-free whipped topping*
2 (4-ounce) packages chocolate instant pudding mix	*1/2 cup chunky peanut butter*
	1 (9-inch) graham cracker pie shell

Combine the ice cream, pudding mix, whipped topping and peanut butter in a large mixing bowl and mix well. Pour into the pie shell. Freeze for 2 hours or longer. Yield: 6 to 8 servings.

Kathryn D. Brown, Laureate Epsilon Theta
St. Petersburg, Florida

SNICKER SQUARES

1 pint chocolate fat-free frozen yogurt, softened	*1 small package sugar-free fat-free chocolate instant pudding mix*
1 cup fat-free whipped topping	*1/4 cup peanut butter Confectioners' sugar*

Combine the frozen yogurt, whipped topping, pudding mix and peanut butter in a large bowl and mix well. Spoon into an 8×8-inch dish. Freeze for 2 hours. Cut into squares and dust lightly with confectioners' sugar. Yield: 6 to 8 servings.

Ramona Brown, Preceptor Alpha Delta
Henderson, Nevada

SPUMONI

This is a traditional Italian treat for special occasions.

3 pints chocolate ice cream, softened	*1/2 pound mixed candied fruit*
1 pint pistachio ice cream, softened	*2 teaspoons rum extract*
2 pints vanilla ice cream, softened	*1 1/2 cups heavy whipping cream, whipped (optional)*

Place a 2 1/2-cup melon mold in the freezer. Beat the chocolate ice cream in a mixing bowl until smooth. Spread across the mold, forming a 1-inch shell. Freeze until firm. Beat the pistachio ice cream in a bowl until smooth. Spread evenly over the chocolate layer. Freeze until firm. Combine the vanilla ice cream, candied fruit and rum flavoring and mix well. Pack into the center of the mold. Freeze until firm. Invert onto a serving plate and decorate with the whipped cream. Yield: 12 servings.

Donna Clapton, Preceptor Delta Alpha
Revelstoke, British Colombia, Canada

PHONY SPUMONI

1 quart vanilla ice cream, softened	*1/3 cup quartered red and green maraschino cherries*
8 ounces whipped topping	*1 tablespoon chopped toasted almonds*
1 tablespoon chopped candied orange peel	

Spread the ice cream across the bottom and side of a 6-cup mold or 4×8-inch dish. Freeze until almost firm. Place the whipped topping in a bowl. Fold in the orange peel, cherries and almonds. Spoon into the ice cream shell. Freeze for 8 hours or longer. Invert onto a serving plate. Yield: 6 to 8 servings.

Shirley J. Bird, Xi Alpha Nu
Eureka Springs, Arkansas

FROZEN STRAWBERRY PIE

2 (16-ounce) packages frozen strawberries	*1 (6-ounce) package strawberry gelatin*
1 (14-ounce) can sweetened condensed milk	*8 ounces whipped topping*
	2 (9-inch) graham cracker pie shells

Combine the strawberries, condensed milk and gelatin and mix well. Fold in the whipped topping. Pour into the pie shells. Freeze for 8 to 10 hours. Yield: 16 servings.

Nancy Barton, Laureate Zeta Xi
Austin, Texas

❖ FROZEN STRAWBERRY MARGARITA PIE

1¼ cups finely crushed pretzels
½ cup (1 stick) plus 2 tablespoons butter, melted
¼ cup sugar
1 (14-ounce) can sweetened condensed milk
1 cup sliced strawberries (can use frozen)

¼ cup lime juice concentrate
3 to 4 tablespoons tequila
2 tablespoons orange-flavored liqueur
2 to 4 drops red food coloring
1 cup heavy whipping cream, whipped

Mix the pretzel crumbs, butter and sugar in a bowl. Press onto the bottom and side of a lightly buttered 9-inch pie plate. Combine the next 6 ingredients in a large bowl and mix well. Fold in the whipped cream. Spoon over the pretzel layer. Freeze for 4 hours or until firm. Remove from the freezer 10 minutes before serving. Yield: 8 to 10 servings.

Storm Gonzalez, Delta Omega
Albuquerque, New Mexico

TEXAS-SIZE SUNDAES

This was a favorite dessert of mine at Crystal's Restaurant in Corpus Christi, Texas, that closed last winter after many years of serving our area.

12 flour tortillas
Vegetable oil
½ gallon vanilla ice cream

1 jar hot fudge or caramel topping
8 ounces whipped cream
1 cup chopped nuts

Fry the tortilla shells in hot oil, pressing the center of the tortillas down to form a bowl shape; drain on paper towels and cool completely. Fill each tortilla bowl with the desired amount of ice cream. Top with hot fudge or caramel topping, whipped cream and chopped nuts. Yield: 12 sundaes.

Barbara Bond, Delta Kappa Master
Corpus Christi, Texas

TIA MARIA PIE

1 quart coffee ice cream, softened
2 ounces Tia Maria coffee liqueur
1 (9-inch) graham cracker pie shell

1 (22-ounce) bottle chocolate syrup
1 cup chopped pecans

Combine the ice cream and liqueur in a bowl and mix well. Spoon into the pie shell. Freeze until firm. Pour a thin layer of chocolate syrup over the pie and sprinkle with the pecans. Freeze until just before serving. Yield: 8 servings.

Catherine Neville, Preceptor Zeta
Vero Beach, Florida

WHITE CHOCOLATE MOUSSE PIE

This pie is well worth the extra effort it takes. If you don't have a springform pan, use two pie plates.

1 (12-ounce) package vanilla wafers, finely crushed
½ cup (1 stick) butter or margarine, melted
½ teaspoon cinnamon
½ cup (3 ounces) white chocolate chips
½ cup heavy whipping cream
1½ cups (9 ounces) white chocolate chips
2 tablespoons crème de cacao

1 teaspoon vanilla extract
½ cup sugar
¼ cup water
4 egg whites, at room temperature
1½ cups heavy whipping cream
2 packages frozen strawberries or raspberries
1½ tablespoons Triple Sec or Grand Marnier
Confectioners' sugar
Shaved chocolate

Combine the vanilla wafer crumbs, butter and cinnamon in a small bowl and mix well. Press onto the bottom and side of a greased 9-inch springform baking pan. Bake at 325 degrees for 6 minutes. Cool completely. Sprinkle with ½ cup white chocolate chips. Bring ½ cup cream to a boil in a small saucepan over medium-high heat. Reduce the temperature to low. Add the 1½ cups white chocolate chips and stir until smooth. Remove to a medium bowl and stir in the crème de cacao and vanilla. Cool completely. Combine the sugar and water in a small saucepan. Bring to a boil over medium heat, stirring until the sugar dissolves. Cook for 5 minutes or to 238 degrees on a candy thermometer. Beat the egg whites in a large bowl until soft peaks form. Add the hot sugar syrup to the egg whites in a steady stream, beating until stiff peaks form. Cool completely. Fold into the egg whites in two batches. Whip 1½ cups cream in a mixing bowl until soft peaks form. Fold gently into the chocolate mixture. Pour into the prepared pan. Freeze for 5 hours or longer. Combine the strawberries, Triple Sec and a small amount of confectioners' sugar in a blender and process until smooth. Press through a fine sieve to remove the seeds if desired. Swirl a small amount of the raspberry purée on each serving plate. Top with a slice of the pie. Spoon more purée over the top and sprinkle with shaved chocolate. Yield: 16 servings.

Sally Blaisdell-Field, Preceptor Kappa
South Thomaston, Maine

YOGURT PIE

4 tablespoons peanut butter	1 quart frozen yogurt, softened
1 tablespoon honey	Chocolate syrup
1½ cups crisp rice cereal	(optional)
1 banana, sliced	

Microwave the peanut butter and honey in an 8-inch pie plate on Medium, stirring once or twice until smooth. Stir in the rice cereal. Press onto the bottom and side of the pie plate. Freeze until firm. Layer the banana, yogurt and chocolate syrup over the cereal layer. Freeze until firm. Yield: 8 servings.

Elaine M. Wilson, Laureate Beta
Warwick, Rhode Island

BLUEBERRY SHERBET

2 cups fresh or thawed frozen blueberries	1 tablespoon fresh lemon juice
1 cup fat-free buttermilk	½ teaspoon vanilla extract
½ cup sugar	

Combine the blueberries, buttermilk, sugar, lemon juice and vanilla in a blender and process until smooth. Pour into a 9×9-inch dish. Freeze, covered, for 4 hours or until firm. Process in batches in the blender until smooth. Freeze, covered, for 4 hours or until firm. Garnish with mint sprigs if desired. Yield: 6 servings.

Mary Ellen Grossman, Laureate Beta Nu
Lawrenceburg, Indiana

LEMON SHERBET

1 cup lemon juice	2 cups heavy whipping cream
2½ cups sugar	4 cups milk

Combine the lemon juice and sugar in a bowl and stir until the sugar dissolves. Chill until cool. Whip the cream in a mixing bowl until stiff peaks form. Stir in the lemon mixture and milk. Pour into an ice cream freezer container. Freeze using the manufacturer's directions. Yield: 2 quarts.

Elizabeth Madden, Xi Beta Sigma
Natchitoches, Louisiana

EASY STRAWBERRY SHERBET

Try this recipe with other fresh fruits. It's especially good with peaches.

4 cups strawberries, sliced	2 cups sugar
	2 cups buttermilk

Combine the strawberries and sugar in a bowl. Let stand for 1 hour. Mash the strawberries. Add the but-termilk and mix well. Pour into a plastic container and freeze until firm. Remove to a bowl and beat until smooth. Freeze until firm. Scoop into balls to serve. Yield: 6 to 8 servings.

Jane McDaniel, Laureate Beta Gamma
Tyler, Texas

LAYERED RAINBOW SHERBET DESSERT

2 cups heavy whipping cream	1 (12-ounce) package vanilla wafers, crushed
3 tablespoons confectioners' sugar	1 cup chopped nuts
1 teaspoon vanilla extract	½ gallon rainbow sherbet, softened

Whip the cream, confectioners' sugar and vanilla in a mixing bowl until stiff peaks form. Fold in the crushed vanilla wafers. Spread half the cream mixture across the bottom of a 9×13-inch dish. Sprinkle with ½ cup of the nuts. Top with the sherbet. Cover with the remaining cream mixture and sprinkle with the remaining nuts. Freeze until firm.
Yield: 12 to 15 servings.

Shirley Welch, Alpha Delta Master
Mesa, Arizona

❖ BLUEBERRY SORBET

8 cups blueberries, rinsed and dried	¼ cup lemon juice
¾ cup sugar	½ cup water

Purée the blueberries in a blender. Remove to a medium saucepan. Add the sugar, lemon juice and water. Bring to a boil over medium heat, stirring until the sugar dissolves. Press through a sieve over a bowl. Cool completely. Pour into an ice cream freezer container. Freeze using the manufacturer's directions. Yield: 6 to 8 servings.

Cindy Johns, Laureate Iota
Raleigh, North Carolina

CHOCOLATE SORBET

3⅓ cups water	10 tablespoons chocolate liqueur
1⅛ cups sugar	
1¾ cups baking cocoa	

Combine the water and sugar in a saucepan. Cook over medium heat, stirring occasionally. Bring to a boil. Boil for 3 to 4 minutes, stirring constantly. Stir in the baking cocoa. Cook for 5 minutes longer. Remove to a bowl to cool completely. Stir in the liqueur. Pour into an ice cream freezer container. Freeze using the manufacturer's directions. Yield: 8 servings.

Linda Nixon, Zeta Beta
Madras, Oregon

STRAWBERRY MARGARITA SQUARES

1¼ cups crushed
  pretzels
¼ cup (½ stick) butter
  or margarine, melted
1 (14-ounce) can
  sweetened
  condensed milk

1 cup puréed
  strawberries
½ cup lime juice
8 ounces whipped
  topping

Mix the crushed pretzels and butter in a small bowl. Press onto the bottom of a 9×13-inch dish. Chill. Combine the condensed milk, strawberries and lime juice in a bowl and mix well. Fold in the whipped topping. Spoon over the pretzel layer. Freeze for 6 hours or longer. Remove from the freezer 10 to 15 minutes before serving. Cut into squares and garnish with extra strawberries. Yield: 12 to 15 servings.

Pam Niederhauser, Preceptor Pi
Columbia, Missouri

FREEZER SUNDAES

2 cups crisp rice cereal
1 cup flaked coconut
¼ cup packed brown
  sugar
½ cup chopped nuts

½ cup (1 stick) butter or
  margarine, melted
½ gallon vanilla ice
  cream, softened
Hot fudge topping

Combine the cereal, coconut, brown sugar, nuts and butter in a bowl and mix well. Press half the cereal mixture onto the bottom of a 9×13-inch dish. Layer half the ice cream, the remaining cereal mixture, and remaining ice cream over the top. Freeze until firm. Remove from the freezer 10 minutes before serving. Serve with hot fudge topping. Yield: 8 to 10 servings.

Mary Stiles, Laureate Delta Beta
Princeton, Missouri

ICE CREAM PEPPERMINT TORTE

1½ to 2 cups vanilla
  wafer crumbs
2 ounces unsweetened
  chocolate
½ cup (1 stick)
  margarine
2 egg yolks, beaten

2 cups confectioners'
  sugar
2 egg whites
½ gallon vanilla ice
  cream, softened
Crushed peppermint
  candies

Press the vanilla wafer crumbs over the bottom of a greased 9×13-inch dish. Melt the chocolate with the butter in a heavy saucepan over low heat. Add the yolks and confectioners' sugar, stirring constantly. Bring to a boil. Boil for 2 minutes, stirring constantly. Remove from the heat and cool slightly. Beat the egg whites in a mixing bowl until soft peaks form. Fold into the chocolate mixture. Pour over the crumb layer. Freeze until firm. Top with half the vanilla ice cream. Sprinkle with crushed peppermint candy. Repeat the layers. Freeze until firm.
Yield: 8 to 10 servings.

Camille Wilson, Xi Delta Epsilon
Kendallville, Indiana

BISCUIT TORTONI

This light and tasty little dessert is the perfect conclusion to a big Italian meal.

½ gallon vanilla ice
  cream, softened
½ package coconut
  macaroons, crumbled

½ jar maraschino
  cherries, sliced
½ cup roasted almonds,
  chopped

Combine the ice cream, macaroons, cherries and almonds in a large bowl and mix well. Spoon into paper-lined muffin cups. Top each with a sliced cherry. Freeze until firm. Yield: 12 servings.

Donna Musgrave, Laureate Alpha Zeta
Pineville, West Virginia

CHOCOLATE CHIP KAHLÚA FREEZE

½ cup Kahlúa
½ cup milk
2 (1-pound) packages
  chocolate chip
  cookies

32 ounces whipped
  topping

Combine the Kahlúa and milk in a shallow dish. Dip enough of the cookies in the Kahlúa mixture to line a 9×13-inch dish, being careful to dip quickly and not soak the cookies. Top with half the whipped topping. Continue with another layer of dipped cookies and the remaining whipped topping. Crumble any remaining cookies and sprinkle over the whipped topping. Freeze for 2 hours or until firm. Remove from the freezer 30 minutes before serving. Cut into squares. Yield 8 to 10 servings.

Betty Kozley, Preceptor Iota
Henderson, Nevada

---

*Amanda Hudson, Iota Beta, Medicine Lodge, Kansas, makes **Ice Cream Bars** by mixing a crushed package of chocolate sandwich cookies with ½ cup melted margarine in a bowl and pressing the mixture into a 9×13-inch dish. She mixes ½ gallon softened vanilla ice cream and 9 ounces whipped topping in a mixing bowl and spoons the mixture into the dish. She sprinkles crushed chocolate sandwich cookies over the top, freezes until firm, and cuts into bars just before serving.*

FROZEN CHOCOLATE DESSERT

18 chocolate cream-filled
    sandwich cookies,
    crushed
1/4 cup (1/2 stick) butter
    or margarine, melted
1/2 gallon ice cream,
    softened (any flavor)

1 cup sugar
1 cup evaporated milk
2 ounces unsweetened
    chocolate
Whipped topping
    (optional)

Combine the crushed cookies and butter in a bowl
and mix well. Press into the bottom of a 9×13-inch
pan. Freeze for 2 hours. Spoon the ice cream over the
frozen crust and spread lightly. Freeze until firm.
Combine the sugar, evaporated milk and chocolate in
a saucepan. Cook over medium heat until thickened,
stirring constantly. Cool completely. Drizzle over
the ice cream layer. Freeze until firm. Serve with
whipped topping. Yield: 12 servings.

Arlene Radel, Chi Omicron
Naperville, Illinois

MIXED FRUIT FREEZE

1 (16-ounce) can crushed
    pineapple
1 (14-ounce) can
    sweetened
    condensed milk

12 ounces whipped
    topping
1 (21-ounce) can cherry
    pie filling
Chopped nuts (optional)

Combine the pineapple, condensed milk, whipped
topping, pie filling and nuts in a bowl and mix well.
Pour into a loaf pan. Freeze, covered, for several
hours or until firm. Slice just before serving.
Yield: 12 servings.

Lorraine DeLaReintrie, Alpha Beta Master
Fairmont, West Virginia

PINEAPPLE STRAWBERRY FREEZE

I offer this recipe in memory of my grandfather,
Charles Hoffman, and my father, Donald Sanders,
who loved this dessert.

8 ounces cream cheese,
    softened
3/4 cup sugar
1 (20-ounce) can crushed
    pineapple, drained

1 (10-ounce) package
    frozen strawberries
1 cup chopped nuts
12 ounces whipped
    topping

Beat the cream cheese and sugar in a bowl until light
and fluffy. Stir in the pineapple, strawberries and
nuts. Fold in the whipped topping. Spoon into a
9×13-inch dish and freeze until firm.
Yield: 12 servings.

Kendra Craig, Xi Mu Chi
Ramsey, Illinois

ICE CREAM SQUARES

30 graham crackers,
    crushed
1/2 cup (1 stick) butter,
    melted

1 (4-ounce) package
    gelatin (any flavor)
1 cup boiling water
1 pint vanilla ice cream,
    softened

Mix the crushed graham crackers and butter in a bowl.
Press into the bottom of an 8×8-inch pan. Combine
the gelatin and water in a large bowl and stir until
the gelatin dissolves. Stir in the ice cream. Spread
over the prepared crust. Freeze until firm.
Yield: 10 to 12 servings.

Emma May Weisseneder, Master Gamma
Rothesay, New Brunswick, Canada

LEMON ICEBOX PIE

1 (14-ounce) can
    sweetened
    condensed milk
1/2 cup lemon juice

Grated zest of 1 lemon
2 egg yolks
1 (9-inch) graham
    cracker pie shell

Combine the first 4 ingredients in a bowl and mix
well. Pour into the pie shell. Freeze until firm. Note:
If you are concerned about using raw eggs, use eggs
pasteurized in their shells, which are sold at some
specialty food stores, or use an equivalent amount of
pasteurized egg substitute. Yield: 8 servings.

Barbara Melton, Eta Beta
Stonewall, Louisiana

CRISPY PEANUT BUTTER SQUARES

1 cup peanut butter
1 cup confectioners'
    sugar
2 tablespoons
    margarine, softened

2 cups crisp rice cereal
1/2 gallon vanilla ice
    cream, softened
Chocolate syrup

Mix the peanut butter, confectioners' sugar and margarine in a bowl. Stir in the cereal. Spread over the
bottom of a 9×13-inch dish. Spread the vanilla ice
cream over the cereal layer. Freeze until firm.
Remove from the freezer just before serving. Cut into
squares and drizzle with chocolate syrup.
Yield: 12 to 15 servings.

Kathy Hilton, Laureate Zeta
Mitchell, South Dakota

RoseMarie Peterson, Laureate Alpha Alpha, Merrill,
*Wisconsin, shared her recipe for **Ireland Nightfall**, an*
ice cream treat for adults. She scoops coffee ice cream
into a glass and tops with 1 1/2 ounces Kahlúa. She
garnishes the dessert with chocolate shavings and
pirouline cookies.

Garden Party

SWEET BREADS, FRUIT DESSERTS AND SALADS

BANANA BREAD

2³/4 cups sifted all-purpose flour	10²/3 tablespoons butter or margarine, softened
2 teaspoons baking powder	1¹/3 cups sugar
1 teaspoon baking soda	2 eggs, well beaten
¹/2 teaspoon salt	1²/3 cups mashed bananas
1¹/2 teaspoons cinnamon	2 teaspoons vanilla extract
³/4 teaspoon nutmeg	
¹/4 teaspoon ground cloves	

Sift the flour, baking powder, baking soda, salt, cinnamon, nutmeg and cloves together three times. Beat the butter and sugar in a bowl until light and fluffy. Beat in the eggs. Beat in the dry ingredients alternately with the bananas. Stir in the vanilla. Pour into 2 greased loaf pans. Bake at 350 degrees for 35 minutes or until the bread tests done. Cool in the pans for 10 minutes. Remove to a wire rack to cool completely. Yield: 24 servings.

Delores D. Roberts, Preceptor Beta
Butte, Montana

BANANA NUT BREAD

2 cups all-purpose flour	1 cup sugar
1 teaspoon baking soda	2 eggs
¹/2 teaspoon salt	1 teaspoon vanilla extract
¹/2 teaspoon cinnamon	
¹/2 cup (1 stick) butter or margarine, softened	¹/2 cup chopped nuts
	3 bananas, mashed

Combine the flour, baking soda, salt and cinnamon in a bowl. Beat the butter and sugar in a bowl until light and fluffy. Beat in the eggs and vanilla. Add the dry ingredients and mix well. Stir in the nuts and bananas. Pour into a greased 5×9-inch loaf pan. Bake at 350 degrees for 1 hour or until the bread tests done. Cool in the pan for 10 minutes. Remove to a wire rack to cool completely. Yield: 12 servings.

Vineta Mickie Reass, Xi Nu
Winter Haven, Florida

❖ BLACKBERRY BREAD

2 cups all-purpose flour	1¹/4 cups vegetable oil
1 teaspoon baking soda	¹/2 cup milk
1 teaspoon salt	1 teaspoon vanilla extract
¹/2 teaspoon cinnamon	2 cups fresh or frozen blackberries
¹/4 teaspoon nutmeg	
¹/4 teaspoon allspice	1 cup black walnuts, chopped
2 cups sugar	
4 eggs, beaten	

Combine the first 7 ingredients in a bowl. Add the eggs, oil, milk and vanilla and mix well. Stir in the blackberries and walnuts. Pour into 2 well greased 5×9-inch loaf pans. Bake at 350 degrees for 60 to 70 minutes or until the bread tests done. Cool in the pans for 5 to 10 minutes. Remove to a wire rack to cool completely. Yield: 24 servings.

Billie Ann Waite, Preceptor Lambda Iota
Jefferson City, Missouri

---

*Gigi Savona, Xi Delta Nu, Mandeville, Louisiana, makes a healthy **Grape Pecan Surprise** by whipping 8 ounces softened cream cheese with ¹/2 cup sour cream and 4 tablespoons Splenda in a bowl. She folds in 2 cups seedless red grapes, smoothes the top, and covers the mixture with ¹/2 cup pecan halves.*

BLACKBERRY GINGERBREAD

1¹/2 cups frozen
    blackberries
1 tablespoon
    all-purpose flour
1 (14¹/2-ounce) package
    gingerbread mix
¹/3 cup sugar
¹/4 cup (¹/2 stick) butter
¹/4 cup half-and-half or
    light cream

Combine the blackberries and flour in a bowl and toss to coat. Prepare the gingerbread mix using the package directions. Fold in the blackberries. Pour into a greased 9×9-inch baking pan. Bake using the package directions. Cool in the pan for 5 minutes. Remove to a wire rack to cool. Combine the sugar, butter and half-and-half in a saucepan. Bring to a boil over medium heat, stirring constantly. Reduce the heat and simmer for 2 minutes, stirring constantly. Drizzle over warm blackberry gingerbread and garnish with additional thawed blackberries.
 Yield: 9 to 12 servings.

Jacky Breitenbach, Laureate Beta Omicron
Prescott, Arizona

BOSTON BROWN BREAD

My mom always served this after Christmas Eve services.

1 pound raisins
2 cups boiling water
2 teaspoons baking soda
2 tablespoons butter
2 eggs, beaten
2 cups sugar
4 cups all-purpose flour,
    sifted
1 teaspoon cinnamon
1 teaspoon salt
¹/4 cup pecans, chopped

Mix the raisins, water, baking soda and butter in a large bowl. Cool completely. Add the eggs, sugar, flour, cinnamon and salt and mix well. Stir in the pecans. Grease 7 clean 16-ounce cans and fit a circle of waxed paper into the bottom of each can. Divide the batter evenly across the cans. Bake at 350 degrees for 1 hour or until the bread tests done. Cool in the cans for 10 minutes. Remove to a wire rack to cool completely. Serve with cream cheese.
Yield: 32 servings.

Patti Ann Pickhard, Mu
Oklahoma City, Oklahoma

LEMON LOAF

1¹/2 cups all-purpose
    flour
1 teaspoon baking
    powder
¹/2 cup (1 stick) butter or
    margarine, softened
1 cup sugar
2 eggs
Grated zest of 1 lemon
Juice of 1 lemon
¹/2 cup milk
¹/2 cup sugar

Combine the flour and baking powder. Beat the butter and 1 cup sugar in a bowl until light and fluffy. Add the eggs, lemon zest and 2 teaspoons of the lemon juice and mix well. Stir in the dry ingredients alternately with the milk. Pour into a nonstick loaf pan. Bake at 325 degrees for 50 to 60 minutes or until the bread tests done. Cool in the pan for 15 minutes. Mix ¹/2 cup sugar and the remaining lemon juice in a bowl. Drizzle over the bread. Cool for 10 minutes. Remove the bread to a wire rack to cool. Serve warm, at room temperature or wrap and freeze.
Yield: 12 servings.

Gwen M. Goodridge, Beta Master
Winnipeg, Manitoba, Canada

PEACH BREAD

2 cups all-purpose flour
1 teaspoon baking
    powder
1 teaspoon baking soda
¹/2 teaspoon salt
¹/2 teaspoon cinnamon
1 cup chopped nuts
2 cups chopped peeled
    peaches
1¹/2 teaspoons lemon
    juice
¹/2 cup (1 stick) butter,
    softened
1 cup sugar
¹/2 teaspoon almond
    extract
2 eggs, beaten

Sift the flour, baking powder, baking soda, salt and cinnamon together. Add the nuts. Combine the peaches and lemon juice in a bowl and toss to mix. Beat the butter, sugar and almond extract in a mixing bowl until light and fluffy. Beat in the eggs. Stir in the dry ingredients alternately with the peaches. Spoon into a greased and floured 5×9-inch loaf pan. Bake at 350 degrees for 55 to 60 minutes or until the bread tests done. Cool in the pan for 10 minutes. Remove to a wire rack to cool completely. Yield: 12 servings.

Sarah Kapla, Chi Omicron
Romeoville, Illinois

PEACHES AND CREAM QUICK BREAD

¹/2 cup fat-free sour
    cream
1 egg
2 egg whites
2 tablespoons extra-
    virgin olive oil
1 teaspoon almond oil
1¹/2 cups all-purpose
    flour
³/4 cup whole wheat
    flour
¹/4 cup toasted wheat
    germ
³/4 cup sugar
1 teaspoon baking soda
¹/2 teaspoon salt
2 peaches, peeled and
    chopped

Combine the sour cream, egg, egg whites, olive oil and almond oil in a bowl and mix well. Combine the all-purpose flour, whole wheat flour, wheat germ, sugar, baking soda and salt in a large bowl. Make a well in the center and pour in the egg mixture.

Stir just until combined. Fold in the peaches. Spoon into a greased 5×9-inch loaf pan and smooth the top of the batter. Bake at 350 degrees for 1 hour or until a wooden pick inserted in the center comes out clean. Cool in the pan for 10 minutes. Remove to a wire rack to cool completely. Yield: 16 servings.

Irja Hansen, Gamma Zeta
Ramore, Ontario, Canada

PERSIMMON NUT BREAD

This makes a wonderful Christmas gift for neighbors and keeps well in the refrigerator.

3¹/₂ cups all-purpose flour	1 cup raisins
¹/₂ teaspoon baking powder	¹/₂ cup chopped walnuts
2 teaspoons baking soda	3 cups sugar
2 teaspoons salt	1 cup vegetable oil
1 teaspoon cinnamon	4 eggs
1 teaspoon allspice	2 cups soft persimmon pulp
1 teaspoon ground cloves	²/₃ cup water

Combine the flour, baking powder, baking soda, salt, cinnamon, allspice, cloves, raisins and walnuts. Mix the sugar, oil, eggs, persimmon pulp and water in a large bowl. Add the dry ingredients and mix well. Fill 2 or 3 greased 5×9-inch loaf pans ³/₄ full. Bake at 325 degrees for 1 hour or until a wooden pick inserted in the center comes out clean. Cool in the pans for 10 minutes. Serve warm with whipped topping or dust with confectioners' sugar.
Yield: 24 to 36 servings.

Carole Emge, Laureate Iota Sigma
Vallejo, California

PUMPKIN BREAD

1 cup corn oil	1¹/₂ teaspoons salt
4 eggs, beaten	1 teaspoon nutmeg
²/₃ cup water	1 teaspoon cinnamon
2 cups canned pumpkin	3 cups sugar
3¹/₃ cups sifted all-purpose flour	1 cup golden raisins
2 teaspoons baking soda	1 cup nuts, chopped

Combine the oil, eggs, water and pumpkin in a large bowl and mix well. Stir in the flour, baking soda, salt, nutmeg, cinnamon and sugar. Stir in the raisins and nuts. Pour into 2 greased and floured loaf pans. Bake at 350 degrees for 1 hour or until the bread tests done. Cool in the pans for 10 minutes. Remove to a wire rack to cool completely. Yield: 24 servings.

Valerie Rankin, Laureate Epsilon Theta
Pinellas Park, Florida

APPLE SHORTBREAD

1 cup all-purpose flour	¹/₂ teaspoon cinnamon
¹/₂ cup packed brown sugar	¹/₂ cup (1 stick) butter
	28 ounces applesauce

Mix the flour, brown sugar and cinnamon in a bowl. Cut in the butter until crumbly. Spread the applesauce over the bottom of a 7×11-inch baking dish. Sprinkle the flour mixture evenly over the applesauce and press lightly. Bake at 375 degrees for 40 minutes or until golden brown. Remove to a wire rack to cool completely. Yield: 8 servings.

Beverley Adams, Laureate Alpha Theta
Coquitlam, British Columbia, Canada

PINEAPPLE UPSIDE-DOWN BISCUITS

1 (10-ounce) can crushed pineapple	10 maraschino cherries
¹/₂ cup packed light brown sugar	1 (10-count) can refrigerated buttermilk biscuits
¹/₄ cup (¹/₂ stick) butter, softened	

Drain the pineapple, reserving the juice. Mix the pineapple, brown sugar and butter in a bowl. Divide the mixture among 10 greased muffin cups. Top each with a cherry. Place one biscuit on top of the cherry in each muffin cup. Spoon 1 teaspoon of the reserved pineapple juice over each biscuit. Bake at 400 degrees for 12 to 15 minutes or until golden brown. Cool in the pan for 2 minutes. Invert onto a serving plate and serve warm. Yield: 10 servings.

Carol Fielder, Laureate Kappa
Beatrice, Nebraska

BLUEBERRY CRUNCH

1 (20-ounce) can crushed pineapple	1 (2-layer) package yellow cake mix
2 cups fresh or frozen blueberries	¹/₂ cup (1 stick) butter, melted
³/₄ cup sugar	1 cup chopped pecans
	¹/₄ cup sugar

Spread the pineapple over the bottom of a nonstick 9×13-inch baking pan. Scatter with the blueberries and sprinkle with ³/₄ cup sugar. Sprinkle the cake mix over the top. Drizzle with the melted butter. Mix the pecans and ¹/₄ cup sugar in a bowl. Sprinkle over the top. Bake at 350 degrees for 45 to 50 minutes. Remove to a wire rack to cool for 25 minutes. Press gently on the surface with the back of a spoon to submerge any dry areas. Yield: 15 servings.

Margaret Budney, Preceptor Eta Phi
Indian Harbour Beach, Florida

CINNAMON CREAM CHEESE DANISH

2 (8-count) cans
    refrigerated crescent
    rolls
16 ounces cream cheese,
    softened
1 cup confectioners'
    sugar

1 teaspoon vanilla
    extract or water
    (optional)
1/2 cup (1 stick) butter,
    melted
Brown sugar to taste
Cinnamon to taste

Unroll 1 can of crescent dough and fit in the bottom of a nonstick 9×13-inch baking pan. Press the seams to seal. Beat the cream cheese, confectioners' sugar and vanilla in a bowl. Spread over the dough in the pan. Unroll the remaining can of crescent dough and press the seams to seal. Place on top of the cream cheese mixture. Drizzle with the melted butter. Mix the brown sugar and cinnamon in a bowl. Sprinkle over the top. Bake at 375 degrees for 25 minutes. Remove to a wire rack to cool completely.
Yield: 12 servings.

Anita Greene, Xi Alpha Pi
Mount Airy, North Carolina

CINNAMON BUN CAKE

1 (2-layer) package
    yellow cake mix
3/4 cup vegetable oil
4 eggs
1 cup sour cream
1 cup packed brown
    sugar

1 tablespoon cinnamon
2 cups confectioners'
    sugar
1/4 cup milk
1 tablespoon vanilla
    extract

Combine the cake mix, oil, eggs and sour cream in a bowl and stir until no lumps remain. Pour half the batter into an ungreased 9×13-inch baking dish. Mix the brown sugar and cinnamon in a bowl. Sprinkle over the batter. Pour the remaining batter evenly over the brown sugar mixture. Swirl a knife through the batter so that it resembles a bun. Bake at 325 degrees for 40 minutes or until the cake tests done. Remove to a wire rack to cool. Combine the confectioners' sugar, milk and vanilla in a bowl. Whisk until smooth. Pour evenly over the warm cake. Yield: 12 servings.

Jean Kraft, Alpha Eta Master
New Albany, Indiana

SINFUL CINNAMON BUNS

1/4 cup chopped nuts
    (optional)
3/4 cup packed brown
    sugar
1/2 cup (1 stick) butter
1 tablespoon cinnamon

1 (4-ounce) package
    butterscotch
    pudding mix
1 package refrigerated
    pizza dough,
    partially frozen

Sprinkle the nuts over the bottom of a greased bundt pan. Combine the brown sugar, butter and cinnamon in a saucepan. Cook over medium heat until the butter melts, stirring frequently. Remove from the heat. Pour the pudding mix into a small bowl. Cut the pizza dough into 2-inch pieces. Dip the dough pieces into the butter mixture and coat with the pudding mix. Arrange in the prepared pan. Sprinkle with the remaining pudding mix and pour the remaining butter mixture evenly over the top. Cover with a towel and let rise in a warm place for several hours. Bake at 350 degrees for 25 to 30 minutes. Cool in the pan for 10 minutes. Invert onto a rimmed serving plate and serve warm. Yield: 12 servings.

Karen Ives, Xi Theta Alpha
Grimsby, Ontario, Canada

APPLE COFFEE CAKE

2 1/4 cups all-purpose
    flour
2 teaspoons baking
    powder
1 teaspoon cinnamon
3/4 teaspoon nutmeg
1/2 teaspoon ground
    cloves
1/2 cup (1 stick) butter,
    softened
1 cup granulated sugar

1/2 cup packed brown
    sugar
2 eggs
1 cup buttermilk
3 cups chopped apples
3/4 cup chopped nuts
1/4 cup packed brown
    sugar
2 tablespoons
    granulated sugar
1 1/2 teaspoons cinnamon

Combine the flour, baking powder, 1 teaspoon cinnamon, nutmeg and cloves. Beat the butter and 1 cup granulated sugar in a large bowl until light and fluffy. Beat in 1/2 cup brown sugar. Beat in the eggs. Stir in the dry ingredients alternately with the buttermilk. Fold in the apples. Pour into a greased 9×13-inch baking pan. Mix the nuts, 1/2 cup brown sugar, 2 tablespoons granulated sugar and 1 1/2 teaspoons cinnamon in a bowl. Sprinkle over the top. Bake at 350 degrees for 45 minutes or until the cake tests done. Remove to a wire rack to cool. Serve warm or cold. Yield: 12 to 15 servings.

Diane Ogden, Tau Alpha
Paradise, California

BLUEBERRY COFFEE CAKE

2 cups sifted all-purpose
    flour
2 teaspoons baking
    powder
1/2 teaspoon salt
1/4 cup (1/2 stick) butter,
    softened
3/4 cup sugar

1 egg
1/2 cup milk
2 cups fresh or frozen
    blueberries
1/2 cup sugar
1/4 cup all-purpose flour
1/2 teaspoon cinnamon
1/4 cup (1/2 stick) butter

Combine 2 cups flour, the baking powder and salt. Beat 1/4 cup butter and 3/4 cup sugar in a bowl until light and fluffy. Beat in the egg. Beat in the milk. Stir in the dry ingredients. Fold in the blueberries. Spoon into a greased 9×9-inch baking pan. Mix the 1/2 cup sugar, 1/4 cup flour and cinnamon in a bowl. Cut in 1/4 cup butter until crumbly. Sprinkle over the top. Bake at 375 degrees for 45 minutes or until the center springs back when lightly touched. Remove to a wire rack to cool. Serve warm or at room temperature. Yield: 9 servings.

Ruth Molzan, Xi Epsilon Mu
Leamington, Ontario, Canada

CHERRY STREUSEL COFFEE CAKE

2 cups sifted all-purpose flour	2 eggs
2 teaspoons baking powder	1/4 cup milk
1/2 teaspoon salt	1 (21-ounce) can cherry pie filling
18 tablespoons butter, softened	1 cup sugar
1 1/4 cups sugar	1 cup all-purpose flour
	2 teaspoons cinnamon
	1/2 cup (1 stick) butter

Sift 2 cups flour, the baking powder and salt together. Beat 18 tablespoons butter and 1 1/4 cups sugar in a bowl until light and fluffy. Beat in the eggs 1 at a time. Stir in the dry ingredients alternately with the milk. Pour half the batter into a nonstick 9×13-inch baking pan. Spread the pie filling evenly over the top. Cover with the remaining batter. Mix 1 cup sugar, 1 cup flour and the cinnamon in a bowl. Cut in 1/2 cup butter until crumbly. Sprinkle evenly over the batter. Bake at 350 degrees for 45 to 55 minutes or until the cake tests done. Remove to a wire rack to cool completely. Yield: 12 servings.

Kathy Smith, Laureate Alpha Sigma
Tilbury, Ontario, Canada

CRANBERRY ORANGE COFFEE CAKE

2 cups all-purpose flour	2 cups chopped fresh or frozen cranberries
1 cup sugar	2 tablespoons grated orange zest
1 1/2 teaspoons baking powder	8 ounces cream cheese, softened
1/2 teaspoon baking soda	1/3 cup sugar
1/2 teaspoon salt	1 egg
3/4 cup orange juice	1 teaspoon vanilla extract
1/4 cup (1/2 stick) margarine, melted	Crumb Topping
1 teaspoon vanilla extract	
1 egg, beaten	

Mix the flour, 1 cup sugar, baking powder, baking soda and salt in a large bowl. Stir in the orange juice, margarine, 1 teaspoon vanilla and 1 egg. Fold in the cranberries and orange zest just until combined. Pour into a nonstick 9-inch springform pan. Beat the cream cheese and 1/3 cup sugar in a bowl until light and fluffy. Beat in 1 egg and 1 teaspoon vanilla. Spoon evenly over the batter in the pan and spread lightly. Sprinkle with Crumb Topping. Bake at 350 degrees for 65 to 75 minutes or until the center springs back when lightly touched. Remove to a wire rack to cool for 15 minutes. Loosen from the side of the pan with a sharp knife and remove the side. Cool completely. Dust with confectioners' sugar before serving. Yield: 12 servings.

CRUMB TOPPING

3/4 cup all-purpose flour	1/2 cup (1 stick) margarine
1/2 cup sugar	

Combine the flour and sugar in a bowl. Cut in the margarine until crumbly.

Laurene Atherton, Laureate Alpha Iota
Qualicum Beach, British Columbia, Canada

CREAM CHEESE DANISH

2 (8-count) cans refrigerated crescent rolls	1 (21-ounce) can peach, cherry or apple pie filling
8 ounces cream cheese, softened	1/2 cup confectioners' sugar (optional)
1/4 cup confectioners' sugar	2 to 3 teaspoons water (optional)
1 egg yolk	

Unroll 1 1/2 cans of the crescent dough on a large lipped baking stone or in a 9×13-inch baking pan. Press the seams to seal. Beat the cream cheese, 1/4 cup confectioners' sugar and egg yolk in a bowl until smooth. Spread evenly over the unrolled dough. Spread the pie filling evenly over the cream cheese mixture. Unroll the remaining dough on a work surface and cut into 3 strips. Lay the strips over the pie filling, sealing the edges. Bake at 350 degrees for 25 to 30 minutes. Remove to a wire rack to cool completely. Mix 1/2 cup confectioners' sugar and water in a bowl. Drizzle over the cooled danish. Yield: 12 servings.

Pamela Altis, Xi Beta Upsilon
Sedalia, Missouri

*Marian R. Brumley, Chi Master, Topeka, Kansas, enjoys making **Gelatin Shots**. She prepares a package of gelatin using the package directions, substituting rum for water. She pours the gelatin in a 9×13-inch dish and chills until it is set. Just before serving, she cuts the "shots" into 3-inch squares.*

CRANBERRY SWIRL CAKE

2 cups all-purpose flour	1 teaspoon almond extract
1 teaspoon baking powder	1 (16-ounce) can cranberry sauce
1 teaspoon baking soda	1/2 cup chopped nuts
1/2 teaspoon salt	3/4 cup confectioners' sugar
1/2 cup (1 stick) butter or margarine, softened	1 tablespoon warm water
1 cup granulated sugar	
2 eggs	1/2 teaspoon almond extract
2 cups sour cream	

Sift the first 4 ingredients together. Beat the butter and granulated sugar in a bowl until light and fluffy. Beat in the eggs one at a time. Beat in the dry ingredients alternately with the sour cream at low speed. Stir in 1 teaspoon almond extract. Pour half the batter into a greased 9-inch tube pan. Stir the cranberry sauce in a bowl until softened. Dollop half the cranberry sauce over the batter in the pan and sprinkle with half the nuts. Pour the remaining batter evenly over the nuts. Dollop with the remaining cranberry sauce and sprinkle with the remaining nuts; do not swirl. Bake at 350 degrees for 50 minutes or until the cake tests done. Cool in the pan for 10 minutes. Remove to a wire rack to cool completely. Mix the remaining ingredients in a bowl. Drizzle over the cooled cake. Yield: 8 to 12 servings.

Carol E. Twining, Beta Master
Ludlow, Massachusetts

LEMON BREAKFAST CAKE

1 1/2 cups all-purpose flour	2 eggs
1 cup sugar	1/2 cup milk
1 teaspoon baking powder	1/2 cup vegetable oil
1/2 teaspoon salt	Grated zest of 1 lemon
	Juice of 1 lemon
	1/3 cup sugar

Combine the flour, 1 cup sugar, baking powder and salt. Beat the eggs, milk, oil and lemon zest in a bowl. Add the dry ingredients and stir to combine. Pour into a greased 7×11-inch baking pan. Bake at 350 degrees for 30 minutes or until the cake tests done. Remove to a wire rack. Pierce the cake with a fork. Combine the lemon juice and 1/3 cup sugar in a saucepan. Cook over medium heat until the sugar dissolves, stirring constantly. Pour evenly over the hot cake. Cool for 10 minutes. Serve with lemon slices and a dusting of confectioners' sugar. Yield: 10 servings.

Shirley M. Williams, Preceptor Alpha Theta
Shady Side, Maryland

CHEESE DANISH

2 (8-count) cans refrigerated crescent rolls	1 teaspoon vanilla extract
1 egg yolk	1 1/4 cups sugar
16 ounces cream cheese, softened	1 egg white
	1/4 cup sugar

Unroll 1 can of crescent dough and fit in the bottom of a nonstick 9×13-inch baking pan. Press the seams to seal. Beat the egg yolk in a bowl. Add cream cheese, vanilla and 1 1/4 cups sugar and beat until smooth. Spread over the dough in the pan. Unroll the remaining can of crescent dough and press the seams to seal. Place on top of the cream cheese mixture. Beat the egg white in a bowl until stiff peaks form. Spread evenly over the dough and sprinkle with 1/4 cup sugar. Bake at 350 degrees for 30 to 35 minutes or until golden brown. Remove to a wire rack to cool completely. Yield: 12 to 15 servings.

Donna Aven, Preceptor Alpha Alpha
Pearl River, New York

LOW-FAT APPLESAUCE MUFFINS

1 1/4 cups all-purpose flour	1/2 cup chunky applesauce
1 tablespoon baking powder	1/2 cup packed brown sugar
1 teaspoon cinnamon	2 tablespoons margarine, melted
1/4 teaspoon salt	1/2 cup raisins or sweetened dried cranberries
1 cup Grape-Nuts cereal	
1 cup skim milk	
1 egg, lightly beaten	

Combine the flour, baking powder, cinnamon and salt. Combine the cereal and milk in a bowl and let stand for 3 minutes. Add the egg, applesauce, brown sugar, margarine and raisins and mix well. Add the dry ingredients and stir just until moistened; the batter will be lumpy. Fill 12 greased muffin cups 2/3 full. Bake at 400 degrees for 20 minutes or until the muffins test done. Cool in the pan for 5 minutes. Remove to a wire rack to cool completely. Yield: 12 servings.

Diane Kobrin, Preceptor Eta Omega
Port Saint Lucie, Florida

MIRACLE WHIP BANANA MUFFINS

1/2 cup granulated sugar	1 teaspoon baking soda
1/2 cup Miracle Whip Dressing	1/2 cup packed brown sugar
1/2 cup mashed bananas	1 teaspoon cinnamon
1 cup all-purpose flour	

Combine the granulated sugar, Miracle Whip, bananas, flour and baking soda in a bowl and mix well. Fill 10 to 12 nonstick muffin cups 2/3 full. Mix the brown sugar and cinnamon in a bowl. Sprinkle evenly over the muffins. Bake at 350 degrees for 20 minutes or until the muffins test done. Cool in the pan for 5 minutes. Remove to a wire rack to cool completely. Yield: 10 to 12 servings.

Kathie Connor, Laureate Delta Mu
Oshawa, Ontario, Canada

BANANA BRAN CHOCOLATE CHIP MUFFINS

1 cup whole wheat flour	1/4 cup molasses
1 cup bran	1/4 cup packed brown
2 1/2 teaspoons baking	sugar
powder	1/2 cup skim milk
1 teaspoon cinnamon	1 1/4 cups mashed
1 egg	bananas
2 tablespoons canola oil	1/4 cup chocolate chips

Mix the whole wheat flour, bran, baking powder and cinnamon in a bowl. Beat the egg, oil, molasses, brown sugar, milk and bananas in a bowl. Add the dry ingredients and stir just until combined. Fold in the chocolate chips. Fill 10 to 12 greased muffin cups 2/3 full. Bake at 350 degrees for 40 to 45 minutes or until a wooden pick inserted in the center comes out clean. Cool in the pan for 10 minutes. Remove to a wire rack to cool completely. Yield: 10 to 12 servings.

Jacki Dyment, Theta
Trail, British Columbia, Canada

OLD-FASHIONED BLUEBERRY MUFFINS

My husband, who is diabetic, loves these muffins.

2 cups all-purpose flour	1/4 cup honey
2 teaspoons baking	2 eggs
powder	1 teaspoon vanilla
3/4 teaspoon salt	extract
1/2 cup (1 stick) light	1/2 cup skim milk
margarine, softened	1 cup fresh or frozen
1 cup Splenda	blueberries

Sift the flour, baking powder and salt together. Beat the margarine, Splenda and honey in a bowl until light and fluffy. Add the eggs 1 at a time, beating well after each addition. Stir in the vanilla. Stir in the dry ingredients and milk. Fold in the blueberries. Fill 10 paper-lined muffin cups 2/3 full. Bake at 350 degrees for 25 to 30 minutes or until golden brown. Cool in the pan for 10 minutes. Remove to a wire rack to cool completely. Yield: 10 servings.

Diane Heil, Laureate Kappa
Knoxville, Arkansas

RHUBARB PECAN MUFFINS

This recipe won the "Best Muffin Across Canada" contest and once you taste them, you'll know why.

2 cups all-purpose flour	1 egg
3/4 cup sugar	1/4 cup vegetable oil
1 1/2 teaspoons baking	2 teaspoons grated
powder	orange zest
1/2 teaspoon baking soda	3/4 cup orange juice
1 teaspoon salt	1 1/4 cups finely chopped
3/4 cup chopped pecans	rhubarb

Combine the flour, sugar, baking powder, baking soda, salt and pecans in a large bowl. Beat the egg in a bowl. Beat in the oil, orange zest and orange juice. Add to the dry ingredients and stir just until combined. Fold in the rhubarb. Fill 12 lightly greased muffin cups 3/4 full. Bake at 350 degrees for 25 to 30 minutes or until the muffins test done. Cool in the pan for 5 minutes. Remove to a wire rack to cool completely. Yield: 12 servings.

Ginette Hunter, Xi Theta
Niagara Falls, Ontario, Canada

GLUTEN-FREE FRENCH BREAKFAST PUFFS

If you are not concerned about gluten, you may substitute 1 1/2 cups all-purpose flour for the rice flour mix, sweet rice flour, sorghum flour and xanthan gum.

3/4 cup rice flour mix	1/2 teaspoon salt
1/4 cup sweet rice flour	1/4 teaspoon nutmeg
1/4 cup sorghum flour	1/3 cup shortening
1 teaspoon xanthan gum	1/2 cup sugar
1 1/2 teaspoons baking	1 egg
powder	1/2 cup milk

Combine the first 8 ingredients in a bowl. Beat the shortening, sugar and egg in a bowl until light and fluffy. Add the dry ingredients and milk and mix well. Fill 8 greased muffin cups 2/3 full. Bake at 350 degrees for 20 to 25 minutes or until the muffins test done. Cool in the pan for 5 minutes. Remove to a wire rack to cool completely. Yield: 8 servings.

Betty Doubravsky, Laureate Delta Beta
Dove Creek, Colorado

Christine Berry, Delta Phi, Adrian, Missouri, shared her recipe for **Cake Mix Muffins**. *She chooses any flavor cake mix (such as spice or carrot) and mixes it with one 15-ounce can pumpkin in a bowl. She spoons the mixture into muffin cups and bakes the muffins at 350 degrees for 20 minutes.*

DANISH PUFF

1 cup all-purpose flour	1 cup all-purpose flour
1/2 cup (1 stick) butter or margarine	3 eggs
2 tablespoons water	1 teaspoon vanilla extract
1/2 cup (1 stick) butter or margarine	Almond Glaze
1 cup water	Ground walnuts

Place 1 cup flour in a bowl. Cut in 1/2 cup butter until crumbly. Add 2 tablespoons water and stir to form a dough. Shape the dough into a ball, cut in half and place on a nonstick baking sheet. Pat each portion into a 3×12-inch rectangle, leaving 3 inches between the rectangles. Combine 1/2 cup butter and 1 cup water in a saucepan. Bring to a boil over medium heat, stirring occasionally. Add 1 cup flour and remove from the heat. Stir until smooth. Remove to a bowl. Add the eggs one at a time, beating well after each addition. Add the vanilla and beat until smooth. Spread evenly over the dough strips and smooth the tops. Bake at 350 degrees for 55 minutes. Remove to a wire rack to cool. Spread the Almond Glaze over the cooled puffs and sprinkle with ground walnuts. Yield: 15 servings.

ALMOND GLAZE

2 cups confectioners' sugar	2 tablespoons milk
1/4 cup (1/2 stick) butter, softened	1/2 teaspoon almond extract

Beat the confectioners' sugar and butter in a bowl until light and fluffy. Add the milk and almond extract and beat until smooth.

Patti Maier, Phi Master
Joseph, Oregon

HOT APPLE ROLLS

2 cups all-purpose flour	1/2 cup milk
2 teaspoons baking powder	2 cups chopped apples
1/4 teaspoon salt	1/2 cup chopped pecans (optional)
1/2 cup (1 stick) margarine	2 cups water
1 egg, beaten	2/3 cup sugar
	1 teaspoon cinnamon

Mix the flour, baking powder and salt in a bowl. Cut in the margarine until crumbly. Add the egg and milk and stir to form a dough. Roll out the dough on a floured work surface to 1/4-inch thickness. Top with the apples and pecans. Roll to enclose the filling. Cut into 1-inch slices. Arrange the slices, cut side down, in a nonstick 9×13-inch baking pan. Combine the water, sugar and cinnamon in a saucepan. Bring to a

boil over medium heat and cook until clear, stirring constantly. Pour around the rolls in the pan, but not directly on the rolls. Bake at 400 degrees for 25 minutes. Remove to a wire rack to cool completely. Yield: 12 servings.

Janet Bagley, Preceptor Eta
Milford, Maine

CHERRY CHIP SCONES

3 cups all-purpose flour	1/4 cup milk
1/2 cup sugar	1 1/3 cups dried cherries or chopped dried apricots
2 1/2 teaspoons baking powder	
1/2 teaspoon baking soda	2/3 cup vanilla or white chocolate chips
6 tablespoons butter	2 tablespoons milk
1 cup vanilla yogurt	

Mix the flour, sugar, baking powder and baking soda in a bowl. Cut in the butter until crumbly. Mix the yogurt and 1/4 cup milk in a small bowl. Add to the flour mixture and stir just until moistened. Fold in the dried cherries and vanilla chips. Pat into a 9-inch circle on a greased baking sheet. Cut into 8 wedges and separate. Brush with 2 tablespoons milk. Bake at 400 degrees for 20 to 25 minutes. Remove to a wire rack to cool. Serve warm. Yield: 8 to 16 servings.

Flora Kremin, Phi Master
Riverview, Michigan

ORANGE WHIRLIGIGS

2 cups baking mix	1/2 cup confectioners' sugar
1/2 cup water, milk or orange juice	1/2 teaspoon grated orange zest
3 tablespoons butter, softened	1 teaspoon butter, softened
2 teaspoons grated orange zest	Orange juice or milk
2 teaspoons cinnamon-sugar	

Combine the baking mix and water in a bowl. Stir to form a dough. Knead 6 to 8 times on a floured work surface. Roll into a 1/2-inch thick rectangle. Spread with 3 tablespoons butter. Sprinkle with 2 teaspoons orange zest and the cinnamon-sugar. Roll up lengthwise to enclose the filling and cut into 1-inch slices. Arrange the slices, cut side down, in a nonstick 9×11-inch baking pan. Bake at 425 degrees for 10 to 15 minutes. Remove to a wire rack to cool completely. Combine the confectioners' sugar, 1/2 teaspoon orange zest and 1 teaspoon butter in a bowl. Stir in enough juice to make a glaze. Drizzle over the cake. Yield: 12 servings.

Nancy Purkey, Pi Iota
Overland Park, Kansas

MAPLE PECAN CRESCENT TWISTS

2 (8-count) cans
refrigerated crescent
rolls
2 tablespoons butter,
melted
1/2 cup chopped pecans

1/4 cup granulated sugar
1 teaspoon cinnamon
1/2 cup confectioners'
sugar
2 tablespoons maple
syrup

Separate the crescent dough into 8 rectangles and press the seams to seal. Brush with the butter. Mix the pecans, granulated sugar and cinnamon in a bowl. Sprinkle evenly over the rectangles. Roll up each rectangle lengthwise and pinch the edges to seal. Cut one roll in half lengthwise with a sharp knife to form 2 strips. Overlap the strips, cut side up, two times to form a twist shape. Pinch the ends of the twist to seal. Repeat with the remaining 7 rolls. Arrange the twists on a greased baking sheet. Bake at 375 degrees for 12 to 15 minutes. Remove to a wire rack to cool. Mix the confectioners' sugar and maple syrup in a bowl until smooth. Drizzle over the warm twists.
Yield: 8 servings.

Jeanne Wilson, Laureate Epsilon Theta
Belleville, Ontario, Canada

ZUCCHINI LEMON LOAF

This is so moist and good that I have used it to make wedding cakes.

3 cups all-purpose flour
1 teaspoon salt
1 teaspoon baking
powder
1 teaspoon baking soda
3 eggs
2 cups granulated sugar
1 cup vegetable oil
Grated zest of 1 lemon

Juice of 1 lemon
2 teaspoons vanilla
extract
1 cup chopped nuts
2 cups shredded zucchini
Additional lemon juice
1 cup confectioners'
sugar

Sift the flour, salt, baking powder and baking soda together. Beat the eggs in a bowl until thick and pale yellow. Beat in the granulated sugar and oil. Beat in the lemon zest, lemon juice and vanilla. Beat in the dry ingredients. Fold in the nuts and zucchini. Pour into 2 greased and floured 5×9-inch loaf pans. Bake at 350 degrees for 1 hour or until the bread tests done. Cool in the pans for 10 minutes. Remove to a wire rack. Place the confectioners' sugar in a bowl. Add enough lemon juice to make a glaze. Drizzle over the warm loaves. Yield: 40 servings.

Elizabeth Franks, Laureate Iota
Moose Jaw, Saskatchewan, Canada

APPLE AMBROSIA DUMPLINGS

1 cup granulated sugar
1 cup water
1/2 teaspoon red food
coloring
8 cups sliced peeled
apples
1 1/2 cups all-purpose
flour
1/2 teaspoon salt

2 teaspoons baking
powder
1/4 cup shortening
3/4 cup milk
2 tablespoons butter,
melted
2 tablespoons brown
sugar
1/2 teaspoon cinnamon

Combine the granulated sugar, water and food coloring in a medium saucepan and bring to a boil over medium heat. Cook until the sugar dissolves, stirring occasionally. Place the apples in an even layer in a greased 9×13-inch baking dish. Pour the sugar syrup over the apples. Sift the flour, salt and baking powder into a large bowl. Cut in the shortening until crumbly. Stir in the milk just until the mixture forms a dough. Drop by large spoonfuls onto the apple mixture to form dumplings. Make a shallow indentation in the top of each dumpling with a tablespoon. Combine the butter, brown sugar and cinnamon in a small bowl and mix well. Spoon the sugar mixture into the indentations. Bake at 450 degrees for 25 to 30 minutes or until the dumplings are golden and the apples are tender. Yield: 16 servings.

Wendy Horton, Xi Epsilon Theta
Port Perry, Ontario, Canada

APPLE CRISP

No one will guess that this delicious dessert is low in fat and light in calories—only 180 per serving.

6 small apples, peeled
and sliced
1/4 teaspoon grated
lemon zest
2 tablespoons lemon
juice
1/2 cup all-purpose flour

2 tablespoons light
brown sugar
1 teaspoon cinnamon
1/4 teaspoon allspice
1/4 cup (1/2 stick)
margarine

Place the apples in a greased 9-inch pie plate. Sprinkle with the lemon zest and lemon juice. Combine the flour, brown sugar, cinnamon and allspice in a medium bowl. Cut in the margarine until crumbly. Sprinkle over the apples. Bake at 350 degrees for 30 to 40 minutes or until the topping is brown and the apples are tender. Yield: 6 servings.

Patricia Fordem, Preceptor Mu Sigma
Borrego Springs, California

NUTTY APPLE CRISP

This has long been my family's favorite dessert. It's my mother's recipe from a 1941 newspaper clipping.

1 cup sugar	6 cups thinly sliced
3/4 cup all-purpose flour	peeled tart cooking
1 teaspoon cinnamon	apples
3/4 teaspoon salt	3/4 cup chopped walnuts
1/2 cup (1 stick) butter or	or chopped pecans
margarine	

Sift the sugar, flour, cinnamon and salt into a large bowl. Cut in the butter until crumbly. Place the apples in a greased 9×9-inch baking pan. Top with the walnuts and the crumb mixture. Bake at 350 degrees for 45 minutes or until the apples are fork tender. Serve with vanilla ice cream or whipped topping if desired. Yield: 9 servings.

Linda Isbell, Omicron Xi Preceptor
Flower Mound, Texas

APPLE DEW COBBLER

2 (8-count) packages	1 cup (2 sticks) butter
refrigerated crescent	1 cup packed brown
rolls	sugar
2 Granny Smith apples,	1 teaspoon cinnamon
peeled and sliced into	1 (12-ounce) can
8 wedges	Mountain Dew

Separate the rolls into triangles. Place an apple wedge at the large end of each triangle and roll up. Arrange the rolls in a 9×13-inch baking pan. Melt the butter in a medium saucepan and add the brown sugar and cinnamon. Cook over medium heat until smooth, stirring occasionally. Pour over the rolls. Pour the Mountain Dew evenly over the top. Bake at 350 degrees for 40 minutes or until brown and bubbly. Cool slightly before serving. Serve with vanilla ice cream or whipped cream if desired. Yield: 16 servings.

Barbara Savage, Laureate Tau
Jacksonville, Arkansas

APPLE FRITTERS

3 or 4 apples, peeled	2 tablespoons
and cored	granulated sugar
2 egg yolks	1/4 teaspoon salt
4 cups milk	2 egg whites, at room
1 tablespoon lemon	temperature
juice	1/8 teaspoon salt
1 tablespoon butter,	Vegetable oil for
melted	deep-frying
1 cup all-purpose flour	Confectioners' sugar

Cut the apples crosswise into 3/8-inch slices, forming rings. Beat the egg yolks and milk in a large bowl until blended. Stir in the lemon juice and butter. Sift the flour, granulated sugar and 1/4 teaspoon salt into the bowl. Stir just until combined. Beat the egg whites and 1/8 teaspoon salt in a bowl until stiff peaks form. Fold into the batter. Dip the apple rings in the batter to coat. Fry, a few at a time, in 375-degree oil until light brown. Remove with a slotted spoon. Drain on paper towels. Sprinkle with confectioners' sugar. Yield: 6 servings.

Nancy Auf DerHeide, Pi Iota
Shawnee, Kansas

APPLE SCALLOP

My grandmother made this recipe when I was a child. With plenty of apples in the orchard, the ingredients were always at hand.

1 cup sifted all-purpose	1/2 cup (1 stick) butter or
flour	margarine
1/4 cup packed brown	4 cups sliced peeled
sugar	cooking apples
	Dash of cinnamon

Combine the flour and brown sugar in a bowl. Cut in the butter until crumbly. Place the apples in a greased 9×9-inch baking pan. Sprinkle with the cinnamon. Top with the flour mixture. Bake at 375 degrees for 45 minutes or until the apples are tender. Yield: 6 servings.

Edna Faye Williams, Delta Omicron
Kennett, Missouri

APPLE PIE BARS

3 cups all-purpose flour	12 cups thinly sliced
1 teaspoon baking	peeled apples
powder	1 cup granulated sugar
1 teaspoon salt	1 teaspoon cinnamon
1 cup shortening	Vanilla Glaze
1/3 cup milk	

Sift the flour, baking powder and salt into a large bowl. Cut in the shortening until crumbly. Stir in the milk just until a dough forms. Shape into a ball and divide in half. Roll half the dough into a 10×15-inch rectangle on a lightly floured surface. Place the rectangle in a 10×15-inch baking pan or onto a baking sheet. Mix the apples, granulated sugar and cinnamon in a large bowl. Spread over the dough. Roll the remaining dough into a 10×15-inch rectangle and place over the filling. Seal the edges. Prick the top crust with a fork. Bake at 400 degrees for 30 minutes or until golden brown. Drizzle with Vanilla Glaze. Cool and cut into bars. Yield: 15 servings.

VANILLA GLAZE

1 cup confectioners'
  sugar
2 tablespoons hot water

1/4 teaspoon vanilla
  extract

Combine the confectioners' sugar, water and vanilla in a small bowl and stir until smooth.

Karol Scott, Xi Omicron Kappa
Camarillo, California

BAKED BANANAS WITH COCONUT CREAM

1 cup heavy whipping
  cream
1 cup grated coconut
  (fresh preferred)
5 large firm bananas

1/4 cup (1/2 stick) butter,
  melted
1/2 cup sugar
1/2 cup lemon juice
1 tablespoon cinnamon

Whip the cream in a bowl until stiff peaks form. Fold in the coconut. Chill, covered, for 30 minutes. Place the bananas in a greased 9×13-inch baking dish. Mix the butter, sugar, lemon juice and cinnamon in a bowl. Pour over the bananas. Bake at 350 degrees for 30 minutes or until hot and bubbly. Serve hot with the coconut cream. Yield: 6 to 7 servings.

Jeanne Gordon, Preceptor Epsilon Pi
Trenton, Ontario, Canada

LAYERED BANANA PINEAPPLE DESSERT

You can use sugar-free pudding and fat-free whipped topping.

1 1/2 cups graham cracker
  crumbs
1/4 cup sugar
1/3 cup butter or
  margarine, melted
3 bananas, sliced
8 ounces cream cheese,
  softened

3 1/2 cups 2% milk
2 (4-ounce) packages
  vanilla instant
  pudding mix
1 (20-ounce) can crushed
  pineapple, drained
8 ounces whipped
  topping

Combine the graham cracker crumbs, sugar and butter in a bowl and mix well. Press onto the bottom of a 9×13-inch baking dish. Arrange the banana slices over the crust. Beat the cream cheese in a large bowl until fluffy. Beat in the milk gradually until combined. Add the pudding mix and mix well. Spread evenly over the bananas. Spoon the pineapple over the pudding layer. Spread the whipped topping evenly over the top. Chill for 3 hours or until just before serving. Yield: 15 servings.

Jackie Altman, Preceptor Tau
Fairview, Oregon

CHERRY PIZZA

2 (8-count) packages
  refrigerated
  crescent rolls
8 ounces cream cheese,
  softened
1 egg yolk

1/4 cup confectioners'
  sugar
1/2 teaspoon vanilla
  extract
1 (21-ounce) can cherry
  pie filling
1 egg white

Separate the rolls into 16 triangles. Arrange 12 of the triangles on a pizza pan to form a round crust and press the edges together. Bake at 350 degrees for 10 minutes. Cool. Combine the cream cheese, egg yolk, confectioners' sugar and vanilla in a bowl and beat until smooth and fluffy. Spread over the crust. Spread with the pie filling. Beat the egg white in a small bowl until stiff peaks form. Spread over the pie filling. Cut the remaining 4 crescent roll triangles in half lengthwise. Roll each piece of dough into a bread stick shape and arrange on top of the pizza. Bake at 350 degrees for 20 minutes or until light brown. Yield: 8 servings.

Sue Boland, Beta Delta Master
Warrensburg, Missouri

MOCK CLOTTED CREAM

1 cup heavy whipping
  cream
1/3 cup softened cream
  cheese or sour cream

1 teaspoon
  confectioners' sugar
1 teaspoon vanilla
  extract

Place all the ingredients in a blender or food processor and process until thick and smooth. Store, covered, in the refrigerator for up to 4 days. Yield: 1 1/2 cups.

Joycee Davis, Laureate Alpha Epsilon
Lowell, Arkansas

EASY COBBLER

1/2 cup (1 stick) butter or
  margarine, melted
1 cup sugar
1 1/2 teaspoons baking
  powder

1 cup all-purpose flour
3/4 cup milk
3 cups chopped fresh or
  canned fruit
1/2 to 3/4 cup sugar

Pour the butter in an 8×8-inch baking dish. Combine 1 cup sugar, baking powder, flour and milk in a bowl and mix well. Drizzle over the melted butter. Combine the fruit with sugar to taste in a bowl and mix well. Spoon over the batter. Bake at 350 degrees for 50 minutes or until golden and bubbly. Yield: 4 to 6 servings.

Liz Smith, Preceptor Alpha Gamma
Brookfield, Missouri

OLD-FASHIONED FRUIT COBBLER

4 cups fresh fruit, or 3 (15-ounce) cans fruit, drained	1/2 teaspoon salt
Cinnamon	1/2 cup (1 stick) butter, melted
Nutmeg	1 cup milk
2 cups all-purpose flour	3/4 cup sugar
1 1/4 cups sugar	1 tablespoon cornstarch
2 teaspoons baking powder	1/4 teaspoon salt
	1 cup boiling water

Place the fruit in a 9×13-inch baking pan and sprinkle lightly with cinnamon and nutmeg. Combine the flour, 1 1/4 cups sugar, baking powder, 1/2 teaspoon salt, butter and milk in a large bowl and mix well. Pour over the fruit. Combine 3/4 cup sugar, the cornstarch and 1/4 teaspoon salt in a small bowl and mix well. Sprinkle over the batter. Pour the boiling water evenly over the top. Bake at 350 degrees for 1 hour or until golden and bubbly. Yield: 12 to 15 servings.

Becky Rogers, Kappa Kappa
Meriden, Kansas

FRUIT COBBLER

My mother, now deceased, gave me this recipe 40 years ago. Whenever I make it, I always think of her.

1/4 cup (1/2 stick) butter, softened	1/4 teaspoon salt
1/2 cup sugar	1/2 cup milk
1 cup sifted all-purpose flour	4 cups fresh or canned fruit
2 1/2 teaspoons baking powder	1/4 to 1 cup sugar
	1 cup fruit juice or water

Combine the butter and 1/2 cup sugar in a bowl and beat until smooth. Add the flour, baking powder, salt and milk and mix well. Pour into a greased 9×13-inch baking dish. Top with the fruit and sugar to taste. Pour the juice evenly over the top. Bake at 375 degrees for 45 to 50 minutes or until golden and bubbly. Yield: 6 to 8 servings.

Elizabeth Fuller, Preceptor Theta Mu
Stuart, Florida

BERRY APPLE COBBLER

2 (12-ounce) packages frozen mixed berries, thawed and drained	1/2 cup sugar
	1 1/2 teaspoons cinnamon
1 (21-ounce) can apple pie filling	1 (20-ounce) package refrigerated sugar cookie dough

Combine the berries, pie filling, sugar and cinnamon in a large bowl and mix well. Pour into a greased 8×8-inch baking dish. Crumble the cookie dough evenly over the fruit mixture. Bake at 350 degrees for 45 minutes or until the crust is crisp and golden and the filling is bubbly. Serve warm with vanilla ice cream if desired. Yield: 8 servings.

Joan Lutz, Laureate Alpha Eta
Oneonta, New York

COOKIE APPLE COBBLER

8 cups sliced peeled apples	2 tablespoons lemon juice
1 cup packed brown sugar	1 (20-ounce) package refrigerated sugar cookie dough
2 tablespoons all-purpose flour	2 tablespoons granulated sugar
1 teaspoon cinnamon	1/2 teaspoon cinnamon
1/2 teaspoon allspice	

Combine the apples, brown sugar, flour, 1 teaspoon cinnamon, allspice and lemon juice in a large bowl and mix well. Spoon into an ungreased 9×13-inch baking dish. Crumble the cookie dough evenly over the apples. Combine the granulated sugar and 1/2 teaspoon cinnamon in a small bowl and mix well. Sprinkle over the dough. Bake at 350 degrees for 35 to 45 minutes or until the top is golden brown and the apples are tender. Yield: 8 servings.

Berlita Anderson, Laureate Kappa
Beatrice, Nebraska

BLACKBERRY COBBLER

2 1/2 cups blackberries	2 to 3 tablespoons butter or margarine, melted
1 tablespoon orange liqueur	
3/4 cup packed brown sugar	1 teaspoon baking powder
3/4 cup granulated sugar	1/2 teaspoon salt
1 cup all-purpose flour	1 tablespoon cornstarch
1/2 cup milk	3/4 cup boiling water

Place the blackberries in an 8×8-inch baking dish. Sprinkle with the liqueur. Combine the brown sugar and granulated sugar in a small bowl. Combine the flour, half the sugar mixture, the milk, butter, baking powder and salt in a large bowl and mix well. Spread over the berries, covering completely. Stir the cornstarch into the remaining sugar mixture. Sprinkle over the batter. Pour the boiling water evenly over the top, covering completely. Bake at 350 degrees for 1 hour and 10 minutes or until the crust is golden brown. Serve warm with ice cream if desired. Yield: 6 to 8 servings.

Mary E. McGriff, Xi Beta Kappa
Columbia, South Carolina

BISCUIT-TOPPED BLUEBERRY COBBLER

My mom made this for my son for many years. Now that she is gone, I make it for him.

2/3 cup sugar	*2 tablespoons fresh*
2 tablespoons	*lemon juice*
cornstarch	*Biscuit Dough*
1/4 teaspoon freshly	*2 teaspoons sugar*
grated nutmeg	*1/8 teaspoon freshly*
2 1/2 pints blueberries	*grated nutmeg*
(5 1/4 cups)	
2 teaspoons grated	
lemon zest	

Whisk together the sugar, cornstarch and 1/4 teaspoon nutmeg in a large bowl. Stir in the blueberries, lemon zest and lemon juice. Pour into a 9×13-inch baking dish and cover tightly. Bake at 400 degrees for 20 minutes. Uncover and stir the berries. Divide the Biscuit Dough into 8 mounds and drop onto the berries. Mix 2 teaspoons sugar and 1/8 teaspoon nutmeg in a small bowl. Sprinkle over the dough. Bake for 35 minutes or until the biscuits are golden and the filling is bubbly. Cool. Serve warm or at room temperature. Yield: 8 servings.

BISCUIT DOUGH

2 cups all-purpose flour	*2 cups heavy whipping*
3 tablespoons sugar	*cream*
2 teaspoons baking	*2 teaspoons grated*
powder	*lemon zest*
1/2 teaspoon salt	

Whisk together the flour, sugar, baking powder and salt in a medium bowl. Add the cream and lemon zest, stirring just until a very soft dough forms.

Carlene VanBlaricum, Laureate Upsilon
Carolina Shores, North Carolina

PEACH COBBLER

For a wintertime dessert, use canned pie filling instead of fresh fruit and omit the sugar.

3/4 cup all-purpose flour	*1/2 cup (1 stick) butter or*
2 teaspoons baking	*margarine, melted*
powder	*2 cups sliced peaches or*
Dash of salt	*other fruit*
1 cup sugar	*1 cup sugar*
3/4 cup milk	

Sift the flour, baking powder and salt into a large bowl. Stir in 1 cup sugar. Stir in the milk gradually until smooth. Pour the butter into a 9×13-inch baking dish. Drizzle the batter over the melted butter. Do not stir. Combine the peaches and sugar in a bowl and mix well. Spoon the fruit over the batter. Bake at 350 degrees for 1 hour or until golden and bubbly. Yield: 8 to 12 servings.

Helen (Suzi) Boggs, Xi Theta Upsilon
Riverview, Florida

CRANBERRY PEACH COBBLER

1 (2-layer) package	*1 cup chopped nuts*
yellow cake mix	*2 (16-ounce) cans peach*
1 teaspoon cinnamon	*pie filling*
1 teaspoon nutmeg	*1 (16-ounce) can whole*
1/2 cup (1 stick) butter or	*cranberry sauce*
margarine	*Vanilla ice cream*

Combine the cake mix, cinnamon and nutmeg in a large bowl and mix well. Cut in the butter until crumbly. Stir in the nuts. Pour the pie filling and the cranberry sauce into an ungreased 9×13-inch baking pan and stir to combine. Sprinkle with the crumb mixture. Bake at 350 degrees for 45 to 50 minutes or until golden brown. Serve with vanilla ice cream. Yield: 12 servings.

Sandra E. Moody, Preceptor Eta Sigma
Trinity, Florida

SOUTHERN DEEP-DISH PEACH COBBLER

2 cups all-purpose flour	*1/2 teaspoon cinnamon*
1 teaspoon salt	*Dash of salt*
3/4 cup shortening	*9 cups sliced peaches*
1/4 cup cold water	*3 tablespoons butter*
2 1/4 cups sugar	*1 tablespoon sugar*
4 1/2 tablespoons	*1/4 to 1/2 teaspoon*
all-purpose flour	*cinnamon*

Combine 2 cups flour and 1 teaspoon salt in a bowl. Cut in the shortening until crumbly. Stir in the water gradually to form a dough. Shape into a ball and divide in half. Roll out each half on a lightly floured surface to a 9×9-inch square. Combine 2 1/4 cups sugar, 4 1/2 tablespoons flour, 1/2 teaspoon cinnamon and a dash of salt in a large bowl and mix well. Add the peaches and stir gently to coat. Spoon half of the peaches in a 9×9-inch baking pan. Dot with half the butter. Top with 1 of the crusts and cut vents. Bake at 375 degrees for 15 to 20 minutes. Remove from the oven and top with the remaining peaches. Dot with the remaining butter. Top with the remaining crust and cut vents. Combine 1 tablespoon sugar and 1/4 teaspoon cinnamon in a small bowl and mix well. Sprinkle over the crust. Return to the oven and bake for 40 to 50 minutes or until golden brown and bubbly. Yield: 8 to 10 servings.

LaVonda Wentworth, Laureate Omega
Enid, Oklahoma

EASY STRAWBERRY COBBLER

This recipe offers a refreshing change from chilled strawberry pie—with much less effort. Frozen berries work well if fresh aren't available.

1/2 cup (1 stick) butter or margarine, melted	1 cup milk
1 cup all-purpose flour	3 cups sliced strawberries
1 cup sugar	1 cup sugar
1 tablespoon baking powder	1 cup water
1/2 teaspoon salt	Cinnamon to taste (optional)

Pour the butter in 9×13-inch baking dish. Combine the flour, 1 cup sugar, baking powder and salt in a large bowl and mix well. Stir in the milk gradually until smooth. Drizzle over the melted butter. Combine the strawberries, 1 cup sugar and the water in a large bowl and stir gently to dissolve the sugar. Pour over the batter and sprinkle with the cinnamon. Bake at 350 degrees for 45 minutes or until golden brown. Cool. Cut into squares. Serve with ice cream, frozen yogurt or whipped topping if desired. Yield: 8 to 12 servings.

Sandra Beard, Laureate Theta Theta
San Antonio, Texas

HOT FRUIT CASSEROLE

1 (20-ounce) can pineapple slices	1 (29-ounce) can pear halves, drained
1/4 cup green maraschino cherries, drained and halved	1 (16-ounce) jar spiced apple rings, drained
1/4 cup red maraschino cherries, drained and halved	1 cup sugar
	1/2 cup all-purpose flour
1 (29-ounce) can peach halves, drained	1/2 cup (1 stick) margarine
	1/2 cup cooking sherry

Drain the pineapple and reserve 1/2 cup of the juice. Place the maraschino cherries, pineapple slices, peaches, pears and apple rings in a greased 9×13-inch baking dish. Combine the sugar, flour, reserved pineapple juice and margarine in a heavy saucepan. Cook over medium heat until smooth, stirring constantly. Stir in the sherry. Remove from the heat and pour over the fruit. Chill, covered, for 24 hours. Bake at 350 degrees for 40 minutes or until hot and bubbly. Yield: 8 to 10 servings.

June Turner, Laureate Rho
Fountain Inn, South Carolina

❖ FRUIT SALSA

1 pound strawberries, sliced	1 Granny Smith apple, peeled and chopped
3 kiwifruit, sliced	2 tablespoons apple jelly
1/3 cup chopped celery	

Combine the strawberries and kiwifruit in a bowl. Add the celery, apple and apple jelly and mix well. Spoon into an airtight container and chill until just before serving. Yield: 4 to 6 servings.

Kathy Kuper, Xi Xi Tau
Lubbock, Texas

GLACÉ BAKED FRUIT

This recipe makes a large amount—perfect for potlucks and family dinners.

1 (21-ounce) can apple pie filling	1 (12-ounce) package pitted dried plums (prunes)
1 (21-ounce) can cherry pie filling	1 (11-ounce) can mandarin oranges, drained
1 (16-ounce) can peach slices, drained	Salt
1 (16-ounce) can pear halves	3 to 4 tablespoons butter or margarine
1 (15-ounce) can pineapple tidbits, drained	

Combine the pie fillings, peaches, pears, pineapple, prunes and mandarin oranges in a 9×13-inch baking dish. Sprinkle with salt and dot with butter. Bake at 350 degrees for 1 hour or until hot and bubbly. Serve hot, warm or chilled. Yield: 12 to 16 servings.

Janice W. von Riesen, Omicron Master
Manhattan, Kansas

FRUIT COCKTAIL PUDDING WITH BUTTER SAUCE

This recipe can be cut in half and baked in an 8-inch square pan. The pudding can be made one day in advance.

1 (29-ounce) can fruit cocktail in light syrup	2 cups sugar
2 eggs	2 teaspoons baking soda
2 cups all-purpose flour	1 teaspoon salt
	Butter Sauce

Drain the fruit cocktail syrup into a large bowl. Add the eggs and beat well. Combine the flour, sugar, baking soda and salt in a bowl and mix well. Add to the egg mixture and mix well. Fold in the fruit cocktail. Pour into a greased 9×13-inch baking pan. Bake at 375 degrees for 35 to 45 minutes or until golden. Drizzle with warm Butter Sauce. Yield: 15 to 20 servings.

BUTTER SAUCE

1 cup (2 sticks) butter
2 cups sugar
1 (12-ounce) can evaporated milk

Combine the butter, sugar and evaporated milk in a large saucepan. Cook over medium heat for 5 minutes or until the sugar dissolves and the mixture is smooth, stirring constantly.

E. Joan Neill, Master Gamma
Saint John, New Brunswick, Canada

FROZEN FRUIT SLUSH

This refreshing make-ahead dessert is a great choice for summer cookouts.

2 bananas, chopped
1 cup sugar
1 (6-ounce) can frozen orange juice concentrate, thawed
1 (8-ounce) can crushed pineapple
3 tablespoons lemon juice
2 cups lemon-lime soda

Combine the bananas, sugar, orange juice concentrate, pineapple, lemon juice and soda in a large bowl and mix well. Pour into a 9×9-inch pan. Freeze for 1 1/2 to 2 hours. Remove from the freezer. Scoop the frozen mixture into a large bowl and beat until slushy. Return to the pan and freeze. Remove from the freezer 20 minutes before serving. Yield: 8 to 9 servings.

Carol Ann Johannigmeier, Alpha Gamma Master
Fort Collins, Colorado

GRAPE DESSERT

For a smaller crowd, halve the recipe and use an 8×8-inch pan.

8 ounces cream cheese, softened
1 cup sour cream
1/2 cup granulated sugar
1/2 teaspoon vanilla extract
2 pounds each seedless green grapes and seedless red grapes, rinsed and patted dry
1 cup chopped pecans
2 cups packed brown sugar

Combine the cream cheese, sour cream, granulated sugar and vanilla in a large bowl and beat until smooth. Fold in the grapes. Pour into a 9×13-inch dish. Combine the pecans and brown sugar in a bowl and mix well. Sprinkle over the grape mixture and press lightly. Chill, covered, for 24 hours.
Yield: 18 to 20 servings.

Diana A. Burge, Laureate Gamma Theta
Niles, Michigan

CHILLED FRUIT AND CREAM SQUARES

2 (6-ounce) packages apricot gelatin
1 (20-ounce) can crushed pineapple
3 or 4 bananas, sliced
1 cup miniature marshmallows
1 egg
1/2 cup sugar
3 tablespoons all-purpose flour
8 ounces cream cheese, softened
8 ounces whipped topping
Miniature chocolate chips
Chopped walnuts

Prepare the gelatin using the package directions and 3/4 cup less water. Pour into a bowl and chill until partially set. Drain the pineapple and reserve the juice. Fold in the pineapple and bananas and pour into a greased 9×13-inch dish. Top with the marshmallows and chill until firm. Beat the egg and the reserved pineapple juice in a medium saucepan. Add the sugar and flour. Cook over medium heat for 5 minutes until thickened and smooth, stirring constantly. Remove from the heat and stir in the cream cheese until smooth. Cool. Place the whipped topping in a large bowl. Fold in the cream cheese mixture. Spread over the gelatin layer. Sprinkle with the chocolate chips and walnuts. Chill until firm. Cut into squares. Yield: 16 servings.

Marie Umbriac, Preceptor Alpha Upsilon
Tamaqua, Pennsylvania

ORANGE PINEAPPLE CREAM

For a lighter version of this dessert, use sugar-free gelatin, light sour cream and whipped topping.

1 (6-ounce) package orange gelatin
2 cups boiling water
1 cup sour cream
1 (8-ounce) can crushed pineapple
1 (11-ounce) can mandarin oranges, drained
Whipped cream or whipped topping

Combine the gelatin, boiling water and sour cream in a large bowl. Stir for 2 minutes or the gelatin dissolves. Chill until partially set. Stir in the pineapple and mandarin oranges. Chill. Spoon into sherbet dishes and top with whipped cream. Yield: 6 servings.

Sharon L. Saundry, Laureate Alpha Iota
Qualicum Beach, British Columbia, Canada

*Carla McDaniel, Preceptor Delta, Centralia, Illinois, makes a creamy **Fruit Dip** by mixing 1 jar marshmallow creme and 8 ounces softened cream cheese in a bowl. She likes to serve the dip with kiwifruit, strawberries, apples, and grapes.*

ORANGE CREAM SQUARES

Try other fruit and gelatin variations on this light, refreshing dessert.

2 (6-ounce) packages
   sugar-free orange
   gelatin
6 cups boiling water
1 (12-ounce) can frozen
   orange juice
   concentrate

1 (15-ounce) can
   mandarin oranges,
   drained
12 ounces fat-free
   whipped topping

Combine the gelatin and boiling water in a large bowl. Stir for 2 minutes or until the gelatin dissolves. Add the orange juice concentrate and mix well. Chill for 1 hour or until partially set. Stir in the mandarin oranges. Chill for 30 minutes. Fold in the whipped topping. Pour into a greased 9×13-inch dish. Chill until firm. Yield: 12 to 15 servings.

Marjorie Werner, Xi Delta
Farmington, Michigan

RASPBERRY YOGURT DESSERT

3 (3-ounce) packages
   raspberry gelatin
1¹/2 cups boiling water
18 ice cubes
1 (12-ounce) package
   frozen raspberries,
   thawed

2¹/2 cups whipped
   topping
12 ounces raspberry
   yogurt

Combine the gelatin and boiling water in a large bowl. Stir for 2 minutes or until the gelatin dissolves. Add the ice cubes and stir until the gelatin begins to set. Remove any remaining ice cubes. Stir in the raspberries. Pour half the gelatin mixture into a glass serving bowl or trifle dish. Add 1 cup of the whipped topping to the remaining gelatin and beat until smooth. Pour over the gelatin in the serving bowl. Mix ¹/2 cup whipped topping with the yogurt in a bowl. Spread on top of the gelatin. Spread the remaining 1 cup whipped topping over the yogurt layer. Chill until set. Yield: 10 to 12 servings.

Rose Mary Coakes, Laureate Alpha Rho
Marshall, Michigan

Carolyn Cunningham, Laureate Beta Gamma, Flint, Texas, enjoys making **Fruit Fondue** *for her grandchildren. She combines 16 ounces chopped milk chocolate and 8 ounces chocolate chips in a double boiler and cooks until smooth, stirring often. She adds 1 cup half-and-half and ¹/4 teaspoon cinnamon and warms the mixture through. She serves the fondue with an assortment of fruit.*

LEMONADE DESSERT SQUARES

This cool, refreshing dessert is especially good in the summer.

2 cups crushed club
   crackers
¹/2 cup (1 stick)
   margarine, melted
2 tablespoons sugar
1 (14-ounce) can
   sweetened
   condensed milk

1 (6-ounce) can frozen
   lemonade
   concentrate, thawed
1 (8-ounce) can crushed
   pineapple, drained
12 ounces whipped
   topping

Combine the crushed crackers, margarine and sugar in a bowl and mix well. Press onto the bottom of a 9×13-inch pan. Combine the condensed milk, lemonade concentrate and pineapple in a large bowl and mix well. Fold in the whipped topping. Pour over the crust. Chill for several hours to overnight. Cut into squares. Garnish with a dollop of whipped topping, a strawberry and a sprig of mint if desired.
Yield: 15 to 18 servings.

Martha Norcross, Laureate Beta Mu
Macomb, Illinois

ORANGE DREAM

This has become our traditional dessert at Easter.

3 cups water
1 (3-ounce) package
   orange gelatin
1 (3-ounce) package
   vanilla instant
   pudding mix
1 (3-ounce) package
   tapioca pudding mix

1 (15-ounce) can
   mandarin oranges,
   drained
1 (8-ounce) can crushed
   pineapple, drained
8 ounces whipped
   topping

Bring the water to a boil in a large saucepan. Whisk in the gelatin and pudding mixes until smooth. Bring to a boil over medium heat, stirring constantly. Boil for 1 minute. Remove from the heat and cool completely. Fold in the mandarin oranges, pineapple and whipped topping. Spoon into a glass serving dish. Chill, covered, for 2 hours. Yield: 12 to 14 servings.

Sharon Brockmeier, Beta Gamma Master
Saint Louis, Missouri

ORANGE PINEAPPLE DESSERT

2 cups graham cracker
   crumbs
¹/2 cup (1 stick)
   margarine, melted
1 (8-ounce) can crushed
   pineapple

1 small package sugar-
   free orange gelatin
12 ounces whipped
   topping
Additional graham
   cracker crumbs

Combine 2 cups graham cracker crumbs and the margarine in a bowl and mix well. Press onto the bottom of a 9×9-inch baking pan. Bake at 350 degrees for 10 minutes. Cool on a wire rack for 5 minutes. Chill. Combine the pineapple and gelatin in a small saucepan and mix well. Bring to a boil over medium heat. Boil for 2 minutes, stirring constantly. Remove from the heat and cool completely. Fold in 1/2 cup of the whipped topping. Spread over the crust. Spread the remaining whipped topping over the gelatin layer. Sprinkle with additional graham cracker crumbs. Chill until set. Yield: 8 to 9 servings.

Madonna McGrath, Preceptor Gamma
Lower Sackville, Nova Scotia, Canada

ORANGE PINEAPPLE CREAM CHEESE SQUARES

1 (6-ounce) package orange gelatin	1 1/2 cups graham cracker crumbs
1 1/2 cups boiling water	1/2 cup (1 stick) butter or margarine, melted
1 cup cold water	
1 (20-ounce) can crushed pineapple	8 ounces cream cheese, softened
1 (11-ounce) can mandarin oranges, drained	1/4 cup sugar
	2 tablespoons milk
1/4 cup sugar	12 ounces whipped topping

Combine the gelatin and boiling water in a large bowl. Stir for 2 minutes or until the gelatin dissolves. Stir in the cold water, pineapple and mandarin oranges. Chill for 1 1/4 hours or until slightly thickened. Combine /4 cup sugar, graham cracker crumbs and butter in a bowl and mix well. Press onto the bottom of a 9×13-inch pan. Chill. Combine the cream cheese, 1/4 cup sugar and the milk in a large bowl and beat until light and fluffy. Fold in 2 cups of the whipped topping. Spread evenly over the crust. Spoon the gelatin mixture evenly over the cream layer. Chill for 2 hours or until firm. Garnish with the remaining whipped topping. Yield: 15 servings.

Vera Todd, Delta Xi
Niagara Falls, Ontario, Canada

ROASTED PEACHES

1/2 cup packed brown sugar	1 tablespoon orange-flavor liqueur
2 tablespoons butter	4 peaches, halved and pitted
3 tablespoons water	
1 teaspoon vanilla or orange extract	Vanilla ice cream

Place the brown sugar, butter and water in a 9×13-inch baking dish. Place in a 350-degree oven for about 6 minutes or until the butter melts and the sugar dissolves. Remove from the oven and whisk in the vanilla and liqueur. Place the peach halves, cut side down, in the sugar mixture. Bake for 15 minutes or until tender. Remove from the oven and carefully remove the peach skins. Spoon into serving dishes and top with vanilla ice cream. Yield: 4 servings.

Dorothy Bieshelt, Epsilon Tau
Columbiana, Ohio

POACHED PEARS

5 cups water	4 pears, peeled and halved
1 cup sugar	
Grated zest of 2 lemons	4 to 8 tablespoons chocolate syrup
Juice of 2 lemons	
2 cinnamon sticks	

Combine the water, sugar, lemon zest, lemon juice and cinnamon sticks in a large saucepan. Bring to a boil. Cook over medium heat for 5 minutes or until the sugar dissolves, stirring constantly. Add the pears to the boiling syrup. Reduce the heat to medium-low and simmer gently for 15 to 20 minutes or until the pears are almost tender. Remove from the heat and let the pears cool in the syrup. Drain and pat dry with paper towels. Drizzle with the chocolate syrup. Yield: 8 servings.

Sandi Davison, Alpha Gamma Master
Kansas City, Missouri

SPICED PEARS IN RED WINE

A slow cooker makes preparation of these blushing poached pears simple and fuss-free.

1 cup red wine	12 cloves
1/2 cup sugar	1 cinnamon stick
6 pears, peeled	

Combine the wine and sugar in a slow cooker. Heat on High until the sugar dissolves. Add the pears, cloves and cinnamon. Cover and cook on Low for 3 to 4 hours or until tender, basting occasionally with the syrup. Serve with ice cream or whipped cream if desired. Yield: 6 servings.

Vicki Collister, Preceptor Tau
Troutdale, Oregon

Julia Gatsos, Laureate Beta Omicron, New Albany, Indiana, entertains with **Fresh Fruit with Yogurt Dip.** *She mixes 8 ounces low-fat vanilla yogurt, 1/4 cup unsweetened applesauce and 1/8 teaspoon cinnamon in a small serving bowl. She spears assorted fresh fruit with decorative picks and places them on a serving platter.*

BAKED PINEAPPLE

This recipe can also be served as a side dish with ham.

2 eggs
1 (20-ounce) can crushed
  pineapple
1/3 cup sugar
1 tablespoon cornstarch
2 tablespoons butter
Cinnamon

Beat the eggs in a large bowl until frothy. Add the pineapple, sugar and cornstarch and mix well. Pour into a greased 1-quart baking dish. Dot with the butter and sprinkle with the cinnamon. Bake at 325 degrees for 1 hour or until hot and bubbly. Yield: 4 to 6 servings.

Mary Beth (Betsy) Schmitz, Laureate Zeta Beta
Fairview, Pennsylvania

COUNTRY PINEAPPLE CASSEROLE

1/2 cup (1 stick) butter or
  margarine, softened
2 cups sugar
8 eggs
3 tablespoons lemon
  juice
2 (20-ounce) cans
  crushed pineapple,
  drained
10 slices day-old white
  bread, cubed

Beat the butter and sugar in a large bowl until light and fluffy. Beat in the eggs 1 at a time. Stir in the lemon juice and pineapple. Fold in the bread cubes. Pour into a greased 9×13-inch baking dish. Bake at 325 degrees for 35 to 40 minutes or until golden and set. Yield: 8 to 10 servings.

Cid Knight, Preceptor Zeta
Carthage, Missouri

PINEAPPLE PRETZEL FLUFF

1 cup crushed pretzels
1/2 cup sugar
1/2 cup (1 stick) butter,
  melted
8 ounces cream cheese,
  softened
1/2 cup sugar
1 (20-ounce) can crushed
  pineapple, drained
12 ounces whipped
  topping

Combine the pretzels, 1/2 cup sugar and butter in a large bowl and mix well. Spread into a 9×13-inch baking pan or onto a baking sheet. Bake at 400 degrees for 7 minutes. Cool. Beat the cream cheese and 1/2 cup sugar in a large bowl until light and fluffy. Fold in the pineapple and whipped topping. Chill. Stir the pretzels into the cream cheese mixture just before serving. Yield: 10 to 12 servings.

Marjorie Snyder, Laureate Zeta Xi
Cedar Creek, Texas

FRUIT SALAD

1 (29-ounce) can peach
  slices
1 (20-ounce) can
  pineapple chucks
1 (15-ounce) can
  mandarin oranges
1 (3-ounce) package
  lemon instant
  pudding mix
2 bananas, sliced
Maraschino cherries
  (optional)

Drain the peaches, pineapple and mandarin oranges, reserving the juices. Place the fruit in a large bowl. Add the pudding mix and stir gently to coat. Chill, covered, for 6 hours to overnight. Stir in the bananas. Add the reserved fruit juice if a thinner consistency is desired. Pour into a glass serving bowl. Top with the maraschino cherries. Yield: 10 servings.

Norma Borgmann, Preceptor Delta
Centralia, Illinois

APRICOT GELATIN SALAD

1 (20-ounce) can crushed
  pineapple
1 (6-ounce) package
  apricot gelatin
2 cups buttermilk
16 ounces whipped
  topping
1 cup chopped pecans

Pour the pineapple into a saucepan and bring to a boil over medium heat, stirring constantly. Remove from the heat and add the gelatin. Stir for 2 minutes or until the gelatin dissolves. Pour into a large bowl and cool. Add the buttermilk and mix well. Chill until partially set. Fold in the whipped topping. Pour into a glass serving bowl. Top with the pecans. Chill until set. Yield: 10 to 12 servings.

Irene G. Berghoff, Pi Master
Bethalto, Illinois

CRANBERRY AND CREAM CHEESE SALAD

1 (6-ounce) package
  raspberry gelatin
1¼ cups boiling water
1 (20-ounce) can crushed
  pineapple
1 (16-ounce) can whole
  cranberry sauce
8 ounces cream cheese,
  softened
1 cup sour cream
1/2 cup walnut pieces

Combine the gelatin and boiling water in a large bowl. Stir for 2 minutes or until the gelatin dissolves. Stir in the pineapple and cranberry sauce. Pour into a 7 x 11-inch pan. Chill until firm. Combine the cream cheese and sour cream in a bowl and beat until fluffy. Spread over the gelatin layer. Sprinkle with the walnuts. Cut into squares just before serving. Yield: 8 to 12 servings.

Ginger Sauter, Xi Beta Lambda
Chambersburg, Pennsylvania

ORANGE SALAD SUPREME

1 egg
1/3 cup sugar
3 tablespoons tapioca
1/8 teaspoon salt (optional)
1 (3-ounce) package vanilla instant pudding mix
1 (3-ounce) package orange gelatin
2 cups hot water
8 ounces whipped topping
1 (11-ounce) can mandarin oranges, drained

Beat the egg in a large saucepan until frothy. Stir in the sugar, tapioca and salt. Let stand for 5 minutes. Add pudding mix and gelatin. Stir in the water. Bring to a boil over medium heat. Cook for 5 minutes or until thickened, stirring constantly. Pour into a large bowl and cool completely. Fold in the whipped topping and the mandarin oranges. Pour into a mold if desired. Chill until set. Yield: 12 to 18 servings.

Twila B. Tomlinson, Xi Iota Sigma
Archie, Missouri

SUGAR-FREE FRUIT SALAD

1 (15-ounce) can crushed pineapple
1 large package sugar-free orange gelatin
2 cups buttermilk
1 cup shredded coconut
12 ounces fat-free whipped topping
1 cup chopped pecans

Pour the pineapple into a saucepan and bring to a boil over medium heat, stirring constantly. Remove from the heat and add the gelatin. Stir for 2 minutes or until the gelatin dissolves. Pour into a large bowl and cool. Stir in the buttermilk and coconut and mix well. Fold in the whipped topping and pecans. Pour into a serving bowl and chill until set. Yield: 12 to 15 servings.

Mary L. Reardon, Omicron Master
Maryville, Missouri

STRAWBERRY RIBBON GELATIN

2 (3-ounce) packages strawberry gelatin
1 1/2 cups boiling water
2 (10-ounce) packages frozen strawberries
1 (8-ounce) can crushed pineapple
2 bananas, mashed
2 cups sour cream

Combine the gelatin and water in a large bowl. Stir for 2 minutes or until the gelatin dissolves. Add the strawberries, pineapple and bananas and mix well. Pour half the fruit mixture into a 9×13-inch dish. Chill for about 40 minutes or until almost set. Spread half the sour cream over the gelatin layer. Spoon the remaining fruit mixture over the sour cream and spread lightly.

Top with a layer of the remaining sour cream. Chill until firm. Cut into squares. Yield: 12 to 15 servings.

Ruth Modl, Beta Pi Master
Paris, Texas

STRAWBERRY PRETZEL SALAD

2 cups crushed pretzels
3 tablespoons sugar
3/4 cup (1 1/2 sticks) butter, softened
1 (6-ounce) package strawberry gelatin
2 cups boiling water
2 (10-ounce) packages frozen strawberries
1 (20-ounce) can crushed pineapple, drained
8 ounces cream cheese, softened
1 cup sugar
8 ounces whipped topping

Combine the pretzels, 3 tablespoons sugar and butter in a bowl and mix well. Press onto the bottom of a 9×13-inch baking pan. Bake at 400 degrees for 7 minutes. Cool. Combine the gelatin and water in a bowl. Stir for 2 minutes or until the gelatin dissolves. Stir in the strawberries and pineapple. Chill until partially set. Beat the cream cheese and sugar in a large bowl until light and fluffy. Fold in the whipped topping. Spread over the cooled crust. Spoon the strawberry mixture over the cream cheese layer and spread evenly. Chill until firm. Yield: 15 to 20 servings.

Ila May O'Farrell, Laureate Delta Xi
Needles, California

SEVEN-LAYER GELATIN SALAD

7 (3-ounce) packages assorted flavors gelatin
4 1/2 cups boiling water
4 1/2 cups cold water
1 (12-ounce) can evaporated milk
8 ounces whipped topping

Dissolve 1 packet of the gelatin in 3/4 cup of the boiling water in a bowl. Add 3/4 cup of the cold water and mix well. Pour into a 9×13-inch dish coated with nonstick cooking spray. Chill for 40 minutes or until partially set. Dissolve a second packet of the gelatin in 1/2 cup of the boiling water in a bowl. Add 1/2 cup of the cold water and 1/2 cup of the evaporated milk and mix well. Pour over the first layer. Chill for 40 minutes or until partially set. Repeat the procedure five times, alternating plain gelatin with creamy gelatin and chilling each layer until partially set. Spread with the whipped topping just before serving. Garnish with fresh mint, sliced strawberries and/or sliced kiwifruit if desired. Yield: 15 to 20 servings.

Kris Boersna, Xi Alpha
Sioux Falls, South Dakota

PINEAPPLE BREAD PUDDING

5 slices bread, crusts trimmed and cubed	1 (20-ounce) can pineapple chunks
1/2 cup (1 stick) butter or margarine, melted	2 eggs
	3/4 cup sugar

Place the bread in a large bowl. Drizzle with the butter and toss until the bread is completely moistened. Drain the pineapple, reserving the juice. Beat the eggs, sugar and pineapple juice in a bowl. Add the egg mixture and pineapple to the bread, mixing just until combined. Pour into a buttered 9×9-inch baking dish. Bake at 350 degrees for 45 to 50 minutes or until light brown and set. Yield: 4 to 6 servings.

Sharon Rhoden, Alpha Beta Upsilon
Crestview, Florida

CHILLED STRAWBERRY SOUP

3 cups buttermilk	1 quart strawberries, hulled
3/4 cup sour cream	
3 tablespoons kirsch	3/4 cup sugar
1 cup buttermilk	

Combine 3 cups buttermilk, the sour cream and kirsch in a large bowl and mix well. Place 1 cup buttermilk, the strawberries and sugar in a food processor or blender, in batches if necessary, and process until smooth. Pour into the buttermilk mixture and mix well. Chill, covered, until just before serving. Garnish with mint sprigs and strawberry fans if desired. Yield: 12 to 15 servings.

Ellen A. O'Bryan, Preceptor Gamma
Hannibal, Missouri

FOUR-FRUIT COMPOTE

1 (20-ounce) can pineapple chunks	2 tablespoons cornstarch
1 (11-ounce) can mandarin oranges, drained	1/3 cup orange juice
	1 tablespoon lemon juice
	3 or 4 apples, chopped
1/2 cup sugar	2 or 3 bananas, sliced

Drain the pineapple, reserving 3/4 cup juice. Combine the reserved juice, sugar, cornstarch, orange juice and lemon juice in a saucepan. Bring to a boil over medium heat, stirring constantly. Boil for 1 minute or until thickened, stirring constantly. Remove from the heat. Combine the pineapple, oranges, apples and bananas in a bowl. Pour the warm juice mixture over the fruit. Stir gently to coat. Cool completely. Store, covered, in the refrigerator. Yield: 12 to 16 servings.

Sylvia Cornell, Alpha Gamma Master
Mount Vernon, Ohio

FRUIT AND CREAM AMBROSIA

1 (20-ounce) can fruit cocktail, drained	1 cup shredded coconut
1 (11-ounce) can mandarin oranges, drained	1 (8-ounce) can crushed pineapple
	2 cups sour cream
1 cup miniature marshmallows	16 ounces whipped topping

Combine the fruit cocktail, mandarin oranges, marshmallows, coconut, pineapple and sour cream in a large bowl, stirring just until combined. Fold in the whipped topping. Pour into a glass serving dish. Chill until ready to serve. Yield: 16 to 20 servings.

Mary L. Geyer, Preceptor Gamma Phi
Mill Hall, Pennsylvania

FRUIT COCKTAIL TORTE

1 (20-ounce) can fruit cocktail, drained	1/2 teaspoon salt
1 cup all-purpose flour	1 egg
1 cup granulated sugar	2 to 3 tablespoons brown sugar
1 teaspoon baking soda	

Combine the fruit cocktail, flour, granulated sugar, baking soda, salt and egg in a large bowl and mix well. Pour into a greased 9-inch baking pan. Sprinkle with the brown sugar. Bake at 350 degrees for 45 minutes or until a wooden pick inserted in the center comes out clean. Serve warm with whipped topping if desired. Yield: 8 servings.

Mary Iseman, Preceptor Alpha Alpha
Nanuet, New York

BRANDIED ORANGES

8 oranges	1/4 cup brandy
1 cup sugar	1/4 cup orange-flavor liqueur
2/3 cup water	

Cut the peel and pith from the oranges using a sharp serrated knife. Cut the oranges along each membrane to remove the segments. Place the segments in a bowl. Squeeze any juice from the remaining parts of the oranges into the bowl. Combine the sugar and water in a small saucepan. Cook over medium-low heat until the sugar dissolves, stirring constantly. Bring to a boil. Boil for 2 minutes, stirring constantly. Cool. Stir in the brandy and liqueur. Pour over the orange segments. Chill, covered, for up to 1 day. Serve with ice cream. Yield: 8 servings.

Marilyn M. Olsen, Delta Delta Master
Eureka, California

Goody Bag
MISCELLANEOUS SWEETS

ALMOND DESSERT

1 cup all-purpose flour
1 (7-ounce) package
  flaked coconut
1/4 cup packed brown
  sugar
1 (2-ounce) package
  slivered almonds

1/2 cup (1 stick)
  margarine, melted
2 (3½-ounce) packages
  vanilla instant
  pudding mix
3 cups milk
8 ounces whipped
  topping

Mix the flour, coconut, brown sugar and almonds in a bowl. Add the margarine and mix well. Scatter over the bottom of a nonstick 9×13-inch baking pan. Bake at 350 degrees for 15 minutes or until light brown, stirring occasionally. Remove to a wire rack to cool completely. Remove ¾ cup of the almond mixture to a bowl and set aside. Spread the remaining almond mixture evenly over the bottom of the baking pan. Whisk the pudding mix and milk in a bowl for 2 minutes. Fold in the whipped topping. Pour evenly over the almond mixture in the pan. Sprinkle with the reserved almond mixture. Chill, covered, until just before serving. Yield: 15 servings.

Mary Sandholdt, Gamma Delta
Oskaloosa, Iowa

APPLE ENCHILADAS

4 to 6 (8-inch) flour
  tortillas
1 (21-ounce) can apple
  pie filling
1 teaspoon cinnamon

1/2 cup (1 stick) butter
1/2 cup granulated sugar
1/2 cup packed brown
  sugar
1/2 cup water

Lay the tortillas on a work surface. Spoon a heaping ¼ cup of pie filling down the center of each tortilla. Sprinkle with the cinnamon. Roll up the tortilla. Place, seam side down, in a single layer in a greased 2-quart baking dish. Combine the butter, granulated sugar, brown sugar and water in a saucepan. Bring to a boil over medium-high heat, stirring constantly. Boil for 3 minutes, stirring constantly. Pour evenly over the tortillas. Let stand for 30 minutes. Bake at 350 degrees for 30 minutes or until golden brown. Serve with vanilla ice cream if desired.
Yield: 4 to 6 servings.

Trudy Weare, Pi Omicron
Council Bluffs, Iowa

BAKLAVA

1 pound walnuts,
  finely ground
1 cup sugar
1½ cups (3 sticks) butter
  or margarine, melted

1 (16-ounce) package
  frozen phyllo dough,
  thawed
2 (16-ounce) jars honey

Combine the walnuts and sugar in a bowl and mix well. Pour enough of the butter into a 10×15-inch baking pan to cover the bottom. Place one-third of the phyllo dough sheets in the baking pan. Sprinkle with half the walnut mixture. Repeat the layers. Cover with the remaining phyllo dough. Cut diagonally with a sharp knife into 1½-inch diamond shapes. Pour the remaining melted butter evenly over the baklava. Bake at 350 degrees for 1 hour or until light brown. Remove to a wire rack and pour the honey evenly over the baklava. Cool completely. Yield: 36 servings.

Jo Culp, Xi Delta
Livonia, Michigan

BANANA SPLIT CAKE WITH COCONUT

1 (11-ounce) box vanilla wafers, crushed	3 bananas, sliced
1/2 cup (1 stick) margarine, melted	1 (20-ounce) can crushed pineapple, drained
12 ounces cream cheese, softened	1 cup shredded coconut
1 (1-pound) package confectioners' sugar	12 ounces whipped topping
	Chopped nuts

Combine the crushed vanilla wafers and margarine in a bowl and mix well. Press into a 9×13-inch dish. Beat the cream cheese and confectioners' sugar in a mixing bowl until light and fluffy. Spread into the prepared pan. Top with the bananas. Spoon the pineapple over the bananas and spread lightly. Sprinkle with the coconut. Cover with the whipped topping and sprinkle with nuts. Yield: 12 servings.

Bonnie Willis, Omicron Eta
Orland, California

BANANA TORTILLAS

2 (8-inch) flour tortillas	1/4 cup packed brown sugar
1 tablespoon butter, melted	1 tablespoon water
4 bananas, cut into 1/4-inch slices	1/2 teaspoon cinnamon
	1/4 cup (1/2 stick) butter

Brush each side of the tortillas with 1 tablespoon butter. Arrange in a 10×15-inch baking pan. Bake at 450 degrees for 7 to 8 minutes or until golden brown. Place the banana slices in concentric circles on the tortillas. Cook the brown sugar, water and cinnamon in a saucepan over medium heat until the sugar dissolves, stirring constantly. Stir in 1/4 cup butter until smooth. Brush over the bananas. Bake at 450 degrees for 10 minutes or until the bananas are shiny. Cut into wedges. Serve warm with ice cream if desired. Yield: 4 servings.

Kathleen Callery, Laureate Delta Psi
Kingston, Ontario, Canada

BANANA SPLIT CAKE

2 cups graham cracker crumbs	6 bananas, thinly sliced
1 1/2 cups (3 sticks) margarine, melted	12 ounces whipped topping
2 cups confectioners' sugar	1 (15-ounce) can crushed pineapple, drained
1 teaspoon vanilla extract	1 1/3 cups chopped walnuts
2 eggs	Maraschino cherries

Mix the graham cracker crumbs and 1/2 cup of the margarine in a bowl. Press into a 9×13-inch dish. Beat the confectioners' sugar, vanilla, remaining 1 cup margarine and eggs in a bowl for 20 minutes. Spread in the prepared dish. Cover with bananas. Spread the pineapple over the bananas. Cover with whipped topping. Sprinkle with nuts and cherries. Chill, covered, for several hours or longer. Note: If you are concerned about using raw eggs, use eggs pasteurized in their shells, which are sold at some specialty food stores, or use an equivalent amount of pasteurized egg yolk substitute. Yield: 12 to 14 servings.

Penny Williams, Preceptor Mu Omicron
Fountain Valley, California

BLUEBERRY LEMON CREAM CRISP

1 cup all-purpose flour	1/2 cup chopped walnuts
1/2 cup packed brown sugar	1 (14-ounce) can sweetened condensed milk
1/2 teaspoon cinnamon	
1/2 teaspoon salt	2 eggs
1/2 cup (1 stick) margarine, softened	4 teaspoons grated lemon zest
1 teaspoon vanilla extract	1/4 cup lemon juice
	1/4 teaspoon salt
1 cup flaked coconut	1 (21-ounce) can blueberry pie filling
1/2 cup quick-cooking oats	

Combine the flour, brown sugar, cinnamon, 1/2 teaspoon salt, margarine and vanilla in a bowl and mix until crumbly. Stir in the coconut, oats and walnuts. Remove 2 1/2 cups to an ungreased 9×9-inch baking pan and press lightly. Bake at 375 degrees for 12 minutes. Remove to a wire rack. Beat the condensed milk, eggs, lemon zest, lemon juice and 1/4 teaspoon salt in a bowl for 2 minutes. Pour evenly over the coconut mixture in the baking pan. Spoon the pie filling evenly over the lemon mixture. Sprinkle with the remaining coconut mixture. Bake at 375 degrees for 16 to 18 minutes or until light brown. Remove to a wire rack to cool. Yield: 9 to 10 servings.

Dottie Kollar, Gamma Zeta
Vallejo, California

Norma Herbold, Sequim, Washington, prepares **Heavenly Hot Fudge Sauce** *by melting 1/2 cup (1 stick) butter and 4 ounces unsweetened baking chocolate in a large saucepan over medium-low heat. She adds 3 cups sugar 1/4 cup at a time, stirring constantly. As the chocolate mixture thickens, she adds a pinch of salt and gradually stirs in a large can of evaporated milk. She cooks the mixture for about 8 minutes, stirring constantly. Two teaspoons vanilla extract are added after the sauce is removed from the heat. The sauce is served with ice cream.*

BUGLE TREATS

My family had a contest to see who could come up with a new recipe for the holidays. My youngest daughter won with this recipe.

1 (7¹/2-ounce) package
   Bugle corn snacks
³/4 cup sliced almonds
1 cup (2 sticks)
   margarine

1 cup sugar
¹/4 cup water
2 tablespoons light
   corn syrup

Mix the Bugles and almonds in a bowl. Combine the margarine, sugar, water and corn syrup in a heavy saucepan. Cook over medium heat for 40 minutes or until the mixture begins to brown, stirring constantly. Stir into the Bugle mixture slowly. Spread the mixture evenly over a nonstick baking sheet. Break into pieces while warm. Cool completely. Store in an airtight container. Yield: 6 dozen pieces.

Linda Jean Shreffler, Xi Zeta Pi
Pryor, Oklahoma

BUTTERSCOTCH DELIGHT

1 cup all-purpose flour
¹/2 cup (1 stick) margarine
¹/2 cup chopped pecans
8 ounces cream cheese,
   softened
1 cup confectioners'
   sugar
1 cup whipped topping

2 (3¹/2-ounce) packages
   butterscotch instant
   pudding mix
3 cups milk
2 cups whipped topping
Additional chopped
   pecans

Place the flour in a bowl. Cut in the margarine until crumbly. Stir in ¹/2 cup pecans. Press into the bottom of a 7×12-inch baking dish. Bake at 350 degrees for 15 to 20 minutes. Remove to a wire rack to cool completely. Beat the cream cheese and confectioners' sugar in a bowl until light and fluffy. Stir in 1 cup whipped topping. Spread over the cooled crust. Whisk the pudding mix and milk in a bowl for 2 minutes. Pour evenly over the cream cheese mixture. Chill, covered, until set. Cover with 2 cups whipped topping. Sprinkle with additional chopped pecans. Chill, covered, until just before serving. Yield: 20 servings.

Sharon Leech, Preceptor Gamma Beta
Hartford City, Indiana

ANGINETTI CANNOLI

1¹/4 cups ricotta cheese
1 tablespoon vanilla
   instant pudding mix
¹/4 cup confectioners'
   sugar
¹/2 teaspoon vanilla
   extract

¹/4 cup miniature
   semisweet
   chocolate chips
1 (5-ounce) package
   Anginetti cookies

Mix the ricotta cheese, pudding mix, confectioners' sugar and vanilla in a bowl. Stir in the chocolate chips. Split the cookies horizontally. Spread 1 tablespoon of the cheese mixture over the bottom half of cookie and replace the tops. Serve immediately or chill, covered, for up to 2 hours. Yield: 6 servings.

Cheryl Ledger, Laureate Epsilon Kappa
Wintersville, Ohio

CARAMEL COOKIE DELIGHT

25 chocolate sandwich
   cookies, crushed
1 (14-ounce) package
   caramel candies
²/3 cup evaporated milk
¹/2 cup (1 stick) butter
3 ounces cream cheese,
   softened

1 cup confectioners'
   sugar
¹/4 teaspoon vanilla
   extract
12 ounces whipped
   topping
12 chocolate sandwich
   cookies, crushed

Press the 25 crushed cookies into the bottom of a nonstick 9×13-inch baking pan. Combine the caramels, evaporated milk and butter in a saucepan. Cook over medium heat until smooth, stirring often. Pour into the prepared pan and spread evenly. Beat the cream cheese and confectioners' sugar in a bowl until light and fluffy. Stir in the vanilla and 2 cups of the whipped topping. Spread over the caramel layer. Cover with the remaining whipped topping and sprinkle with 12 crushed cookies. Chill, covered, until just before serving. Yield: 10 to 15 servings.

Jennifer Sanderson, Xi Delta Tau
Quitman, Louisiana

BROWN BAG CARAMEL CORN

14 cups popped popcorn
1 cup packed brown
   sugar
¹/2 cup (1 stick) butter
¹/4 cup light corn syrup

¹/2 teaspoon salt
1 teaspoon vanilla
   extract
¹/2 teaspoon baking soda

Place the popcorn in a large brown paper bag. Combine the brown sugar, butter, corn syrup and salt in a large microwave-safe bowl coated with nonstick cooking spray. Microwave on High for 2 minutes; stir. Microwave on High for 3 minutes. Stir in the vanilla and baking soda. Pour immediately over the popcorn in the bag. Fold the top of the bag several times to close. Shake the bag vigorously to mix. Microwave the bag on High for 1¹/2 minutes. Spread the popcorn mixture over waxed paper. Let stand until cool. Break into pieces. Store in an airtight container. Yield: 8 to 10 servings.

Kathy Rand, Xi Alpha Pi
Madison, Wisconsin

CHOCOLATE BUNDLES

1 sheet frozen puff
   pastry
1 cup (6 ounces)
   semisweet
   chocolate chips

1/4 cup chopped walnuts
4 teaspoons liqueur, any
   flavor (optional)
Confectioners' sugar

Thaw the pastry at room temperature for 30 minutes. Roll into a 12-inch square on a floured work surface. Cut into four 6-inch squares. Place 1/4 cup chocolate chips, 1 tablespoon walnuts and 1 teaspoon liqueur in the center of each square. Bring the four corners of each square together and twist to seal. Spread the corners of each square to open slightly. Arrange the squares on an ungreased baking sheet. Bake at 425 degrees for 10 to 15 minutes or until golden brown. Remove to a wire rack and cool for 10 minutes or longer. Sprinkle with confectioners' sugar. Yield: 4 servings.

Pat Windholz, Preceptor Delta Chi
Hays, Kansas

CHOCOLATE CHEESE BALL

18 ounces cream cheese,
   softened
1/2 cup (3 ounces)
   chocolate chips,
   melted

1 tablespoon almond-
   flavored liqueur
1/4 teaspoon cinnamon
Chopped pecans

Combine the cream cheese, chocolate, liqueur and cinnamon in a bowl and mix well. Shape into a ball and place on a plate. Chill until firm. Roll in chopped pecans and place on a serving plate. Chill, covered, until just before serving. Serve with chocolate wafer cookies. Yield: 36 servings.

Beverly Gooch, Preceptor Gamma
Memphis, Tennessee

CHOCOLATE ÉCLAIR CAKE

2 small packages sugar-
   free vanilla instant
   pudding mix
3 cups skim milk
8 ounces fat-free
   whipped topping

1 (14-ounce) package
   graham crackers
1 container chocolate
   frosting, warmed

Combine the pudding and milk in a bowl. Whisk for 2 minutes. Fold in the whipped topping. Fit the graham crackers in a single layer into a 9 x 13-inch pan. Spoon half of the pudding mixture over the crackers and spread lightly. Cover with a single layer of graham crackers. Top with the remaining pudding mixture. Cover with a single layer of graham crackers.

Spread the frosting over the crackers. Chill until just before serving. Yield: 12 servings.

Jody Arsenault, Iota Sigma
Englewood, Tennessee

CHOCOLATE HOT POTS

3/4 cup semisweet
   chocolate chips
1/2 cup (1 stick) unsalted
   butter
2 eggs

3/4 cup sugar
3 tablespoons
   all-purpose flour
1/2 cup (3 ounces) white
   chocolate chips

Place a 10×15-inch baking pan in a cold oven. Preheat the oven to 400 degrees. Melt the semisweet chocolate chips and butter in a large microwave-safe bowl in the microwave or in a double boiler. Stir until smooth. Cool completely. Beat the eggs, sugar and flour in a bowl. Add the chocolate mixture and mix well. Stir in the white chocolate chips. Divide the mixture evenly among 4 buttered ramekins. Remove the baking pan from the oven carefully. Place the ramekins in the hot pan. Bake at 400 degrees for 20 minutes or until the tops are cracked and shiny and the centers are very soft. Remove the ramekins to a wire rack to cool. Yield: 4 servings.

Pat Crockett, Laureate Alpha
Myrtle Creek, Oregon

CHOCOLATE LUSH

1 cup all-purpose flour
1/2 cup (1 stick) butter or
   margarine, melted
3/4 cup chopped walnuts
8 ounces cream cheese,
   softened
1 cup confectioners'
   sugar

1 cup whipped topping
2 (31/2-ounce) packages
   chocolate instant
   pudding mix
3 cups milk
2 cups whipped topping

Mix the flour, butter and walnuts in a bowl. Press into the bottom of a nonstick 9×13-inch baking pan. Bake at 350 degrees for 15 minutes. Remove to a wire rack to cool completely. Beat the cream cheese and confectioners' sugar in a bowl until light and fluffy. Stir in 1 cup whipped topping. Spread over the cooled crust. Beat the pudding mix and milk in a bowl for 2 minutes. Pour evenly over the cream cheese mixture. Chill, covered, until set. Spread 2 cups whipped topping evenly over the chocolate pudding. Chill, covered, until just before serving. Yield: 12 servings.

Cheryl Johnson, Laureate Pi
Sandy, Utah

TRIPLE CHOCOLATE MESS

1 (2-layer) package
   chocolate cake mix
2 cups sour cream
³/4 cup vegetable oil
4 eggs
1 (3¹/2-ounce) package
   chocolate instant
   pudding mix
1 cup water
1 cup (6 ounces)
   chocolate chips
1 (16-ounce) can
   chocolate syrup
1 (14-ounce) can
   sweetened
   condensed milk

Combine the cake mix, sour cream, oil, eggs, pudding mix and water in a bowl and mix well. Stir in the chocolate chips. Pour into a slow cooker coated with nonstick cooking spray. Cook on Low for 6 to 8 hours or until the cake tests done. Combine the chocolate syrup and condensed milk in a saucepan. Cook over medium heat until hot, stirring frequently. Spoon the cake into serving bowls and top with the chocolate syrup mixture. Serve with vanilla ice cream if desired. Yield: 10 to 12 servings.

Judy T. Judy, Preceptor Omega
Cynthiana, Kentucky

CHOCOLATE MINT DESSERT

17 unsalted saltine
   crackers, crushed
1 cup granulated sugar
1 cup finely chopped
   nuts
4 egg whites, stiffly
   beaten
1 cup (2 sticks) butter,
   softened
2 cups confectioners'
   sugar
4 ounces unsweetened
   chocolate, melted
2 teaspoons vanilla
   extract
1 teaspoon peppermint
   extract
4 egg yolks

Mix the crushed crackers, granulated sugar and nuts in a bowl. Fold in the egg whites. Spoon into the bottom and up the side of 24 nonstick miniature muffin cups. Bake at 325 degrees for 20 minutes or until slightly crisp. Cool in the pan on a wire rack. Beat the butter and confectioners' sugar in a bowl until light and fluffy. Beat in the melted chocolate, vanilla and peppermint extract. Add the egg yolks 1 at a time, beating for 3 minutes after each addition. Spoon into the muffin cups. Chill, covered, until firm. Garnish with whipped cream and chocolate curls. Freezes well. Note: If you are concerned about using raw eggs, use eggs pasteurized in their shells, which are sold at some specialty food stores, or use an equivalent amount of pasteurized egg yolk substitute. Yield: 12 servings.

Evelyn Baziuk, Preceptor Beta Mu
Kamloops, British Columbia, Canada

MINTY CHOCOLATE CUPS

8 ounces milk chocolate,
   chopped
¹/4 cup (¹/2 stick)
   margarine
1 (3-ounce) package lime
   gelatin
1 cup boiling water
2 cups chocolate chip or
   vanilla ice cream
3 tablespoons crème
   de menthe
1 cup whipped topping

Microwave the chocolate and margarine in a 2-cup microwave-safe measuring cup until melted. Stir until smooth. Divide the chocolate mixture among 12 paper-lined muffin cups, spreading the mixture over the bottom and up the side of the paper with the back of a spoon. Chill for 1 to 2 hours or until set. Dissolve the gelatin in the boiling water in a bowl. Add the ice cream and stir until smooth. Stir in the crème de menthe. Chill for 30 minutes or until thickened. Beat until smooth. Fold in the whipped topping. Divide among the chilled chocolate cups. Chill for 1 to 2 hours or until set. Peel the paper off carefully and place the cups on serving plates. Garnish with chocolate curls or whipped topping and a maraschino cherry. Yield: 12 servings.

Cricket Turley, Laureate Beta Xi
Dodge City, Kansas

CHOCOLATE CINNAMON NACHOS

Salad shells are found in the refrigerated section of the grocery store with the tortillas.

1 (5¹/2-ounce) package
   bake & fill salad
   shells
¹/2 cup sugar
1 teaspoon cinnamon
¹/2 cup (3 ounces)
   semisweet chocolate
   chips
1 tablespoon shortening

Let the shells stand at room temperature for 10 minutes to soften. Cut each shell into 8 wedges. Arrange on a nonstick baking sheet. Bake at 375 degrees for 4 to 7 minutes or until golden brown. Remove the wedges to a wire rack to cool completely. Combine the sugar and cinnamon in a sealable plastic bag. Seal the bag and shake to mix. Spray the wedges lightly with nonstick cooking spray. Add a few wedges at a time to the bag and shake to coat. Remove the coated wedges to a wire rack. Melt the chocolate chips and shortening in a microwave-safe bowl in the microwave or in a double boiler. Stir until smooth. Dip the wide end of each coated wedge into the chocolate mixture and place on a waxed paper-lined baking sheet. Chill until firm. Serve with berries or toasted nuts. Yield: 8 servings.

Kathy Rand, Xi Alpha Pi
Madison, Wisconsin

CHOCOLATE PASSION BOWL

2 (3½-ounce) packages
    chocolate instant
    pudding mix
3 cups milk
8 ounces French vanilla
    whipped topping

1 baked (9×9-inch) pan
    brownies, cut into
    1-inch squares
2 cups raspberries

Whisk the pudding mix and milk in a bowl for 2 minutes. Fold in 1 cup of the whipped topping. Spread half of the brownie cubes over the bottom of a 2-quart serving bowl. Pour half the pudding over the brownies and sprinkle with half the raspberries. Spread half the remaining whipped topping over the raspberries. Repeat the layers. Chill, covered, for 1 hour or longer. Yield: 16 servings.

Mary F. Ross, Xi Beta Upsilon
Sedalia, Missouri

GERMAN CHOCOLATE PIZZA

6 frozen unbaked dinner
    rolls, thawed and
    risen
1 cup (6 ounces)
    chocolate chips

1 cup flaked coconut
1 cup chopped pecans
1 (14-ounce) can
    sweetened
    condensed milk

Shape the dough into a ball. Pat into a 13-inch circle on a lightly floured work surface. Fit into a 12-inch pizza pan coated with nonstick cooking spray, turning up the edge of the dough to form a rim. Bake at 400 degrees for 5 minutes. Sprinkle with the chocolate chips, coconut and pecans. Drizzle evenly with the condensed milk. Bake at 350 degrees for 20 minutes. Remove to a wire rack to cool. Serve warm. Yield: 8 servings.

Barb Sanders, Xi Alpha Omega
Oelwein, Iowa

CHRISTMAS WREATHS

This can also be made as one large wreath using a gelatin mold coated with nonstick cooking spray.

½ cup (1 stick) butter
35 large marshmallows
1 teaspoon vanilla
    extract

1 teaspoon (or more)
    green food coloring
3½ to 4 cups cornflakes
Red cinnamon candies
Small edible silver balls

Melt the butter and marshmallows in a double boiler, stirring until smooth. Stir in the vanilla and food coloring. Pour over the cornflakes in a large bowl coated with nonstick cooking spray. Stir gently with a spatula coated with nonstick cooking spray until coated. Form the mixture into small wreaths with wet fingers and place on waxed paper. Press cinnamon candies and silver balls lightly into the wreaths to decorate. Let stand until firm. Yield: 25 to 30 wreaths.

Kathy Rand, Xi Alpha Pi
Madison, Wisconsin

COCONUT CREAM DESSERT

1¼ cups all-purpose
    flour
½ cup (1 stick) butter,
    softened
½ cup chopped nuts
8 ounces cream cheese,
    softened

1 cup confectioners'
    sugar
1 cup whipped topping
2 (4-ounce) packages
    coconut cream
    pudding mix
2½ cups milk
2 cups whipped topping

Place the flour in a bowl. Cut in the butter until crumbly. Stir in the nuts. Press into the bottom of a nonstick 9×13-inch baking pan. Bake at 350 degrees for 15 minutes. Remove to a wire rack to cool completely. Beat the cream cheese and confectioners' sugar in a bowl until light and fluffy. Stir in 1 cup whipped topping. Spread over the cooled crust. Combine the pudding mix and milk in a saucepan and cook using the package directions. Cool but do not let set. Pour evenly over the cream cheese mixture. Chill, covered, until set. Spread 2 cups whipped topping evenly over the pudding. Sprinkle with additional chopped nuts if desired. Chill, covered, overnight. Yield: 16 servings.

Joyce Ayers, Chi Master
Ft. Myers, Florida

❖ COCONUT TOAST TRIANGLES

These taste like coconut macaroons and make a unique finger food for receptions.

1 loaf sliced white
    bread, crusts removed
½ cup (1 stick)
    margarine
1 cup sugar

1 teaspoon vanilla
    extract
1 cup packed flaked
    coconut
1 egg

Fit the bread in a single layer into one or two 10×15-inch baking pans. Combine the margarine, sugar, vanilla and coconut in a saucepan. Cook over medium heat until the sugar dissolves, stirring often. Beat the egg in a bowl until foamy. Stir the egg gradually into the coconut mixture. Spread evenly over the bread slices, one tablespoon at a time. Bake at 350 degrees for 15 to 20 minutes or until golden brown. Remove to a wire rack to cool slightly. Remove one slice at a time to a cutting board and cut diagonally into four triangles. Yield: 4½ dozen triangles.

Louise Sledge, Delta Omicron
Lexington, South Carolina

COOKIE SALAD

2 (3½-ounce) packages
  vanilla instant
  pudding mix
2 cups buttermilk
1 (20-ounce) can crushed
  pineapple

8 ounces whipped
  topping
1 (11½-ounce) package
  fudge stripe
  shortbread cookies,
  crushed

Whisk the pudding mix and buttermilk in a bowl for 2 minutes. Stir in the pineapple and whipped topping. Fold in the crushed cookies. Serve immediately or chill, covered, until just before serving.
Yield: 12 servings.

Tammy Johnson, Theta Epsilon
Slater, Iowa

CORN CHIP BARS

1 (10-ounce) package
  corn chips
1 cup sugar

1 cup light corn syrup
1 cup peanut butter

Arrange the corn chips over the bottom of a nonstick 9×13-inch baking pan. Combine the sugar and corn syrup in a saucepan. Bring to a boil over medium heat and cook until the sugar dissolves, stirring constantly. Remove from the heat and stir in the peanut butter until smooth. Drizzle evenly over the corn chips. Let stand until firm. Cut into bars.
Yield: 12 to 15 servings.

Karen Head, Xi Phi
Council Bluffs, Iowa

CRANBERRY ORANGE CHEESE BALL

8 ounces cream cheese,
  softened
1 (1-pound) package
  confectioners' sugar
½ cup sweetened dried
  cranberries

2 teaspoons grated
  orange zest
⅛ teaspoon cranberry
  extract
1 teaspoon orange juice
1 teaspoon lemon juice

Beat the cream cheese and confectioners' sugar in a bowl until smooth. Add the cranberries, orange zest, cranberry extract, orange juice and lemon juice and mix well. Shape into a ball and wrap in plastic wrap. Chill until firm. Serve with vanilla wafers.
Yield: 24 servings.

Faye Evans, Delta Master
Hendersonville, Tennessee

*Lynette VanOyen, Chi Omicron, Oswego, Illinois, makes **Pumpkin Dip** by placing 1 cup pumpkin butter in a large bowl and folding in 2 cups whipped topping. She serves the dip with vanilla wafers and stores it in the refrigerator.*

CREAM PUFF SQUARES

1 cup water
½ cup (1 stick)
  margarine
1 cup all-purpose flour
4 eggs
8 ounces cream cheese,
  softened
2½ cups milk

2 (3½-ounce) packages
  vanilla instant
  pudding mix
8 ounces whipped
  topping
Magic Shell ice cream
  topping

Bring the water and margarine to a boil in a saucepan over medium-high heat, stirring occasionally. Add the flour and mix well. Remove from the heat and cool completely. Add the eggs 1 at a time, beating well after each addition. Spread into a greased 9×13-inch baking pan. Bake at 400 degrees for 30 to 40 minutes or until golden brown. Remove to a wire rack to cool completely. Beat the cream cheese, milk and pudding mix in a bowl until thickened. Spread over the baked layer. Spread the whipped topping evenly over the pudding mixture. Drizzle with Magic Shell. Cut into squares. Yield: 15 servings.

Nancy A. Rahal, Kappa Lambda
Edenton, North Carolina

DOUBLE CHERRY TARTS

28 vanilla wafers
4 ounces cream cheese,
  softened
¼ cup sugar
6 ounces cherry yogurt

8 ounces whipped
  topping
1 (21-ounce) can cherry
  pie filling

Place one vanilla wafer, flat side down, in the bottom of each of 14 paper-lined muffin cups. Beat the cream cheese and sugar in a bowl until smooth. Add the yogurt and mix well. Fold in the whipped topping. Spoon half the mixture into the muffin cups. Top with the remaining vanilla wafers. Spoon the remaining mixture over the wafers. Chill for 3 hours or until set. Spoon 2 tablespoons of the pie filling over each muffin cup. Chill until just before serving.
Yield: 14 servings.

Silvia Gunderson, Alpha Beta
Fort Frances, Ontario, Canada

*Debbie Martin, Psi Pi, Minooka, Illinois, shared her simple recipe for **Blonde Bombers**. She combines 15 ounces graham cracker crumbs, 2 cups semisweet chocolate chips, and two 14-ounce cans sweetened condensed milk in a bowl and mixes well. She spreads the mixture in a greased 9×13-inch baking pan. She bakes the bars for 20 to 30 minutes, and cools them for 15 minutes. The dessert should be cut into squares just before serving.*

RUSSIAN CREAM

2 envelopes unflavored gelatin	1 1/2 cups sour cream
1/2 cup cold water	1 teaspoon vanilla extract
1 3/4 cups light cream	Fresh or frozen raspberries
1 cup sugar	

Soften the gelatin in the cold water in a bowl. Heat the cream and sugar in a saucepan until hot and the sugar dissolves, stirring frequently. Stir into the gelatin mixture. Chill until slightly thickened. Beat the sour cream and vanilla in a bowl until thick and fluffy. Fold into the gelatin mixture. Pour into individual molds or sherbet glasses. Chill until set. Unmold onto serving plates and top with raspberries. Yield: 6 to 8 servings.

Susie Harbers, Laureate Iota Eta
Yoakum, Texas

MEXICAN CHOCOLATE CRÈME BRÛLÉE

1 tablespoon unsalted butter, melted	4 eggs
1 cup milk	3 egg yolks
1 cup heavy cream	2 tablespoons coffee-flavored liqueur
4 ounces semisweet chocolate, chopped	1/3 cup sugar
1/4 cup baking cocoa	1/2 teaspoon vanilla extract
3/4 teaspoon espresso powder or instant coffee granules	Pinch of salt
	1/2 cup sugar
3/4 teaspoon cinnamon	4 teaspoons grated orange zest

Brush 8 small ramekins with the butter. Set the ramekins in a baking pan. Combine the milk and cream in a microwave-safe bowl. Microwave on High for 1 1/2 minutes or until very hot. Add the chocolate, baking cocoa, espresso powder and cinnamon. Whisk until smooth. Cool completely. Whisk the eggs and egg yolks in a bowl until slightly thickened. Stir in the chocolate mixture, liqueur, 1/3 cup sugar, vanilla and salt. Divide among the prepared ramekins. Add enough hot water to the baking pan to come halfway up the side of the ramekins. Bake at 300 degrees for 30 minutes or until barely set; the centers will be very soft. Remove the baking pan to a wire rack to cool completely. Remove the ramekins and cover with plastic wrap. Chill for 2 hours or longer. Mix 1/2 cup sugar and the orange zest in a bowl. Sprinkle over the top of the custards. Place under a broiler for 2 to 4 minutes or until the sugar is bubbly. Serve immediately or chill, covered, for up to 3 hours. Yield: 8 servings.

Joyce Crippen, Xi Nu Eta
Carbondale, Illinois

CRÈME CARAMEL

1 cup sugar	4 cups hot milk
6 eggs, lightly beaten	1 teaspoon vanilla extract
2/3 cup (or less) sugar	
1/2 teaspoon salt	

Cook 1 cup sugar in a heavy saucepan over medium-low heat until the sugar dissolves and is caramel colored, stirring often. Divide the mixture among 8 to 10 small ramekins. Mix the eggs, 2/3 cup sugar and the salt in a bowl. Whisk in the hot milk gradually. Stir in the vanilla. Divide the milk mixture among the ramekins. Place the ramekins in a baking pan. Add enough boiling water to the baking pan to come halfway up the side of the ramekins. Bake at 350 degrees for 1 hour or until a knife inserted in the center of the custards comes out clean. Remove the ramekins carefully to a wire rack to cool completely. Chill, covered, for 3 hours or longer. Invert onto individual serving plates. Yield: 8 to 10 servings.

Judy Parsons, Preceptor Beta
Corner Brook, Newfoundland, Canada

BLACK FOREST CREPES

1 cup all-purpose flour	3 tablespoons butter, melted
2 tablespoons sugar	
2 tablespoons baking cocoa	1 (21-ounce) can cherry pie filling
3 eggs, lightly beaten	Fudge Sauce
1 1/4 cups buttermilk	Whipped cream

Combine the flour, sugar and baking cocoa. Combine the eggs, buttermilk and butter in a bowl and mix well. Add the dry ingredients and mix well. Chill, covered, for 1 hour. Heat a lightly greased 8-inch nonstick skillet over medium heat. Add 2 tablespoons crepe batter to the pan and tilt the pan to coat the bottom of the skillet. Cook until the top of the crepe appears dry. Flip and cook for 15 seconds. Remove to a plate and keep warm. Repeat with the remaining crepe batter. Spoon 2 tablespoons pie filling in the center of each crepe. Fold the crepe over the filling. Arrange the crepes, seam side down, in a greased 9×13-inch baking pan. Bake at 225 degrees for 15 minutes. Remove to serving plates. Drizzle with warm Fudge Sauce and top with whipped cream. Yield: 6 servings.

FUDGE SAUCE

3/4 cup sugar	1/4 cup (1/2 stick) butter
1/3 cup baking cocoa	1 teaspoon vanilla extract
2/3 cup evaporated milk	

Combine the sugar and baking cocoa in a saucepan. Whisk in the evaporated milk. Add the butter. Bring to a boil over medium heat, stirring frequently. Boil for 1 minute, stirring constantly. Remove from the heat and stir in the vanilla. Cool slightly.

Sue Langhoff, Xi Delta Nu
Litchfield, Illinois

❖ CARAMEL BANANA PECAN CREPES

4 bananas, sliced	1/3 cup caramel topping
Lemon juice	6 (9-inch) prepared crepes
2 tablespoons butter	3 tablespoons caramel
1/4 cup chopped pecans	topping

Sprinkle the bananas with lemon juice. Melt the butter in a skillet over medium-high heat. Add the pecans and sauté for 1 minute. Add the bananas and sauté for 2 minutes. Add 1/3 cup caramel topping and sauté for 1 minute. Remove from the heat. Arrange the crepes on a work surface. Spoon 1/3 cup of the banana mixture onto the center of each crepe. Fold in the sides and roll up the crepes. Arrange, seam side down, on serving plates. Drizzle 3 tablespoons caramel topping over the crepes. Yield: 6 servings.

Joyce Fred, Alpha Iota Master
Springfield, Illinois

FUDGE PIES

1 cup (2 sticks) margarine, softened	1/2 cup baking cocoa
2 1/2 cups sugar	1 cup chopped pecans
2 cups all-purpose flour	1 teaspoon vanilla extract
4 eggs	Dash of salt

Beat the margarine and sugar in a bowl until light and fluffy. Add the flour, eggs and baking cocoa and mix well. Stir in the pecans, vanilla and salt. Spoon into 24 greased muffin cups. Bake at 350 degrees for 20 to 25 minutes or until pies test done. Cool in the pan for 10 minutes. Remove to a wire rack to cool completely. Yield: 24 servings.

Jean A. Bunyard, Epsilon Tau
Carthage, Texas

MOCHA CREPES

1 cup all-purpose flour	2 tablespoons butter, melted
4 1/2 teaspoons sugar	Additional butter
Pinch of salt	2 cups heavy whipping cream
4 1/2 teaspoons baking cocoa	1/4 cup sugar
4 1/2 teaspoons instant coffee powder	1/4 cup light rum
2 eggs, beaten	Hot Fudge Sauce
1 1/2 cups milk	

Sift the flour, 4 1/2 teaspoons sugar, salt, baking cocoa and coffee powder into a bowl. Stir in the eggs. Whisk in the milk and 2 tablespoons butter until smooth. Strain through a wire mesh sieve into a bowl. Let stand for 2 hours. Melt a small amount of butter in a 6 to 8-inch skillet over medium heat. Add 2 to 3 tablespoons crepe batter to the pan and tilt the pan to coat the bottom of the skillet. Cook for 1 minute per side or until golden brown. Remove the crepe to a work surface. Repeat with the remaining crepe batter. Whip the cream in a bowl until soft peaks form. Add 1/4 cup sugar gradually, beating until stiff peaks form. Fold in the rum. Spoon equal amount of the whipped cream mixture down the center of the crepes and fold the sides over the filling. Place on a platter. Chill, covered, until just before serving. Place the crepes on serving plates and top with the Hot Fudge Sauce. Yield: 12 servings.

HOT FUDGE SAUCE

1 cup (2 sticks) butter	4 ounces unsweetened chocolate, chopped
4 1/2 cups confectioners' sugar	

Melt the butter in a double boiler. Stir in the confectioners' sugar until smooth. Add the chocolate and stir until smooth. Cook for 30 minutes without stirring. Remove from the heat and stir until creamy.

Lenora VanDusen, Laureate Gamma
Steady Brook, Newfoundland, Canada

MOCK FRUIT CAKE

1 (10-ounce) jar maraschino cherries	1 cup (2 sticks) butter
1 (14-ounce) package graham crackers, crushed	32 ounces pecans, chopped and toasted
1 (10-ounce) package marshmallows	1 (15-ounce) package raisins

Drain the cherries, reserving 2 tablespoons juice. Chop the cherries and place them in a bowl. Combine the marshmallows and butter in a saucepan. Cook over low heat until smooth, stirring often. Pour over the cherries. Add the graham crackers, pecans and raisins and mix well. Spoon into a waxed paper-lined loaf pan. Chill for several hours. Slice just before serving. Yield: 12 servings.

Jo Smith, Delta Master
Franklin, Tennessee

FRUIT CREPES

4 eggs, lightly beaten	2 tablespoons sugar
1¹/₃ cups milk	¹/₂ teaspoon salt
2 tablespoons butter, melted	Melted butter
	2 cups sliced fruit
1 cup all-purpose flour	Whipped cream

Whisk the eggs, milk, 2 tablespoons melted butter, flour, sugar and salt in a bowl until smooth. Heat a medium skillet or crepe pan over medium heat. Brush with melted butter. Add 3 tablespoons crepe batter to the pan and tilt the pan to coat the bottom of the skillet. Cook for 1 to 2 minutes per side or until golden brown. Remove to a serving plate, spoon fruit into the center and roll to enclose the filling. Repeat with the remaining crepe batter. Serve immediately topped with whipped cream. Yield: 8 servings

Susan Geberl, Xi Alpha Theta
Beamsville, Ontario, Canada

IRISH CREAM CREPES

1 (3¹/₂-ounce) package vanilla instant pudding mix	6 tablespoons Irish cream liqueur
	1 cup heavy whipping cream, stiffly whipped
2 teaspoons instant coffee granules	
¹/₂ cup milk	12 prepared crepes

Beat the pudding mix, coffee granules and milk in a bowl until light and fluffy. Add the liqueur and beat at high speed for 1 to 2 minutes. Reserve 2 tablespoons of the whipped cream. Fold the remaining whipped cream into the pudding mixture. Arrange the crepes on a work surface. Spoon 2 tablespoons of the pudding mixture down the center of each crepe and fold the sides over the filling. Place on serving plates, top with the reserved whipped cream and garnish with chocolate shavings. Yield: 6 servings.

Delma Waller, Laureate Delta Lambda
Waterloo, Ontario, Canada

CREPES SUZETTE

¹/₂ cup (1 stick) unsalted butter	2 oranges, peeled and sectioned
³/₄ cup sugar	¹/₂ cup orange-flavored liqueur
2 tablespoons grated orange zest	
	8 prepared crepes
²/₃ cup orange juice	3 tablespoons orange-flavored liqueur

Cook the butter, sugar, orange zest and orange juice in a large skillet over low heat for 20 minutes, stirring occasionally. Stir in the orange sections and ¹/₂ cup liqueur. Add one crepe and baste with the liquid. Roll into a cylinder on a warm plate. Repeat with the remaining crepes. Pour 3 tablespoons liqueur into the skillet. Ignite with a long match. Spoon the sauce over the crepes. Yield: 4 servings.

Gail Burton, Laureate Psi
De Winton, Alberta, Canada

DATE ROLL

2 pounds pitted dates, chopped	1 cup pecans, chopped
	8 ounces mixed candied fruit
1 (16-ounce) package marshmallows, chopped	
	1¹/₂ cups heavy whipping cream, whipped
1 cup graham cracker crumbs	2 cups graham cracker crumbs

Combine the first 5 ingredients in a bowl and mix well. Add the whipped cream and mix gently with hands. Shape into 3 logs. Roll the logs in 2 cups graham cracker crumbs to coat. Wrap tightly in foil and chill. Slice just before serving. Yield: 30 servings.

Ruth York, Nu Tau
Oologah, Oklahoma

FRYING PAN COOKIES

¹/₄ cup (¹/₂ stick) butter or margarine	1¹/₂ cups pitted dates
	¹/₄ teaspoon salt
2 eggs, beaten	3 cups crisp rice cereal
1 cup sugar	¹/₂ cup chopped nuts
¹/₂ teaspoon vanilla extract	1 cup shredded coconut

Combine the butter, eggs, sugar, vanilla, dates and salt in a skillet. Cook over medium heat for 10 minutes, stirring constantly. Remove from the heat. Stir in the cereal and nuts. Shape by spoonfuls into balls with buttered hands. Roll in coconut and place on waxed paper. Let stand until firm. Store in the refrigerator. Yield: 2 dozen servings.

Mary A. Chamberlain, Beta Epsilon Master
Fort Myers, Florida

DONUT HOLES

3 cups all-purpose flour	6 tablespoons vegetable oil
2 teaspoons baking powder	
	1¹/₂ teaspoons vanilla extract
1 teaspoon baking soda	
1 teaspoon salt	1 cup buttermilk
¹/₂ teaspoon nutmeg	Vegetable oil for frying
3 eggs, beaten	Additional granulated sugar
1 cup sugar	

Combine the first 5 ingredients in a bowl. Mix the eggs, 1 cup sugar, 6 tablespoons oil and vanilla in a bowl. Beat in the dry ingredients alternately with the buttermilk. Drop scant teaspoonfuls of batter, a few at a time, into 370-degree oil. Cook until golden brown, turning once during frying. Remove with a slotted spoon to paper towels to drain. Coat in granulated sugar. Yield: 4 dozen donut holes.

Sandy Bartholomew, Xi Epsilon Iota
Ballwin, Missouri

POPCORN CAKE

1/2 cup (1 stick) butter
1/4 cup vegetable oil
1 (10-ounce) package
* marshmallows*
1 small can nuts

1 (16-ounce) package
* "M & M's" Chocolate*
* Candies*
16 cups popped popcorn
Gumdrops to taste
* (optional)*

Combine the butter, oil and marshmallows in a large saucepan. Cook over low heat until smooth, stirring occasionally. Remove from the heat. Stir in the candies, nuts, popcorn and gumdrops. Pat into a buttered bundt pan. Cool completely in the pan. Invert onto a serving plate. Yield: 12 servings.

Charlotte Young, Xi Alpha Zeta
Price, Utah

POPCORN MIX

10 cups popped popcorn
3 cups Rice Krispie
* Treats cereal*
1 cup honey roasted
* peanuts*

1 (12-ounce) package
* white almond*
* bark, melted*
2 tablespoons peanut
* butter*

Combine the popcorn, cereal and peanuts in a large bowl. Combine the almond bark and peanut butter in a small bowl and mix well. Drizzle over the popcorn mixture. Stir gently to coat. Place on waxed paper. Let stand until firm. Store in an airtight container. Yield: 24 servings.

Kathy Stevens
West Terre Haute, Indiana

EASTER NESTS

4 cups chow mein
* noodles*
1/2 cup light corn syrup
1/2 cup sugar

3/4 cup peanut butter
Jelly beans or other
* small egg-shaped*
* candy*

Break the noodles into a bowl. Combine the corn syrup and sugar in a saucepan. Cook over medium heat until the sugar dissolves and the edges of the mixture begin to bubble, stirring constantly. Stir in the peanut butter until smooth. Pour over the noodles and toss to coat. Cool slightly. Shape 1/4 cupfuls into tight balls with buttered hands. Make an inden-tation in each ball so that it resembles a bird nest. Place the nests on waxed paper. Let stand until firm. Place 2 or 3 jelly beans into each indentation. Yield: 1 dozen nests.

Mary Cook, Eta Master
Beckley, West Virginia

ÉCLAIR DESSERT

1 cup water
1/2 cup (1 stick) butter
1 cup all-purpose flour
4 eggs
11 ounces cream cheese,
* softened*
3 cups milk

2 (31/2-ounce) packages
* vanilla instant*
* pudding mix*
8 ounces whipped
* topping*
Chocolate syrup

Bring the water and butter to a boil in a saucepan over medium-high heat. Add the flour and mix well. Remove from the heat and cool completely. Mix in the eggs 1 at a time. Spread into a nonstick 9×13-inch baking pan. Bake at 350 degrees for 20 minutes. Remove to a wire rack to cool completely. Beat the cream cheese, milk and pudding mix in a bowl until thickened. Spread over the baked crust. Cover with the whipped topping. Chill, covered, until cold. Drizzle with chocolate syrup. Yield: 12 servings.

Patricia Schnitker, Iota Epsilon
Clarinda, Iowa

PRESSURE COOKER FLAN

1/2 cup sugar
5 to 6 pitted prunes
13/4 cups milk
1 (14-ounce) can
* sweetened*
* condensed milk*

3 eggs
4 to 8 ounces cream
* cheese, softened*
1 teaspoon vanilla
* extract*

Cook the sugar in a heavy saucepan over medium heat until the sugar dissolves and is caramel colored, stirring constantly. Pour evenly over the bottom of a 9-inch baking pan. Arrange the prunes over the caramelized sugar. Process the milk, condensed milk, eggs, cream cheese and vanilla in a blender. Pour over the prunes. Cover the pan with foil. Pour 3/4 cup water into the bottom of a pressure cooker fitted with a rack. Place the baking pan on the rack in the pressure cooker; seal. Cook at 15 pounds pressure for 7 to 9 minutes, using the manufacturer's directions. Turn off the heat and let the pressure return to zero before removing the lid. Remove the flan carefully to a wire rack to cool completely. Loosen from the side of the pan with a sharp knife and invert onto a serving plate. Yield: 8 servings.

Lisa Robles, Zeta Gamma
Franklin, North Carolina

FOUR-LAYER DESSERT

1 cup all-purpose flour
1/2 cup (1 stick)
   margarine, softened
1 cup chopped nuts
8 ounces cream cheese,
   softened
1 cup confectioners'
   sugar
1 cup whipped topping

1 (3¹/₂-ounce) package
   chocolate instant
   pudding mix
1 (3¹/₂-ounce) package
   vanilla instant
   pudding mix
3 cups milk
2 cups whipped topping

Combine the flour, margarine and nuts in a bowl and mix well. Press into the bottom of a nonstick 9×13-inch baking pan. Bake at 350 degrees for 20 minutes. Remove to a wire rack to cool completely. Combine the cream cheese, confectioners' sugar and 1 cup whipped topping in a bowl and mix well. Spread over the cooled crust. Whisk the chocolate pudding mix, vanilla pudding mix and milk in a bowl for 2 minutes. Pour evenly over the cream cheese mixture. Spoon 2 cups whipped topping over the pudding layer and spread lightly. Garnish with shaved chocolate or chopped nuts. Yield: 12 servings.

Virginia A. Potter, Eta Master
Seattle, Washington

FRUIT-FILLED PHYLLO CUPS

8 sheets phyllo dough
1 small package fat-free
   sugar-free vanilla
   instant pudding mix
4 ounces reduced-fat
   cream cheese,
   softened

1 (16-ounce) package
   frozen mixed fruit,
   thawed and drained
8 ounces light whipped
   topping
1/2 cup butterscotch
   topping

Spray the outside of 8 ramekins with nonstick cooking spray and place upside-down on a baking sheet. Cut the phyllo sheets in half. Fit one half-sheet over each ramekin. Fit a second half-sheet over each ramekin, laying it the opposite direction. Bake at 350 degrees for 5 minutes or until golden brown. Remove to a wire rack to cool completely. Remove the baked shells from the ramekins carefully and place the shells upright on serving plates. Prepare the pudding mix using the package directions. Stir in the cream cheese. Divide the pudding mixture among the phyllo cups and top with a spoonful of fruit. Spoon the whipped topping over the fruit and drizzle each with a tablespoon of butterscotch topping. Yield: 8 servings.

Michele D. VanDyke, Alpha Mu
Crete, Nebraska

LEMON LUSH

1¹/₂ cups all-purpose
   flour
³/₄ cup (1¹/₂ sticks) butter
   or margarine, melted
1/2 cup chopped nuts
8 ounces cream cheese,
   softened

1 cup confectioners'
   sugar
1 cup whipped topping
2 (3¹/₂-ounce) packages
   lemon pudding mix
1 cup whipped topping
1/2 cup chopped nuts

Combine the flour, butter and 1/2 cup chopped nuts in a bowl and mix well. Press into the bottom of a 9×13-inch baking dish. Bake at 350 degrees for 20 minutes or until golden brown. Remove to a wire rack to cool completely. Beat the cream cheese and confectioners' sugar in a bowl until light and fluffy. Stir in 1 cup whipped topping. Spread over the cooled crust. Prepare the pudding mix using the package directions. Cool but do not let set. Pour evenly over the cream cheese mixture. Cover with 1 cup whipped topping and sprinkle with 1/2 cup chopped nuts. Chill, covered, until just before serving. Yield: 12 to 16 servings.

Janice DiBeneditto, Theta Master
Waterbury, Connecticut

BLACK FOREST MOUSSE

1¹/₂ cups milk
1 (3¹/₂-ounce) package
   chocolate instant
   pudding mix
8 ounces whipped
   topping

16 chocolate sandwich
   cookies
1¹/₂ cups cherry pie
   filling

Whisk the milk and pudding mix in a bowl for 2 minutes. Stir in 1 cup of the whipped topping. Crumble 10 of the cookies and stir into the pudding mixture. Spoon half the pudding mixture into a 1¹/₂-quart serving bowl. Spread with 1 cup of the whipped topping. Spread with 1 cup of the pie filling. Spread with the remaining pudding mixture and top with the remaining whipped topping. Drop the remaining pie filling by spoonfuls over the whipped topping. Crumble the remaining cookies and sprinkle around the outer edge. Yield: 12 servings.

Patricia Delesandro, Xi Eta Eta
Greensburg, Pennsylvania

---

*Darla Wooldridge, Psi Pi, Dwight, Illinois, shared her easy recipe for **Snicker Salad**. She chops 5 large Granny Smith apples and places them in a bowl. She chops one 12-ounce package miniature Snickers and adds them to the bowl. She folds in 12 ounces whipped topping and chills until just before serving.*

CHOCOLATE MOUSSE

6 ounces semisweet
  chocolate, chopped
2 to 3 tablespoons water
  or coffee
1 tablespoon butter
1 tablespoon rum, or
  1/2 teaspoon vanilla
  extract

3 egg yolks
3 egg whites
1/2 cup heavy whipping
  cream, whipped

Combine the chocolate and water in a double boiler. Cook until the chocolate is thick and creamy, stirring frequently. Remove from the heat and stir in the butter and rum. Add the egg yolks 1 at a time, stirring well after each addition. Beat the egg whites in a bowl until stiff peaks form. Fold into the chocolate mixture. Spoon into serving dishes. Chill, covered, overnight. Top with whipped cream just before serving. Note: If you are concerned about using raw eggs, use eggs pasteurized in their shells, which are sold at some specialty food stores, or use an equivalent amount of pasteurized egg yolk and pasteurized egg white. Yield: 4 to 6 servings.

Kellie Raven, Alpha Zeta
White Rock, New Mexico

CHOCOLATE MOUSSE WITH RASPBERRY SAUCE

1 (3 1/2-ounce) bar
  premium semisweet
  chocolate, chopped
1 (3 1/2-ounce) bar
  premium dark
  chocolate, chopped
1/4 cup sugar
2 tablespoons butter
2 extra-large eggs,
  beaten

1/3 cup milk
2 cups heavy whipping
  cream
1 teaspoon vanilla
  extract
1/2 cup sugar
Raspberry Sauce

Combine the semisweet chocolate, dark chocolate, 1/4 cup sugar and the butter in a heavy saucepan. Cook over low heat until smooth, stirring constantly. Whisk the eggs and milk in a bowl. Stir a small amount of the hot mixture into the eggs; stir the eggs to the hot mixture. Cook over low heat for 5 minutes or until thickened, stirring constantly. Pour into a bowl and let stand for 45 to 60 minutes. Whip the cream in a mixing bowl until soft peaks form. Add the vanilla and 1/2 cup sugar gradually, whipping until stiff peaks form. Fold into the chocolate mixture. Spoon into serving dishes. Chill, covered, for 2 to 4 hours. Drizzle with Raspberry Sauce and garnish with raspberries. Yield: 8 servings

RASPBERRY SAUCE

1 (10-ounce) package
  frozen raspberries in
  syrup, thawed

2 teaspoons cornstarch
2 tablespoon sugar

Purée the raspberries in a blender. Strain, if desired, and pour into a saucepan. Whisk in the cornstarch. Stir in the sugar. Bring to a boil over medium heat, stirring constantly. Boil for 1 minute, stirring constantly. Remove from the heat and cool completely. Pour into a bowl. Chill, covered, until just before serving.

Connie Warner, Theta Epsilon
Julesburg, Colorado

CHOCOLATE MOUSSE NAPOLEONS

This comes from a cookbook of family recipes that my brother compiled as a Christmas present.

1 sheet frozen puff
  pastry
1 cup heavy whipping
  cream
1/4 teaspoon cinnamon

1 cup (6 ounces)
  semisweet chocolate
  chips, melted
Confectioners' sugar

Thaw the pastry at room temperature for 30 minutes. Unfold the pastry on a floured work surface. Cut into thirds along the fold lines. Cut each third into 6 rectangles. Arrange on a nonstick baking sheet. Bake at 400 degrees for 12 minutes or until golden brown. Remove the rectangles to a wire rack to cool completely. Whip the cream and cinnamon in a bowl until stiff peaks form. Fold in the chocolate, reserving a small amount for garnish. Split the baked pastries horizontally in half. Spread the cream mixture over the bottom halves of the pastries and cover with the top halves. Place on a serving platter. Chill, covered, for up to 4 hours. Drizzle the reserved chocolate over the napoleons and dust with confectioners' sugar. Yield: 18 servings.

Tina Lauer, Alpha Zeta Theta
St. Peters, Missouri

*Ruth Delap, Xi Alpha Mu, Flagstaff, Arizona, shared her tasty recipe for **Hot Buttered Rum**. She combines 1 quart softened French vanilla ice cream, 2 cups softened butter, one 1-pound package brown sugar, one 1-pound package confectioners' sugar, 2 teaspoons nutmeg, and 2 teaspoons cinnamon in a bowl and mixes well. She shapes the mixture into a ball, wraps it in plastic wrap, and freezes it. When she's ready to serve, she spoons 3 tablespoons of the frozen mixture into a mug. She stirs in 6 ounces boiling water and 1 1/2 ounces rum and garnishes it with a cinnamon stick.*

❖ CHOCOLATE GRAND MARNIER MOUSSE

1¼ cups heavy cream	1½ teaspoons grated
1⅓ cups (8 ounces)	orange zest
semisweet chocolate	1½ teaspoons vanilla
chips	extract
⅓ cup sugar	¼ cup (½ stick) butter,
5 egg yolks	softened
1 tablespoon Grand	
Marnier	

Heat the cream in a saucepan over medium heat until small bubbles appear around the edge. Combine the chocolate chips, sugar, egg yolks, liqueur, orange zest and vanilla in a blender or food processor. Add the hot cream and process at high speed for 1 minute. Add the butter 1 tablespoon at a time, processing well after each addition. Pour into serving dishes. Chill, covered, for 3 hours or longer. Yield: 6 servings.

Dianne V. Benn, Alpha Eta Master
Victoria, British Columbia, Canada

FROZEN LEMON MOUSSE

1 tablespoon	⅛ teaspoon cream
vegetable oil	of tartar
¼ cup ground almonds	⅛ teaspoon salt
4 egg yolks, at room	¾ cup sugar
temperature	1½ cups heavy
¼ cup sugar	whipping cream,
4½ teaspoons grated	whipped
lemon zest	1 (10-ounce) package
½ cup fresh lemon	frozen raspberries in
juice	syrup, thawed
4 egg whites, at room	2 tablespoons orange-
temperature	flavored liqueur

Spread the oil evenly over the bottom of an 8-inch or 9-inch springform pan. Sprinkle with the almonds. Combine the egg yolks, ¼ cup sugar, the lemon zest and lemon juice in a large bowl and mix well. Beat the egg whites in a bowl until foamy. Add the cream of tartar and salt and beat until soft peaks form. Add ¾ cup sugar 1 tablespoon at a time, beating until stiff peaks form. Fold into the lemon mixture. Fold in the whipped cream. Pour into the prepared pan. Freeze, covered, for 8 to 10 hours. Loosen from the side of the pan with a sharp knife and remove the side. Mix the raspberries and liqueur in a bowl. Strain through a wire mesh sieve into a bowl. Serve over the lemon mousse and garnish with fresh raspberries, strawberries or sliced kiwifruit. Note: If you are concerned about using raw eggs, use eggs pasteurized in their shells, which are sold at some specialty food stores,

or use an equivalent amount of pasteurized egg yolk and pasteurized egg white. Yield: 10 to 12 servings.

Lauraine Wilson, Preceptor Mu Sigma
Borrego Springs, California

LEMON STRAWBERRY PARFAIT

½ cup sugar	¼ cup lemon juice
2 teaspoons cornstarch	1 cup heavy whipping
1 egg	cream, whipped
2 egg yolks	1 (21-ounce) can
1 tablespoon lemon zest	strawberry pie filling

Mix the sugar and cornstarch in a heavy saucepan. Whisk in the egg, egg yolks, lemon zest and lemon juice. Cook over medium heat for 3 to 5 minutes or until the mixture boils and thickens, whisking gently. Reduce the heat to medium-low and cook for 2 minutes, whisking constantly. Remove to a bowl. Chill, covered, for 1 hour. Fold in the whipped cream. Alternate layers of the lemon mixture and pie filling in 4 parfait glasses. Garnish with a dollop of whipped cream and fresh strawberries. Yield: 4 servings.

Hazel Sterchi, Xi Delta Beta
Olney, Illinois

❖ PANNA COTTA WITH RASPBERRY COULIS

I fell in love with this classic Italian dessert on a trip to Italy. Try serving it with chocolate or caramel sauce for a truly decadent dessert.

1 envelope unflavored	1 teaspoon vanilla
gelatin	extract
½ cup milk	1 (10-ounce) package
½ cup sugar	frozen raspberries in
½ cup milk	syrup, thawed
3 cups heavy cream	1 tablespoon sugar, or
	to taste

Soften the gelatin in ½ cup milk in a measuring cup. Let stand for 10 minutes. Combine ½ cup sugar, ½ cup milk and the cream in a heavy saucepan. Bring to a simmer over medium heat, stirring occasionally; do not boil. Add the gelatin mixture and cook until the gelatin dissolves, stirring constantly. Stir in the vanilla. Pour into ramekins or heatproof stemmed glasses. Chill, covered, for 4 hours or until set. Purée the raspberries and 1 tablespoon sugar in a blender or food processor. Strain through a wire mesh sieve into a bowl. Spoon over the panna cotta just before serving. Yield: 8 servings.

Barbara Henson, Iota Master
Calgary, Alberta, Canada

RUM MOUSSE

2 envelopes unflavored
    gelatin
1/2 cup cold water
4 egg yolks
5 tablespoons sugar

2/3 cup rum
2 cups heavy whipping
    cream, whipped
Brandied Cherry Sauce

Soften the gelatin in the water in a double boiler. Cook until the gelatin dissolves. Beat the egg yolks and sugar in a bowl until thick and pale yellow. Stir in the gelatin mixture and rum. Let stand for a few minutes or until it begins to thicken. Fold in the whipped cream. Pour into an 1 1/2-quart ring mold or bowl. Chill, covered, until set. Unmold onto a serving plate and serve with Brandied Cherry Sauce. Note: If you are concerned about using raw eggs, use eggs pasteurized in their shells, which are sold at some specialty food stores, or use an equivalent amount of pasteurized egg yolk. Yield: 8 servings.

BRANDIED CHERRY SAUCE

2 teaspoons cornstarch
1 (16-ounce) can pitted
    sweet cherries

1 tablespoon brandy

Dissolve the cornstarch in a small amount of water in a saucepan. Stir in the cherries. Cook over medium-low heat until thickened, stirring gently. Remove from the heat and stir in the brandy. Pour into a bowl. Chill, covered, until cold.

Rose C. Gaspari, Beta Chi Master
Santa Rosa, California

WHITE CHOCOLATE MOUSSE

4 ounces white
    chocolate, chopped
1/2 cup (1 stick) butter,
    cut into small pieces

3 egg yolks, beaten
3 egg whites
1/4 cup sugar

Place the white chocolate in a double boiler. Cook until the chocolate begins to melt, stirring occasionally. Stir in the butter a few pieces at a time. Cook until smooth, stirring constantly. Remove from the heat. Stir in the egg yolks gradually. Chill for 10 minutes. Beat the egg whites in a bowl until soft peaks form. Beat in the sugar gradually until stiff peaks form. Fold into the chocolate mixture. Spoon into serving dishes. Chill until just before serving. Note: If you are concerned about using raw eggs, use eggs pasteurized in their shells, which are sold at some specialty food stores, or use an equivalent amount of pasteurized egg yolk and pasteurized egg white. Yield: 4 servings.

Darice Tiffany, Preceptor Beta Gamma
Scottsdale, Arizona

CARAMEL CHOCOLATE SAUCE

30 caramel candies
2/3 cup evaporated milk
1/2 cup (1 stick) butter

1 cup (6 ounces)
    semisweet
    chocolate chips

Combine the caramels, evaporated milk, butter and chocolate chips in a microwave-safe bowl. Microwave on High for 2 minutes; stir. Microwave on High for 1 minute and 40 seconds; stir. Microwave on High until smooth, stirring every minute. Cool completely. Pour into a pint canning jar or another airtight container. Store in the refrigerator. Serve over ice cream. Yield: 2 cups.

Heidi L. Wicks, Xi Theta Xi
Spirit Lake, Iowa

CARAMEL RUM SAUCE

2 cups packed brown
    sugar
1/4 cup cornstarch
1 1/3 cups half-and-half
    or cream
1 cup water

1/2 cup light corn syrup
1/4 cup (1/2 stick) butter
1/4 cup rum
2 teaspoons vanilla
    extract

Mix the brown sugar and cornstarch in a saucepan. Stir in the half-and-half, water and corn syrup. Cook over medium heat until thickened and bubbly, stirring constantly; the mixture may appear curdled. Cook for 2 minutes, stirring constantly. Remove from the heat and stir in the butter, rum and vanilla until smooth. Cool completely. Pour into 4 half-pint canning jars or other airtight containers. Store in the refrigerator for up to 2 months. Serve over ice cream or use as a frosting for yellow cake. Yield: 4 cups.

Fredith Skaife, Gamma Alpha Epsilon
Yuba City, California

HEAVENLY MILK CHOCOLATE SAUCE

1 (11 1/2-ounce) bar
    premium milk
    chocolate, chopped
1 teaspoon vanilla
    extract

1 (14-ounce) can
    sweetened
    condensed milk
Cream or milk

Combine the chocolate, vanilla and condensed milk in a saucepan. Cook over low heat until smooth, stirring frequently. Stir in a small amount of cream to thin the sauce. Serve hot over ice cream or cool completely and pour into an airtight container. Store in the refrigerator. Yield: 2 cups.

Judy A. Bennett, Laureate Rho
Powell, Wyoming

PEANUT BUTTER HOT FUDGE SAUCE

1 (4-ounce) package
  chocolate pudding mix
3/4 cup water
3/4 cup light corn syrup
1/8 teaspoon salt
1 teaspoon vanilla
  extract
1 tablespoon butter
1/3 cup peanut butter
  (may use chunky)

Combine the pudding mix, water, corn syrup and salt in a saucepan and mix well. Bring to a boil over medium heat, stirring constantly. Remove from the heat and stir in the vanilla, butter and peanut butter until smooth. Serve warm over ice cream, angel food cake or strawberries. Yield: 2 cups.

Michelle Steffen, Preceptor Beta Pi
Concordia, Kansas

VANILLA CARAMEL SAUCE

1/2 cup packed brown
  sugar
1/3 cup evaporated milk
1 teaspoon vanilla
  extract
1/4 cup chopped nuts

Combine the brown sugar, evaporated milk and vanilla in a saucepan. Bring to a boil over medium heat, stirring frequently. Boil for 4 minutes, stirring constantly. Stir in the nuts. Serve over pound cake or your favorite dessert. Yield: 1 cup.

Glenda Martin, Xi Iota Delta
Denver City, Texas

PEANUT BUTTER APPLE DESSERT

1 1/2 cups graham cracker
  crumbs
1/2 cup packed brown
  sugar
1/2 cup peanut butter
1/4 cup (1/2 stick) butter,
  melted
8 ounces cream cheese,
  softened
3/4 cup granulated sugar
16 ounces whipped
  topping
2 (21-ounce) cans apple
  pie filling
3/4 cup confectioners'
  sugar
1 teaspoon cinnamon
1/3 cup peanut butter

Combine the graham cracker crumbs, brown sugar, 1/2 cup peanut butter and butter in a bowl and mix well. Press half the mixture into the bottom of a nonstick 9×13-inch baking pan. Beat the cream cheese and granulated sugar in a bowl until smooth. Fold in the whipped topping. Spread half of the mixture over the graham cracker layer. Spoon 1 can of the pie filling evenly over the top. Combine the confectioners' sugar, cinnamon and 1/3 cup peanut butter in a bowl and mix until crumbly. Sprinkle half over the pie filling layer. Repeat the layers. Chill, covered, until just before serving. Yield: 20 servings.

Jamie Phipps, Iota Beta
Medicine Lodge, Kansas

PEANUT BUTTER CHOCOLATE SLICE

1 1/2 cups all-purpose
  flour
3/4 cup (1 1/2 sticks)
  margarine, softened
1/2 cup peanut butter
8 ounces cream cheese,
  softened
1 cup confectioners'
  sugar
16 ounces whipped
  topping
2/3 cup chopped peanuts
2 (3 1/2-ounce) packages
  chocolate instant
  pudding mix
3 cups cold milk

Place the flour in a bowl. Cut in the margarine until crumbly. Press into the bottom of a nonstick 9×13-inch baking pan. Bake at 350 degrees for 20 minutes. Remove to a wire rack to cool completely. Combine the peanut butter and cream cheese in a bowl and mix well. Add the confectioners' sugar and mix until smooth. Stir in half the whipped topping. Spread over the cooled crust. Sprinkle with the peanuts, reserving a small amount for garnish. Whisk the pudding mix and milk in a bowl for 2 minutes. Pour evenly over the peanut butter layer. Cover with the remaining whipped topping. Sprinkle with the reserved peanuts. Chill, covered, for 2 hours or longer. Yield: 12 to 15 servings.

Carolyn S. Nagie, Preceptor Theta Rho
Mount Dora, Florida

PINEAPPLE RICE DESSERT

1 (20-ounce) can crushed
  pineapple
8 ounces cream cheese,
  softened
2 tablespoons sugar
3 cups miniature
  marshmallows
2 cups cooked rice
1 (10-ounce) jar
  maraschino cherries,
  drained and quartered
1 cup heavy whipping
  cream, whipped
1 cup chopped pecans

Drain the pineapple, reserving 1 to 2 tablespoons of the juice. Beat the cream cheese and reserved pineapple juice in a bowl until smooth. Stir in the pineapple and sugar. Stir in the marshmallows, rice and cherries. Fold in the whipped cream and pecans. Chill, covered, until just before serving. Yield: 8 servings.

Judy Knight, Epsilon Alpha
Mesquite, Texas

Matti Schomaker, Xi Eta Xi, Edinboro, Pennsylvania, makes an easy **Mock Coffee Mousse** *with just three ingredients. She dissolves 24 marshmallows in 1 cup hot strong coffee and lets the mixture cool to room temperature. She then whips 1 cup heavy whipping cream and folds it into the coffee mixture. She chills the mousse until firm and serves it in wine glasses.*

SPANISH POPOVERS

2 eggs
2 tablespoons
  granulated sugar
1 teaspoon vanilla
  extract

Pinch of salt
2 cups ricotta cheese
1 cup all-purpose flour
Vegetable oil for frying
Confectioners' sugar

Beat the eggs in a bowl. Stir in the granulated sugar, vanilla and salt. Add the ricotta cheese and mix well. Add the flour and mix well. Drop teaspoonfuls of batter, a few at a time, into the hot oil. Cook until golden brown on both sides. Remove with a slotted spoon to paper towels to drain. Dust with confectioners' sugar. Yield: 2 to 3 dozen popovers.

Patricia S. Barker, Xi Theta Upsilon
Tampa, Florida

PECAN PUMPKIN CRUMBLE

1 cup sugar
1 1/2 teaspoons cinnamon
2 eggs, beaten
1 (16-ounce) can
  pumpkin
1 (12-ounce) can
  evaporated milk

1 (2-layer) package
  yellow cake mix
1/2 cup (1 stick) butter,
  melted
1 cup chopped pecans

Combine the sugar, cinnamon, eggs, pumpkin and evaporated milk in a large bowl and mix well. Pour into an ungreased 9×13-inch baking pan. Sprinkle the cake mix evenly over the top. Drizzle with the butter and sprinkle with pecans. Bake at 350 degrees for 40 to 50 minutes or until golden brown. Remove to a wire rack to cool. Serve with ice cream or whipped cream if desired. Yield: 15 to 20 servings.

Nicole Rayfield, Kappa Kappa
Colonial Heights, Virginia

SNICKERS DESSERT

2 cups graham cracker
  crumbs
3 tablespoons sugar
1/2 cup (1 stick)
  margarine, melted
1 (12-ounce) jar hot
  fudge topping,
  warmed

3/4 cup milk
2 (3 1/2-ounce) packages
  vanilla or chocolate
  instant pudding mix
16 ounces whipped
  topping
6 to 7 (2-ounce) Snickers
  candy bars, chopped

Mix the first 3 ingredients in a bowl. Press into the bottom of a nonstick 9×13-inch baking pan. Pour the hot fudge topping over the crust. Cool completely. Combine the next 3 ingredients in a large bowl. Beat for 2 to 3 minutes or until stiff peaks form, scraping the side of the bowl often. Stir in three-fourths of the Snickers. Spread over the crust. Sprinkle with the remaining Snickers. Chill, covered, for 4 hours or longer. Yield: 15 servings.

Kathy Drake, Nu Chi
Bolivar, Missouri

CHOCOLATE SOUFFLÉ

Butter
5 ounces bittersweet
  chocolate, chopped
3 egg yolks, at room
  temperature

3 egg whites
Pinch of salt
1/3 cup sugar

Butter a 6-cup soufflé dish generously and dust with sugar. Melt the chocolate in a double boiler, stirring until smooth. Remove from the heat and cool slightly. Add the egg yolks and mix well. Beat the egg whites and salt in a bowl until soft peaks form. Beat in 1/3 cup sugar gradually until stiff peaks form. Fold the egg whites into the chocolate mixture, one cup at a time. Spoon into the prepared soufflé dish. Bake in the center of the oven at 375 degrees for 24 to 26 minutes or until puffed and crusty on top but the center is very soft. Serve immediately with whipped cream. Yield: 6 servings.

Rachelle Flanik Loree, Preceptor Nu
Walla Walla, Washington

LEMON SOUFFLÉ

1/2 cup sugar
2 tablespoons
  all-purpose flour
1 tablespoon margarine,
  softened

2 egg yolks, beaten
Grated zest of 1 lemon
Juice of 1 lemon
1 cup milk
2 egg whites

Sift the sugar and flour into a bowl. Add the margarine and beat until smooth. Add the egg yolks, lemon zest and lemon juice and mix well. Add the milk and mix well. Beat the egg whites in a bowl until stiff peaks form. Fold into the lemon mixture. Pour into a greased 9×9-inch baking pan. Place the baking pan in a larger pan. Add enough hot water to the larger pan to come 2 inches up the side of the baking pan. Bake at 325 degrees for 1 hour. Remove the baking pan carefully from the hot water and serve immediately. Yield: 9 servings.

Rosemary Chorney, Laureate Alpha Alpha
Surrey, British Columbia, Canada

❖ LIGHT TIRAMISU

1 cup cold water
1 (14-ounce) can
 fat-free sweetened
 condensed milk
1 small package fat-free
 sugar-free vanilla
 instant pudding mix
8 ounces reduced-fat
 cream cheese, softened
12 ounces light whipped
 topping

1 cup hot water
1/2 cup coffee-flavored
 liqueur
1 tablespoon instant
 espresso powder or
 2 tablespoons instant
 coffee granules
24 ladyfingers, split
 lengthwise
3 tablespoons baking
 cocoa

Whisk the cold water, condensed milk and pudding mix in a bowl. Chill, covered with plastic wrap, for 30 minutes or until firm. Add the cream cheese and mix well. Fold in the whipped topping. Combine the hot water, liqueur and espresso powder in a bowl. Stir until the espresso dissolves. Arrange 16 ladyfinger halves in the bottom of a trifle bowl. Drizzle with one-third of the espresso mixture and spread with one-third of the pudding mixture. Dust with 1 tablespoon of the baking cocoa. Repeat the layers 2 more times. Chill, covered, for 8 hours or longer. Yield: 12 servings.

Nan Rutkowski, Xi Beta Lambda
Gold Canyon, Arizona

TSUNAMI TIRAMISU

1 (12-ounce) package
 vanilla wafers
2 teaspoons instant
 coffee granules
2 tablespoons hot water
32 ounces cream cheese,
 softened

1 cup sugar
1 cup sour cream
4 eggs
1 tablespoon instant
 coffee granules
1 tablespoon hot water

Line a 9×13-inch pan with foil, extending the foil over the edges of the pan. Arrange half the vanilla wafers in a single layer over the bottom of the pan. Dissolve 2 teaspoons coffee granules in 2 tablespoons hot water in a small bowl. Brush half the coffee over the wafers in the pan. Beat the cream cheese and sugar in a bowl until light and fluffy. Beat in the sour cream. Add the eggs 1 at a time, beating just until blended after each addition. Remove 3 1/2 cups batter to a bowl. Dissolve 1 tablespoon coffee granules in 1 tablespoon hot water in a small bowl. Add to the 3 1/2 cups batter and mix well. Pour over the wafers in the pan. Arrange the remaining wafers in a single layer over the top. Brush with the remaining coffee. Pour the remaining batter evenly over the wafers. Bake at 325 degrees for 45 minutes. Remove to a wire rack to cool completely. Chill, covered, for 3 hours.

Garnish with a layer of whipped cream, drizzle with hot fudge sauce and sprinkle with raspberries. Yield: 16 servings.

Joy Syretz, Preceptor Delta Nu
Butler, Pennsylvania

TANTALIZING TIRAMISU

16 ounces cream cheese,
 softened
3/4 cup confectioners'
 sugar
1 cup heavy whipping
 cream, whipped
3 tablespoons coffee-
 flavored liqueur

1 cup strong coffee
24 ladyfingers, split
 lengthwise
3 1/2 cups sliced fresh
 strawberries
2 teaspoons baking
 cocoa

Beat the cream cheese and confectioners' sugar in a bowl until smooth. Fold in the whipped cream. Stir the liqueur into the coffee in a small bowl. Arrange one-third of the ladyfingers, cut side up, in the bottom of an 8×8-inch baking dish. Drizzle with one-third of the coffee mixture. Spread one-third of the cream cheese mixture over the top. Arrange one-third of the strawberries over the cream cheese layer. Repeat the layers 2 more times. Chill, covered, for 1 hour or longer. Sift the baking cocoa over the top and garnish with sliced strawberries. Yield: 8 servings.

Cyndy Auman, Xi Beta Nu
Susanville, California

TORTILLA FRUIT ROLLUPS

12 flour tortillas
2 (21-ounce) cans pie
 filling (any flavor)
1 cup water
2 cups sugar

1 cup (2 sticks)
 margarine
1/4 cup sugar
1 teaspoon cinnamon
1/2 cup chopped pecans

Arrange the tortillas on a work surface. Spread equal portions of the pie filling over the tortillas and roll to enclose the filling. Place, seam side down, in a single layer in a nonstick 9×13-inch baking pan. Combine the water, 2 cups sugar and the margarine in a saucepan. Cook over medium heat until smooth, stirring frequently. Pour evenly over the tortillas. Cover with foil and let stand for at least 2 hours. Bake, covered, at 350 degrees for 30 minutes. Remove to a wire rack. Combine 1/4 cup sugar, the cinnamon and pecans in a bowl and mix well. Sprinkle over the hot tortillas. Bake, uncovered, for 10 minutes longer. Remove to a wire rack to cool completely. Serve with whipped topping or ice cream. Yield: 12 servings.

Margaret Parker, Rho Master
Raton, New Mexico

Merit Winners

Dianne V. Benn, 200
*Chocolate Grand Marnier
Mousse*

Sylvia H. Carpenter, 148
Chocolate Peanut Clusters

Colette Culver, 118
Coffee Meltaways

Joyce Fred, 195
*Caramel Banana Pecan
Crepes*

Storm Gonzalez, 163
*Frozen Strawberry
Margarita Pie*

Juanita W. Gray, 29
Triple Lemon Pie

Dianne Harris-Wakeling, 78
Tobelerone Cake

Sandra Hatala, 74
Praline Pumpkin Cake

Barbara Henson, 200
*Panna Cotta with
Raspberry Coulis*

Penny Holloman, 96
Baked Lemon Pudding

Cindy Johns, 164
Blueberry Sorbet

Kathy Kuper, 180
Fruit Salsa

Beverly Morgan, 113
*White Chocolate Macadamia
Nut Cookies*

Ellen Osachoff, 81
Apple Crisp Cheesecake

Jane Owen, 88
*Pumpkin Chocolate
Cheesecake Bars*

Kimberly Pague, 158
Raspberry Ice Cream Dessert

Eugenia Richardson, 150
White Chocolate Popcorn Crunch

Nan Rutkowski, 204
Light Tiramisu

Jackie H. Sanders, 92
*Piña Colada Bread Pudding
with Coconut Rum Sauce*

Sheila Simmons, 118
Molasses Strips

Louise Sledge, 192
Coconut Toast Triangles

Eleanor Strecker, 126
Butter Pecan Turtle Bars

Gloria Thrasher, 22
Sour Cream Apple Pie

Billie Ann Waite, 167
Blackberry Bread

Ann Walters, 55
Mexican Chocolate Cake

Honorable Mention

Laurene Atherton, 171
Patricia S. Barker, 203
Wendy Bennett, 158
Joyce Bjork, 31
Sally Blaisdell-Field, 163
Joan Brode, 138
Freda Bush, 34
Jeanne Caimano, 35
Yvonne Campbell, 112
Sylvia Cole, 76
Joyce Crippen, 194
Sandi Davison, 110
Linda DellaRossa, 39
Marjorie M. Douglas, 49
Linda Duncan, 72

Carole Emge, 169
Bertie Farabee, 23
Ginette Hunter, 173
Sharon Ingram, 63
Sally J. King, 152
Judy Latta, 81
Erin A. Lollis, 110
Carolyn Marshall, 29
Jan Meredith, 102
Ellen A. O'Bryan, 186
Judy Parsons, 194
Delores D. Roberts, 122
Verla R. Rosequist, 129
Carolyn H. Schott, 129
Jean Sebert, 71

Janet Singleton, 80
Patricia Soard, 44
Rosemary Souleyrette, 47
Ruth Stevens, 134
Marian Stubbs, 32
Kristie Sturrock, 145
Barbara Summerfield, 50
Deborah Tyler, 56
Connie Warner, 199
Kris Weishaupt, 159
Shirley Welch, 69
Linda Fae Wiedeman, 69
Marilyn A. Williams, 115

Metric Equivalents

Although the United States has not converted to metric measurements, most other countries, including England and Canada, use the metric system. The following chart provides convenient approximate equivalents for allowing use of regular kitchen measures when cooking from foreign recipes.

Volume

These metric measures are approximate benchmarks for purposes of home food preparation.
1 milliliter = 1 cubic centimeter = 1 gram

Liquid	Dry
1 teaspoon = 5 milliliters	1 quart = 1 liter
1 tablespoon = 15 milliliters	1 ounce = 30 grams
1 fluid ounce = 30 milliliters	1 pound = 450 grams
1 cup = 250 milliliters	2.2 pounds = 1 kilogram
1 pint = 500 milliliters	

Weight

1 ounce = 28 grams
1 pound = 450 grams

Length

1 inch = $2^1/_2$ centimeters
$^1/_{16}$ inch = 1 millimeter

Formulas Using Conversion Factors

When approximate conversions are not accurate enough, use these formulas to convert measures from one system to another.

Measurements	Formulas
ounces to grams:	# ounces x 28.3 = # grams
grams to ounces:	# grams x 0.035 = # ounces
pounds to grams:	# pounds x 453.6 = # grams
pounds to kilograms:	# pounds x 0.45 = # kilograms
ounces to milliliters:	# ounces x 30 = # milliliters
cups to liters:	# cups x 0.24 = # liters
inches to centimeters:	# inches x 2.54 = # centimeters
centimeters to inches:	# centimeters x 0.39 = # inches

Approximate Weight to Volume

Some ingredients which we commonly measure by volume are measured by weight in foreign recipes. Here are a few examples for easy reference.

flour, all-purpose, unsifted	1 pound = 450 grams = $3^{1}/_{2}$ cups
flour, all-purpose, sifted	1 pound = 450 grams = 4 cups
sugar, granulated	1 pound = 450 grams = 2 cups
sugar, brown, packed	1 pound = 450 grams = $2^{1}/_{4}$ cups
sugar, confectioners'	1 pound = 450 grams = 4 cups
sugar, confectioners', sifted	1 pound = 450 grams = $4^{1}/_{2}$ cups
butter	1 pound = 450 grams = 2 cups

Temperature

Remember that foreign recipes frequently express temperatures in Centigrade rather than Fahrenheit.

Temperatures	Fahrenheit	Centigrade
room temperature	68°	20°
water boils	212°	100°
baking temperature	350°	177°
baking temperature	375°	190.5°
baking temperature	400°	204.4°
baking temperature	425°	218.3°
baking temperature	450°	232°

Use the following formulas when temperature conversions are necessary.

$$\text{Centigrade degrees} \times {}^{9}/_{5} + 32 = \text{Fahrenheit degrees}$$
$$\text{Fahrenheit degrees} - 32 \times {}^{5}/_{9} = \text{Centigrade degrees}$$

American Measurement Equivalents

1 tablespoon = 3 teaspoons	12 tablespoons = $^{3}/_{4}$ cup
2 tablespoons = 1 ounce	16 tablespoons = 1 cup
4 tablespoons = $^{1}/_{4}$ cup	1 cup = 8 ounces
5 tablespoons + 1 teaspoon = $^{1}/_{3}$ cup	2 cups = 1 pint
	4 cups = 1 quart
8 tablespoons = $^{1}/_{2}$ cup	4 quarts = 1 gallon

Index

To order additional copies of

Sweet Endings

call 1-800-251-1520